The Art of Reasoning

A popular Exposition of The Principles of Logic,
Inductive and Deductive,
with an Introductoby
OUTLINE OF THE HISTORY OF LOGIC
and An Appendix on Recent Logical Developments,
with Notes

Samuel Neil

MAVEN BOOKS

Chennai   Trichy   Tirunelveli   New Delhi

MAVEN BOOKS

An Imprint of **MJP Publishers**

Maven Books

All rights reserved   No. 44, Nallathambi Street,
Printed and bound in India   Triplicane, Chennai 600 005

© Publishers, 2020

Publisher : C. Janarthanan

This book is a reproduction of an important historical work. Maven Books uses state-of-the-art technology to digitally reconstruct the work, preserving the original format whilst repairing imperfections present in the aged copy. In rare cases, an imperfection in the original, such as a blemish or missing page, may be replicated in our edition. We do, however, repair the vast majority of imperfections successfully; any imperfections that remain are intentionally left to preserve the state of such historical works.

PREFACE.

Gentle Reader,—It is fitting that you, who are about to peruse the following work, should know the design which the Author had in composing it. In looking at the works on Logic now generally read, he observed that they constituted two great classes,—1st. Those which were strictly formal in their character, and which, consequently, appeared to the general reader tedious, precise, dry, dull, and uninviting. 2nd. Those which, aiming at popularity, overstepped the legitimate bounds of the science—denuded it of its rigidly-formal and abstract nature—spread their observations over a widely-discursive field —and thus, by their very vagueness and indefinity, rendered their precepts vain, nugatory, unmeaning, and impracticable. No one appeared to him sufficiently adapted, in manner and in matter, to the spirit of "the age in which we live." To write a Logic which would be the *synthesis* of these—which would be popular in its method of exposition, without abating "one jot or tittle" of that abstract and formal austerity which science invariably assumes—was the aim of the Author. The projection —in 1850—of a new Serial, "The British Controversialist," to which the Author was invited to contribute, afforded him the opportunity of essaying to work his thought into realization. He drew up an outline plan, presented it to the Editors of that Serial, who were pleased to express their belief that such a work, combining accurate thought with attractiveness and popularity of exposition, was suited to the wants of our time. Accordingly the work was begun, and regularly every month during 1850 and 1851 a paper on "The Art of Reasoning" appeared in that Serial from the pen of the Author. These papers are here reprinted in a revised and greatly extended form, with the addition of an "Introductory Outline of the History of Logic," and an Appendix on "Recent Logical Developments;" a few "Notes" have also been added,—all of which he hopes may be found useful to his readers. It has been difficult to free the work from all appearance of having been issued in a serial form, although considerable pains had been taken, in the revisal, to effect that end. In this work I have not *affected* originality—as the number of my quotations and references will show—but I should not like it to be understood, from this, that I consider there is nothing in it which may be so denominated. Those who are accustomed to such speculations will readily perceive the points of divergence from the usual course pursued by Logical writers. I have made no scruple in differing, occasionally, from men highly renowned in philosophical pursuits; and did I not believe that the attainment of Truth, on these topics, was the most ardent desire of their soul, I might be tempted to apologize for intruding the *adversaria* of a fameless writer, upon such speculations, on the notice of the public. I am very far, indeed, from asserting that the execution of the task which I undertook, has reached the excellence of my ideal of such a work. It is one thing to plan, another to execute. How can it be otherwise? The plan rises before the mind's eye, captivating by its beauty and originality; takes no account of the frequent falterings which one must feel in essaying an untried path, allows nothing for interruptions from sickness, sorrow, or fatiguing professional pursuits, takes not within its ken the contingencies of life, the occasional procrastination in which the mind *will* indulge, and the disadvantages which distance from the press, disjunctness of publication, and the imperative demands of the printer's familiar, may concur in producing. All these several points I am able to plead in excuse of the many imperfections and blemishes, "the faults of omission and commission," with which this literary effort is chargeable. How far I have succeeded the public *will* judge—how far I have fallen below my own estimate, none *can* know. That it has been so far successful in meeting "the wants of the times," the favourable notices which, unsolicited, the newspaper press has bestowed on it, as well as the frequent receipt of congratulatory letters from private individuals—some of them of considerable standing in the literary world—abundantly testify. To those who have thus encouraged me—who strengthened my heart to proceed—I owe a debt of gratitude. And to you, gentle reader, for your patience and forbearance, how much shall I be indebted?

SAMUEL NEIL.

London, September, 1853.

CONTENTS.

PAGE

PART THIRD—RATIOCINATION.

PART FOURTH—METHOD.

APPENDIX.

A.

B.

AN OUTLINE SKETCH

OF THE

HISTORY OF LOGIC.

CHAPTER I.

INTRODUCTION.—PRE-ARISTOTELIAN LOGIC.

LITERARY HISTORY presents to the student few phenomena more singular than the rise and subsequent progress of Logic. The condition of Man as a dependent being, connected by various and almost innumerable interrelations with Nature and Society, must earlily have called forth in him the desire to know how Truth might with certainty be found. This desire, developed into a systematic study, resulted in the science of Logic. It is not to be supposed that this, any more than any other science, sprang from the brain of any projector clothed with the attributes of perfection. The human mind can only proceed gradually in the work of Conception—facts and data must have accumulated, generalization and reasoning must have been exercised, and many internal discoveries must have been made before the great Architect of the science—Aristotle—could have built up his " Organon," and given it " the very form and pressure" which it has now assumed. Who can forbear from thinking that an outline of the History of this Science—so essentially necessary to humanity—originating as it did, in its formal development at least, amongst the most intellectual people of ancient times—being embodied, as it was, in a scientific treatise by one of the most eminent philosophers of Greece—wielding, as it did, a sway over men's minds more lasting and permanent than the dynasty of "the Imperial Cæsars"—and interwoven, as it is, with the web of human thought and language ; being at once " a venerable piece of antiquity, and a great effort of human genius," and indicating, as it does, " a remarkable period in the progress of human reason"—should excite some interest and merit some attention.   The uses and advantages, too, of a true and genuine Logic are so great, in so far as the direction and government of the human mind, while employed in thinking, are concerned, that these of themselves should be powerful enough to induce us to read, with anxiety, the record of its somewhat chequered career, in order that we may learn in what its utility consists, and what purpose it has served in the betterment of humanity.   We have no desire to raise our voice in absurd laudations, or extravagant and preposterous praise.   We have no intention of subscribing to the fantastic encomiums of the schoolmen who represented Logic as "The divine art, the irrefragable canon, the eye of the intellect, the art of arts, the science of sciences, the organ of organs, the instrument of instruments, the servant, the key, the containing vessel, the bulwark of philosophy, the chief master in teaching and in speaking, the umpire and judge of the true and the false," or exclaim in the rapturous accents of verse—

> " Utque supra Ethereos Sol aureus emicat ignes
>   Sic artes inter prominet hæc Logica;
> Quid?   Logica superat Solem ; Sol namque, diurno
>   Tempore, dat lucem, nocte sed hancce negat:
> At Logicæ sidus nunquam occidit; istud in ipsis
>   Tam tenebris splendet, quam redeunte die."

Although, however, we do not wish thus fulsomely to hymn the praises of a favourite pursuit, we are desirous of placing the labours of those great men who have spent their studious hours in calm self-inquisition, in elaborating the science of correct thinking, in pointing out the dangers to be encountered in our researches, and in constructing " the scale and chart of Truth,"—in their true light.   To give a fair, candid, and impartial account of the progressive developments of this science, and thus enable our readers to form for themselves an accurate estimate of the influence and worth of Logic, is the object of the present "outline sketch."

Philosophical pursuits are not the earliest in which the mind engages, although the problems with which Philosophy concerns itself, speedily develop themselves within the human soul.   The actual and the real, rather than the speculative, attract the earnest attention of men.   Consciousness does not become reflective until there exist intervals of sensational repose—until we become habituated to the occurrences which continuously operate around us.   *Then*, when excitement has subsided, Reason wakes and self-interrogation commences, Memory is stored, the real is idealized, thought is exerted, and Truth is sought.   What are the means by which *that* may be attained—what are the habitudes of mind most favourable to the ascertainment of an accurate knowledge of man's relation to the Universe? Minute precision and the careful adjustment of investigative processes are not, at this early period of social existence, capable of an easy and definite settlement. The Mind must go out tentatively and gather an harvest of experience. When *that* is obtained the man of the age will arise and gird himself to the task of theoretically arranging the science of thought.

Let us observe how and by whom some of the earlier experiments in "the Art of Reasoning" were made.

Accepting it as true that the human mind must act according to certain laws, and hence that there is in each man a "natural Logic," however untrained and undeveloped, and that a rigidly systematic observation of the *modus operandi* of the Intellect while fulfilling these laws, through the medium of consciousness, by making us acquainted with the method in which the mind acts, will furnish us with "the elements of thought" accurately enough elaborated to form the beginnings of a methodology of scientific inquiry, and sufficiently formal to constitute the basis of a Logic systematically arranged in such a manner as to be *subjectively* correct, let us proceed to examine the specific attempts made to attain this object, confining ourselves for the present to the Pre-Aristotelian era.

There can be little doubt but that the general consciousness of men, while specific diversities excited, was sufficiently explicit in giving evidence regarding certain generic operations, the ordinary manifestations of which were alike, or nearly alike, in all; any philosopher, therefore, who chose to investigate the subject would commence his disquisition at the level of these revelations and gradually proceed onward, receiving these as indisputable facts in the science of thought—as the premisses from which he shall start. Hence it is that we do not find, at the earliest notices of its birth, that Logical Science was encogitated from its elements, but rather that we find ZENO THE ELEATIC (born in the lxvii. Olympiad, *i.e.*, about 590 B.C.) mentioned as the inventor of "Dialectic," and as

> "Skilled to argue on both sides
> Of any question,"

not because he taught any dogmatic doctrine of Logic, but because he invented logical puzzles, which necessitated the study and exposition of the laws of thought, in order that they might be properly controverted. Thus he became the earliest theoretical expounder of Logic—the logic of controversy—a logic which held it indispensably necessary to the attainment of Truth that each problem should be looked at on all sides, that all the difficulties attending its solution ought to be considered, and these being duly weighed the assent of the understanding should be given to that which has the balance in its favour.

Few good things have ever made their advent in the world without being followed by some counterfeit productive of evil; and so was it with Logic. No sooner had certain of its dogmata been settled than there arose among the people of Greece numerous professed teachers of the much desired art. That study which for awhile attracted all the great minds of Greece, emulous to excel in its practice, soon saw the day of its early glory depart, through the agency of its pseudo-cultivators. Once reduced to didactic form it became possible to give prelections upon it in such a sort as wrested it from its proper uses as a discerner of truth, and made it an instrument of subtle deceit. THE SOPHISTS arose. These men did not all deserve the stigma which was subsequently affixed, by implication, to their name. The earlier professional teachers of "the Art of Reasoning" were honest men, sedulous cultivators of true science; but too soon a race of wordy quibblers, garrulous logomachists, and "men greedy of gain" displaced them, and by their gaudy oratory and vulgar pretensiveness gained the popular ear. "Language as the instrument of power over minds—Language as the imperfect medium of communicating ideas, and therefore the readiest means of mixing and embezzling them in the transfer—Language as the art of pleasing—Language as the never failing subject for etymological ingenuity to anatomize—Language, again, as the natural transcript of the human mind, and the human mind in that low vulgar form, in which alone a popular leader or an expediency-philosopher can see it or wish to see it—Language, in all these lights, was to the Sophists (of this time) everything."[*] Let us be just, however, even to these apparent enemies of human progress. Let us acknowledge that brilliant as was the epoch in which they flourished—an epoch illuminated with the names of Sophokles, Euripides, Thukydides, Phidias, &c.; they were, in a great measure, the result of the times in which they lived. The power of eloquence to flatter popular passion and thus assist in gaining the aims of ambitious men, by captivating the reason or seducing it with spark-

---

[*] Sewell's "Horæ Platonicæ," chap. vii., p. 51. For differing estimates of the character of the Sophists see Plato's " Protagoras" and "Euthydemus;" Aristotle's "Organon," in the Book of Sophistical Elenchi; Xenophon's " Memorabilia," i. 6, 13; Maurice's "Moral and Metaphysical Philosophy," Ancient, chap. vi., dio. ii., sect. i.; Grote's "History of Greece," vol. viii., chap. lxvii.; Carus's "Ideen zu einer Geschichte der Philosophie," p. 493; Wigger's "Life of Sokrates," chap. ii., iv.; Hippeau's "Histoire de la Philosophie," premiere epoque Sophistes, p. 55. We might refer to other sources, but these, we think, will be found sufficient.

ling sophisms,—the litigious spirit of the Greeks, at this period, when wealth and success had led to luxury and extravagance and a general corruption of manners, all formed inducements to the Greeks to study oratory, and this to train a set of men whose only aim was to acquire distinction and wealth by the gaudy frippery of Rhetoric. These men were interested in confounding Truth and Falsehood, in involving all things in an atmosphere of uncertainty and doubt, in contradicting the plainest dictates of consciousness, and in dressing out error in the garments of Truth. Scepticism thus became for a time triumphant; but scepticism is only the resource of shallow minds—whose fears or prudence counsel them to hold their present standing-ground rather than risk defeat or endure the inconveniences of a continued warfare. It is the coward's solace—"the flattering unction" which he lays to his soul to hide his meanness from himself—the passive contentment of a slave to present enjoyments rather than the bravery of soul which arms itself for fight, and resolves rather to "die with harness on his back" than resign himself to a belief in the inevitability of ignorance. Yet was this wordiness—this luxuriance of mere verbiage, not without its use. Nobler minds perceived that *words* were not philosophy, although they contained it, when interpreted and understood with reference to an accurate knowledge of human nature and the universe. There was thus a twofold tendency given to philosophy; one leading to a knowledge of the objective proceeding from *the within* to *the without;* the other seeking an acquaintance with the subjective, inquiring from *the external* what degree of verity was justly attachable to the thoughts which arose within the mind itself. Seeing in *words* the union-point of these—the complement of the knowledge derived from external nature and the excogitations of the human soul. ANTISTHENES (born in the second year of the lxxxix. Olympiad, *i.e.*, about 422 B.C.), a pupil of the Sophist Gorgias, afterwards a student under Sokrates, and the founder of the sect of the Cynics, pointed out the extreme importance of attending to the Art of Definition. Only by careful definition could immunity from erroneous reasonings be found. *This*, as it gave the full essence of any given thought-expression, formed the porch of the temple of Truth. Definition fixed and determined the one essential quality or attribute which, in relation to the question proposed, it was necessary to consider. Hence arose its value as a means to the attainment of the great end of human research—the Truth.

EUKLIDES (date of birth unknown) the Megarean, a student of the works of Parmenides (519 B.C.), and a pupil of Sokrates, ventured upon two branches of speculation which tended to the development of a scientific solution of the question—how may Truth be best found ? and the exemplification of certain formal methods of argumentation. He. rejected analogical reasoning, asserting that if compared things be like, it is better to deal with the originals than with their *analogues;* and if unlike, error must result. He first gave to the *reductio ad absurdum* a formal structure, and not only defended but exemplified its use.

We have mentioned these parties a little anachronistically because we were desirous of treating of the central figures in this era. (Sokrates and Plato) consecutively, in order that the tendency which they gave to logical pursuits might be exhibited uninterruptedly, and that parenthetical divergencies might be avoided.

Of SOKRATES (the son of Sophroniskus and Phenarete, born in the fourth year of the lxxvii. Olympiad, *i.e.,* about 468 B.C.) we have now to speak, but this only in reference to his Logical Method. As a dialogist and dialectician Sokrates is famous. His method was critical and eclectic. Experience—the whole assemblage of sensations, emotions, prejudices, &c., which constituted the mental state of a man— formed the starting-point for him. Lofty abstractions and air-thin speculations suited him not; *the real* thoughts of a man, whether right or wrong, charmed him to discourse; *here* he found a place upon which he could erect the permanent foundations of Truth and Virtue. To him philosophy manifested herself in her practical work-a-day dress, as the servant of man and the ministrant to his happiness. "Men are too apt to think and talk of Sokrates as if he had (had?) the works of Bacon and Bentham to guide him—at least, as if he had come after, and not preceded, the works of Plato, Aristotle, and Zeno (!?). We are too apt to forget that Sokrates had to build up Moral Philosophy, *implying the settling of an intellectual system* (for men must know what is true before they can be convinced of what is right), upon the shifting sands of mythologists and poets, cosmogonists and sentence-makers; that is, he had to distinguish what was sound and good from what was unsound and evil." * * * "To lay that foundation had been an herculean task, equalled only by the judgment shown in the selection of materials; but by some critics, nay, by some philosophers, that work, because it has become hidden under the surface, is to be undervalued." *

It will be observed that the logical teaching of Sokrates was not of a theoretically dogmatic and positive character, but lay latent in his method of inquisition and disquisition. His practical sagacity led him

* Potter's "Greek Philosophers," article—"The Philosophy of Sokrates," page 65.

to adopt a right method, his adoption of that method led his pupils to speculate upon the *reasons* on which its efficiency depended, and hence to deduce the theoretical laws which govern these mental operations. His *Elenchus* was adopted in opposition to the Sophists, who sought power solely through the aid of words. Clearly to perceive the true significance of words—by eliciting from each the sense in which he understood them while expressing their ideas—was with him an object of paramount importance. To drive men back to Consciousness to seek *there* the meaning of the idea-symbols he employed, and thus, as he himself jocosely remarks, by a kind of mental obstetricism make men *bring forth* the Truth, was his chief aim; hence his argumentative methodology, which consisted of a series of reasonings proceeding from the conclusions sought to be proven to the total demolition of the premisses on which they were founded, and hence the invalidation of the argument, and the necessity of proceeding to a re-discussion of the question at issue in the light derived from the new premisses then gained. His Logic was thus *negative* in so far as it oppugned error, and *positive* in so far as it led to a new course of Reasoning.

His disciple PLATO (the son of Aristo and Pericthone, born in the third or fourth year of the lxxxvii. Olympiad, *i.e.*, about 429 or 430 B.C.) continued this manner, and adopted much of its spirit. He wished to clear the soul from all preconceptions. Ignorance he pronounced the true start-point for science. Sensations, notions, and ideas constitute the three things which furnish The Intelligence: *Sensations* refer to individualities with all their variableness; *Notions* to generalizations, also variable; *Ideas* concern themselves only with the invariable and universal. Then follow Definition, Division, and Hypothesis. Definition, what in each thought is knowable, essential, and universal. Division separates ideas from each other according to their intrinsic differences, and enables the mind to gather them together by Generalization, and to arrange them in groups by classification. Hypothesis lays down the principles on which they may be accounted for, and Deduction informs us of the conclusions to which Hypothesis leads. As there are three species of elements which enter into and constitute thought, so there are three kinds of Logic, thus:

Knowledge consists of

Ideas		Notions		Sensations,
		which respectively produce a		
		Logic—		
Apodictic,		Epicheirematic,		Enthymematic,
or absolute,		or probable,		or imperfect;

the operations of each of which are—
1, Definition; 2, Division; 3, Generalization; 4, Classification; 5, Hypothesis; 6, Deduction.
These lead the mind to the attainment of
1, Truth; 2, Opinion.

Words are the instruments of thought, not substitutes for it. Truth is the educt of the consentaneous and proper exercise of all the mental faculties, and is not transitory, as the mere result of sensations must be, but eternal, and capable of being transmitted from age to age, because derived from the innate spontaneity of the soul. Thus we see that a gradual accumulation of materials was preparing the way for a systematic exhibition of the principles of thought. Our next chapter will inform how this was effected, and by whom.

CHAPTER II.

ARISTOTELIANISM.

THE Greeks were a most remarkable people—intelligent and debate-loving. Among them, wisdom-worship attained its fullest development. Their intellect seems to have been peculiarly scientific, and to them can be traced the earliest attempts to accomplish the systematization of knowledge. To them, at an early period, the fact became apparent, that man is possessed of many endowments peculiarly his own—endowments which are unshared by the objectivities around him. The origin of their being—the purpose of their existence—the occult nature of their future fate—the Whence, Why, and Whither, lay before them, dark, inexplicable enigmas. These they set themselves about anxiously to solve. But Mystery refused to lift her veil—the Sphinx was unwilling to "read her riddle"—the Oracle was dumb. Yet they did not succumb; they determined to persevere. One sage after another rose to explore the hidden ways of wisdom, that he might become master of her treasures. Every avenue was attempted—every apparent outlet was tried; and yet "shadows, clouds, and darkness" rested as before upon their path. Nothing could they perceive "about, above, around," but the hideous and intolerable gloom of Ignorance. "All that is known is, nothing can be known," seemed to be the only answer their questioning could elicit, and the wail of Empedocles seems to be but an improvisatore version of the heart-feeling of the Greeks at that time :—

> " Swift-fated and conscious, how brief is life's pleasureless portion !
>   Like the wind-driven smoke, men are carried backwards and forwards,
>   Each trusting in nought save what his Experience vouches,
>   On all sides distracted: yet *wishing to find out the whole truth*
>   *In vain ;* perceptible to man neither by eye nor by ear,
>   *Nor to be grasped by his mind :* And thou, when thus thou hast wandered,
>   Wilt find, that *the knowledge of mortals no farther forth reaches.*"

Then began the several attempts, mentioned in the previous chapter, to " cut the Gordian knot " which Philosophy was unable to unloose, that led to the popularity of the Sophists, and the prevalence of a general spirit of disputation.   At this crisis in speculation—in this dilemma— in this time of eager inquiry, when each one was greedily thirsting to learn how and where the Truth on these matters could be found, and none were able to answer, Socrates, Plato, and Aristotle successively appeared, and, each after his own fashion, strove to satisfy the craving appetite of their countrymen. With the speculations of the former two we need not now concern ourselves, as we have already, in the preceding chapter, given a brief abstract of the chief items which they had either directly or indirectly contributed towards the elements of this science : the opinions of the latter constitute our present subject. How did he answer the query? He said, Truth is the natural product of correct thought : if then we can ascertain the precise process in which the mind invariably performs the operation of thinking, and in all our cogitations follow that method, the problem will be solved. This, then, is the task he sets himself—let us see how he proceeds in the execution of it. Words are the signs of ideas, the formulæ in which we express our notions, judgments, and reasonings. Hence arises the necessity of Definition, of Categories, of Predicables. Words must be bounded, so that the limits of their signification may not be overstepped. Sensation gives the elements of thought, and is correct and trustworthy as sensation ; but thought is predication :—every individual idea which Sensation yields is true ; but when we predicate one idea of another, that predication may be false ;—Error, then, lurks in affirmation or negation. Each affirmation or negation, however, constitutes a proposition ; the *false* is therefore an incorrect predication, the true a correct one. Speech is of two kinds—predicative and non-predicative. Logic concerns itself with the former, Rhetoric employs the latter. Reasoning is just a series of predicative propositions, so put together, that from the truth or falsehood of the premised propositions the proof of the new inference inevitably results. In the adjustment and disposition of these propositions, therefore, lies another source of Error. There are therefore two sources of Error,—1st, Our affirmation may be untrue—may be an incorrect expression of the fact; 2nd, Our method of conjoining propositions may be incorrect, and thus our deductions will be spurious. With regard to the first, "every man is to be believed in his own art," for with it he is best acquainted; respecting the second, a method of security may be devised if we can number the legitimate modes in which propositions may be arranged. To Demonstrate is to show the dependence of one truth upon an anterior one: these prior truths are Axioms, Definitions, Hypotheses, &c., as they are self-evident, limitative, pre-supposed, &c., as the case may be. All human knowledge is made up of two parts—viz., the τοῦ ὅτι—knowledge *that* things are, and are in some manner; and the τοῦ διότι—knowledge *why* they are so. We can know *about* things, though we cannot know them *per se*—*i.e.*, as they are *in themselves*. All Demonstration therefore is of two kinds—viz., *à posteriori*—from the *effect* observed, to the *cause* unknown; and *à priori*, from the *cause* observed or assumed, to the resultant *effect*. There are thus, it would appear, three parts, and only three parts, virtually present in every act of Demonstration or ratiocination—1st, the prior truth; 2nd, the experienced, imagined, or defined thing; 3rd, the thing proven. This constitutes a syllogism. But all the qualities of substances are either necessarily or inseparably inherent in them—contingently conjoined to them—or so disjoined that certain properties can never by any possibility be connected with certain substances. In the first and third, experience is our informant; and when we understand our experience sufficiently well to make correct predications regarding what it tell us, no error can evolve itself; in the second, we are always liable to mistake, as our reasonings can only result in probability. There is therefore a necessity for care and attention, so that we may not deceive ourselves in accepting *probable* reasoning where *certainty* is attainable; and it is a mistake to demand certainty where probability alone can be acquired by the mind.

Such is in general terms a roughly-sketched outline—a rude draft of the Reasoning of Aristotle, and the way in which he attempted the solution of the question—How and Where may Truth be found? We have been induced to give this running abstract, in order that our readers may see the general tendency of his teaching, and the purpose which presided over the execution of the "Organon," that they may follow us with eagerness and zeal—rough as the pathway, steep as the ascent may be—through a more minute examination of the several portions of that work. This we shall precede with the following tabular as translated in the "Penny Cyclopedia," art. Logic) :—

Aristotle's Organon, viz. :

Logic is conversant about the Syllogism, and hence "TheOrganon" explains,	I. The parts of a Syllogism, and that	1st. With reference to primary notions,	i.e., "The Categories."
		2nd. With reference to secondary notions,	i.e., On Interpretation.
	II. The Syllogism,	1st. Generally = Prior Analytics.	
		2nd. Specially	i. Demonstrative = Post. Analy. ii. Dialectical = The Topics. iii. Sophistic = The Sophistical Elenchi.

I. THE CATEGORIES. The book of the Categories commences with a few remarks on the distinctions of Terms, the logical division of things and their attributes, and the connexion between the subject and the predicate. It then proceeds to specify "The Categories"—ten in number—viz., Substance, Quantity, Quality, Relation, Where, When, Position, Possession, Action, and Passion.* This topic is sufficiently discussed in Chapter XIII. of "The Art of Reasoning," and need not be farther spoken of here. To the Categories succeed the theory of the Predicables; these also are treated in the chapter referred to, which see.

II. OF INTERPRETATION. Much of what this book contains is now considered to belong more properly to Grammar than to Logic, as it relates chiefly to words as the signs of thought. Language is articulate sound made significant by the common consent of those who use it. It is of two kinds, predicative and non-predicative. The former we use in Reasoning, and with it Logic concerns itself. The consideration of the latter belongs to Rhetoric and Poetry. Predicative speech consists of propositions. Definitions of the chief distinctions of propositions we give in Chapter V., and as they are essentially similar to those contained in Aristotle's "*De Interpretatione*," this reference will save time, space, and repetition.†

III. PRIOR ANALYTICS. This book, as well as that which succeeds it, received its title from the fact that the object which its author had in view in its composition, was to *analyze* the process of the reasoning

---

* The authorship of the Categories has led to some debate. See on this topic, Brandis' article "Ueber die Schicksale der Aristotelischen Buecher," &c., in Niebuhr's "Rheinisches Museum," vol. i., Bonn and London, 1827; Stahr's "Aristotelia;" Jonseins' "De Historiæ Philosophicæ Scriptoribus." While regarding the worth of the categorical classification, see Locke's "Essay;" Harris' "Philosophical Arrangements;" Kant's "Kritik der Reinen Vernunft," p. 79; Cousin's "Histoire de Philosophie;" Hamilton's "Reid," p. 686; also his "Discussions," see under the word "Categories," in the Index, p. 750, &c.

† See farther on this subject, B. St. Hilaire's "Sur la Logique d'Aristote," vol. ii.

faculty, and by this means to explain the elemental parts of which an act of reasoning consists. It begins by treating of the "conversion of propositions;" but this portion of its contents we have laid before our readers in Chapter XIII., in order that they may have, in one continuous, comprehensive, and consecutive whole, an abridged account of the doctrine of Propositions; and that we might be able, consecutively and at once, to present an outline of the Syllogistic Theory.

Then follows a development, in detail, of the doctrine and practical application of the syllogisms, and a complete exposition of all the possible forms in which assertions may be made, and arranged into syllogistic forms, in order that valid conclusions may be deduced from them. Afterwards he makes a few judicious and ingenious remarks upon the possibilities of error arising from these arrangements. We have left little space to point out the many wise, ingenious, and forethoughtful sayings, the acute distinctions and philosophical remarks with which these books abound. A hasty and very imperfect line-sketch is all that we can present to our readers. The remainder of this treatise contains instructions for the discovery of middle terms; the general principle laid down is, to examine the question so as to ascertain what is the point to be proven; then, to seek out such a term as shall bear the relation required in the mood or figure to be employed, as the rules of syllogism demand: after this, he occupies some chapters in showing the method of resolving propositions into their several parts, so that the truth of each individual part may be tested with care and caution, and concludes with a general description of the powers of syllogisms, their uses, and the most effective means of employing them in disputation.

IV. POSTERIOR ANALYTICS. This book is a most important one, and we are sorry that our limits will not permit us to give more than what may be termed an *index* of its contents. It commences with a dissertation on the distinction between the *form* and *matter* of a proposition; with this, however, we have made our readers, in Chapter X., acquainted. He then divides syllogisms into three sorts: —1st, Apodictical, or possessed of true premisses, and duly *formal* in construction; 2nd, Dialectical, or possessed of only probable premisses, and accurate as to the *form* in which it is cast; 3rd, Sophistical, or those which, while apparently true and formal, are really neither of the two. The principles of evidence afterwards engage his attention, but on this we have also enlarged, Chapter VIII., and therefore need not here trouble our readers with remarks on them. Causes he divides into—efficient, material, formal, and final; and then proceeds to treat in a most lucid and acute manner on Demonstration,—the general principle is, that there must be truths necessary, and external, which, either as the result of mere thought—evolution, or the influence of experience, naturally germinate in the mind, and are the seeds of all our future thought-blossomry,—that from these truths we derive others, but that each derivative truth is less surely evident than those from which they are derived,—that Experience in its widest sense, Analogy, and Testimony, are the three "sources of evidence,"—and that all human thought is included in the threefold classification of Truth, Opinion, and Faith.

V. The succeeding book contains the TOPICA, or a treatise on the Art and Method of Conducting Discourse; but, as this department is now usually consigned to the other branch of the *Trivium* Rhetoric, and, as it has been slightly noticed in the division, *Method*, Chapters XIX. and XX., we will not seek to synopsize it here.

VI. The next book, DE SOPHISMATIBUS, or an Essay on the Causes of Error, and the nature of Fallacy, we purposely omit noticing, as it occupies a whole chapter in the body of this work.

Here, now, our analysis must terminate.

CHAPTER III.

POST-ARISTOTELIAN LOGIC—TILL THE CHRISTIAN ERA.

THUS have we seen the germ-seeds of early thought becoming developed, improved, and ripened. Not yet to its highest possible perfection has it reached, but skilled culture may now be applied to its betterment. The studies of the "scientific wonder" of Greece have been so successfully prosecuted that the laws of the growth of thought may now be pretty readily understood and applied. All hail to the grand triumvirate of Greek philosophers, in whom the largest development of man-gained truth blossomed and fructified! Chiefly to him who manfully systematized the discursive and disjointed items which prior geniuses contributed to the upbuilding of a science, be praise cheerfully accorded. Laud is the meed of each heroic soul, and he was one of the unquestionably brave.

It remains for us now only, in this chapter, to trace the progress and onward marching of the science by which truth may be tested, from the Aristotelian to the Christian era.

The earlier successors of Aristotle were chiefly engaged in comment-
ing on his philosophy—re-stating, with trifling alterations and greater
formalism, their master's dogmas. Neglecting the consideration of the
grand and comprehensive views developed in the tenets of their
teacher, they reduced it more and more to a system of technicalities.
The chief of these were Theophrastus, Endemus, Strato, Ariston, and
Critolaus, but we can only speak of their tendencies, not of their distinguishing dogmas.

While Plato and Aristotle were engaged in laying the foundations of
a philosophy of thought, one arose whose influence also was to be wide
and lasting—Pyrrho (about B.C. 340)—although more a destroyer
than a builder—the founder of the Sceptics. *Doubt*—Uncertainty—
Vagueness were the watchwords of his sect. Suspend your Judgment
till Truth speaks in plain, not doubtful, language. Sense and Thought
utter antitheses, and all their teachings contradict each other : which
shall we believe? Where such differences are, there can be no criterion,
for that itself requires demonstration, and that another *ad infinitum.*
All is contradictory, therefore all is false, seems to have been his reasoning. He had apparently not observed that if it is true that "all is
false," this also must be false, and if not false, then something is true,
i.e., not false; either way the Sceptic is wrong—of two contradictions
one must be true, the other false. The tendencies of this school were
further developed, without, however, eliciting anything worthy of
remark, by his pupil Timon, the Phliasian (about B.C. 324), with great
sophistic skill.

Zeno of Citium (about B.C. 362), the founder of the Stoics, embraced
in his system a Logic which he believed to be, at once, the director of
reason, and the regulator of language, and which was consequently
more extensive than that of Aristotle, being no less than a science for
the right use of Intellectual power. Sense yields particulars, Intellect
produces, from these, general notions, and thus the truths of sense and
intelligence become unicalized and reconciled. Objectivities possess,
1st, a substrate or essence ; 2nd, a fixed and therefore differentiating
quality ; 3rd, general relations ; and 4th, individual, temporary, and
transitory relations. His doctrines regarding essences were far from
being settled, and his general system was more than of technical
formality, the result of strong, masculine common sense.

His immediate successor, Cleanthes (about B.C. 320), displayed no
great subtlety or keenness of mind. Chrysippus, the pupil of Cleanthes, however (about B.C. 280), was a man of superior mind and
ready dialectic power. He added much to the Logic of the Stoics. All

human knowledge is derived from Sensation, generalized and operated upon by the Intellect. True knowledge has the following characteristics, viz.:—1st. It is the product, originally, of a sensible object. 2nd. It presents a correct idea of that object. 3rd. It cannot be produced by a different object. Perceptions and ideas come purely into relation with the cognition, and hence their truth is irresistible. He criticised the Logic of Aristotle, and is said to have simplified the art of Argumentation.

EPICURUS, an Athenian (born about B.C. 341), desired to simplify the Aristotelic " Organon," by substituting instead of his arduous process a few general and precise rules. There are three *criteria* of Truth— 1st, Sensations ; 2nd, Anticipations, *i.e.*, general ideas ; 3rd, Emotions. The following are the rules for correct thinking :—I. Sensations never really deceive. II. Error originates in opinion. III. Opinion is true when sensations confirm or do not contradict it, and false when they contradict or do not confirm them. IV. All general ideas are received through the senses. V. General ideas are the elements of reasoning. VI. Whatever is not evident in itself ought to be demonstrated by reference to something which is self-evident. VII. Whatever our emotions accept gratefully, the same is good and true, and ought to be sought after ; whatever they dislike is evil and false, and should be avoided. We do not think it necessary here to allude to his moral " canonics," although it will be seen that its vitiating tendency enters into his Logic. In consequence of his placing the foundation of his system in general maxims, little innovation or change was introduced into his theory by his successors—the chief of whom were Metrodorus, Hermachus of Mitylene, whom Epicurus nominated as his successor, Polystratus, Dionysius, Zeno of Sidon, Diogenes of Tarsus, &c. Lucretius, the Roman poet (born 95, and died 51 B.C.), one of the pupils of Zeno of Sidon, in a poem of great power, excellence, and beauty, entitled " *De Rerum Natura*," has thrown around Epicurianism the vestment of the Muses, and Ovid has predicted truly that

> " Carmina sublimis tunc sunt peritura Lucreti
> Exitio terras cum dabit una dies." *

For the exposition of the logical tenets of Epicurus see " *De Anima Natura*," book iv.

What has been called " *The New Academy*," was instituted by ARCE-SILAUS (born at Pitane about B.C. 316). He is said to have received

---

* " Lucretius' lofty song shall live in deathless fame
Till Fate destroys, at once, this universal frame."

instructions from Theophrastus, the successor of Aristotle, Crantor, a Platonist, Diodorus, the Megarean, and Pyrrho, the Sceptic. Having thus made "the grand tour" of all the philosophies of the age, he placed himself at the head of a new school, in which were combined in varying proportions the Sokratic inquisition, the Platonic idealism, and the Zenoic suspension of Judgment. The manifold negations which every opinion met rendered dogmatism inadvisable, and probability was all that we could infer from the appearances of things. This doctrine was still more fully developed by one of his successors, Carneades (born about B.C. 215, at Cyrene). His eloquence and logical skill were most marvellous. He was the embodied genius of controversy—a perfect impersonation of the Logician of Butler,—

> "On either side he could dispute,
>   Confute, change hands, and then confute."

There can be no *absolute* criterion of Truth; for that criterion must either be sought in the impressions made on the mind, or in the judgments of the mind; but the judgments of the mind result from sensations, and they are the representations of fleeting, uncertain, and transitory things. Every general idea has a twofold reference; the one to the object, the other to the subject—or mind of the observer. We cannot, however, refer to the object for proof, for that would necessitate a prior knowledge of the object, which is the matter in dispute; we can only, therefore, refer to the mind. It may have three degrees of proof: 1st. The clearness of the conception. 2nd. The agreement of appearances one with another. 3rd. The appearance of the object itself when examined under various aspects and in different circumstances. Any one of these gives probability, but not truth, and a combination of all three yields the highest degree of probability ($\tau\grave{o}$ $\epsilon\ddot{v}\lambda o\gamma o\nu$). If discordances arise between these proofs and the object, Improbability is the result. Between true and false ideas there is an infinite number of degrees, but no sensible line of demarcation. After Carneades no great name illustrated the annals of this school. Philo and Antiochus were timid spirits, unworthy of their predecessors,—demi-sceptics, unable to strive after truth, and hopeless of finding it.

Thus stood the ancient world,—Speculation had winged its loftiest flights, and found no sure rest for the sole of its foot; Platonism, Aristotelianism, Stoicism, Epicurism, had all merged into one fatal tendency to Scepticism; and Cicero, the most eloquent of Romans (born at Arpinum about 106 B.C.), and the noblest of the later disciples of the New Academy, seems to sum up the state of ancient speculations in a few words, when he says, "All knowledge is environed with difficulties." # # # "As seamen, in a tempest-tost ocean, fix themselves to a rock, so do men attach themselves to some favourite system." # Thus it is uncertainty still hangs its dark cloud-curtain between human eyes and the goddess Truth; nor will she yet deign to give other than faint and shadowy glimpses of her heavenly form. Surely when the veil is rent Truth will be eagerly embraced! When? Ah woeful, because uncertain when!

CHAPTER IV.

CHRISTIANITY AND LOGIC.

"THE fulness of time" has come. "The way, THE TRUTH, and the life" have been revealed. "He came unto his own"—to those who having ever possessed the truth—in some heaven-revelation—needed not a speculative science to determine upon the criterion of Truth—"and they received him not." They had had no keen discipline of thought —no earnest combatings with error—no struggle for light—no contestings with the vague uncertainties which threw their gloom over the souls of the sages of Greece—they felt not the damp dews of despair upon their brows when, after all their energies were spent, the response of the oracle had been denied, and Death became the only chance of obtaining a solution of the problems which their active minds had evolved. To them had been committed "the oracles of God," but their "vain imaginations" and their age-reverent prejudices lead them to misinterpret the plainest teachings of these oracles, and when "God manifest in the flesh" came to bring "life and immortality to light in the gospel," "they crucified the Lord of Glory and put him to open shame." Not so was he received when, in the person of his apostles, he appealed to those who for ages had been pursuing investigations regarding the *criteria* of Truth. Widely as their opinions regarding criteria differed, he was eagerly accepted. God-given and Heaven-descended Truth, judged by a man-attained standard, was received with welcome and embraced with gladness. This is at once an evidence of the Truth of Christianity and of the utility of Logic which, in reflecting upon this portion of literary history, suggested itself to our minds and seemed worthy of the notice and consideration of our readers.

* "*De Finibus*," ii. 12.

A Logical System to be valuable must be capable, in its results, of adding to man's positive knowledge. Truths which no Logic was able to discover might, when revealed, be convincingly in accordance with the requirements of a true Logic—might be logically consecutive and sequentive, might be truly consistent from its rudimental germs to its highest teachings—and hence be received as of unspeakable importance. This seems to have been the case with Christianity. A true Logic mingles with " all objects of all thought"—with all that enters into man's intellectual and moral life; and the christian ethics, containing, as they did, all-comprehensive prescriptions for correct conduct, afforded full exercise for the formalizing systematization in which Logic delights. This placed a pole-star in the heaven of speculation, by which men were enabled to steer their course safely. Truth-attainment is the object of logical science; Love of Truth the wise man's glory; the worship of the Truth the Christian's delight. These are all closely and indissolubly united, and whatsoever affects one beneficially must affect all in like manner, and aid them all. Christianity did this; Christianity introduced certain definite and authoritative truths which it became its disciples to teach—to teach these effectually it was necessary to show their accordancy with right reasoning, and hence to exhibit them logically.

Hence originated the logical system of " the Fathers" of the Church. Accepting the *matter* of Christianity, and approving of the *manner* of truth-investigation and truth-exposition given in the Logic of Greek philosophy, they applied them unitedly to the regulation of the ideas and lives—the thoughts and actions of men. The chief of those who deserve mention are, Justin Martyr (born at Sichem, in Samaria, about A.D. 89, and died a martyr's death at Rome in 167), Tatien, his friend and disciple (born in Syria about A.D. 130, embraced Christianity at Rome 160, and died 176), Tertullian (born at Carthage A.D. 160, died 245), St. Clement of Alexandria (flourished 190—220 A.D.), Origen (born at Alexandria about A.D 185, died in Tyre in 255), Eusebius of Cæsarea (born A.D. 268, died 338), and St. Augustine (born at Tagaste, in Africa, A.D. 354, died 430). The general tendency of these authors —whose writings are very voluminous—was to establish the harmony of Reason and Faith. This they attempted in two forms, the Polemical and the Didactic: the former they employed in debating with the opponents of Christianity; the latter, while they sought to expound their own systems. Their centre-truth was revelation; this they strove to prove it was necessary that man should receive and believe, and then they aimed at constructing a scheme of thought consistent at once with revelation and human nature. Philosophy was with them the means to an end—that end the plucking up of the tares of doubt and implanting the seeds of true and genuine virtue. For this purpose two things were to be done:—1st, Pagan Creeds and Philosophies required, so far as they were erroneous, to be expurgated from the mind; and 2nd, All the sciences required to be organized and systematized in the light derivable from the great centre-truths which Christianity revealed. Only thus could they hope to render their doctrines acceptable, or even suitable, to humanity. Great deeds may fail, but they are at least indications of great minds. "The decline and fall of the Roman Empire" prevented the full realization of their wishes. Their labours, however, remain with us; may we prize them as the bequeathments of intellectual heroes—men who dared to grapple boldly with "the questions of all times."

Christianity did not exercise a less beneficial influence on logical studies, in the positive manifestation which it sought, than in the negative spirit which it aroused. The same weapon—Reason—required to be employed by both; the same rules of war—the same tactics—Logic—were obeyed by both. Thus arose a stimulant to the practical study "The Art of Reasoning," in both its phases, constructive and destructive—a detector of error and a defender of truth. Though

> " That everlasting spring
> Of which philosophy so long had dreamt,
> And seemed rather to wish than understand,"

had been revealed as "a well of water springing up into eternal life," there were spirits who could not submit to accept such a revelation. Of these we shall hereafter speak; in the meantime, we are desirous of tracing a little farther the tenets of the Pyrrhonistic School. The hopelessness of discovering truth, in which most of the ancient philosophists were compelled to acquiesce, gave a passive triumph to scepticism. This passive resting in doubt and hesitancy, not being formalized, was unsuited to the congregation of a sect, and opinions are never so powerful as when well organized. Hence a desire arose to constitute a doctrine or dogmatic form of scepticism! This was first efficiently attempted by Ænesidemus (born probably about A.D. 16), but more successfully at a subsequent time by Sextus Empiricus (flourished about the commencement of the 3rd century, A.D.), many names of less note filling up the intervenient period. The general tendency of the efforts of these men may be very briefly summed up. Logicians have usually advocated three sources, through the agency of which Truth may be gained—1st, The Reason which judges; 2nd, The means by which man gains the material for judgment—viz., the senses; 3rd, The means by which man applies these—viz., Attention. Man is a compound being, hence his mental operations cannot be accurately known—the senses give variable and contradictory evidence—attention is not always equally sustained. These constitute the elements of the criterion of truth. Now we must either demonstrate their truthfulness or not; if we do, that demonstration requires proof, and so on for ever; if we do not, then we accept it at hazard; either way we have not truth. Perceptions are uncertain; Logic deals with the results of perceptions, and hence partakes of their uncertainty. Definitions explain words, but definitions result from perceptions, and are hence, if possible, less to be depended on than they. Generalization proceeds from particulars, *i.e.*, perceptions; Reasoning depends on Generalization; therefore, Reasoning is more uncertain than the perceptions from which it results. All that we suppose is knowledge fades away and perishes from the mind when exposed to contemplation, and scepticism only accepts the same premisses as other men to prove that they do not yield positive or trustworthy conclusions.

Another manifestation of thought has received the name of the Neo-Platonic, Eclectic, or Alexandrian school. The prime aim of this sect was to unite the Greek philosophy and the Oriental dogmas into one grand whole, by a deeper insight and more profound interpretation than had yet been given them. Taking Platonism as its foundation, it sought to eclectize whatever of truth might be gained from other sources. Ammonius Saccas seems to have been the earliest of these teachers, although it was not till his pupil and disciple, Plotinus (born at Lycopolis, in Upper Egypt, 205 A.D.), justly styled the inaugurator of the Alexandrian school, arose, that an encyclopediac eclecticism strove to join nasent Christianity, flourishing Orientalism, and decadent Graecism—all schools of all civilizations—into one harmonious unity. Porphyry, his pupil, followed, then Iamblichus and Hierocles, and lastly, Proclus (born 412, died 483), a man of mighty mind, closes the register of the chief masters of Alexandrianism. Plotinus was the metaphysician; Porphyry, the logician; Iamblichus, the theosophist; and Proclus, the systematizer of this school. A decree of the Emperor Justinian ordained the closing of all profane schools, and dispersed the Alexandrians. Of Porphyry, as a name great in logical science, much reverenced in the middle ages, we may venture to say a word. He says, The intelligence has two modes of knowing—the sensuous, which yields science; the supersensual, which confers faith and virtue. Ideas are— 1st, seminal; 2nd, conceptive; 3rd, rational; 4th, intellectual; and 5th, supersensual. Sensation-seminal becomes conceptive by attention and imagination, rational by memory, intellectual by generalization, and supersensual by the action of the Reason, which contains within itself latently all possible ideas. To these possible ideas the Aristotelic Categories agree, and when the objects of intelligence thus fill up the capacities of the intelligence, Truth is ours.

Of Gnosticism we need say little here, as it did not much influence Logic scientifically. "They took such portions of the Gospel as suited their views or struck their fancy, but these rays of light they mixed up and buried under such a chaos of absurdity, that the Apostles would hardly have recognised their own doctrines." * And herein they practically violated the laws of correct thinking; but an exposition of their fallacious reasonings would be out of place here, and without that their influence on logical science could not be understood.

Despite of the sceptics, Neo-Platonists, and the Gnostics, however, the knowledge of the true God, and of Jesus Christ whom He hath sent, "mightily grew and prevailed." *The True* having submitted himself to human judgment, and presented himself for human acceptance— having said, "Come, let us reason together"—was tried by the standard —the highest standard of truth-testing which the sages of the ancient world were capable of elaborating—by men habituated to its use and well-trained in employing it—and found "worthy of all acceptation." This chapter of the history of "The Art of Reasoning" proves that in the cabinet of the Eternal a mission was given it to perform, and that the wisest purposes of God have been, and are, aided in their development by its free use and culture—teaches us somewhat of the enduring dignity of humanity—the intrinsic potency of the mind-powers of man, and the intense significance of the duty of self-improvement.

<hr>

CHAPTER V.

SCHOLASTICISM.

SCHOLASTIC Philosophy is a subject of such vast extent, that it is impossible, in one brief chapter, to do more than capitulate, in a very rough chalk outline, the chief points of doctrine and modifications of thought which most nearly concern our more immediate topic, referring in a note to the chief sources of farther information of which we possess any knowledge.† The successful apostolate of Christianity, noticed in

* Dr. Burton's "Inquiries into the Heresies of the Apostolic Age," p. 15.

† Cousin's "Histoire de la Philosophie," vol. ii., leçon ix.; "Fragments Philosophique," vol. iii.; Rousselot's "Etudes sur la Philosophie dans le moyen age;"

our previous chapter, was a most propitious event for man. One light, and that an heavenly one, illuminated the moral pathway of our race. The irruptions of the Goths and Vandals—the incursions of the Saracens—the proscription of secular studies by Pope Gregory the Great—the burning, by the Saracens, of the immense library at Alexandria, as well as the destruction, by order of Gregory, of the library of the Palatine—were influences adverse to the advance of knowledge. In this imminent darkness Christian light alone shone. Philosophy only played like a meteor around the horizon of "the Night of Ignorance." So far Christianity was a beneficent conservator of morality and purity of thought as well as, being truth-continent, a productive agency, after a time, in again bringing forth knowledge.

The architectonic arts—those whose formal principles govern other arts, inasmuch as they give law to those others—are valuable and important. To find the logical unity which every thought possessed with every other, it was needful to know those principles of thought which regulated all intellectual exertion. These found, Truth must necessarily result. A perfect machinery of thinking, capable of reducing all thought to regular system, inasmuch as it would render this ultimate unity of all truth evident, was much to be desired, and hence it was much striven after. It constituted the great object of search to the schoolmen, and was the basis of their erudite discussions. Scholasticism passed through three important eras, which may be thus enumerated—1st. The employment of Philosophy, as *the form* of thought, in the service of faith and under the superintendence of Religion. 2nd. The alliance of Religion and Philosophy—Realism. 3rd. The disseverance of Philosophy from Religion—Nominalism.

In the transition period, between the decadence of ancient philosophy and the birth-season of scholastic speculation, one or two names of note occur; among these are Boethius (470—526), a Roman senator, one of the students of Proclus, and the translator of several of the treatises of Aristotle;* the venerable Bede, the master of Alcuin (673—735), an

---

Haureau's "De la Philosophie Scholastique;" Remusat's "Abailard;" and Brucker's "History of Philosophy," vol. iii.; Tenneman's, vol. viii.; Buhle's, vols. v. and vi.; Ritter's, vol. iv.; Blakey's "History of the Philosophy of Mind," vol. ii., chap. 1—4; Enfield's "Philosophy"—a careless and often inaccurate abridgment of Brucker's "*Historica Critica Philosophiæ*," book vii.; Hallam's "Literature of the Middle Ages," vol. i.

* We observe in Sir William Hamilton's "Discussions on Philosophy," p. 142, &c., that some "original logical treatises" are attributed to Boethius, especially a work on "Hypotheticals." Of these we know nothing, and therefore cannot expound his own peculiar system. We wish we could find information upon this subject.

erudite and learned compiler, whose abstracts of ancient knowledge and speculation were of much service. After this period, with the reign of Charlemange (768—814), who instituted *scholæ* and made them the depositories of all then existing science, whether physical or mental, Scholasticism may be said to have begun.

The ascendancy which Christianity had attained rendered it impossible, at that time, for philosophy to exist independently. The doctrines of the Church were the Truth, and all that philosophy could be permitted to do was to discover the best *forms* of arrangement and exposition. This was the prominent duty of the philosophic schoolmen of the first era.

Deserving of earliest mention is Alcuin, the bosom friend of Charlemagne (at York 735, at Tours 804). He was a diligent cultivator of the knowledge of the times, and enthusiastic in his love of information. Several of his works possess great merit, *e.g.*, a small tractate on "The Nature of the Soul," another on "Virtues and Vices," together with one or two dialogues on Grammar, Rhetoric, and Logic: these are written with considerable skill, although they do not exhibit much originality.

John Scotus Erigena was a man of superior mental power (early in the ninth century—886). He was more of a metaphysician than a logician or theologian. The senses are the messengers of the mind which bear the reports of the phenomena to the Reason—which is continually searching for the godlike. His work, "*De Divisione Naturæ*," exhibits singular dialectic skill, although the chief opinions are tinged with Orientalism. As, however, an abstract of his doctrines would be necessary to show his logical system, we can only here say that he seems to consider the human mind capable of attaining Truth, by adhering strictly to the laws of division, definition, analysis, and demonstration. His works had the honour of being placed in the "*Index Expurgatorius.*"

Lanfranc (1005—1089) was a teacher of Logic, and a subtile disputationist. We know of none of his works in which his logical tenets are expounded.

St. Anselm (at Aost 1033—1109 at Canterbury), one of Lanfranc's pupils, was a most distinguished logician. His method is practically exemplified in "*The Monologium,*" in which he attempts to show how an ignorant man, by the power of thought alone, might construct for himself a system of true and rational cognitions. There are two modes of cognition—1st, Faith; 2nd, Science. To the latter, however, he, in this work, confines himself. Science must initiate from an idea at once subjectively and objectively true; that idea is infinite perfection—God. The external senses yield truth—God is Truth; the object of science is to show the coincidence of these truths, one in God, though dual in man. Logic is the art of reasoning soundly and justly. To do so we must gain a knowledge of substances and qualities, and compare the sense-gained manifestations with the intellectual notions which faith forms. The real and the ideal must agree. His *proslogium* is the inverse. He supposes himself possessed of Truth, and endeavours to prove that his opinions agree with the formula of thought. His tract, "The Grammarian," is an able essay on Reasoning.

Roscellinus of Compeigne (flourished 1080), the originator of the grand middle-age discussion between Nominalism and Realism, which soon became the pivot of all philosophic thought, was a man of acute mind. None of his works, so far as we are aware, remain. The question about *nominals* and *reals*—universals and particulars, originated in the Greek philosophy, though it was not developed till the ninth century. Plato maintained that universals existed in archetypes in the bosom of God; Aristotle, that they were abstractions and generalizations from experience,—the former, that they were *à priori*; the latter, that they were *à posteriori*. To determine the legitimate employment and positive value, as well as the genesis of general ideas, had now become the key of philosophy; for if particulars are the only realities, the senses are the only sources of knowledge, and the way to scepticism is paved, for absolute affirmation becomes impossible; and if general ideas are the only realities, and individuals only post-existent forms or appearances, where are we to stop short of Pantheism? The verity and value of human reason are involved in this debate! The same question has arisen in all ages. What is the foundation of human knowledge? has always been a pertinent interrogatory. Roscellinus adopted the opinion that universals were mere words—names of conceptions, not conceptions themselves. This, as it led to certain real or supposed heresies, brought upon him the *odium theologicum*, and he was obliged, *metu mortis*, to retract some dangerous, if not fallacious, opinions.

William of Champeaux (died 1120), having studied under Roscellinus, became the opponent of his doctrines, and maintained the realistic doctrines with great zeal and ability. His fame was amazing—Paris required to be enlarged to contain his pupils. This was the Augustan age of Scholastic Logic.

Coeval with him arose Abelard (1079—1142), his pupil, and afterwards his antagonist. His is one of the most celebrated names of the middle ages. He believed that in the domain of Science thought should be free, Faith should be *directed* by the light of Reason. He reverenced the wise men of antiquity. He was not a man likely to be silent in a stirring time; nor was he. He eagerly entered the lists for contest: Nominalism and Realism, choose ye! "I advocate Nominalism," he replied, "but not as of yore it has been defended." Words are the expressions of thoughts; thoughts result from the mutual action of mind and matter—the intuition or conception and the things conceived. Words include and comprise both—the essence being given by thought, the accidents by experience. Realism unites with the spirit to produce Words, and Names are the exponents of both united. This seems to have been his view, though his polemic life left him little opportunity for impartially elaborate exposition.

At this time logical studies were everywhere in the ascendant—the Platonic dialectic here, the Aristotelic there; but a revolt was at hand. This ever revolving of thought without advancement could not satisfy the soul hungering after truth. And so it came. A new Methodology was required.

Hugo St. Victor (1097—1141) was a contemporary of Abelard. Logic did not satisfy the *whole* soul. The intellect was surfeited, the heart famished. Man was created to *love* as well as *to know*. Purity of heart is the condition of acquiring Truth. Reasoning is progressive; sensation gives a knowledge of the external, imagination of the internal; memory registers and preserves these cognitions; judgment decides upon the agreement of sensation and imagination; reason goes forth under the direction of these decisions to search after the unknown, and hence results faith: all these consentaneously satisfied give us wisdom.

Richard St. Victor (1109—1172), a member of the same monastery —St. Victor—resembled his brother monk very much in his course of thought. Experience, Reason, and Faith are the three sources of knowledge. Experience relates to temporal knowledge, Reason and Faith to heavenly conceptions. The prior leads us to know what accords with reason—reason being the middle term of thought; the last leads us to what transcends reason, although it does not contradict it.

Peter Lombard, the Master of Sentences, recalled men's minds to positive studies, by abridging and collecting the opinions of the early fathers upon Theology and Philosophy.

John of Salisbury (1120—1180), an erudite and intelligent critical historian, defended Logic as a means, not as an end, and opposed the contentious and superficial learning of his time.

Amaury de Chartres and David de Dinant deduced from Logic a theory of pantheistic tendency.

A new element was introduced into Scholasticism in the latter part of the tenth century, viz., the complete works of Aristotle and the philosophy resulting from their study among the Arabians, especially the works of Avicena and Averroes. Several names of note occur which we cannot stay even to catalogue. Bonaventura (1221—1274) strove to unite Logic and Intuition. Philosophy is either Rational, Natural, or Moral,—Rational when in relation to ideas as apprehended, *i.e.*, Grammar, in asserting regarding ideas, *i.e.*, Logic, in exciting emotions through ideas, *i.e.*, Rhetoric,—Natural when relating to physical existences,—Moral when relating to duty. Wisdom is both unical and multiform; Science and Faith are unitive; phenomena are multiplex. Negation cannot exist independent of affirmation, *i.e.*, every idea implies its opposite. Individualities result from the union of *matter* and *form*. Reflection and Judgment are only possible on perception of difference. All reasonable souls are destined to know the good and the true.

Thomas Aquinas (1227—1274), the greatest philosopher of the middle ages. The church had found heresy in Nominalism, and blasphemy in Realism, and still the question was, What is the Real—the True? It is, answers our philosophist, the precise agreement between *fact* and *thought*. Reason, the gift of God, shines in each heart—a ray of true light dissipating darkness and error. The perfectionment of man is the end of science. Science consist of *matter* and *form*. A knowledge of the matter of Science is derived from experience—the form is the educt of the mind. Experience and Reason coinciding produce Truth.

The inefficacy of merely mental exercitations in the fields of science began now to be felt; the excessive importance attached to the formalizing power of the mind began to wane—other modes of thought were sought for, and the necessity for experimentalization began to be acknowledged.

Roger Bacon (at Ilchester, 1214—1294) observed that the logical categories conveyed no real knowledge of physical objects, and that the art of observation necessitated experimental processes. Clear, distinct, and adequate thoughts can only be attained by these means. His "*Opus Majus*" is a work of great subtilty and power, justly entitled to rank as the precursor of the "*Novum Organum*" of his still more illustrious successor.

Duns Scotus (1274—1308), *the Subtile Doctor*, was the steady opponent of Thomas Aquinas, and the chief of one of the two great sects into which scholasticism was now dividing itself, viz., Thomists and Scotists. Ideas are either sensible or necessary, and absolute. All Truth exists in the latter, the former being the *occasions* not the *causes* of thought. Aquinas supposed that universal *forms really* dwelt in individuals. Scotus maintained that universal and individuative entities existed independently, and that by their junction the nature of things was determined. Universals reside in the mind as *powers*; sensation brings them forth into *acts*. Excessive division and subdivision is the vice of this philosophist and his followers.

Raymond Lully (1235—1309) was the strangest genius of Scholasticism. In him all kinds of contradictory elements were actively mingled. Chivalry, Pedantry, Mysticism, Logical accuracy, Innovation, and Conservatism were all manifested by him. He reduced Logic to a mechanical contrivance. The "*Ars Magna*" contains an *à priori* determination of all the possible forms and combinations of thought—a key to all possible reasonings—and a mechanical contrivance for resolving all possible questions by a simple mechanism. We must, however, refer to the notices of this Art which appeared in "Les Memoires de l'Academie des Inscriptions et Belles-Lettres," by Degérando, 1814—1819, for a complete detail. We may remark, however, that some have believed that it was a quiet sarcasm upon the formalism of the schools.

William Occam (died 1328), a pupil of Duns Scotus, was an *invincible* opponent of Realism. His "*Summa Logices*" is a work of considerable merit. Pope John XXII. prohibited the teaching of his logical system.

The combination of words, without attaining to the truth of things, now began to be considered absurd, and the reaction against the *abuse* of logical forms operated detrimentally upon the science of thought. The practical good was not equivalent to the mental activity educed. Men's philosophic tastes, however, could not slumber, and many works of importance were written during this period. The names of De Cusa, Paracelsus, Van Helmont, Telesio, Campanella, and Jordano Bruno, deserve mention. Renchlin (1455—1522), Lodovicus Vives (1492—1540), and Peter Ramus (1515—1572), were opposed to the general scholastic system. Ramus daringly controverted some of the chief tenets of Aristotelianism, and was for that publicly condemned of being "rash, impudent, arrogant, and ignorant." Hereupon Boileau issued a satiric petition, craving an interdict against Reason and Experience, who would no longer submit to the Aristotelic Laws. This satiric *jeu d'esprit* produced good results, and the disciples of Ramus became very numerous. Montaigne, Charron, Sanchez, Levayer, Wilson, and Pascal also aided in turning the formal Logic of Scholasticism into disrepute. The Church, which had homologated Aristotelianism, also felt the shock, and few of the Reformers were less enthusiastic in amending the Art of Reasoning than in revolutionizing the doctrines of religion; Logic here again becomes a witness to the Truth. A corrupt church requires a corrupt Logic; before a pure Logic it cannot stand. The reaction was complete. Who has strength of mind sufficient to remould the thought-science of the age in accordance with its Spirit? We shall see!

CHAPTER VI.

THE INSTAURATION OF THE SCIENCES.

WE left philosophy struggling for emancipation. Who achieved its freedom? Authority and Reverence held it in bondage. Men seldom hold "the golden mean;" they fly to extremes. Slavery is grievous, but perfect independence is impossible. To settle new and better modes of obtaining Truth it was not necessary to ignore all former aids; yet this was in a great measure done. The leaders in this reform were chiefly Bacon, Descartes, Hobbes, Gassendi, Spinoza, Leibnitz, the Port-Royalists, Mallebranche, Bayle, and Locke. We shall briefly sketch the tendencies which these introduced into logical pursuits.

The two first were minds of "gigantic powers and almost inexhaustible resources." They were the founders of a philosophy which is one in spirit—a unity of method—the Analysis of Nature, *i.e.*, of external phenomena and internal consciousness. Of their peculiar doctrines it is not necessary here to offer an abstract, as in the body of this work these will be found sufficiently outlined.* Bacon (1561—1626) gave his chief attention to the Sensational means of knowledge-attainment, and gave such laws as enabled man to guard the avenues of sense and interrogate aright the messengers who entered them. Descartes (1596—1650) principally applied his vast powers to the fittest means of restraining the mind from error-paths. The method of Analyzing Nature was taught by Bacon, the method of Analyzing Thought was speculated on by Descartes. The method is one—the result one.

* See, for Bacon, Chapters VIII. and IX.; for Descartes, Chapter XIX.

These are the two series of facts given to man: Truth can be gained from no other source, revelation excepted.*

Hobbes (1588—1679), a friend of Lord Bacon, and a strictly nominalistic Logician, is a well known *name*, but little known *author*. His "*Computatio sive Logica*" contains his doctrines on the Art of Reasoning, although scattered references to his logical tenets are to be found in all his writings. Truth is in *words*, not in *things*. Exact definitions of words are necessary to attain the end of science—demonstrative knowledge. Reasoning is a sort of arithmetic applied to the combining of words, and through words of ideas. Science, properly speaking, is a knowledge of consequences. Syllogism is the instrument of demonstration and instruction. What sap is to a tree, evidence is to Truth. Sense is the only source of evidence. Science is the evidence of Truth. Knowledge is Truth supported by evidence. The just addition and subtraction of ideas is correct reasoning, and its result Science.

Gassendi (1592—1655), in his "*Exercitationes paradoxicæ adversus Aristoteleos*," and in the two first books of his "*Syntagma Philosophicum*," bravely attacks the Aristotelic Logic. He is called by Tenneman, "the most learned amongst philosophers, and the most philosophic among the learned." The latter work contains an Historical Sketch of Logic, and a dissertation on the Criterion of Truth. Logic has four topics, Ideas, Propositions, Syllogisms, and Method. Sensation gives ideas, ideas constitute facts, facts compared yield propositions, propositions compared result in principles, axioms, &c. Method expounds these.

Clanberg (1622—1665), "a very solid and judicious German philosopher," in his "*Logica Vetus et Nova*," and "*Initiatio Philosophi*," expounded the Cartesian doctrines with great clearness, and applied the Baconian tenets to the improvement of Logical Methodology.

Spinoza (1632—1677) aided the progress of Logic more by the rigour of his method of exposition than by any direct influence. Clear and distinct ideas ought to constitute the basis of science. Reasoning attaches effects to causes, reduces phenomena to law, knowledge to general principles; by the aid of analysis and synthesis it rises from particulars to generals, and descends from generals to particulars. It does this infallibly but blindly. It cannot explain *why* these laws

* Ready access may now be had to the opinions of Bacon and Descartes. Of the former, Bohn's Library will supply the student with the chief works; and there is a very accurate and excellent translation of Descartes' "Discourse on Method," and "The Meditations," published by Sutherland and Knox, Edinburgh. See also Lewes' "Biographical History of Philosophy," vol. iii. This is a book every student of philosophy should *study*.

are infallible. Thought is a regular chain, but to what is the first link fastened? Unless intellectual intuition unifies our thoughts when thought and fact are set face to face, there is no certainty.

Locke (1632—1704) was an opponent of Syllogistic Logic, and regarded it as a useless and cumbrous machine for teaching us to do what we cannot help doing. Ideas enter the mind by two sources, Sensation and Reflection. Knowledge is the agreement of ideas. Truth is the correspondence of thought and fact. Knowledge may differ in its objects, nature, and origin. Knowledge can only exist when we have ideas, and when these ideas are seen to agree or disagree. Knowledge is either intuitive, sensitive, or demonstrative. Reasoning consists of—1st. Discovering proofs, *i.e.*, Aristotelically, Middle terms. 2nd. Arranging them properly, *i.e.*, placing them in Syllogisms. 3rd. Perceiving their mutual connexion (how?). 4th. Employing them correctly. Reason is the superintendent of the whole machinery of thought.

Leibnitz (1646—1716) exercised a beneficial influence on logical philosophy, especially in Germany. Descartes had shown *where* Truth was likely to be found, although the Egoistic basis which *he* gave was too narrow. On *that* alone it was impossible to build up an external world. The soul needs another source of knowledge than Experience yields—some power which will "teach us not only what happens, but what *must happen*." Hence he adds to the maxim of the Lockeists, "*Nihil est in Intellectu nisi quod prius in sensu*," the words "*nisi Intellectus ipse*," meaning to intimate thereby, the region of Faiths or Intuitions, which form the necessary and unquestionable *principia* of Thought. Every principle must either be demonstrable by and to the Understanding, or must rest on Faith—the elementary dogmata of the mind itself. To avoid absolute Idealism, we must negotiate with Intuitionalism. He posits as his Thesis that Nature exists according to a "pre-established harmony," which the Uncreated and Supreme has ordained shall rule the whole. The Syllogism, although only the natural *modus operandi* of the mind in thinking, ought to be studied in order that expertness in thinking rightly, and dexterity in arguing wisely, may be acquired. Two *criteria* of Truth exist, viz., 1st, *The principle of contradiction;* 2nd, Of sufficient reason.

Mallebranche (1638—1715) has been called the Christian Plato. He was first inclined to philosophical thinking, by reading Descartes' "Traité de l'homme." His system is based upon Theology. Union with God is the source of our knowledge of the Truth. Sin has alienated our souls from God; hence error. Ideas are the perceptions of the mind; to be seen, they must exist, and that not as modifications of the soul, but as apart from it. Sentiments are the results of modifications of the soul. Sentiments and Ideas are therefore distinct. Philosophy is the perception of the connexions of ideas. To God the whole of our ideas may be attached, for in Him they primarily exist. All things, therefore, are seen in God.

Book I. of the "Recherche de la Vérité" treats of "the errors of the senses." Book II., in two parts, treats "of the Imagination." Book III. relates to "the Understanding, or pure Intellect." Book IV. expounds the philosophy "of the Inclinations." Book V. discusses the errors of the passions. And Book VI. shows "the Method" by which man may free himself from the dominion of error.* This last book contains copious rules for correct thinking, of which the following are among the more important :—1st. Reason on those things upon which clear and distinct ideas may be attained. 2nd. Understand distinctly the point to be inquired into. 3rd. Try to discover one idea, or several ideas, which may be used as a mean or means of knowing the relations of those things regarding which we are thinking. 4th. Subduct all unnecessary considerations during the process of examination. 5th. Arrange thoughts in their natural order, and proceed from the more simple to the more complex. The whole work deserves diligent perusal, and will amply repay it.

Blaise Pascal (1623—1662), Arnauld (1612—1694), and Nicole (1625—1695), members of the Port-Royal, and collaborateurs in the elevation of man, as authors of the "Art of Thinking," deserve very honourable mention. This work is an ingenious attempt to unite the Aristotelic syllogism with the Cartesian philosophy, upon a basis of what might be termed, in allusion to a subsequent philosophical development, common-sense principles. An analysis of this work is scarcely required, as a most excellent translation has lately been edited by T. S. Baynes, and our limits necessitate retrenchment.

Bayle (1647—1706), a man of acute mind and high logical cultivation, author of the "Historical and Critical Dictionary," since so famous as a manifestation of philosophic scepticism, has given in his different works ("Oeuvres diverses") a few hints to a new-development of logic, as well as an outline of his thoughts on that topic. He believed, and may we not say exemplified, that the mind is keen-sighted enough to detect error, although unable, of itself, easily to attain to a knowledge of the truth. His views are a compound of Aristotelianism and Cartesianism. The chapter on "Method" is the most valuable part of this tractate.

* See his own abstract, book i., chapter iv., in Edition Paris, 1674, or Taylor's English translation, 1694, London and Oxford.

Our great Milton (1608—1674) ought not to be forgotten in this connexion. His master-mind saw the importance of logical studies. He published his "*Artis Logicæ plenior institutio, ad Petri Rami methodum concinnata*" in 1672. Logic is the chief of arts, and is of two sorts :—Natural, the faculty of reason in the human mind; Artificial, rules for directing the operations of that faculty. Sense, Observation, Induction, and Experience are the means of knowledge. There are two parts in Logic, Invention and Disposition. In the first book he treats of the elements, objects, matter, and form of arguments; in the second he teaches us the proper method of arranging them. Ideas of the same class and leading to the same truths should be classed together. It belongs to Logic to lead us from universals to particulars, from that which is known, to that which is yet unknown. The first part of Method is Synthesis; the second, Analysis.

Wolff (1679—1764), the friend of Leibnitz, and the continuator of his philosophic system, in his "*Philosophia Rationalis sive Logica,*" has exhibited the principles of this science with wonderful philosophic skill. Logic is either *empirical* or *pure.* The former relates to the matter furnished by sensation, the latter to that furnished by the mind itself. Men *may* reason without a knowledge of formal rules, but they can neither do so well nor comprehensively. There are three kinds of knowledge—Historical, of facts whether of sensation or intuition; Philosophical, of causes or reasons; Mathematical. Philosophy is the science of the existent and the possible. It has three objects—God, the Human Soul, Matter. The soul has two powers—knowing and willing: that seeks *the true;* this, *the good.* To direct their exercise two sciences are needful—Logic and Practics. Practics consists of Morals and Politics. Logic is divided into two parts—1st, Theoretical; 2nd, Practical: that treats of the principles of Logic—conceptions, judgments, reasonings; this, of the employment of Logic—in intellectual studies and ordinary life. The sufficient reason and the principle of contradiction of Leibnitz figure prominently in his system. He is profound and clear, forcible and concise in exposition, and his influence throughout the Continent was very great. Other names, *e.g.,* the Digbys, Norris, Wallis, Oldfield, Burgersdicius, Foucher, Derodon, Fontenelle, Marrioti, Tschirnhausen, Thomasius, Rudiger, Plocquet, Davies, and Lambert, might be mentioned by us in a mere outline such as this, but *cui bono?*

We have seen a great work consummated. Philosophy reformed, her independence secured, her progress well sustained. Bacon and Descartes—the methodologists of this era—have imparted the duplex tendency, *sensuousness* and *idealism*, which was necessary to a true philosophy for a being at once sensuous and intellectual. Leibnitz attempted to unify them, and to construct a philosophy which should fulfil all the conditions of a search after truth. Phenomena without, and consciousness within, these are now the elements of philosophy— the objective and the subjective as sources of knowledge are recognised. How are these to yield Truth? is now the problem. What means shall be taken to decide that? The Human Mind must labour, however unsatisfying the results. There is some virtue in an honest doubt, not in despair. The perennial lesson taught humanity is "Learn to *labour* and to *wait*."

CHAPTER VII.

THE LOGIC OF THE EIGHTEENTH CENTURY.

THE impulse given to true philosophy, by the establishment of the new method, continued its quickening influence still farther, and disciplined the intellect of the eighteenth century. Thought became more intensely directed towards the evolution of the truth of Reality and the reality of Truth. How can the *logically* true—the thinkable—the possible in thought, become harmonized to, and coincident with, the fact-truth of objectivities? How may the truth-seeker be successful in his search? Thought is evidently the means of Truth-attainment; How direct the faculties of thought that they may succeed? It will be necessary to settle, first, what must be believed, what are the mental *substrata* upon which all thought must rest. The settlement of this problem was attempted by a French Jesuit, Buffier (1661—1737), in his "Traité des Vérités Premières." "First Truths" are necessary, they result from " Common Sense "—that capacity with which all men are alike endowed, by which they think of the same subjects in the same manner in so far as their judgments do not rest on prior judgments. Without acknowledging these, the simplest processes of thought are impossible. The following are examples of these truths—viz.,

1st. There are other beings and men than ourselves in the world.

2nd. There are in men certain qualities called truth, wisdom, prudence.

3rd. We find in ourselves certain qualities called *mind*, and certain other qualities, which are not mind, and are called *body*.

4th. What men in all ages and countries think and say is called Truth.

5th. All men have not agreed to deceive and impose upon us.

6th. Non-intelligence cannot produce all the effects of intelligence.

Buffier endeavoured to combine Lookeism and Cartesianism.

In our own country, Isaac Watts (1674—1748) published two excellent and well-known treatises—viz., "Logic, or Right Use of Reason," and "The Improvement of the Mind," in which he most judiciously selects the most useful doctrines of Aristotle, the Schoolmen, Bacon, and Locke, and made them both popular and instructive. William Duncan (1717—1760), Regius Professor of Philosophy of Aberdeen, upon a more decided Lockeian basis, wrote "The Elements of Logic;" a work which even yet may be unhesitatingly recommended. It deserves, although it has not had, greater popularity than Watts' treatise. A work was published in 1713 intitled "*Clavis Universalis*, or a New Inquiry after Truth," bearing as its motto the following singular antithesis to the opinion of Buffier, extracted from Mallebranche's "Recherche de Vérité"—viz., "*Vulgi assensus et approbatio circa materiam difficilem est certum argumentum falsitatis istius opinionis cui assentitur.*" * The author of this work was Arthur Collier (1680 —1732), one of the earliest of those who wrought out the philosophy of Descartes into absolute idealism. This work contains some judicious remarks on the manner of seeking truth. Bishop Berkeley (1684— 1753), however, had published, three years previously (1710) his "Principles of Human Knowledge;" a work of great value, very little read, and far less studied than it ought to be. Bishop Butler (1692—1752), in his "Analogy of Religion," not only taught, but excellently exemplified the value of analogical reasoning. Hutcheson's (1694—1747) "Logical Compendium" contains many judicious remarks on the scope of the science and the best means of attaining truth. Hume (1711—1776) indirectly aided the advancement of logical studies, and contributed several items towards a more correct science of the art of thinking. He expresses a decidedly favourable opinion on logical studies in his "Treatise of Human Nature." "The only expedient from which we may hope for success in our philosophical researches is * * * to march up directly to the capital or centre of these sciences —to Human Nature itself—which being once masters of, we may everywhere else hope for an easy victory." There is no knowledge without experience; thoughts and impressions constitute the primary divisions

---

* The assent and approval of the common herd about a difficult matter is a certain argument for the falsity of that opinion to which it assents.

of ideas. Impressions result from experience, and thoughts result from impressions. We have no power of affirming the reality of facts. Habit is the origin of our beliefs. Logic concerns itself with the relations of ideas, hence a science of thought is possible, for, as the mind forms the ideas, it can also form a science of the relations by which they are knit together. "Belief is nothing but a conception more intense and steady than what attends the mere fictions of the imagination."

The same sensational foundation for philosophy was advocated by Helvetius (1715—1771) in his "De l'Esprit" and "Traité de l'Homme." Physical sensibility is the origin of all knowledge and of all passion. *The true is the pleasant.*

A still greater mind, that of D'Alembert (1717—1783), the Encyclopedist, was engaged in tracing the relations and connections of human knowledge in the "Preliminary Discourse" to the "Encyclopédie," and therein assumed the same sensational origin of knowledge as Hume and Helvetius; but the great chief of the modern Scotch school of metaphysicians—Thomas Reid (1710—1796)—startled, at once, by the consequences of the idealistic ideas of Berkeley, and the sensualistic philosophy of Hume, had been induced to reconsider anew the grounds of human belief; and, unwitting of the works of Buffier, to analyze the consciousness of man, in order to discover the "Instinctive principles of Belief." We are so formed as to be under the necessity of believing in the reality of external nature. "I despise philosophy, and renounce its guidance: let my soul dwell with common sense." The facts of consciousness are ultimate facts, of which no explanation is or ought to be demandable. Science concerns itself with the demonstrable; all that is indemonstrable *outlies* the province of philosophy. The *regulæ philosophandi* can only be operatively exercised when the *facts* of thought are made their subject. *A priori* chimeras—born from subtile intelligences—are not within, but without, the conditions of science. The nature of thought is, and must always remain, to us, inscrutable, although the forms of thought, their relations and their objects, in whose existence we must implicitly believe, are capable of being inductively philosophized upon. This tendency to rest in Common Sense—the unphilosophical instincts of the race—necessitated the undervaluing of a rigidly formal logic, and hence in his imperfect and one-sided—and we may be allowed to express our belief in one word, wrong-sided—"Brief Account of Aristotle's Logic," he indulges in disparaging remarks regarding the character and ability of this one of

"the great of old,
The dead, but sceptred sovrans, who still rule
Our spirits from their urns,"

unworthy of a great mind, while he seems in many instances to have mistaken the nature and province of a true Logic. Nevertheless, his decided appeal to the facts of consciousness serve the purpose of the logician, for he cannot and does not doubt that his science accurately and adequately expresses the forms in which the mentality exerts itself while reasoning. It is not necessary to detail the elements or principles of Reid's philosophical exposition of his despite of philosophy. The tendency being exhibited, we may refer to that *omnium gatherum* of erudition and acute thought, Sir William Hamilton's "Reid's Collected Writings," in which the antidote to many of the tenets of Reid will be found admirably rendered, and, in many instances, defences more specious than correct addressed to the jury—the reading public. It is unnecessary to do more than mention Beattie, Oswald, Stewart, Brown, Payne, &c., as disciples, adhering more or less tenaciously to the general views of their great master, while adding to or substracting from his fundamental tenets, or, by a more enlarged and comprehensive analysis, resolving the complex facts of consciousness, which Reid had rashly assumed as simple, into more elementary and primary psychologic experiences.

Dr. Campbell's "Philosophy of Rhetoric" (1762) deserves honourable mention as a work of great talent, containing many judicious views on points of Logic, although denying, mistakenly, the advantages or necessity of a science of Syllogism. Lord Burnet, of Monboddo, on the other hand, is an ardent admirer of the Aristotelic Logic, and protests warmly—in his "Ancient Metaphysics" (1779)—against the views entertained by the Common Sense School of philosophers. Lord Kaimes' (Home) "Introduction to the Art of Thinking" is of no logical value; but his "Sketches of the History of Man" (1770) contains a book (iii.) well worth reading "On the Progress of the the Sciences." About this time Dr. Gillies translated the works of Aristotle, and Mr. John Bruce developed the principles of Locke and Bacon in his lectures to the students in the Edinburgh University.

The influence of Hume was not confined to Britain and France; he aroused the intellect of Germany also. Kant (at Koenigsberg, in Prussia, April 22nd, 1724—February 12th, 1804), alarmed at the abyss to the edge of which philosophy had been brought by the sceptical speculations of Hume, especially those portions which relate to the principle of Causation,[*] strove to save her from the imminent destruction with which she was threatened. Our notice of his *method* must necessarily be brief, indicative of tendencies rather than results.

[*] See the 4th, 5th, and 7th Sections of Hume's "Inquiry concerning the Human Understanding."

Before we can effectively search after Truth we must learn our, potential, ability of knowing and believing; hence the necessity of " a critique of pure Reason," in the first instance, and, by an inevitable sequence, "A critique of practical Reason."

Reason*ing* operates upon Judgments. Judgments result from impressions. Judgments are of two kinds, primarily, viz., (1) *à priori*, *i.e.*, necessary and regulative; (2) *à posteriori*, *i.e.*, experience-given and constitutive. Again, they are by-divisive into—I. Analytical, *i.e.*, expositive of what is already conceived of as contained in the subject; II. Synthetical, *i.e.*, attributive of more than is already conceived of as contained in the subject.

When knowledge is to be unfolded—elucidated, Analytical Judgments suffice; when it is to be added to—advanced, Synthetical Judgments are needful. Knowledge is of two kinds, viz., (*a*) of experimentally discovered connexions—*à posteriori* judgments; (*b*) reason-discovered and necessary connexions—*à priori* judgments. The physical sciences generally illustrate the one, the mathematical the other. Experience *causes* our belief in the former, and *occasions* our belief in the latter. Experience, whencesoever derived, must be conformed to our mental laws; *it* gives the matter, *these* give the moulds. All things must be thought of as occupying *Space*, and existing in *Time*. An intellect destitute of experience has no object to mould to the forms of thought. Experience envisaged gives impressions; these impressions, however, must be intuited, or beheld, by the Reason, according to its own forms, and hence knowledge is the result of the co-operation of the inward and outward. Hence are educed the Kantean Categories (explained in Chapter XX.). Sensation and Judgment yield the matter of Reason*ing*, and all Reason*ing* is Syllogistic, *i.e.*, either Categorical, Hypothetical, or Disjunctive. The first relates to the actual and necessary=*is* and *must be;* the second to the probable = *may* or *can be;* the third to the actual or necessary *plus* uncertainty which. The critical question, "What can I know?" is solved by the acceptance of the Syllogistic forms, and tracing premiss back to premiss until we arrive at a subject which cannot in its turn be made a predicate—a cause which is not itself caused—a unity in which the actual and the necessary coincidently dwell. *The Absolute* is that which concentres all these unitive ideas in himself, and is at once the source and end of Truth—in which the thesis and antithesis are synthethized. It were vain to attempt to explain the points of differentiation between the several disciples of Kant, and the amount of their divergence from his tenets. Schultz, Beck, Dietz, Jacob Keisewetter, Hoffbauer, Fuerbach, Born, Kinker, Staeudlin, &c., might all be mentioned as adhering to and advocating the principles of Kantism, with slight and, so far as their tendencies were concerned, unimportant differences and deviations.

Fichte (1762—1814) with intense logical acumen demonstrated the Categories which Kant had assumed as given, and maintained that the destination of the truth-seeker is to pass from doubt to knowledge, and thence to belief. His logical system is inseparable from his psychologic speculations; their general tendency, however, was to legitimate the Kantean Logic.

Schelling (born 1775) has employed Logic as a constructive science in order to combine the elementary ideas of Spinozism, Kantism, and Fichteism, into an ideal exposition of All Knowledge—God, Man, Nature.

The Logic of Hegel (1770—1831) is an exposition of the Truth, in itself—the true and only science of Being; not a merely formal science, but one whose forms are filled, whose *contents* are given in the very fact of having thoughts. Every conception involves its contradictory; thought is dichotomous. The unity of these two conceptions yields a third; this implies a new opposite and a new resultant thought. The first is a subject, the second a predicate, and the third a middle term. So we go on in unending series, continually educing plurality from unity, and a new unity as the result, until the totality of thought is exhausted, all the possible has been discovered, then thought externalizing itself becomes the real, the actual, and all that is not thus realized is the probable, *i.e.*, the-to-be-expected and the-ought-to-be.

The names of Krause, Herbert, Sigwart, might be introduced as able and excellent writers on Logical Science, while several other great men, *e.g.*, Fries, Bardili, Formey, Frederic de Hardenberg (under the pseudonym of Novalis), Schlegel, Schleiermacher, might be named, whose labours have tended to give stability to the foundations of knowledge, accuracy to our acquaintance with the laws of thought, and readiness to our perception of error.

In this series of brief chapters on the History of Logic, we have been compelled to omit much, either on account of want of information, oversight, or the necessary requirements of conciseness. We have sought, in general, rather to trace tendencies than to expound, in detail, the opinions of the great minds which have devoted their talents to the evolution and perfectionment of a science of thought. Closely knit as Psychology and Logic are, it was, in many instances, impossible to do more than indicate the method of the philosophic school from which the logical tendency of the Time sprung. We hope that, short

as the present abstract is, it will not be destitute of use in showing
how steadily a progress has been making towards exhausting all the
possible solutions of the problems of the Intellect, and hence of increasing the likelihood that the future cultivators of the science, by
an extensive inductive survey of all these theories, a wider generalization of systems, and a clearer perception of what *may be* the truth,
shall be capable of educing an accurate and trustworthy Logic. We
could have wished to exhibit, in greater detail, the correlation between
free thought and logical culture, and hence to educe signs of hope for
the future from the increased ardency with which such studies are
now being pursued; but such an attempt would have exceeded the
limits of an Introductory Essay, which is all that these brief chapters
pretend to be.

We shall finish our task for the present by directing attention to
"The Appendix on Recent Logical Developments," attached to the
succeeding work, and referring our readers for farther information on
the History of Logic to the following works, viz. :—

Franck's "Esquisse d'une Histoire de la Logique;" B. Saint Hilaire's
"Logique d'Aristote;" Blakey's "Historical Sketch of Logic;" D. F.
Toleti's "*Introductio in Universam Aristotelis Logicam;*" Reid's
"Brief Account of Aristotle's Logic;" Sir William Hamilton's "Discus-
sions;" Tatham's "Chart and Scale of Truth," vol. i.; Dugald Stewart's
"Elements of the Philosophy of the Human Mind," vol. ii.; Brown's
"Lectures," lect. 4; Campbell's "Philosophy of Rhetoric;" Kant's
"Critic of Pure Reason," and "Fallacy of the Four Figures of Syllo-
gism;" Jardine's "Outlines of a Philosophical Education;" Cousin's
"Histoire de la Philosophie." See also an able article "On Indian
Logic," by Professor Max Müller, appended to Thomson's "Laws of
Thought;" Trendelenburg's "Geschichte der Kategorienlehre;" Hau-
reau's "Philosophie Scholastique," &c., &c.

THE ART OF REASONING.

CHAPTER I.

INTRODUCTION.

THE present age is one of progress and inquiry. Society is undergoing rapid and important changes. The aspect of the world is becoming altered. The large eye of humanity is gazing on the future with expectancy. Force, wealth, fraud, and prejudice are losing their supremacy, and intellectuality is steadily advancing and becoming dominant. Mind is gaining an upward and elevating tendency. We seem as if we had attained the verge of a new era. Truth is the object of earnest search and serious investigation. Thought is reaping richer fruits, and *thinking* men are less scarce than formerly. In the faith of this elevation, progressiveness, and desire for truth, the following chapters have been written.

The nature of man has always been a favourite study; and well may he be pardoned for the apparent self-love which this fact seems to indicate. What object in the visible universe is so worthy of diligent and enlightened investigation?—His frame so exquisitely constructed, so wondrously fitted for his situation, so admirably adapted to his internal and external relationships! When we compare ourselves with the existences around, we feel that in many things our homogeneity is evident; but when we read our own consciousness, and feel the power of thought exerting itself within us, we readily perceive the basis of the exclamation, "How noble a thing is man!" The generic distinction of the human race is Reason—by this faculty have men been led to speculate upon the world beyond them, and the still more wondrous phenomena within—by this have the foundation facts and primary elements, upon which the glorious superstructure of science and art has been upbuilt, been discovered and applied—by this has the star-typed page of the evening sky been read, the hieroglyphics of the fossilized strata been discovered, and the mysterious language of nature been understood, interpreted, and taught—by this has science been originated, advanced, and applied—by this the progression of humanity has been effected, and by it greater and more glorious triumphs will yet be proposed and successfully accomplished. New facts, new inferences, new results, and applications, thus in unending series proceed the operations of the rational faculty. True, error is incident to humanity. True, the nightly watchers on Chaldea's plains imagined that some occult influence was eliminated from the gems which deck eve's lustrous mantle, and ruled, as they thought, the fate of all the children of mortality! True, the alchymist, with anxious beating breast, sat o'er his crucibles and watched the processes and transmutations which occurred within them, in the illusory hope that wealth untold would gleam before his eyes, and an uncounted treasure be extracted from the earthy ores. But even then the "light which led astray was light from heaven." After long years of tedious watching and persevering observation, the inquiries of the astrologer resulted in the deduction so ably expressed by our own poet—

> " The fates, dear Brutus, are not in our stars,
> But in ourselves, that we are underlings."

After long years of "patient expectation," many years of unrequited toil and self-deceiving hopes, when experiment had been repeated ten thousand thousand times, and still the hope was blighted, the futility of the attempt became too evident, and from the wreck of these imaginary sciences has arisen that magnificent body of truths which Astronomy unfolds and Chemistry reveals. "Newton brought down the old divinities from their starry thrones, and converted lovely Venus and potent Jove into silent monitors of the lapse of time, or friendly guides of the adventitious navigator on a lonely ocean; Judicial Astrology was for ever confuted, and men learned to gaze unmoved on the comet which they once thought

> ' From his horrid hair
> Shook pestilence and war.' "*

Light has now been thrown on the profoundest secrets of nature, and as the eye becomes accustomed to the brilliancy, how glorious shall the disclosures and discoveries of the future be! But in all this, Reason must be our guide, and observation and experiment her handmaids. In this manner have all the discoveries and inventions of modern times been effected. The circulation of the blood, vaccination, the steam engine, the telegraph, with all their advantages, applications, and effects, what are they but the results of observation and experiment, guided and controlled by the deductions of reason? But it is not alone in the elevated walks of science and philosophy that reason gains her

* STODDART's Universal Grammar, p. 80.

triumphs; it is not alone amid the far distant planetary orbs, in the dim caverns of the earth, or on the surface of the plant-covered globe, that she may be found. She may not only be seen poring over the glyphography of the eternal-seeming hills, classifying the myriads of the flowers, searching, scalpel in hand, for the arcana of life, arranging a cabinet of ocean shells or earth's treasury of minerals, sitting in a museum of natural history, and "counting the number of the stars," but also unfolding the scroll of a nation's laws, summing huge columns of statistical accounts, revealing the prerequisites of a sanitary condition, and conducting the business of ordinary life. And what were life without her all-needful aid? A series of sensations, feelings, passions, yielding delight, it is true, but a delight short-lived and transitory. How frequently do we wander "unweeting of the perilous way," bewildered amid mere present impressions, the delicious nature of which we feel, but the insidious character of which we think not of attempting to discover! What is the origin of error? In what manner do we solve the strange and startling enigma of *vice*, if we admit not that *unreflectiveness* bears a share in the divergence of the unwary from the track of well-doing and well-being? if we do not believe, with the poet, that

> " Evil is wrought by want of thought,
> As well as want of heart?"

Correct principles of thought, accurate habits of reasoning, cannot but be advantageous; they enable us to examine the chart of life with care, to elude the insidious snares which seek to lure us into error, and preserve us from being " like a vessel tossed upon the waters, rudderless and without a compass, with no port to make for, and no stars to steer by." They enable us to regulate our thoughts, to test the accuracy of arguments, to refute sophisms, and to adopt rules for our conduct in every-day life. They teach us to keep our eye constantly fixed on the focus of truth, and preserve us from all wavering and fluctuation.

In the above remarks we have argument sufficient to justify our present attempt to simplify and place within the reach of all a knowledge of " The Art of Reasoning." In what branch of life is this unrequired? In what position in society can we exist without its exercise? In the operations of the farm, in the labours of the loom, the lathe, the sledge-hammer, in the management of machinery, in the pursuit of literature, in the advocacy of truth, and in the multifarious topics of controversy and conversation, it is equally necessary. But in the present crisis, when the weal or woe of our nation seems about to be more entrusted to the guardianship of each member of the community, how exceedingly important is it that we should find some means to prevent ourselves from being tossed about by every wind of doctrine! We must become acquainted, so to speak, with the mechanism of thought, the understanding must be anatomized—the method of its action ascertained and applied to the constantly recurring difficulties of thought and practice. Whether, therefore, we speak to men of speculative disposition, to men of business or of trade, the subject of our prelections will be seen to be equally indispensable to success. But, we may be told, common sense is the best logic; and we answer, we do not wish to dispense with common sense, but to *train* it, to habituate it to the best, nay, the *only legitimate* method which the mind can take in the examination of any question in philosophy, science, literature, or business. Which artizan will argue that natural talent alone will suffice to enable any one successfully to perform the peculiar duties belonging to any walk of industrial exertion? But this innate ability operated upon by the *training* undergone during the period of apprenticeship, sufficiently capacitates any moderately gifted person to follow his calling in a tolerable manner. Here no new faculty is imparted, but the inherent ability improved by continuous exercise and attention, enables him to perform his duties. In like manner, Logic bestows no new sense, no additional mental faculty, but superinduces improvement, refinement, and skill, on the already and previously existent capacity. The powers of the mind we possess by nature, and these do in some sort instinctively exert themselves. But we know that there is false as well as true reasoning—that some men are conspicuous for the accuracy and clearness of their ideas and their power of perspicuous exposition, persons who can "thread the labyrinth" of intricate and interblended investigations, and present them to the "mind's eye" with order and clearness, while some are precisely the reverse—people who confound facts, misconstrue statements, garble thoughts, mystify plain and obvious distinctions, and are almost incapable either of perceiving things accurately themselves, or of presenting them in a lucid or intelligible form to others.

"The Art of Reasoning" pre-supposes the *substratum* of reason to be already existing, and endeavours to explain *how* some men succeed in elucidating thought, while others fail. To watch the procedure of the intellect when exerted correctly in the search for truth, or the investigation of phenomena, to describe this examinative process, to point out the sources of error, and the method of avoiding mistakes, are all that logic, properly so called, pretends to perform. By thus describing, explaining, and exemplifying the correct use of the investigative powers, we place before those who are desirous of becoming adepts in its application, comparing their several acts with the means of the *formulæ* to which all true reasoning must perforce conform. We show them how to trace thought from its most rudimentary form to its completion as an act of ratiocination. We explain how thought succeeds thought, and what relations and connections are pre-supposed or implied in them. By this means the vigour of the mind is increased, its vigilance and acumen kept on the alert, and its perceptive powers quickened and refined. In short, we heartily subscribe to and endorse the opinion of J. S. Mill, pithily expressed in the following sentence :—"If a science of logic exists, or is capable of existing, it must be useful. If there be rules to which every mind conforms, in every instance in which it judges rightly, there seems little necessity for discussing whether a person is more likely to observe those rules when he knows the rules, than when he is unacquainted with them." What can be more valuable as an agent in strengthening the intellect, in enlarging knowledge, and promoting our own welfare and prosperity, than to possess a gauge of our own powers, and an acquaintance with the best method of employing them ?

We do not intend to treat with dry and uninteresting frivolousness of the *questiones vexatæ* of the schools ; we do not intend to attempt the solution of the mystery-involved verbiage of the dark ages ; we will not talk of "intention and remission, proportion and degree ; infinity, formality, quiddity, and individuality," and a dozen other " occult qualities and imaginary essences;" but while we aim at lucidity of expression, conciseness, and philosophical accuracy, we will endeavour to fit our lucubrations for the purposes of ordinary life and the necessities of the thinking masses.

Every " Art" depends upon some theory, some principle or collection of principles which underlie, and form the substratum of, the practices of those who employ it. Theory thus appears to be essential to the successful prosecution of any *art*. As it is a systematised series of all the most important observations and rules, deduced from the most approved method of procedure adopted by the most eminent speculators and operators, it would appear evident that, after the theory is fully developed and accurately studied, nothing farther is necessary than to habituate the mind and accustom the intellectual powers to promptitude and precision in the processes which it describes and explains. By this we see what others have done ; how they did it ; what measure of success attended their efforts ; what obstacles they overcame ; with what difficulties they wrestled ; how the victory was gained ; and how

error, vanquished, left the field. Man should live at perpetual enmity
with ignorance. It is the bane of life, and the antagonist of well-
being; every conquest of truth is another addition to the average
happiness of our race; every error refuted is an obstacle to man's progressiveness removed and foiled. If men desire a diminution of pain,
and an increase of delight, ignorance is the first foe to be attacked;
against this must we continually engage in an inveterate warfare.
Ignorance, however, is either positive or negative; negative ignorance
is the absence of *knowledge* in the soul. We are all born negatively
ignorant: the soul, philosophically considered, is an unwritten volume
on which perception and reflection write the accumulated mass of facts
of which life is composed; positive ignorance is the absence of truth, is
error, crime, wrong-doing, and wrong-thinking. The former supposes
the mind a "*tabula rasa*," a series of blank forms to be filled up; the
latter looks on it as "scribbled o'er" with notions needful of deletion,
and, to continue the figure, in this up-filling of the mental manuscript
errors must be erased, emendations introduced, revisal and correction
are necessary, new facts must be registered, old ideas re-examined, and
new ones submitted to the ordeal of trial and experiment. In such cir·
cumstances it is that logic is required; and here let us admit that the
task is difficult and the study abstruse. To keep watch and ward over
the avenues of the soul, to detect the entrance of inaccurate impressions,
to guide the evolutions of the intellect, and curb the wayward wish by
the stern reign of *will*, is no easy task. There *is* no "royal road" to
certitude of thought, there *is* no intellectual mastery attained but by
courageous effort. We do intend to simplify, but not so much as to
render thought unnecessary. We desiderate a thoughtful, self-inquiring
soul; to *him* we will unfold our thoughts, and in the light of his own
spirit shall he view them and feel their truth. Study, then, the following concise abstract of our subject, and criticise as you proceed, feel that
each step is accurately taken, and we doubt not you will reap the fruit
of your exertions in correctness of thought, accuracy of reasoning, and a
clear perception of truth.

Logic properly signifies discourse; and, as the mind is that which
employs discourse, logic, as a SCIENCE, includes a theory of mind so far
as its operations are necessary for the purposes of speech, or the inter-
communication of ideas. All discourse is *educative*, and should have
for its object the outleading and upbuilding of the intellect. All the
mind's intercommunications ought to be employed either in the discovery of the truth, or the imparting of it, in the attainment of knowledge hitherto unpossessed, or the exposition and explication of some

department of inquiry, either not at all, or imperfectly comprehended by those whom we address. Hence logic, as an ART, teaches the method in which truth *is* discovered, and how the explication of it *must* proceed.

According to the above view of the subject, logic *may be* defined as the *science* which instructs us in the principles of correct reasoning, and the *art* of applying these principles to the discovery and communication of truth. Truth consists in the coincidence of our ideas with the objectivities by which they are originated. The operations of the intellect which are employed for the above-mentioned purposes are Perceptivity, Judgment, Ratiocination, and Method.

Perceptivity is that faculty of the mind by which the impressions which phenomena,—that is, the external appearance of things,—make upon the thinking powers, and the knowledge of the mental operations employed in cogitation, and conveyed to us through the medium of consciousness, are observed and registered. Those impressions and mental operations which are thus noticed by the mind are called perceptions, and these perceptions, when treasured up in the memory, become the objects of *thought* and *knowledge*, and are called ideas.

Judgment is that mental power by which we compare two distinct perceptions, and by this simple comparison predicate agreement or discordancy regarding them. A judgment expressed in words is called a proposition.

Ratiocination is the synthesis of two judgments, or the comparison of two distinct ideas through the intermediatcy of another object or idea. The verbal expression of an act of ratiocination is called a syllogism.

Method is the arrangement of our knowledge, that is, the *results* of our perceptivity, judgment, and ratiocination, so as to be most easily remembered and communicated.

The above-mentioned faculties may be called the integrants of reason. Perceptivity collects and judgment adjusts the materials of thought. Ratiocination builds them, and method displays the edifice of upbuilt fact. We have not felt constrained at present to enter at any greater length upon the explication of the foregoing definitions : in the meantime it behoves our readers to strive after a correct knowledge of the meaning attached to these terms, as they will recur at every step of our future progress. The necessity of definition is obvious ; for words are the mere *circulating medium* of speech, and if their value be not definitively settled, misunderstanding, doubt, and difficulty must arise.

Let these definitions be entered, then, amongst our present verbal currency, and let their value be accurately appreciated now, so shall we

the less require to interlard our future articles with explanatory clauses
and parenthetical divergencies.

In our next chapter we shall proceed to analyse the perceptive powers
of man : this will afford us an opportunity of explaining, illustrating,
and reducing to practical use the primary and rudimentary investigative
faculties of our race. We will endeavour to point out their mode of
action, and the precautions necessary for the attainment of correct ideas,
the basis of all correct reasoning and all true knowledge. You have
seen the necessity for the art of which we have been speaking. You
have attained a glimpse of what it proposes ; will you go along with us
in its attentive study, the results of which must be so advantageous, the
rewards of which will be so great ?

CHAPTER II.

PERCEPTIVITY.

> " So build we up the being that we are—
> Thus deeply drinking in the soul of things,
> We shall be wise."   WORDSWORTH.

WHEN we look around us on the world in which we dwell, we find
ourselves encompassed and surrounded by a multiplicity of objects possessed of the power of originating impressions in our minds, through
the instrumentality of our organs of sense. When we introvert our
thoughts, examine the ideas which are formed in our souls, and flit continually through their chambers, and observe how the mental powers
operate upon them, we become capable of discerning the several states
into which the mind successively enters. By these two investigative
processes—the former of which is called Sensation, the latter Reflection
—we gain the *matériel* from which the Understanding eliminates Truth ;
by these we acquire a knowledge of those objective, *i.e.*, external, and
those subjective, *i.e.*, internal impressions, which the sensorial powers
had communicated to, or originated in, the thinking principle. This
capacity of mind is what we call Perceptivity, and the method in which
it performs its functions is twofold—corporeal and mental. We do not,
however, intend to restrict our consideration to what a mere literal
interpretation of the term might imply, but to view, in conjunction, its
corporeal operations and their mental results. To accomplish this

'properly, we shall classify our remarks into the following departments —viz., Sensation, Perception, Ideas, and Names—each of which we propose, in the briefest possible manner, to bring under your notice.

SENSATION signifies that series of corporeal impressions or influences which external objects and internal feelings produce on Man, and by which all our knowledge of Phenomena, *i.e.*, the outward appearances of things, is conveyed to the mental percipiency. Before any representation of phenomena can be imparted, there are certain *media* through which it must pass in order that it may be rendered cognoscible by the Intellect. The object in which the phenomena inhere must either be in contact with the sensational organ, or with some intervening agent by which the sensative power may be informed—*e.g.*, the pulsations of air, the rays of light, &c.—then follows the excitation of the organism under the appropriate stimuli. This excitement must run the course of the nervous circuit, till it reaches the sensorial centre—the Brain—and, lastly, the brain must, in some unknown and mysterious way, "report progress to the upper house"—the Mind. Properly speaking, the greater part of the above steps belong rather to the Physiology of Man, than to the Philosophy of Mind. But all knowledge is interwoven ; and it were vain to attempt the explanation of our subject, by exhibiting the mind, like an immense picture-gallery, ready furnished, without striving to show, at least, part of the process by which this mental *Daguerreotypy* is effected.

We shall therefore proceed, succinctly, to consider the *modus operandi* of the senses. The Senses are the avenues to the soul, and the routes by which Knowledge arrives at the Mind. All our ideas of external things are derived through our sensational organs : of these, that of sight is by far the noblest and most useful, as it conveys to the sensorium the greatest amount, variety, and diversity of impressions ; it pictures there the world, with all its beauties and sublimity, the varied aspects of humanity and the operations of the laws of the natural world, whilst, since the introduction of the art of printing, it almost supersedes the ear as the receiver of communicated-knowledge. Now, we think it is self-evident that, if we possess sensations at all, they must be originated by substances possessing a sensation producing power ; and although we readily grant that *noumena* or the *essence of things* is inappreciable by our faculties, yet we cannot well conceive of qualities being developed from that in which they are not resident. Be the essence of external objects, however, settled as it may, we cannot for a moment doubt that we are surrounded on all sides by myriads of objects which are not ourselves, but which, by impinging their effects upon our perceptive organs, convey impressions to our minds and realise in them ideas—the germs of thought and action. For if it be maintained that mankind are idealogists, and dwell only in a theatre of shadowy and unreal phantasies, self-begotten in the intellect, and up-built only with the unsubstantial architecture of the imagination, it will be evident that a part, that is, a sensation, cannot contain the whole, that is, sensations; if the eye be only a sensation, it cannot surely contain and realise within itself all visible sensations. Now let this sensation-recipient be shut out from the contact of anything external, and let the mind, the idealogic portion of man, strive to re-paint the landscape upon which the eye has erewhile gazed, and how faint and inadequate will be the portraiture! Reflection upon the idea slightly indicated in the foregoing sentence will, we think, convince any man that there are *beyond* and *without* him objects other than himself, which possess a sensation-imparting power, and that he himself is a sensation-recipient. If these perceptions be imparted by an outward agent, then that agent must be possessed of the quality of which, in the arcana of the intellect, it produces an impression. Do not let it be imagined that we are here arguing for the identity—the *self-sameness* of the qualities of objects with our sensations. We only assert that objects impinge upon our sensational organs impressions of certain qualities of which the perceptions in our minds are the signs, and these signs are the evidences to us of the *inherency* of that quality in the objects thus presented to us. For how can there be a sign without a thing which is signified thereby? If this be not so, why do we, on perceiving the round shadow which the earth throws upon the moon during an eclipse, predicate the rotundity of the globe? Do we not here infer, from the sign of the quality, the existence of the quality itself? Sensations constitute the inarticulate language in which nature converses with the soul. And as words do not present to us the qualities or objects about which speech is employed, but are a series of symbols indicative of these qualities and objects, so sensation does not produce the quality in our mind, but indicates its existence.

Sensation is of two kinds—special and common. Common Sensation is that ordinary Nervile power which is distributed through all the parts of the human framework, charged with the general conservation of the body. By this power we gain the ideas of heat and cold—pleasure and pain—hunger and satiety—exhaustion and lassitude—and perhaps, motion and rest—and other similar general impressions. This power of ordinary sensation may, for the sake of distinction, be called Nervility. Special Sensation is that felt by those *foci* of peculiar nervous ramifications, called the Senses. These are but particular sensational organisms, appropriated to the reception of more peculiar impulsions than those of which Common Sensation takes cognizance, and are commonly reckoned five, viz., Smell, Taste, Touch, Hearing, and Sight.

Smell is that sense by which we receive information of the odours of external objects through the action of scent-yielding effluxes upon the olfactory nerves. The part which this sense plays in the drama of sensation is comparatively insignificant, though, as a conservative instrument, it is very valuable. The perception of those odorous emanations doubtlessly introduces new ideas of the properties of bodies into our mind; and the exquisite pleasure which it thus yields us seems to entitle it to this brief notice of its doings.

Taste is a faculty of the Sensational agency, whose peculiar duty is —so far as our present purpose is concerned with it—to impart to the soul a knowledge of certain qualities of bodies, comprehended under the general term *Sapidity*. The organ by which it conveys these sensations is the upper surface of the tongue, which is possessed of a papilaceous structure, somewhat resembling the pile of velvet, through which the nerve of taste is distributed. The knowledge-imparting power of this organ is feeble, and of little moment.

Taste and smell are chemically-acting senses, and are excited by the action of certain volatile particles of bodies upon the secreted mucus which lubricates the surfaces of these nervous networks. The other senses of which we have to speak are mechanical, operated upon by the pressure of bodies upon the Nervile fibres, and thus stimulated to action.

Touch is one of the chief knowledge-imparting senses. By it we gain our ideas of most of the physical properties of the material universe. The whole Nervile network, which diffuses itself through the human frame, is, in some measure, endowed with this tactual perceptive power; but the chief seats of this faculty are the tips of the fingers, the lips, and the tongue. The ideas which this sense communicates are such as hardness or softness—roughness or smoothness—solidity or liquidity —regularity or irregularity—distance or nearness—figure, magnitude, and viscidity—and, perhaps, motion or rest.

Hearing is the sense by which, through the agency of the ear, we receive the knowledge of sounds. The sensorial impression felt by the auditory nerve is essentially the result of an exquisitely minute and delicate action of the power of touch. There are certain undulatory vibrations of air, occasioned by the percussion of elastic bodies, which, being conveyed to the complicated mechanism of the ear, and concentrated therein, impinge their impulsions on the auditory nerves, and thus produce the sense of sound. To this sense we are indebted for the refined gratification arising from Music, whether sung in "wood-notes wild" by the maiden of our love, the partner of our joys and sorrows, or in the exquisite warblings of the "Swedish Nightingale,"—piped by instruments of varying harmony—sounded by the high-pealing organ, the warlike drum, the piercing fife, the resonant trumpet, or the sounding flute. The rich, delicious melody of the Summer's unhired songsters —the lofty diapason of the thunder—the lay of the loud-resounding sea —bring into exercise this organ of the soul. But the chief value it possesses is its enabling us to listen to those sounds, indicative of thought and feeling, which constitute Language, by which we are enabled to transmit, through posterity, the accumulated treasures of wisdom which the genius of man has discovered or acquired.

Sight is the last, and most important, of the general classification of the senses. The organ of sight is the eye, the retina of which is, as its name imports, a network expansion of the optic nerve. The rays of light, which are reflected from all objects, passing through the eye, come in contact with the retina, and paint thereon a picture of the objects from which they proceed ; the impression thus made is conveyed to the nervous centre—the Brain—and thence mysteriously into the mind. The sensations obtained through this organ are, the external, visible appearances of things, such as superficial extension, shape, apparent magnitude, colour, shade, relative position, distance, &c. As light is the intervening medium through which the sense of sight receives impressions, and as the reflections of light are modified according to the diversity of the texture and material qualities which substances possess, so there is an almost infinite diversity in the sensations which we feel through it. We learn, by habit, the actual magnitude and solid dimension of objects from their distance, and the disposition of light and shade in the objects which we behold ; and we discern distance by the comparison of the apparent magnitude with the known size of bodies, concerning which, either tactually or otherwise, we possess a previous knowledge.

The pleasure as well as the knowledge which we derive from this organic function is incalculable. By it the beauty, sublimity, grandeur, and magnificence of the surrounding world are made ours. We gaze upon a landscape—and the light, greatest of artists, pictures it in our eye, and engraves it on the memory. The giant mountain with cloud-piercing summit, clad with trees, heath, herbage, and overspread with cattle— the river flowing statelily, bearing upon its breast vessels of every imaginable size and burthen—the peaceful rural hamlet built upon its brink

—the towering battlements of some hoary castle—the level meadow— the wooded dell—"the smiling cot, the cultivated farm"—the milkmaid and her swain—the ponderous waggon with its sleeky team—the blue sky and the flower-enamelled grass—with ten thousand other objects of beauty, grace, and grandeur, are instantaneously imprinted on the nervous network in the most delicate tints, and with the most admirable proportion of parts and harmony of colouring. By this sense we examine the productions of nature, scale the heavens and measure the starry host which light them—perceive a world of life and joy and motion in a tiny flower, or a myriad of minute creatures in one liquid water-drop. By it we determine and guide our peripatetic wanderings, glean wisdom from the pages of genius, whether of our own or other countries and times, and gather knowledge from the wide-open beauty-written hieroglyphs of Nature. As Dr. Brown eloquently remarks, "It is not a small expanse of light which we perceive, equal merely to the narrow expansion of the optic nerve. It is the Universe itself. We are present with stars which beam upon us at a distance that converts to nothing the whole wide diameter of the planetary system. It is as if the tie which binds us down to the globe belonged only to the other senses, and had no influence over this, which, even in its union with the body, seems still to retain all the power and unbounded freedom of its celestial original."

By the conjoint agency of these sensation-receiving faculties, we gain our knowledge of external objects. The intellectual powers exist implicitly or unmanifested, sensation developes them and calls them into action. As the acorn possesses the capacity, when light, heat, proper soil, and the other appropriate stimuli are applied, of producing trunk, leaves, branches, &c., so the mind is endowed with the capacity of eliminating perception, thought, &c., as the result of the operation of external existences upon the sensitive organs. So far is it true, that Sensation is the *educer* of thought, that we have no ideas prior to the reception of sensations, and have not even perception coeval with them. Our senses require *education*—development. Though light impresses the retina by its radiations, though pulsations of air vibrate on the auditory nerve, though tactual contiguity be established between our nervous powers and exterior objects, there is at first only a vague, indefinite imprint produced: this becomes more and more distinct, definite, and precise, as repetition *educates* the sensorial agency. Much exercise and excitement, many times repeated, must be undergone before such a feeling be produced as the same object will always excite in the organ of sense. Sensation, therefore, is the *result* of external impressions made on the *educated* senses, and conveyed to the sensorium, the nervous centre, the brain.

PERCEPTION. The subsequent step in the attainment of ideas is the excitement of the intellectual faculties by sensation. The feeling thus produced is called Perception. Sensation is the *corporeal*—Perception the *mental* impression. How this mental *ébranlement*—motivity—is brought about, is inscrutable to us. Yet that it is a fact we can scarcely doubt, for we know that sensations are frequently made upon the organs appropriated to their reception, which, nevertheless, communicate no perceptivity to the *intellection* within, as in the case of any one diligently pursuing his studies or engaged in meditation deep, unwitting of the clock's time-telling voice. The mind, on being excited by the intimations of the senses, immediately becomes *conscious* of the sensation conveyed. This *Consciousness* of the mind causes it to exert its various faculties and powers in different ways, according to the qualities of the object perceived; as, for instance, desire, hatred, fear, willing, believing, doubting, thinking, &c., which are all acts of the mind set in operation by the telegraphic communications of the sensorial powers. The faculty by which we perceive the mind's acts is called Reflection. From the above we see the natural process by which knowledge is acquired. We can have no perception of our own mental acts till they are excited; they cannot be excited unless the perceptive powers are furnished with sensations by which they may be stimulated; these sensations can only be attained through the sensorial avenues which form a part of the animal frame. When, however, the mind is furnished with these representatives of external existences, it proceeds to recal, examine, arrange, combine, and modify them: thus it becomes acquainted with its own operations, creates, so to speak, new objects of thought, and augments indefinitely the sum of its ideas. By the comparison of those ideas, and by combining them in such a manner as shall best suit the object in view, the human understanding is enabled to proceed from the proximate to the remote, until it learns the truth of facts far beyond the reach of man's sensational ken. This exertion of mind, which results in the formation of ideas, we call Perceptivity. "Strange process!" by which Sensation "is converted into thought as the mulberry leaf is converted into satin!"

IDEAS. Thus we have seen that the *corporeal* impression produced by external objects is called Sensation—the *mental* notion originated by this is called Perception—and the mind's consciousness of its own doings is named Reflection—that these, conjointly, constitute Perceptivity, and are the sources whence the intellectual powers derive the elements of thought—Ideas. When an idea conveys to the mind a sense of the present reality of an object, it receives the name of Perception; but when it is accompanied by a sense of remembrance, imagination, or expectancy, it is called a Conception. The word idea, however, in the sense in which we will use it, includes both of these, and signifies—*That apprehension of an object or mental state which is raised in the mind either by perception, memory, or imagination, by and upon which the operation of thought is performed.* Ideas are of two kinds, Sensible and Mental—Sensible Ideas are those gained by the Perception of exterior objects, as of a house, a horse, a tree, a man, &c. Mental Ideas are those which we receive through reflection, as fearing, hating, loving, braving, &c., and those Ideas of *relation* which sense cannot apprehend, but which the mind perceives as *implied* in the sensuous impressions it receives, as space, time, distance, causation, &c. Sensation can only inform the mind of *things*. It can correctly represent to the mental percipiency the *thing* upon which another stands, and the *thing* standing upon it; but the idea, which we may take the liberty of calling *upon-ness*, not being an object of sense, can only be the result of a comparison and judgment instituted, instinctively in many cases it may be, by the powers of the understanding, and hence "every kind of relation is a pure idea of intellect, and can never be apprehended by sense." The mind being furnished with these ideas in the manner already so fully described, the Logician proceeds to classify them into simple and complex—distinct or indistinct—adequate or inadequate—abstract or concrete—particular or general.

A Simple Idea is one which is conceived in the mind as existing unically, *i.e.*, which can be considered only as *one*, being indivisible and without distinct parts. Such are most of our ideas of qualities, as hot, cold, black, white, round, smooth, hard, soft, &c.; many of our notions of tastes and sounds, as bitter, sweet, loud, low, &c.; and many of our ideas of the operations and feelings of our minds, as desire, hunger, pain, perceptivity, thinking, &c. Simple ideas are incommunicable to any one who is destitute of the organic function or faculty empowered to perceive them. A man born blind cannot gain ideas of light and colour, however minute and vivid the description given may be. Neither can an individual, deaf from birth, have any notion of sounds. No ability of the understanding can supply this connate deficiency, for there can be no cumulation of simpler elements by which such an idea might be communicated; and if it were possible to find a man who had never been sensible of thought, will, or desire, the only way in which these ideas could be *educed* would be to excite them in himself.

A Complex Idea is made up of, or contains, two or more simple ideas, into which it may be divided or subdivided, and each of which is *individually* capable of being thought upon, as the idea of a watch, which is made up of many simple ideas combined in one. Most of our ideas of Virtues and Vices, as truth, justice, deceit, &c., all our ideas of figures, as squares, cubes, circles, parallelograms, &c., and of substances constituting what are commonly called "the three kingdoms of Nature," are complex, *i.e.*, made up of simple ideas which the mind is capable of *individualizing*.

A Distinct Idea is one which is so separated and distinguished from others, that we can form a full, clear, and perfect comprehension of *it*, as contradistinguished from others nearly similar—one, of which you can as clearly discern the boundaries and dissimilitudes as if it were a mathematical figure. An Indistinct Idea is the reverse of this—one which we are unable obviously to discern and accurately to perceive, and distinguish as dissociated and apart from those bearing a resemblance to it. In Geometry, Arithmetic, and the other mathematical sciences, our ideas are perfectly clear and distinct; we can with certainty discern the points of agreement and disagreement between them; but in philosophy, religion, business, morals, art, &c., our ideas are in general indistinct to a greater or less degree. In proportion to the distinctness of our ideas is the certainty of our knowledge.

An Adequate Idea is an exact and complete representative of the object originating it; the external object being the prototype or model, the idea, to be adequate, must be its antitype, or precise and corresponding likeness. An Inadequate Idea is not a correct and perfect representation of an object—is one in which *all* the parts and properties of an object are not comprehended. An idea may be distinct and yet inadequate. We may have a distinct conception of all the *parts*, and yet not have an adequate idea of all the *properties* of these parts; thus, we can have a clear idea of a triangle, although our perception of the *properties* of a right-angled, isosceles, or scalene triangle, each of which *implies* peculiar properties of sides and angles, may be exceedingly inadequate. A distinct idea differentiates, an adequate one informs us what is involved and implied in that indication of differences.

Abstract Ideas are formed by comparing any number of objects in two points of view, viz., the coinciding portion, or quality, and the differing one or ones. When we have found that in which they coincide, we abstract or withdraw *that* from the objects in which it inheres, and give it a name, as height, roundness, length, wisdom, &c.; then this becomes an idea transferable from one object to another, one on which the mind can think independently of an object. Concrete ideas are those which express an abstract quality as inherent in or belonging to some object.

Particular ideas represent individual existences; as they are seen in nature unclassified and individuated, they are symbolised by proper names, as Socrates, Victoria, Athens, London, &c., &c.

General Ideas are those which comprehend several classes of individuals under one general representative cognomen, as man, tree, flower, house, &c. Language would be infinite, and communication impossible, were the mind compelled to give every individual object a distinct name; fortunately, however, it is endowed with the power of generalisation, by which it affixes to each class of similar ideas a specific name, which may be applied to any one object comprehended in that class, and distinguishes individuals only when it is necessary for the sake of perspicuity. By this expedient, language is rendered much more easy of acquisition, and more convenient for use. But this subject will be more fully elucidated in our remarks "On Names and Objects able to be named." The utility and advantage of these distinctions will become more obvious as we proceed in our analysis of the processes of thought.

The universe, from which much of our knowledge is obtained, and by which our mental powers are called into action, is an Academic hall, whose portals are never shut, and whose teachers are never unwilling to impart information to the ardent-souled student. And what a glorious body of instructors are there! The sun, in its mid-day glory; the moon, with her meek and chastened smile; those myriad dwellers in the city of splendour—the stars; the mighty ocean, the green-clad earth, the towering mountains, the expansive forests, the nestling vales, the foaming cataracts, the glacial ice-peaks, the majestic river, the murmuring brooklet rambling through the glade, the lightning's electric current, the Borealic coruscations, the comet in its apparently eccentric orbit; those spring-scattered daughters of beauty—the flowers, the glory-hued firmament, the seven-coloured arch of heaven, and all that is rich, rare, lovely, magnificent, and sublime. But man is nature's sole interpreter—the translator of the symbolic language of those soul educators, and it becomes him to beware lest he allow any sinister motive to interpose between their teachings and his perceptions. Every organic function places us in a definite relation and connection with these our *natural* instructors, but self-deception is frequently a favourite pursuit of humanity, and we are too apt to misconstrue the most evident precepts of nature to our own hurt, wherefore it is of the utmost importance that we should guard against prepossessions and prejudices.

From these considerations we take the liberty of prescribing the following practical rules, which are founded upon the foregoing explication of the origin, perception, and classification of ideas.

1st, Endeavour to gain accurate ideas.

Our ideas are inaccurate chiefly from two causes—carelessness in the observation of the objects which produce them, and negligence in acquiring the precise meaning of the words used to denote them. Hence this rule implies carefulness in the comparison of objects with ideas, and of ideas with the words which are used as their signs. Much space need not be occupied in enforcing this rule. If accuracy be not obtained, time, trouble, investigation, are thrown away. If a house be erected upon an unstable foundation, or if it have any *radical* defect, it had better not have been built; so if ideas be formed in the mind which are not coincident with their object, we had better not have had them, for any deductions based upon them will be erroneous, and ignorance is preferable to error. The ignorant man needs only to be instructed, but the errorist must unlearn and relearn. Besides, the possession of erroneous ideas leads us to imagine ourselves well informed when we really are not so; we are thus exposed to the disagreeable feeling of humiliation resulting from detected error, and all those harassing misconceptions of wilful imposture to which this gives rise. Negligence of this rule causes ambiguity of expression, which is the chief cause of debate and controversy. All that is required is patience, attention, and diligent investigation; if we give these to the task, we shall soon reap the rich reward of accuracy of thought, strength of judgment, and mental superiority.

2nd, Gain as many ideas upon every important subject as possible.

If we are correct in our opinion, that soul education is the great object of human existence—if we are right in believing that the universe is expressly and admirably adapted for the *eduction* of thought and the invigoration of the mental powers, the appropriateness and relevancy of this rule will be evident. Knowledge is the sunlight of the world; it is that which beautifies by its rays, illumines by its brilliance, and vivifies and strengthens by its universal prevadency. The world was not wholly formed to nourish the vegetable products which grow upon its surface, to feed the animals which course along its plains, or yield the necessaries of life to the members of the human race. No! it was the design of Providence, that every human soul should hold the germ of wisdom. The soil which produces the fragrance-breathing children of the valley, or the beauteous dwellers on the sun-gilt hill, is not more adapted to its purpose than is the world of which we are the inhabitants, calculated to draw forth the energies latent in the soul, and give them life, vigour, and vitality. As well might the eye see in the absence of light, or the ear hear without the vibratory motions of the air, as the human mind be healthy without knowledge. By this the Astronomer scans the star-decked dome of heaven, and counts therein a multitude of worlds; the Geologist lifts a pebble from the shore, a shell from off the beach, and tells the secrets of the earth when history was dumb. By this we cross the trackless ocean, and wind along the mighty seas which girdle the earth, learn the products of every clime, hear the records of nations long since buried from the human eye, trace the history of the past, observe the aspect of the present, and anticipate the future, watch the progress of humanity, witness its struggles for freedom, its strenuous striving after mental illumination, see the cities men have built, the customs they observed, the hopes they entertained, listen to the noblest sentiments, the most eloquent orations, the highest resolves, and the almost angel-voiced songs of the "monarchs of mind." We should, therefore, seek to gain as many ideas on science, art, nature, society, business, manners, laws, morals, philosophy, religion, as is within our power, and strive to gain great and comprehensive views of men and things. Oh, how dark is that man's soul who has not thus striven after knowledge! Nature is a mass of hieroglyphs, unmeaning and illegible, upon which he gazes in mysterious awe and wonder. Such an one may fittingly employ the melancholy and sublime lamentation of the mighty-soul'd Milton—

> "Ever-enduring dark
> Surrounds me—from the cheerful ways of men
> Cut off—and for the book of knowledge fair
> Presented with a universal blank
> Of nature's works, to me expunged and razed,
> And wisdom, at *its* entrance, quite shut out."

CHAPTER III.

PERCEPTIVITY.

NAMES, AND OBJECTS ABLE TO BE NAMED.

" The reader who would follow a close reasoner to the summit of the absolute principle of any one important subject, has chosen a chamois hunter for his guide. He
cannot carry us on his shoulders ; we must strain our sinews, as he has strained his;
and make firm footing on the smooth rock for ourselves, by the blood of toil from our
own feet."—COLERIDGE.

" La langue est le tableau de la vie ; c'est l'assemblage de toutes les idées d'un
peuple, manifesté au dehors par le sons." *—THOMAS.

NAMES.—Hitherto we have considered Man merely as a knowledge-
recipient, not as a thought-expositor. We have shown how ideas are
acquired, we have now to explain how they are communicated. Thus,
a new object lies before us, a new current is given to our speculations.
The ideas which may enter the mind are numerous and diversified, yet
without Language they remain invisible, unexpressed, and incomprehensible to any but ourselves. Everything in the multiplicity of
objects which surrounds us, and by which we are impressed ; every
feeling of the sentient powers, and every operation of the intellectual
faculties, when brought under the cognizance of our Consciousness,
seeks to be invested with a name, that it may be enabled to pass from
the domain of pure thought to the territory of communicable knowledge. Without Language men would be locked-up boxes of experience,
knowledge, and thought, destitute of the power of

> " Painting in sound the forms of joy and woe,
> Until the mind's eye *sees* them melt and glow."

We have all a thought-treasury of our own, acquired by intercourse
with existences around and without us, and operations continually
progressing within ; but we have social relations to fulfil which require
the interchange of this mental wealth. We are not formed merely for
acquisition and niggardly hoarding, or miserly avariciousness, but for
intellectual commerce. Hence we are endowed with lingual powers,
which capacitate us to symbolize our thoughts in sound, and thus
represent them to the minds of others ; that is, to originate within
their minds, by the action of sounds on the auditory nerves, ideas
similar to those which occupy our own. These marks or signs being

* Language is a picture of life ; it is a collection of all the ideas of a people—exhibited
outwardly by sounds.

once fixed, by a process of mental association, hereinafter to be explained, produce and re-produce each other; that is to say, the view of the object naturally suggests the sign, designation, or name; and the hearing of the name as naturally recalls our conception of the object to the percipient agency. Words are the vehicles of thought-transference, the instruments by which we catalogize and registrate our knowledge, and convey it to the minds of those with whom the social compact places us in relation. Oh, how glorious an endowment is this which we possess, Language! By this have the wisdom-revealments of Socrates, Plato, and Euclid been transmitted to us; by this has old Homer's soul-exciting Epic been given to immortality; by this the thunder-toned eloquence of Demosthenes electrified the Athenians to new life, energy, and struggle; by this did the "Bard of Avon" teach us what he had learned from the many-paged book of human life; and Newton disclose the marvellous secrets which he decyphered on the star-written scroll of the evening sky. Language is the medium through which Science, History, Poetry, and Religion transmigrate from breast to breast, and originate in men those refined and refining influences which they are so admirably adapted to do; and through the agency of words the Thoughts-men of all ages have transfused the brightest, best, and most ennobling portion of their thoughts into the souls of their contemporaries and posterity. They afford a magical facility for the expression of

> "All thoughts, all passions, all delights,—
> Whatever stirs this mortal frame;"

and the communication of those luxuriant trains of thought which "sweep across the mind with angel wing." By them the dim-descried vistas of the intellectual Dreamland of ancient sages are registered, and by the subsequent explorations of future adventurers, in the long course of ages, become the certainties of the future, and are catalogued as *knowable*. By them the irrational puerility of tradition and surmise is exchanged for precise historical detail and demonstrated scientific truth. They are the messengers of thoughts, feelings, and information from man to man, and between the inhabitants of every clime and country. Words are the current coin of mental commercialists, the representatives of the real or acquired intellectual riches of the land of their adoption, and, like the baser circulatory medium to which we have compared them, they must be carried to the exchangers before they can acquire a currency in any other district of the universe. The power of intellection is the same *in kind* in the whole human race; all the objects in the external world coincide in their main characteristics, and impress the mind in a manner somewhat analogous and identical, but the representational media which the different nations of the earth have adopted as expressive of the ideas originated by them, are diverse; hence, we see that though Languages differ, yet the purposes which they serve are the same, and that though our observations are necessarily confined to our own language, as the vestment of thought, yet the principles which we shall elucidate will be such as must, from the constitution of the human mind, be equally applicable to all languages.

Names are vocal sounds, conventionally attached to, and expressive of ideas, the signs or marks which we employ to denote those objects which excite our Perceptivity, and which, being pronounced, or written, produce similar ideas in the minds of others. By this power of imposing names on our ideas, we are able to marshal the several objects in the universe, and pass them in review before ourselves or others. We can bring to our remembrance those friends who have a place in our affections, those parties of whom, from station or intimacy, we find it necessary to converse, and those defaulters who have excited our indignation; everything that may have moved us to pity, awe, or love, that may have instructed or amused us, or been in any way connected with us in the constantly-recurring or ever-varying scenes of life. Thus we register our ideas of all that we have seen or been affected by ourselves, of all that we have heard of or believe on the testimony of others; of all we wish, hope, fear, or doubt. The ever-active mind of man, impressed by everything around, and influenced by everything within, is necessitated to definitize the objects brought within the range of its cognition. Hence man's lexicon of names is vast. The mountain, lifting its snow-clad summit to the ether above, the hollow-sounding, unfathomed, and mysterious main, the illimitable expanse of the many-hued sky, the newly-risen sun, the clouds garmented with beauty, or blackened with storms, the "Queen of Night," the space-careering stars, the foam-crested cataract, the crashing avalanche, the eye-deceiving mirage, the smiling cornfield, the smooth-shaven lawn, the forest, the garden, and the grove, the palatial hall, the far-spread demesne, the rustic village, the mazy, many-streeted city, the instruments of labour, the fruits, the flowers, the trees, the myriad species of the animal kingdom, the destruction-winged tempest, the death-dealing pestilence, the lightning's vivid flash, the thunder's loud reverberation, "the dome of thought, the palace of the soul," the criminal, the depraved, the talented, the good, the great, and ten thousand times ten thousand thought-educing objectivities around and within, are all commemorated and marked by *Names*. Not only so, but man can imagine objects such as never have existed, and give them a cognomen; can designate a number of objects as if they were individuated, and speak of qualities as if they formed separate existences, and were endowed with essentiality. All this is done by Perceptivity, each act of which results in the formation of a thought; each such thought the mind naturally seeks to vesture with a name.

It is needful, for a proper understanding of our subject, to bear in mind, that all our knowledge is perceptual. Of *noumena*, *i.e.* the essences of objects, we know nothing. Of *phenomena*, *i.e.* appearances, all our knowledge is made up and composed, and although there is a continual objectivizing of our thoughts,—a continual inference of their *withoutness* and externality; yet, what knowledge we possess is really subjective, and essentially idealogic. Hence it results, that Names are not marks designative of objects themselves, but of the *conceptions* produced in our mind by them. In saying this we do not deny the existence of external objects, but predicate our incapacity to attain to a knowledge of things in their *essence*, and assert that we perceive existtences as quality-possessors, as appearance-yielding, not as essentiative, not as disclosing their quality-indwelling parts. Names, therefore, are the exponents of our ideas; but were every individuated objectivity to receive a distinct name, words would be indefinitely multiplied, and the purposes of speech be wholly frustrated. Indeed, it would be impossible to give a particular name to everything capable of impressing our sensorial organs or our mental consciousness. Such an effort would far transcend the utmost powers of human ingenuity. Even if it were possible, it would be undesirable, for before we could communicate our notions of anything, we should require to teach the person to whom we spoke the cumbrous machinery of Language which we had constructed; even after this point was attained, and his memory gorged to the full with individual designations, it would be unavailable, for, as Aristotle says—"Of particular things there is neither definition nor demonstration, and, consequently, no science, since all definition is in its nature universal." From this difficulty the mind is enabled to disembarrass itself in a way and by an expedient which we shall endeavour briefly to explain.

The perceptive powers of the mind, on being called into exercise by a number of external objects or inward operations, possess the ability to observe their resemblances, differences, and relations. This capacity of discovering the identities, dissimilarities, and relations of perceptions and ideas, is the elemental power from which science originates.

Observation furnishes the mind with ideas. Generalization classifies them, and we attach names to them when classified. We have spoken of Generalization, we doubt, as if its function were generally understood; but as it is right, in every one assuming the Didactic, to take for granted the ignorance of the majority of his readers—else, Why the necessity of instruction?—we will take the liberty of detailing more at large the important office which Generalization fills in relation to the imparting of names to the objects of cognition. We have seen before that our sensorial and perceptual powers are in want of education: while this educative process is going on, everything appears unconnected, detached, and disunited, but when it is completed—when the isolated sensations and perceptions are reduced to uniformity and coherence, we begin to identify and generalize, to perceive ideas definitely, to compare carefully, to recognise their similarities, to abstract their disagreeing parts, to arrange those which are accordant in their essential peculiarities, and attach names to those which coincide in the production of similar phenomena. This principle it is which assists us in the intricacy, bewilderment, and confusion through which we must grope in our investigative processes. Sights, sounds, feelings, tastes, appetites, odours, jumblingly and inextricably mixed, are primarily impressed on our sensorium; these we gradually begin to disentangle and unwarp, arrange, classify, and name. Thus we reduce the mass of our impressions into similar groups. This systemizing and colligation of ideas is of vast importance in rendering our knowledge perfect, useful, and communicable. In the natural objects which surround us, in the processes of thought, and in the artificial products of human ingenuity, there is much scope for *identification*. Amid almost infinite diversity in the minor peculiarities, or accidental forms and attributes of bodies, there is a vast amount of similarity and resemblance. When, therefore, we examine one object minutely and accurately, and obtain a knowledge of its form, properties, relations, &c., we have much knowledge of all similar objects acquired; for though some of them may be defective, and others superabundant in the accidental peculiarities of their nature, yet our knowledge of these objects, so far as similitude is possessed by them, is certain, and we have now only to ascertain in what their differences consist, to have gained a knowledge of them also. These similar objects Generalization colligates, classifies, and names after the following manner:—Having observed that a number of objects are possessed of some common properties or attributes—in other words, make a somewhat similar impression on the mentality—the mind seeks to indicate this similitude by anatomising the impression; thus it discovers the various conceptions of which it is made up, or into which it may be analysed; it then gives a *name* to the common part, regardless of the differences, and thus are originated what logicians denominate Common Names, or General Terms. This may be instanced thus—Men perceive the Oak, Elm, Beech, Birch, Palm, Fir, Cedar, &c.; observe that they are tapering plants of considerable height, covered with bark, divided into branches, bearing foliage, and producing seed. These may be called the coinciding points. All plants agreeing in these common qualities are called *Trees*, however they may differ as regards size, internal structure, and substance, colour, bark, peculiarity of branches and leaves, and the nature and properties of their seed-bearing parts, &c. Again, the ancient philosophers discovered that *Electron* (Amber), when rubbed or excited, had the power of attracting or repelling small bodies; subsequent inquirers found that other substances, as gumlac, resin, sulphur, talc, glass, the precious stones, silk, the fur of quadrupeds, the atmosphere, &c., were possessed of a similar property; no new name, however, was sought expressive of this wide-spread agency, but the word Electricity, which etymologically signifies *Amberness*, was, and is, indiscriminately applied to that property by whatever body displayed. Here it will be observed that the mind being fixed upon the one distinguishing and coincident quality overlooks all differences, and designates the property common to all these objects by one common name, and this class of objects by one general cognomen, Electricals. Shakspere gives a specimen of Generalization in the address of *Macbeth* to the murderers of *Banquo* :—

> "Ay! in the catalogue ye go for *men*,—
> As hounds, and greyhounds, mongrels, spaniels, curs,
> Shoughs, water-rugs, and demi-wolves, are called
> All by the name of dogs."

Thus it will be seen, that a Common Name may be defined as a word which may be employed, in the same signification, to denote each individual of a class of objects, as Man, River, Horse, Tree, &c.*

Some other distinctions of *names* may be mentioned as in common use among logicians, but upon which we do not intend to dwell longer

---

* "Man is capable of being truly affirmed of John, Peter, George, and other persons, without assignable limits; and it is affirmed of all of them in the same sense, for the word Man expresses certain qualities; and when we predicate it of these persons, we assert that they all possess these qualities. But John is only capable of being truly affirmed of one single person, at least in the same sense; for though there are many persons who bear that name, it is not conferred on them to indicate any quality, or anything which belongs to them in common, and cannot be said to be affirmed of them in any sense at all, consequently not in the same sense."—MILL's *Logic*, Vol. I. p. 33.

than merely to give a brief but comprehensive definition of each. 1st. Proper names are designative of those individual objects which from our social relations we find it necessary to mark out more distinctly than can be done by common names. They consist, for the most part, of Names of Persons and Places, as Plato, Newton, Athens, London, &c. 2nd. Universal Names are such as consist of a single word indicative of an object or attribute, as Star, Bright, &c. 3rd. Multiverbal Names are made up of more than one word expressive of the same object, as,—an equilateral triangle; "The blind old bard of Chios' isle;" Victoria, by the grace of God, Queen of Great Britain, &c. 4th. Collective Names are such as indicate a whole class Unically, *i.e.*, taken as an individual, as Clergy, Army, &c. 5th. Abstract Names are those which are the signs of abstract ideas, as Fineness, Sweetness, &c. 6th. Names which can be applied to only one class, or the individuals comprehended in that class, are called Invariable, as Man, Star, Plant. 7th. Those which can be used as signs of different classes, or the individuals comprising different classes, are called Variable. They comprehend what Grammarians call Pronouns; thus *He* may be employed as the sign of Father, Brother, King, Friend, Lion, Horse, Eagle, &c. 8th. Names of qualities are called Convertible; that is, susceptible of being interchanged from object to object, without altering their truth, as *bright*, which may be truthfully applied to the Sun, a Star, precious stones, metals, and pictures.

OBJECTS ABLE TO BE NAMED.—We have already said that Perceptivity enables us to become acquainted with the qualities and relations of objects, and the operations which these objects superinduce in us. We purpose now to explain and illustrate what is contained in that assertion, and thus, by a classification of those things capable of impressing our *Consciousness*, be enabled to perceive what Goethe calls the "limits of the Knowable." Farther than the impressions made upon Consciousness and the inferences logically deducible from them, man's intellect cannot extend its search. All that we can positively *know* is that which we perceive and that which we infer. We cannot transcend Consciousness—cannot overstep the limits of our nature—cannot *know* that which lies beyond the circle of our intellectual ken. That which does not exist within, or tangentiate upon, that circle, transcends our knowledge—lies beyond the bound of our cognitive powers, and cannot be grasped by our mind, or comprehended in our catalogue of "Objects able to be known." All the knowledge which we possess *immediately*, that is, without any intervening agent, consists of ideas. Ideation is the result of our organic powers, whether physical or psychical, called into action by objectivities which either lie without us, or are supposed to do so. Upon our being placed in certain relations to externalities, our Consciousness becomes excited, and perception is the consequent. This being the case, then, it becomes of importance to know what can excite our ideative powers: thus we shall be able to determine what are the knowable and nameable objects which are capable of impressing our Perceptivity. These may be classified thus:—

1st. Consciousness gives us a knowledge of our sensations, thoughts, desires, will, memory, and all those mental conditions which the phenomena of the intellection presents. Of these the thinking part of our nature has the most immediate and decided knowledge; hence, Consciousness is the most trustworthy basis of certitude. Concerning that which we feel operating within us, and are irresistibly led to observe, we have the most accurate knowledge, and on that we can place the greatest dependence. These form the first great class of knowable and nameable things which our nature is capable of perceiving.

2nd. These phenomena which Consciousness reveals must inhere in some existence possessed of a susceptibility of being thus impressed—this we can infer; and we denominate this impressible, thought-comprehending power—this rational faculty—Mind.

3rd. We have asserted that all knowledge consists of ideas; and it will, perhaps, sound strange and paradoxical in us now to class External Objects as the third great series of objects able to be known and named. Yet we think it will not be denied, that although we have no *immediate* knowledge of objects extrinsic to ourselves, yet we are led by the irresistible laws of our intellectual nature to objectivise our ideas; that is, to suppose our thoughts to be originated in us by objects beyond and external to us. Nay, we think that the existence of external things is susceptible of proof inferential from the facts revealed to us by Consciousness. If it be not so, is thought self-germinative? Is the mind endowed with self-excitativeness? Can it originate thought by innate or connate activity? If it be not self-excitable anterior to thought-eduction, it must be excited by that which lies without. If it be self-excitable previous to the origination of thought, by what strange process did it *think of beginning to think*? Are we to be driven back to the vague, but beautiful and poetic doctrine of Plato,—Reminiscence? Or shall we admit that *mediately*, by the intervention of Consciousness, we have a knowledge of external objects? We accept the latter, and yet adhere to our former assertion, that all knowledge *to us* consists in ideas. For instance, we have an idea of heat, of burning perhaps, and of flame; these are the elements of our knowledge—these we objectivise

—these we infer resulted from some causative agent; but are our conjunct ideas of heat, burning, and flame, indicative of the essence, or the attributes of fire? Of the attributes assuredly; and if of the attributes, whence do we gain our knowledge of objects? By the laws of our mind we are necessarily led to *infer* the existence of an object on the perception of its attributes. External objects, as the originators of thought, as the educators of the mind, fulfil an important end in the economy of Nature. They are capable of impressing our perceptivity as wholes and in their several parts; of these we can form conceptions—to our conceptions we can give names; and thus they take their rank in our catalogue of nominable objects.

4th. The existences which surround us are variously related to ourselves, and to each other; these relations coming under our cognizance originate ideas, and are thus "Objects able to be *named*." The principal relations are Coevality and Succession; Similarity and Dissimilarity; Position and Quality.

Of these four classes of objects are the knowable and nameable composed; other than our feelings, our minds, the ideas resulting from external objects, and their relations, we cannot *know*, for these only can reach the cognitive sphere of finite mortals such as we are. In these all knowledge is comprehended; from these all latent truth may be elicited; and upon these the rational faculty has ample scope to build huge columns of inferential truth. On these as a substratum, a basis—

> "That wondrous force of thought, which, mounting, spurns
> This dusky spot, and measures all the sky,"

has "ample room and verge enough" to construct the bright edifice of science. Excited by the pleasure imparted through this knowledge, the mind widens its speculative track, and

> "Learns, by a mortal yearning, to ascend
> Towards a higher object."—WORDSWORTH.
> "For from the birth
> Of mortal man, the sovereign Maker said,
> That not in humble nor in brief delight,
> Not in the fading echoes of renown,
> Power's purple robe, or Pleasure's flowery lap,
> The soul should find enjoyment—but from these
> Turning disdainful to a *greater* good,
> Through all the ascent of things enlarge her view,
> Till every bound at length will disappear,
> And infinite perfection close the scene."—AKENSIDE.

We shall have occasion to enter more fully into the errors resulting from Language, when we come to treat of the "Idols of the Intellect;"

meanwhile we will close our present chapter with a rule which we consider necessary for the proper conducting of speech regarding "Names, and Objects able to be named :"—

. Always use your words in the proper sense, or at least in the same determinate sense.

By attention to this rule, many, if not all, of those disputes about words, without any distinction of meaning, which have disturbed, deranged, coteried, and sectarianised society, might be avoided. Human life is, surely, far too short to be thus wasted and frittered away in idle logomachy and word-war; hence we should use every effort not only to gain correct ideas, but also to acquire a correct method of expressing these ideas in communicating them to others. As we have already said, there cannot be any communication of simple ideas, it will be evident that our only liability to error will be in the use of words denoting those which are complex; those which involve more than the mere mental operation of perceptivity. When, therefore, we use complex designatives, we should exercise the utmost diligence and caution to sum up in our minds, as accurately and completely as possible, *all* the component ideas of which they are the ordinary signs; and when we find that the conclusions, or inferences, at which we arrive, are incoincident with, or different from, those deduced by the authors whom we read, the friends with whom we converse, or the parties whom we controvert, we should pause, reflect, and re-examine the words used, and the ideas involved in them, and we will most frequently find by this reflection and re-examination the cause of the disagreement, dispute, or controversy. If you write or speak, define your terms—let their import in your mind be understood by those whom you address. This you are bound to do; for if your conception of the meaning of a term differs from that entertained by those whom you seek to convince by your argumentation, how can you expect they will agree to the inferences which you make? How happy would it have been for man had this simple rule been attended to! How much has human happiness been destroyed—how much has human progress been retarded—how much has the advancement of knowledge been impeded by misapprehension and mistake, resulting from the neglect of a rule so obvious and utile! Never seek to deceive, strive never to be deceived by words; scrutinise, examine, and re-examine them. Let no means be left untried to find the true import of a term. Endeavour to find out the meaning attached to words, the ideas of which they are the signs. See that no forgery, no imposition, is practised upon you—that each expression used is genuine. By this means the veil of sophistry will be rent—the equivocation of double-dealing hypocrisy be discovered —the gloss of partizanship, and the colouring of sectarianism, be abraded. The demagogue, the schismatist, the quack, whether medical, moral, social, religious, philosophical, or political, will be unmasked. Then truth, accompanied by Love, and followed by the Graces, will rule a happy world—

> " And man, at whose creation God rejoiced,
> No more in darkness of the spirit dwell,
> But with a bright, recovered soul appear."

CHAPTER IV.

JUDGMENT.

" The truth is, there could be no such thing as art or science, could not the mind of man gather the general natures of things out of the numberless heap of particulars, and then bind them up into such short aphorisms or propositions, that so they may be made portable to the memory, and thereby become ready, or at hand, for *Reason* to apply and make use of, as there shall be occasion."—ROBERT SOUTH, D.D.

THUS far have we proceeded in our consideration of this important subject. We have investigated the action of objects upon our bodily organs—the impressions made by them upon Consciousness—the origination of ideas in the mind through the operation of the perceptive powers. We have dilated upon the necessity and advantage of speech—the method which the mind pursues in the attaching of " Names " to the objects of perception, and, by arranging under appropriate heads the " Objects able to be named," have pointed out the line which bounds the knowable. In all this, however, we have only been employed upon preliminaries. We have been engaged in showing the materials upon which the " Art of Reasoning " is exerted, and the manner in which these materials are obtained. We have not yet been able to do more than give a few general rules, by which accuracy of perception may be promoted, and by which the mind may be aided in its early attempts in the acquisition of Knowledge, and in its initiatory steps in the search for Truth. With mere receptivity, however, the mind cannot long remain satisfied. It is naturally endowed with activity, and a thirst for information, and cannot, without difficulty, content itself in unprogressiveness, *i.e.*, with the unexerted passivity of its perceptual faculties. In the much-complicated, confused, and chaos-like minglement of mental impressions which the mind receives, the ideative powers begin to operate. The "Spirit of order" proceeds to exert itself, it collects, arranges, compares, and colligates the ideas which are being continually educed by objectivities. In so doing, it quickly notices that some of these sensational representations are alike, and some unlike—that some of these mental operations agree in certain modes of action, and some disagree. By this means the mind is enabled to observe all those perceptions and intellectual functions which are coincident, and all those which are incoincident, and can predicate agreement or disagreement regarding them. Whenever we correctly understand the properties of an object, or the characteristics of a mental act, Judgment can be performed with intuitive certainty, for each perception is necessarily possessed of a *specificity* of impression—that is, the power of producing a particular idea. As soon, therefore, as two perceptions are conveyed to the mind, the very fact of their power of specific impressibility irresistibly leads to the mental process of determining their likeness or dissimilarity. This act of the mind is called Judgment; and we have already defined it as "that power by which we compare two distinct perceptions, and by this simple comparison predicate agreement or discordancy between them."

It is in this affirmational process that our liability to error begins to develop itself. Perceptions, as perceptions—that is, as representations of the impressions made upon Consciousness by matter or by mind—are necessarily true *to us;* for as they appear, we perceive—and that which we perceive is the only ultimate ground of certitude *to us;* but when we begin to affirm or deny anything of these appearances, Error may mingle with our assertions. Hence it will appear, that though error may *result* from inadequate or incorrect ideas, yet so long as nothing is predicated of these ideas, Error cannot be *developed.* It is in our affirmations or denials, therefore, that we are to look for the earliest perceptible germination of error and falsehood. If our perceptive powers be defective, this defect will lead to error, but the impressions received by them will be truth *to us;* and it is not until we make an assertion that the divergency can be discovered, or the contrariety found out. For instance: To an individual afflicted with Daltonism (*i.e.*, an affection of the eye, by which it is incapacitated to perceive or distinguish certain colours), it is truth that these colours do not exist. But when he, as Dalton did, asserts that the bright scarlet of a Cambridge Professor's gown, and the leaves of the evergreens which grow in the outer court, are alike in colour, the error becomes manifest. It becomes plain, that what is truth to him, is not the truth of things. So also when the ancient philosophers perceived that the sun, and the other heavenly bodies, *appeared* to move round the earth, it was truth *to them* that they did so move. But when modern philosophy has proved the impossibility and absurdity of this, it is no longer a portion of the truth it had been. It will be seen from this, that error may underlie appearances, and that though perceptions, as perceptions, are true, yet they may not be the absolute truth; and that in our affirmations or negations alone can the latent error be revealed; and hence the necessity of care, examination, and caution, prior to the performance of an act of judgment. This wariness, circumspection, and accuracy, cannot be attained except by attentive observation, watchful experimentation, and a wide Inductive survey of the impressions made by the thought-educing objectivities about which our inquiries are concerned. Of the methods by which this may be accomplished, we shall, in a subsequent chapter, treat more fully under the head "Induction," contenting ourselves, in the meantime, with signalising the fact, that Induction is one mode in which Judgment operates.

In common parlance, the word "Judgment" is used synonymously with penetration, prudence, sagacity, intelligence, opinion; and when thus employed denotes, not a particular operation of the mind, but the appropriate, correct, and harmonious exercise of all its faculties. It is also made use of in courts of justice technically to signify a decision. To the latter signification the term in the manner in which it will be employed by us nearly approximates; for as a Judge, by the examination of the evidence adduced, sums up the arguments on each of the opposing sides, and announces the decision at which he has arrived, so does the mind sit as umpire over its perceptions, and by comparison ascertain what is correct, truthful, and exact.

The characteristic of that mental act which logicians denominate Judgment, is that it compares two perceptions or ideas, so as to arrive at a conclusion regarding their similarity or incoincidence. Its operations may be variously subdivided, according to the method in which the comparison is conducted—as Analytical, Synthetical, Intuitive, or Inferential.

Judgment Analytical signifies the *unloosing* or *separating* of any complex idea into its component parts—"the resolution (to borrow a phrase from chemistry) of a compound into its elements." In this act we add nothing to the ideas which employ our Intellect, but merely decompose them—merely make a transcription of those simple conceptions which, united, form the complex whole: thus, when we say "an equilateral triangle is one which has three sides equal," we make an analytical judgment; in other words, we compare the ideas, triangle, and *equalsidedness*, and find that they agree in, make up, and harmonise with, our idea of an equilateral triangle. Analytical Judgments form Definitions.

Judgment Synthetical imports the *placing together* and *combining* of two separate ideas, the conception of one of which does not *necessarily* involve the idea of the other, in such a manner as to predicate that the one is a constituent element in the mental conception of the other; as when we assert that "Every equilateral triangle is also equiangular." Here we place together the ideas of *triequilaterality* and *equalcorneredness*, the latter of which does not necessarily involve the former, but is common also to a square, &c., and find or decide from this comparison that these, compounded—synthetised—make up and are contained within our notion of an equilateral triangle. Synthetical Judgments, when expressed, are termed Propositions.

Judgment Intuitive is when by merely *looking at* any two ideas, and without any effort of the mind, we can predicate their agreement or disagreement; as when we assert that " It is impossible for the same thing to be and not to be at the same time," it is evident that, if we fully understand the signification of the terms, we can, at a glance, perceive the accuracy of the proposition. And although Hegel has enunciated the startling proposition, that "being and non-being are the same" (*seyn und nichts ist dasselbe*), we do not think that any sane individual will hesitate in granting, that if the terms being and non-being are properly understood, the incoincidence of the ideas must be manifest, and the truth of the prior proposition clear and admissible.

Judgment Inferential is when we deduce the agreement of one idea with another, through the medium of a demonstration; thus, when it is affirmed that "rights and duties are reciprocal," it does not appear evident until it is shown, proved, demonstrated, that these are correlative terms; then it becomes plain that if the relate is not granted, the correlate is undemandable, and *vice versâ*.

The two latter distinctions may be in reality regarded as mere modifications of Synthetical Judgments, yet they are not without their use in showing the line of demarcation between truth based on the certitude of the mere operation of the mental powers, and truth founded on the basis of search, inquiry, and demonstration.

DEFINITION.—The expression of an analytical judgment is called a Definition, from the Latin *Definitio*, the laying down of a boundary, and is, in logic, a sentence which explains any term so as to separate the idea which it expresses from every other, as a boundary does a field. Sounds and characters,—which are the constituent elements of language, whether spoken or written,—when compounded, form words, and these, as we have before said, are the signs of our ideas; but it is quite evident that these signs, though primarily they may have been natural, are now arbitrary: for in different languages diverse marks are employed as designative of the same thought. But, from the necessities of our social state, it is requisite that we should possess, in some degree, the power of mutual intercourse: hence nations of men have found it expedient to adopt a language which, by its power of inducing uniformity in idea-communication, may lead to ease and readiness in the mutual commerce of thought. This purpose must be entirely frustrated and nullified when this uniformity of signification is not rigorously attended to and enforced. Definition, therefore, becomes necessary as an auxiliary to accuracy of thought and communication, by explaining in what sense any term is used, and thus enabling men to perceive whether they attach a similar signification to the same word. Were we always attentive to the thought-process in our own minds, cautious in the observing of our mental impressions, and rigid in the transcription of our ideas into words, much indistinctness might be avoided. But men are by no means so circumspect on this point as they should be: the application of terms is made in a confused, disorderly, and inconstant manner. This want of care leads to much embarrassment and division, for men frequently imagine that there are serious differences between them, when in reality, were their terms properly defined, the difference in meaning would appear quite trivial, or the result of an unconscious extension or contraction of the signification rightly embodied and involved in the terms employed.

Words have a triple reference, and may bear relation—1st, To the ideas which we ourselves entertain. 2nd, To the ideas entertained by others. 3rd, To external objects. When men engage in conversation, writing, lecturing, &c., it is generally for the purpose of being understood: the words which they employ, therefore, ought to be such as, according to their own ideas, best serve to explain their meaning, and give expression to their thoughts: here words have reference to our own ideas. But unless we adopt such phraseology, and converse in such terms as are either originative or representative of similar conceptions in the minds of those whom we address, we shall most certainly be misunderstood: and thus, so far as they are used for thought-communication, words bear reference to the ideas which are entertained by or originable in others. Again: from the power before explained of objectivising our conceptions, men are in the habit of applying the signs of their ideas to that which originates them, and thus our words are made to bear reference to external existences. We have before proved that we have no knowledge of things as they are in themselves—no knowledge of the essentialities of objects; hence we may be able to perceive the erroneousness of the distinction which logicians commonly make between *nominal* and *real* definitions; for if, as we think we have demonstrated, *things* be inappreciable by our minds, there can be no definition of any kind except that which expresses the meaning which we intend shall be understood as affixed to the word which we have chosen as the sign of our mental conception. All definitions are, therefore, in reality, nominal—of the name; not real—of the thing. In observing a fact, law, or thing, we receive an idea. On the reception of this idea, a new impression is made on the mental powers. This new impression requires a name. When this name is originally imposed by us, it cannot pass current until we have explained the component ideas of which it is made up in such terms as shall excite a like notion in the mind of others. Hence definitions can only express in words an analysis of the items comprehended in the complex idea which the word defined implies. The importance of definition may be readily perceived by reflecting that in the interchange of ideas, if there be a difference in that which is comprehended in the symbols of thought, mistake, misunderstanding, and division must arise regarding the conclusions deducible from them.

Definition depends on the observation of identity and diversity—similarity in the Genus, variety in the Species. In defining a term, all that is exuvial in thought is thrown off; all that is inconstituent and non-essential—all that is merely accessory and accidental, is disregarded. Things are explained by the explication of their names; experience is reduced to laws, and these laws, constituting ideas, receive names and become explainable; individuals are generalised, and the ideas comprehended under or involved in these things, experiences, and individualities, are alone considered, by the mind. Every idea which we have, must, to constitute it an idea, have the power of presenting a peculiar appearance to the mind, by which the distinction between it and every other idea may be perceived. In attempting to convey this idea into the mind of another, it is necessary that we present such an analysis of that idea, as shall convey *it* most clearly and unmistakeably; and in so doing we must describe and unfold the precise conception which the use of language attaches to a term, or that idea which we choose shall be affixed to the word employed. A word is the sign of an idea—our business in definition is to explain what compound of simple ideas shall be, or is, involved in its signification; that thus we may indicate, precisely, the quality which distinguishes it, and with how much *that* is to be conjoined. In order to do this effectually, we must make an accurate survey and examination of the idea itself—search into the process of its formation in our own minds, and distinctly observe and mark out the elemental perceptions from which it takes its rise, and of which it is composed—attend to the manner in which these are classified, arranged, and joined together—which are primary and which are subordinate, or secondary; and when in this manner we have anatomised the impression, we have only to transcribe, in their order, these various component simple ideas, and the conception will be excited in the mind of the reader or hearer. But the mental powers are very circumscribed in their range of action, and are unable to retain in their grasp a numerous group of disjointed and detached ideas; hence we are under the necessity of proceeding by gradational advances. We associate them into groups and arrange them into classes; these groups or classes we re-arrange into new combinations, and form conceptions of them; and thus we can proceed, conjoining our ideas, and generalising our conceptions, until, by habit and practice, the mind gains a facility in thinking of them somewhat in the same light as simple ideas, and can use them as component parts of higher and more refined generalisations. We advance from individuals to species—of these species we compose genera—these genera we unite and colligate by some essential and distinctive quality common to all; they then become the species of a new generalisation:—thus we have genera, remote and proximate; and a perfect logical definition consists in the pointing out of the proximate genus and the specific difference: such a definition will always be adequate; but it will not always and necessarily be clear, for the genus may require definition as well as the species. From this it appears that before an idea be unfolded or explained, it may be necessary to define not only the term which we are about to use, but also, as a preliminary step, to define some term which may be involved in the idea of which we are about to give an explanation. Let it here be noticed, also, that occasionally a definition will not fully answer the purpose of communication, nor suffice to satisfy the wants of the mind; for if men be not acquainted with the simple ideas which are comprehended in the complex term employed, these will require to be excited and educed. This may be done by the use of diagrams, description, enumeration, or any other means calculated to originate the desiderated idea.

Diagrams, models, &c., are employed for the purpose of eliciting those ideas which are needful for the understanding of our terms, for the simplification of the acquirement of complex conceptions, or for the explanation of any peculiar ideas which lie at the foundation of any theory or hypothesis.

Description is the definition of an individual, and consists of the genus, specific difference, properties, and accidents; a recapitulation and detail of the parts, properties, and peculiarities of the object described or spoken of.

Enumeration is a recital and particularisation of *all* the simple subordinate ideas which are involved and included in the formation of one which is complex.

Description is generally employed to explain the complex idea originated by, and arising from, objects which are perceivable by the organs of sight. Enumeration is ordinarily used when we do not feel called on to mention the Genus of an object, but are desirous of merely pointing out what we consider may be comprised in the term. Definition is made use of in the explication of complex ideas of every kind, whether they are the symbols of external objects, or internal operations —whether they emanate from matter, or originate in mind. A good Definition consists of two parts, by the former of which we denote the generic part, or the quality which any object possesses in common with others: by the latter we indicate the specific portion, or that which characterises and distinguishes the object defined from every other of a similar kind.

In Definition proper we regard the term employed as the sign of some idea or conception which has been excited within us, to which idea or conception that sign has been annexed either by the custom of the language which we speak, or by our own express choice; and then the duty which falls upon us is to explain that idea or conception in such a manner as shall either excite or re-excite it in the minds of others. To do this effectually we must—

1st. Take an exact and precise view of that idea or conception, reduce it to its simplest elements, and note attentively all the several simple perceptions which form its constituent elements.

2nd. Consider carefully the manner in which these several simple perceptions are conjoined in the idea or conception, and the order which they assume in the mind.

3rd. So transcribe the revelations of Consciousness as to exhibit distinctly the number and order of the primary elements of our idea or conception.

It is evident that as Definitions are merely expositions of the *contents* of ideas, that definition which truly and accurately enumerates, in their proper and precise order, the several simple constituent perceptions in any given idea, must necessarily be perfect of its kind. Logicians, however, do not find it requisite to insist upon our giving verbal expression to each and all of these, but because several objectivities unite in the possession of somewhat resemblant properties, and the mind has a natural tendency to classification and generalisation, it seldom happens that any idea is so solitary as to have no class in which it may be arranged, and no genus with which it may be conjointly thought, or of which it may not be thought, as a part, they consider it quite sufficient, in giving a definition, to do as we have already said, viz., indicate the Genus and specific difference. It is obvious, however, that although this is all we *express*, it is not an exhaustive detail of the whole thought-process of Definition. That must be carried on as above-described, in order that we may really and correctly *know* the genus and specific difference.

The commonly-received distinctions of definitions are the following: viz.—Nominal and real; accidental, physical, and logical. The two former relate to that which the definition *does*—whether it explains the meaning of a word, or informs us of the nature of the thing. The three latter refer to the method taken to accomplish this—whether it enumerates or describes the accidental, or non-essential qualities, the physical attributes, or the generic properties of objects.

A NOMINAL DEFINITION explains the signification of a term—the idea which we intend shall be expressed by it ; *e.g.*, Thermometer, an instrument for measuring the heat, and ascertaining the temperature of bodies ; Algebra, the science of quantity in general, and the art of computing by symbols.

A REAL DEFINITION is one which informs us what is the essence and nature of a thing.

We have before given, we think, ample proof of man's incapacity to gain a knowledge of noumena, essences, the nature of things ; we shall here quote a passage or two from Locke's " Essay on the Human Understanding," Book IV. cap. i., corroborative of our opinion that *ideas*, and not *things*, are the objects of human *knowledge* :—" Since the mind, in all its thoughts and reasonings, hath no other immediate object but its own ideas, which it does or can contemplate, it is evident that our knowledge is only conversant about them." " It is evident that the mind knows not things immediately, but only by the intervention of ideas it has of them." " Knowledge, then, seems to me nothing but the perception of the connexion and agreement, or disagreement and repugnancy, of any one of our ideas." This being our opinion of the case, we hope we may be excused for not giving an example.

AN ACCIDENTAL DEFINITION is one which details the properties and accidents of an object, or describes its causes, appearances, qualities, and effects; as, Socrates, son of Sophroniscus, a Greek philosopher, whom the Athenians, on a charge of immorality and impiety, condemned to drink hemlock.

A PHYSICAL DEFINITION expresses the parts and qualities which make up our ideas of an object; as, Tree, a tapering plant, consisting of root, trunk, branches, leaves, seed-vessels, &c.

A LOGICAL DEFINITION distinguishes one thing from another by its generic qualities and its specific diversity.

The following six rules for securing the accurate and proper use of definitions, will, if attended to, be found of some value and utility:

1st. *Definitions must be adequate;* that is, they must give a complete idea of what is contained in the term; and if the term be the name of a genus or species, it must be sufficiently wide in its signification to comprehend or include all the species of individuals of which these consist, and so exact as to exclude everything which ought not to be comprehended in it. It must not be too narrow—for that will exclude something which is employed in the term. Not too extensive—for that would be to include something which the term is not meant to express. Thus, to define a bird as a feathered animal possessed of the power of flying, would be too narrow: for some birds, as the ostrich, do not possess the power of flying. Again, to define the same word as denoting all those animals who are possessed of wings, would be too extensive, for that would include insects,—a division of the animal kingdom which is not usually expressed by the term employed.

2nd. *Definitions must indicate those characteristics which are properly and peculiarly denoted by the term.* It is the very fundamental principle upon which definitions are based, that they should enable us to discern distinctly the difference between ideas; if therefore we use our words so loosely that the idea meant by us is not, in its own proper and peculiar nature, expressed in the explanation which we give, of what use can our definition be?

3rd. *Definitions must be clear and plain;* i.e., they must not be expressed in obscure, figurative, or ambiguous language. If there be any word or words used in our definitions which are less easily understood, or as much in need of definition as the term itself, our explication will evidently be unsuitable for its purpose. It behoves us, therefore in defining our terms, to use no word in which there is any difficulty; or if it be absolutely necessary that such should be employed, let us graduate our definition by explaining the words which we are about to use, as a preliminary proceeding to the definition of the term with which our subject is concerned. Unless we attend to this rule, we cannot make ourselves intelligible to those whom we address. The following definitions, we humbly depone, sin against this canon. The former was jotted into our note-book from one of those cheap publications in which " Knowledge for the Million " is vended ; the latter is *verbatim et literatim* from the Dictionary of the Great Lexicographer : 1st. Snuff, a certain heterogeneous mixture of odoriferous particles, chiefly composed of granulated or comminuted tobacco, whose use is to produce a titilatory and sternutative effect on the olfactory nerves which lie distributed along the interior of the nasal organ of the human frame ; sometimes medicinally used as a detergating and defecating agent. 2nd. Network, anything reticulated or decussated at equal distances.

4th. *Definitions must consist of the concisest possible appropriate expressions,*—alike free from embarrassing brevity, and tautological prolixity. The chief object which men should have, being to make themselves understood, any want of conciseness will have the tendency of increasing the difficulty of comprehension ; while the repetition of the same idea more than once—unless for the purpose of securing variety to suit a miscellaneous audience, to whose minds access can only be attained by the employment of judiciously-varied phraseology—will be equally prejudicial.

5th. *Definitions must not comprise either the same or synonymous terms.* This would evidently be no aid to the understanding of the term, for the reiteration of the term could communicate no knowledge regarding the object of thought ; while, if the synonymous term is understood, and the term used by you is not so, you are evidently in the wrong to multiply words which do not necessarily indicate a distinction of thought.

6th. *Definitions ought never to be negative when they can by any possibility be made affirmative.* All positive and definite conceptions ought to be capable of affirmative definition. Privative conceptions cannot, of course, be defined otherwise than negatively.

The importance of definition consists in this—that before we can know a thing we must be able to demarcate and distinguish *it* from all that is *not it*. In this process we do two things ; to show what the thing is, we (1) draw a line of limitation round the idea, and by so doing, we (2) point out what it is not. Thus our thoughts are kept free from intertanglement or confusion. We separate the particular thought which we wish to express, from the multitude of other thoughts which lie latent in the mind. But we must avoid the error of supposing that definitions are capable of informing us of *things as they are in themselves (per se)*. The explanation of *terms* is not at all equivalent to the explanation of *things*. The terms we can explain, for we ourselves know all that is employed in their composition and formation; but of things how can the mind explain the essence—that essence of which it has no cognizance? Ideas we may expound, for of ideas our knowledge is composed; of things—of externalities as regards their essence, we *know* nothing, however much we may *believe*. The logical use of definitions is to guard against the use of any term in more than *one* definite and particular sense. Whatever definition affects this purpose is logically correct. Whenever terms are used without definitions, they are understood according to the common use of language.

The following are the laws by which Definitions may be made serviceable in general reasoning, viz.—

1st. To whatever objectivity the definition may be applied, with that the objectivity defined must agree, and *vice versa*.

2nd. With whatever objectivity the thing defined agrees, to that also may the definition be applied.

In our next we shall treat of Propositions, and will then show the reason which inclined us to diverge from the "use and wont" of logicians, by considering definitions as a part of the operation of "Judgment," rather than of "Perceptivity," and point out the distinction between Propositions and Definitions.

For the dry disquisitional style of the present chapter we can offer no apology; abstruseness is necessarily inwoven with our subject. If we speak, as we hope we do, to earnest vigorous-souled inquirers, no such thing will be needful. They know well that it is vain to hope to pluck a rose without a thorn; they can feel and act upon the energy-exciting lines of the American poetess—

> " There is a charm in knowledge best when bought
> With vigorous toil of mind and earnest stretch of thought."

CHAPTER V.

JUDGMENT.—PROPOSITIONS.

" All philosophy is reducible to a few principles, and these principles are comprised
in a few propositions. . . . . . These are the *apices rerum*, the tops and sums, the
very spirit and life of things extracted and abridged, just as the lines drawn from the
vastest circumference do at length meet and unite in the smallest of things—a point ;
and it is a very small piece of wood with which a true artist will measure all the timber
in the world."—SOUTH.

WE resume our didactic labours. We know not how these have
been appreciated by our readers, but for ourselves we can say, that

> " Mid the din
> Of towns and cities, we have owed to them,
> In hours of weariness, sensations sweet,
> Felt in the blood, and felt along the heart ;"

and that our thoughts have been full of anxiety that we might be able
aright to inform the mind how to cultivate and improve

> " That apprehensive power
> By which it is made quick to recognise
> The moral scope and aptitude of things."

Thought is a mysterious agency, whose processes are so subtle that
it is difficult to follow the track of its progress, or investigate its swifter
than electric evolutions ; but we must not give up as inexplicable any
department of inquiry of which we possess the means of solution, however difficult, abstruse, or recondite it may chance to be. And as we
have confessedly the means of prosecuting this study within our own grasp,
even in our own mentality, it seems preposterous to yield, and acknowledge ourselves baffled, defeated, overcome by the arduousness of the
undertaking. Great minds are shown in great deeds, and become manifest by their daring. Weak minds alone can dream of failure. Earnest-
ness is *the* essential to success. Every truth lost is a motive lost ;
therefore let us search for truth that we may increase motives, and let
no difficulty daunt us in the search. If anything should incline us to
adherence to a belief, or incite to the performance of an action, it should
be truth ; and we may rest assured that however occult or mystery-
enwrapped it may be, persevering investigation will reward our toil,
either by unfolding the hidden scroll upon which the hieroglyphics
of nature are inscribed, or informing us of the futility of the attempt.
There are many even of the material effluences of nature which are

enveloped in obscurity, or which operate with so much more than magical speed, that the acutest scientific eye has hitherto failed to penetrate into the secret of their working; *e. g.*, light, heat, actinism, electricity. If such be the subtlety of these matter-affluent properties, —if such be the secrecy of their action, how far more transcendentally swift and inappreciable must the processes of thought be! Let this short signalising of the intricacy of such inquiries certiorate our readers of the necessary abstruseness of our subject, and free us from the stigma of dull companionship. We must perforce enter those "metaphysic depths" which lie before us on our way. We shall, however, "thread the labyrinth" with caution, still keeping our eye fixed on the rich, ripe fields of thought, of which we desire to gain a nearer view. Let those who are inclined to relinquish the study in despair and disgust, because of the "lion in the path," remember that it is the firm foot that gains firm footing, and that difficulty is only a finer name for our weakness.

In our last chapter we promised to explain our reasons for diverging from the usual practice of logicians in treating Definitions as the product of Judgment rather than as the result of Perceptivity, and to point out the distinction between Definitions and Propositions. This promise we shall, in a few brief sentences, endeavour to redeem. We crave pardon, while for this purpose we make a succinct *résumé* of some of our former observations, and from this summary show in what manner they affect the point at issue. When an object is placed in certain relations to the perceptual faculty, it makes an impression on that faculty, and thus originates an idea in the mind. If this idea is complex, it is capable of subdivision,—of being resolved into two or more simpler ideas, of being analysed. This analysation is very simply performed, as it results from the fact that objects possess the power of producing distinct ideas of the attributes by which they become known to us,—a power which we have denominated specific impressibility. This specificality of impression-production we employ as a thought-solvent, and by it we are enabled to perceive the component elements of which complex ideas are made up. So far Perceptivity alone is concerned, and here Definition begins its operations. *We* require no act of judgment to inform us of the simple ideas excited in us by objects. Before, however, we can impart to another the ideas which have been educed in us, a process of thought-analysis must be gone through. We must proceed to define, by comparing two or more simpler ideas together, and predicating their conjoint agreement in one complex idea, to which complex idea we give, or have given, a definite name. We assert that these two or more simpler ideas conjointly fill up the complement of the complex idea which we seek to explain; that when in one idea-originating object these simpler ideas (which in definition we mention or enumerate) are unitedly discoverable, it bears, or shall bear, a certain given designation. For instance, when *we* see a thermometer, we perform a mere act of perceptivity, but if we desire to explain what we mean by the use of the term, we must analyse the idea which the object produced in us; on so doing, we find that " instrument " and " heat-measuring " are the simpler ideas which it originated: comparing these we perceive that in conjunction they compose the elicited idea, and our definition flowing from this exertion of the judgment is, " Thermometer, an instrument for measuring heat." Thus Dr. Whewell is perfectly correct in asserting that " a proposition is always *implied* along with the definition," and we are justified in considering definitions as the result of the operations of the judgment. They are the transcriptions of our experience, the *writing out* of what we have perceived; and the judgment is necessary to decide upon the accuracy of the expression as compared with its antecedent and correlate,—Experience. *A name* is the sign of *an idea;* a definition is an explanation of *a name;* a proposition is the verbal expression of *a fact.*

From what has been said in the foregoing paragraph, we hope it is obvious that we have not causelessly left the beaten track. It will be more easy to point out the distinction between definitions and propositions. Before doing this, however, it will be necessary to inform you what a proposition is.

A proposition may be logically defined as a predicative sentence. A sentence consists of any number of words conveying complete sense. Predicative means asserting, but as we may either assert that a thing *is* or *is not*, predicative signifies affirming or denying, and the more extended definition of *a proposition is, any number of words expressive of an act of judgment in which an affirmation or denial is made regarding the agreement or disagreement of two ideas.* It is worthy of remark, however, that the word " agreement " is employed, logically, in a somewhat uncommon signification; nay, that it does not always and invariably convey the same notion. In regard to numbers, figures, and dimensions, agreement denotes equality; in natural philosophy, property; in moral philosophy, politics, religion, &c., congruity; indeed, it appears to signify any sort of relation which ideas can bear to each other. Disagreement, of course, is the reverse. " A proposition is a portion of discourse in which a predicate is affirmed or denied of a subject. A predicate and a subject are all that is necessarily required to make up a proposition; but as we cannot conclude from merely seeing two names put together that they are a predicate and a subject, *i.e.*, that one of them is intended to be affirmed or denied of the other, it is necessary that there should be some mode or form of indicating that such is the intention,—some sign to distinguish a predication from any other kind of discourse. This is sometimes done by a slight alteration of one of the words, called an *inflection*, as when we say '*Fire burns.*' . . . . But this function is more commonly fulfilled by the word *is*, when an affirmation is intended; *is not*, when a negation." * From this the distinction between definitions and propositions may be readily perceived. Definitions are explanatory, propositions assertive. A definition conveys a new conception or notion, or a more accurate idea than that which we previously possessed : it is a description and expression of an idea, made after a comparison of those things to which it bears an affinity; an effort of the intellect to transfer its own perceptions to the minds of others. A proposition is an affirmation—is the assertion of some principle, or the negation of some relation. A definition refers to a *term*—" gives information only about the use of language." A proposition concerns itself with the expression of matters of fact. The explication of *one* idea makes a definition—the due connexion of *two* ideas constitutes a proposition. A definition shows the elemental parts which *coexistently* enter into the formation of the idea conveyed by a *single* complex term. A proposition indicates the relation which the ideas conveyed by two terms bear the one to the other. A definition is to be *understood* merely. A proposition is not only to be understood, it is also to be *believed* or *doubted*—is employed to influence the mind by its truth or falsity.

A proposition is the vocal expression of a deduction mentally inferred from the juxta-positional comparison of ideas. When thought is embodied in propositions, it becomes truth or falsehood, and gains what may be called mental tangibility; its exactitude may be tested, its certainty or uncertainty inquired into, its practicability experimentalized upon; its conformity with or dissonance to known truths, its onleadings to higher, more generalised, important, and recondite inferences and principles, become perceptible. By observing the concatenation of events, the conjunction of attributes, the colligation of circumstances, the interamalgamation of things and qualities, the mutuality of relationship in objects, the permanent sequences or coincidences of nature, we

* Mill's " Logic," Vol. i. p. 85.

gain knowledge, for *knowledge* is the perception of the agreement or disagreement of our ideas. When this knowledge is correctly expressed in words it becomes truth, for *truth* is the agreement of words with ideas. When, therefore, we assert or deny, we place before the minds of those whom we address a subject of belief or disbelief. Belief is a preliminary to action; it is a motion-excitant, and must necessarily be educed before action can result. Propositions, therefore, are expressive of those believable or doubtful consociations of which man's experience informs him, and are at once the *fulcra* and levers of action. They are not vague, meaningless *formulæ*, but vigour-inspiring, action-educing faiths; as such they are the motor-powers of mind. If we consider how much of our conversation, our reading and discourse, are composed of assertions regarding particular objects or classes of objects, of statements regarding occurrences, and affirmations concerning different subjects, we shall readily perceive the importance of an accurate acquaintance with the theory of propositions. How great a portion of language, of human speech, is made up of them! The results of the inquiries, experiments, cogitations, and actions of the greatest, the wisest, the best, and most renowned of men are all embodied in propositions, and they become the inheritance of their successors. From this acquired knowledge we can glean an acquaintance with all the inquiries to which the men of the past have applied their powers, and learn which of these have been satisfactorily answered: we thus become the inheritors of the experience of the world's thoughtsmen, almost without trouble, anxiety, or toil. We can act on it, trust to it, as if we ourselves had undergone the fatigues, the difficulties, the dangers which they encountered, passed through, braved, and overcame. The mental wealth of sages, experimentalists, travellers, historians, moralists, and poets, thus expressed and bequeathed to us, how rich!—how surpassingly valuable! Such are the speculations of Plato, Aristotle, Bacon, Locke, Brown, and Mill; the scientific revelations of Galileo, Newton, Brewster, and Faraday; the otherland descriptions and discoveries of Columbus, Bruce, Park, and Cook; the recitals of Herodotus, Livy, Hume, Mitford, Niebuhr, Gibbon, Grote, and Alison; the moral theories of Cudworth, Butler, Paley, and Bentham; the world-famous and immortal strains of Homer, Virgil, Tasso, Dante, Milton, Racine, and Shakspere.

Since everything of which we can think or talk may be expressed in propositions; since, in fact, the whole series of our thoughts are but interdependent, consecutive chains of propositions; since, as J. S. Mill says, "all truth and all error lie in propositions," it seems plain that a complete knowledge of propositions would materially aid us in the attainment of an adequate and accurate theory of the "art of thinking." We know that there are some who impugn this opinion—parties who stickle for facts, and pin their faith to the poet's oft-quoted line that "Facts are stubborn things, an' winna ding," as if facts were perfect oracles of wisdom, as if they could produce incontrovertible belief. This is one of the multiform and multiplex "cants of the day." The great facts of physical science have remained the same since creation's natal hour. Still does the sun "rule the day, and the moon rule the night;" still does the former exert its planet-tractive force—still do the stars whirl in their vast ellipses through the celestial pathway, and lighten midnight with their glory—still do the Pleiades rain "sweet influences"—still does "Mazzaroth" come "forth in his season"—still "the bands of Orion" are unloosed, and still "Arcturus, with his sons," requires no human guide: as in the "days of old," do they now wheel through the "dominions of heaven;" and yet, how has astronomy changed! Open to the inspection of all, the operations of nature are so free from mutation that men can rectify chronology by their calculations of the solar eclipses. Her processes are unchanged, unchanging, uniform; her sequences are invariable—yet how varied have been the theories to which these have given rise! Facts, then, do not produce irrefragable, unmistakeable truth. They become only the irreversible criterions and bases of truth when looked upon in the light of a judicious hypothesis; this hypothesis is expressed in a proposition, and from these scientific *axiomata* truths are deducible which facts do not yield, but by which facts may be brought to light. Can we illustrate this better than by a reference to the discovery of the planet Neptune? In propositions past-discovered truth is found—in them present-found facts must be embodied; therefore a knowledge of the elements and uses of propositions must be advantageous and important.

From observations formerly made it will have been observed that a proposition necessarily requires that two things be mentioned—the *something* of which we speak and the *something* which we may say regarding it. But although this is done, it is not enough, for there is an assertive symbol still required—something by which the colligation, the agreement, may be indicated; so that in all there are three parts in a proposition,—the Subject, the Predicate, and the Copula, which we will now proceed to explain :—

1st. Subject. That concerning which we make a statement, either by affirmation or denial—the thing spoken of—the word denoting the idea concerning which we make a predication. This may consist of any of the classes of names, except the convertible; it must always consist of what grammarians denominate substantive nouns, or their equivalents; as, *Wine* is stimulating; *The horse* is swift; *Sir Isaac Newton* was the inventor of fluxions,—in which the italicized words indicate the subject.

2nd. Predicate. The word expressive of the idea which we wish to indicate as bearing a relation to, *i. e.*, as agreeing or disagreeing with, the subject—that which we say of the subject—the notion which we assert to be contained in the subject, or otherwise conjoined to it. This may be composed of any one of the classes of names except the abstract, although most frequently consisting of the convertible; as, Iron is *useful*; Cunning is *the ape of wisdom*; Food is *nourishing*,—in which the italicized words point out the predicate.

3rd. Copula. That word in a proposition which informs us that the subject and predicate are to be connected or disjoined; that by which colligation or asunderness is signified—that which expresses affirmation or denial. In an affirmative proposition, it may be considered as conveying sometimes the same meaning as the algebraic sign, $=$, equivalence or identicality, and at other times that of $+$, more. In a negative proposition, it may be looked upon as representative of $-$, minus, less, or generally as $\frown$, the sign of inequivalence; thus, Cæsar $+$ dead, Cæsar *is* dead; Cæsar $-$ dead, Cæsar *is not* dead. The Duke of Wellington $=$ a man; the Duke of Wellington *is* a man. The exhibition of such a *formula* is rendered necessary by the fact that the generic verb, "AM," is a *relative* word, which conveys not only an assertive force, but occasionally superadds the conception of existence. It is worthy of observation also, that the copula is not always a separate word, but is, in our language, variously combined with the assertion-significant—the verb—for the convenience of succinctly expressing time, will, manner, duty, &c.; thus the sentence, "The sun shines," is equivalent to "The sun is shining." *Is* is called the Affirmative copula; *is not*, the Negative copula; and one or other of them must necessarily be either expressed or implied in every proposition. It is likewise a rule in "Logic" that in every negative proposition the negation must affect the copula; for instance, of the two sentences, "No man is perfectly happy," and "Man is not perfectly happy:" the former is considered an affirmative proposition, the latter a negative one, because it alone conforms to the above-mentioned rule.

The subject and predicate are called the terms of a proposition, because they form its *termini* or boundaries. It is to be remarked that either the subject or predicate may consist of one or more words; but that, however many words may be used, there can only be one thing spoken of, and one thing said about it in each proposition; however numerous the accessories of the idea may be, one, and but one, idea can become the subject of a predication, and one, and but one, idea can be predicated of it. If there be more than one word used to express an idea, it is called a multi-verbal name; if there be more than one subject or one predicate employed, it constitutes a compound proposition, and is capable of analysation. It is not the number of *words*, but the number of ideas with which "Logic" concerns itself; hence in some languages the whole three parts of a proposition may be found in one word, as in the Latin "*legit*," he is reading; the Greek τρέχει, he is running; the German "*Lebe*," I am alive.

As propositions express the relations which objects bear to each other; and the chief ideas of relation of which man has any conception are, as we have already noticed in a former chapter, coevality and succession, similarity and dissimilarity, position and quality; it follows that the chief ideas which propositions can express may be classed in one or other of the foregoing categories.

Of all the higher abstractions Existence appears to be the most generalised and the least complicated: to express the mere possession of *this* quality, one object only may be sufficient, as when we say, "The world exists," although strictly speaking, this may be reduced to the three logical elements, and be considered as equivalent to, "The world is an existence."—This may be very learnedly and acutely controverted; but with regard to the other great mental abstractions, there can be little doubt but that they imply plurality—as the very essence of Coevality, Succession, Similarity, &c., is the existence of some two or more objects which may bear such relations.

IDEAS OF COEVALITY relate to co-existence in time, and are very numerous. Of such propositions History and Chronology are almost entirely composed.

IDEAS OF SUCCESSION are such as bear reference to order in time or place. Of these Geography and History will furnish almost innumerable examples.

A very peculiar series of successions are denoted by the word CAUSATION. Natural Philosophy, Anatomy, Physiology, and Medicine, depend upon this idea for their existence. Unless by some means the conception of causative agency could have entered the mind, how barren would all our speculative sciences have been! Yet upon no one philosophic topic has there been more debate and contention; and though the idea itself be perfectly well understood, it seems strange that no definition and analysis have yet been universally agreed upon. The most general idea of Causation, which we have been able to evolve, may be thus expressed—*The action of the attributes or properties of one body or object upon those of another.* In this idea there are three elements,—antecedence, power, and sequence; in any process in which these *three* elements may be *jointly* perceived, or known, or inferred to be, or to have been, in operation, there, we conceive, a true case of Causation is found. If any one of these be wanting, then, in our opinion, Causation is not predicable.

IDEAS OF SIMILARITY are perfectly distinct from co-existence in time, or contiguity of situation or occurrence, both of which we have already noticed. The ideas of likeness or resemblance are very numerous; and the method of their attainment was pretty fully discussed, and their use pointed out, in a former chapter, when we were engaged in explaining the operation of the generalising faculty. The highest and most complete Similarity is called IDENTITY. Ideas of similarity imply their opposite. The mathematical sciences are wholly based upon our ideas of similarity and dissimilarity.

IDEAS OF POSITION differ from ideas of successive order in place, from their being more absolute. Geography, Astronomy, and Geology are filled with propositions of position.

IDEAS OF QUALITY are exceedingly numerous, and denote a peculiar species of coexistence: in propositions resulting from them, we assert that certain objects are possessed of certain properties; these properties may either be essential or accidental. Natural Philosophy, the Fine Arts, indeed everything which exists upon the globe's wide surface, may yield instances of, and propositions concerning, qualities.

We do not, by any means, assert that the foregoing is an accurate analysis and perfect classification of all the ideas of relation which the mind is able to evolve. If it be but an approximation to such a generalised view of them as shall enable us more readily to apprehend the nature of propositions, and shall render us more capable of accuracy of thought, we shall be pleased, and, we hope, our readers will be satisfied. In our chapter " On the Nature and Sources of Evidence," we shall recur to this topic, when it will be seen the few observations here made are neither " barren nor unfruitful."

Propositions are variously subdivided: as regards their *matter*, they are *true* or *false;* their *substance*, they are *categorical* or *hypothetical;*

their *quantity*, they are *universal* or *particular;* their *quality*, they are *affirmative* or *negative.*

A TRUE PROPOSITION is one in which the expression coincides with the reality of things—one in which the words exactly indicate the concord which the mind perceives between the ideas denoted by them; as, Electricity is excited in bodies by a change of temperature.

A FALSE PROPOSITION is one which does not accurately state the actual coincidences of subject and predicate. Error is an involuntary expression of that which does not accord with the certain and genuine agreement or disagreement of the ideas mentioned in it. Falsehood is "a voluntary spoken divergence from the fact as it stands, as it has occurred, and will proceed to develop itself." * *e. g.*, " All animals are rational," is a false proposition.

A CATEGORICAL PROPOSITION is a simple, pure proposition—one which makes an absolute, direct, positive, and express assertion; as, *Ice is cold; Fire burns; Iron is malleable.*

A HYPOTHETICAL PROPOSITION is one which makes a contingent predication; one which stipulates a condition in conjunction with the affirmation or denial, on the presence or absence, the fulfilment or non-fulfilment, of which the verity of the assertion depends; as, " *If you persevere in your studies, you will succeed.*"

A UNIVERSAL PROPOSITION is one in which we assert that the predicate agrees or disagrees with the *whole* subject and its various significates; *i. e.*, with *all* the ideas which can be comprehended in the term; one in which the assertion is understood to be as general as the idea which the term expresses, and which, indeed, gains all its extension and generality from the wideness of the generalisation which the term indicates; as, *Spain and Portugal form a peninsula; Planets revolve round the sun.*

A PARTICULAR PROPOSITION makes a predication in such a manner as to denote that a *part* only, and not the whole of the significates of the term, is affected by the coincidence or incoincidence which it expresses ;—is one in which the predicate does *not* agree or disagree with the *whole* universal idea denoted by the term, but in which some of the individuals comprehended in a specific name, or the species comprehended in a generic one, according as the name is that of a species or genus, bear the peculiar relation indicated by the predicate. It is a proposition affecting only a *part* of the subject; as, " *Many men are prudent ;*" " *Some students are eminent for perseverance.*"

AN AFFIRMATIVE PROPOSITION is an averment or assertion regarding

* Carlyle's " Stump Orator," p. 36.

the accordancy, conformity, or agreement of a subject and predicate ; as, *All intelligent beings are responsible agents.*

A NEGATIVE PROPOSITION is a sentence which denotes the repugnance, incoincidence, or disagreement of subject and predicate ; as, *Compassion is not a primary moral motive.*

It may be observed, by a glance at the illustrative examples given at the end of these several definitions, that there is no variation of form by which one may unerringly distinguish the class to which a proposition belongs ; and it will be equally evident, that this classification is not one by which an individual may ascertain the *one* category in which any given proposition may be included ; on the contrary, any *one* proposition may be arranged under, and comprehended in, more than one of these categorical distinctions. The *sense*, however, and not the *form*, must be chiefly considered in classifying any proposition under these heads. There are, however, a few distinctions of proposition, according to their form, which it may be advisable to mention : they may be comprised in the following enumeration ; viz., simple, compound, conjunctive, disjunctive, comparative, and casual.

A SIMPLE PROPOSITION has only one subject and one predicate ; as, " *The sun is a luminous body.*"

A COMPOUND PROPOSITION has more than one subject, or more than one predicate—it may either be conjunctive or disjunctive.

A conjunctive proposition asserts that the same predicate agrees with one or more subjects conjoined, or that one or more predicates conjoined, agree with the same subject ; as, " *Queen, Lords, and Commons constitute the Legislature.*"

A disjunctive proposition asserts either that the same predicate may be denied of each of the subjects, or that each of the predicates may be denied of the same subject, or that either one or other of the predicates may be asserted or denied of the same subject, or the same predicate of one or other of the subjects ; as, " *Neither the Queen, Lords, nor Commons can of themselves pass laws ;*" " *That mountain is either Ben Macdhui, or Ben Nevis.*"

A COMPARATIVE PROPOSITION asserts that a higher or lower degree of the predicate belongs to the subject—"*Ice is harder than snow.*"

A CASUAL PROPOSITION is one in which a reason or cause is assigned —"*Ice is harder than snow, because it is colder.*"

Ere closing this chapter, suffer one remark. Let not the above be looked upon as technical puerilities, as inutile and harassing dictinctions. Did they serve no other purpose, they would still be valuable as tending to accuracy of thought and correctness of expression. Beattie somewhere says, "The aim of education should be to teach us rather *how* to think than *what* to think—rather to improve our minds, so as to enable us to think for ourselves, than to load the memory with the thoughts of other men." In endeavouring, therefore, to show how accuracy of thought may be best cultivated, we think that exercise in making subtle distinctions of thought and expression is a great step in progress. It conduces to the orderliness of the intellect, aids the power of arrangement, and acts as an auxiliary in the acumenation of the judgment. Classification, arrangement, generalisation, and the power of analysing and distinguishing, are rare endowments, even among the higher order of intellectualists; and any means by which any advance may be made in their attainment should be welcomed, studied, and perseveringly practised. How necessary is it to discipline the mind! —to quicken its perceptions by exercise, to stimulate and incite its activities by continuous, well-directed, and constant application! To introduce order and clearness into the chaos-like interminglement of facts, hypotheses, suppositions, superstitions, credibilities, falsities, theories, and chimeras which hold a lodgement in the human mentality, is surely desirable! To winnow the chaff from the wheat, to separate the dross from the true ore, to pick out, uproot, and destroy the weeds which overgrow the uncultivated soul, one would suppose must be "a consummation devoutly to be wished." This, however, is only to be done by caution, watchfulness, careful discrimination, and accurate distinguishment. Hence *one* great advantage of the mental training to which the attending to minute subdivisions and classifications of thought, as expressed in propositions, must lead. But they have other and higher advantages, as we will hereafter show. Meanwhile, reverting to an assertion made in a foregoing portion of this chapter, "Every truth lost is a motive lost," let us couple this with the fact, that man is as his thoughts are, and how valuable will propositions become, as thoughts expressed! Propositions, too, are the latent containers of much truth not virtually and verbally expressed in them. If this is doubted, may we ask, Are not all the close-reasoned deductions of mathematics virtually, though latently, inherent in the *axiomata* which it lays down as its foundation-facts? Did not the proposition, "Electricity manifests itself by conduction and the emission of sparks," virtually contain within itself, involved in its significance, the discoveries of Franklin, and the subsequent progress of our knowledge of that wondrous power by which "thought is transmitted, not only with the speed, but by the power of lightning?"* Did not the

* Prince Albert.

proposition containing an expression of "the law of gravitation," involve all the mighty, astonishing, and grand results of modern astronomy? so that even now it may be farther generalised into the poet's stanza—

> " That very law which moulds a tear,
>   And bids it trickle from its source—
>   That law preserves the earth a sphere,
>   And guides the planets in their course."

It is ever so—

> " Nothing in this world is single,
>   All things, by a law divine,
>   In one another's being mingle."

Our intellectual powers are goaded on to higher and higher achievements by the instinctive yearning which we feel to unravel the mystery of our being, and the relations which we and nature bear to each other. When we attain to the disentanglement of one fact from another, there is given us in that a clue, a hint, a connecting link ; some analogous fact starts to our recollection or evolves itself in our experience, to direct our steps to farther advancement.   When we attain the object sought, we not only perceive something beyond it, but also gain a notion of the path.   That which we proposed to ourselves as an *ultimatum* is now seen to be but the primary link of a vast chain, which, link by link, we must examine and verify.   Thus are we led on and on, ever and ever progressing towards the temple of truth, by a beautiful, pleasing, and variegated pathway, gaining pure delight and valuable knowledge at every step, having the tedium of the way beguiled by the innumerable diversities observed around us, to excite our curiosity and gratify our souls, panting for truth and knowledge, yet finding as we go, that

> " All experience is an arch, where through
>   Gleams that untravelled world, whose margin fades
>   For ever and for ever as we move."

CHAPTER VI.

JUDGMENT.—NATURE AND KINDS OF EVIDENCE.

> " Know that the human being's thoughts and deeds
> Are not, like ocean-billows, blindly moved;
> The inner world, his microcosmus, is
> The deep shaft out of which they spring eternally ;
> They grow by certain laws, like the tree's fruit;
> No juggling chance can metamorphose them :
> Have I the human *kernel* first examined ?
> Then do I know the future will and action."
>
> *Wallenstein—Coleridge's Translation.*

" Fail by any sin or misfortune to discover what the truth of the fact is, you are lost, so far as that fact goes. If your thought do not image truly, but do image falsely the fact, you will vainly try to work upon the fact. The fact will not obey you, the fact will silently resist you, and ever with silent invincibility will go on resisting you till you do get to image it truly instead of falsely. No help for you whatever, except in attaining a true image of the fact. * * * *That* is the one thing needful; with that it shall be well with you in whatever you have to do with said fact."—CARLYLE.

> " THE world is too much with us—late and soon,
> Getting and spending we lay waste our powers ;
> Little we see in Nature that is ours,
> We have given our hearts away—a sordid boon."

Hence it is that in an age like the present,—which idolatrises materiality, utilitarianism, and tangibility,—depreciation and vilification are profusely vented against any study which, to the question, *cui bono ?*—what use is it ?—cannot answer by quoting a fair per centage of profit-production, and money-getting. Is it to be wondered at, then, that an inquiry into anything so *immaterial* as the human mind should attract notice, or have any attention bestowed upon it ? Is it matter of surprise that, in this universal vassalage to Mammon, when education itself is matured and systematised only upon the ground of its gainfulness—the pursuits of Logic, Psychology, &c., should languish neglected—that the imperishable dignity of the human intellect should be forgotten, and the great and important problems regarding its nature, operations, and destiny, should be passed by unheeded amid a multitudinous group of studies of less importance and minor moment than the *one* all-absorbing mania of this "*golden age ?*" Positivism contemns the " Philosophy of Mind" as improgressive,—twits " Logic" with the jocular definition that it is "*l'art de s'égarer avec méthode*"—the art of going astray by rule—and plumes itself upon its own conquests and advancement. We have no desire to retaliate these "railing accusations;" but surely this almost deification of positive, and scorn of mental science, is nearly equivalent to the assertion that the dwelling-place of the soul should be more cared for, and more luxuriously treated than the semi-divine resident therein. We do not despise the wondrous discoveries and inventions of Physics. We are rather gratified by the fact, that mind is possessed of such mighty powers and gigantic capabilities; and this serves to show us more and more the utility of spreading a knowledge of the "Art of Reasoning." Lord Bacon has most justly observed, that "abstract contemplation, and the construction and invention of experiments, rest upon the same principles, and are brought to perfection in a similar manner." * Yet there is one great distinction between Physics and Metaphysics, which we think may be justly regarded as accounting for the apparent comparative unprogressiveness of the latter, viz., the greater invariability of the objects upon which they respectively occupy themselves. Discoveries and inventions in Physics, once made, require no renewal or repetition, but descend, with all their advantages, to posterity. The printing-press, the steam-engine, the power-loom, the spinning-jenny, and the electric telegraph, &c., lack no second inventor. The truths of geometry, the facts of chemistry, the circulation of the blood, the law of gravitation, the method of fusing metals, of preparing dye-stuffs, of manufacturing porcelain and glass, the revealments of astronomy, &c., stand in need of no new discoverer. The Pyramids, the sacred bull of Nineveh, the Colossus, have borne witness of the art and physical science of man for thousands of years. The Parthenon, the Coliseum, and the temples of Memphis, attest, even in their ruins, the marvellousness of human skill. Canals, bridges, aqueducts, roads, and railways, machinery, and scientific apparatus, &c., bear evidence of the fertility of his genius. The sculptured monument, the life-resembling statue, the elaborately chiseled specimens of architecture, the pictured landscape, the accurately mimicked scenic representation, the gorgeous historical *tableau*, and the carefully outlined portraiture, display the might and delicacy of his inventive powers, and executive dexterity. In all these, ideas have been incarnated into works, and are become permanent memorials and certificates of what human ingenuity has effected and can accomplish. Everything here is stable, firm, enduring. Every succeeding generation starts from a higher eminence in civilisation than the last. The results of some thousands of years of thought, inquiry, experimentation, and invention,

* Impetus Philosophici, p. 682.

become the inheritance of the earth's future inhabitants. With mind it is far otherwise. Mental Philosophy is not cumulative as Natural Philosophy is. No one can here repose with confidence upon the results of the labours of his predecessors. Self-knowledge can only be attained by self-search. Each succeeding student brings in himself the "raw material," upon which, by experimentalisation, scrutiny, and self-examination, he must build up for himself a knowledge of his mental nature, must free himself from doubt, confusion, and intellectual bewilderment, ascertain for himself the *criteria* of belief and action, and gain an acquaintance with the powers of his own mind, and the limits of his own understanding. Hence we believe that, however much physical science may spread improvement abroad throughout the world, there will still be much to be done by mental philosophy, much in the acquisition of self-knowledge, the analysation of the intellectual faculties, the devising of superior educational methods, and in perfecting our acquaintance with the nature and kinds of evidence upon which our beliefs and actions must necessarily rest.

Evidence is that which elucidates truth, which renders the facts of a case clear, plain, obvious, and manifest ; that which proves the accuracy of our thoughts, opinions, and hypothesis, and on which the mind can rely, as the ground and foundation of its beliefs ; which enables us to ascertain the certainty and correctness of that which passes on within the mind, or is impressed upon it from without. What, then, is that which can give us this certainty ? What is that upon which we *must* rely, as the ultimate ground of certitude ? This is an all-important question. To one whose reliance must be so frequently based upon *data* beyond his own power of attainment, who must trust in the testimony of friends, confide in the avouchments of strangers, credit numerical calculations, prepare for or against contingencies, discriminate between appearances and realities, believe that upon the occurrence or recurrence of a given cause, a given effect will follow ; risk life and fortune on the faith of observation, and the deductions which may be drawn from it ; hazard his happiness and well-being on the correctness of an inference ; nay, endanger his " eternal all " on the validity of proof ; that science which seeks a compass that will guide his way, and attempts the discovery of the pole-star of Truth, ought not surely to be overlooked, or glanced at lightly, and thrown aside as frivolous and futile. Yet it is passing strange, that he who discovers a new, and hitherto unchronicled star, amid that unnumbered host which deck night's coronal of jet, or stand as friendly beacons at heaven's open gate, should gain eternal honour, while he who maps the intellectual hemisphere, and deciphers the true reading of the supersensuous mentality, is passed by unheeded and disregarded, or stigmatised as a mystic, a visionary, a metaphysical jargonist. To demarcate the bounds which separate the true from the false, to distinguish the apparent from the real, to ascertain the difference between inadvertency or error, and certitude or correctness, is a noble aim, and lofty aspiration; and if there be a possibility of discovering the " Nature and sources of Evidence," and classifying these into specific grades, dependent on particular operations of the mind, a great advantage shall be gained, were it but in the knowledge which it would yield of the capacities of the intellection. For Locke truly remarks, " Were the capacities of our understanding well considered, the extent of our knowledge (—*acquiring powers ?*) once discovered, and the horizon found which sets the bounds between the enlightened and dark part of things; between what is, and what is not, comprehensible by us, men would perhaps, with less scruple, acquiesce in the avowed ignorance of the one, and employ their thoughts and discourse with more advantage and satisfaction in the other." * Some such attempt we will now essay, in the hope that, imperfect as it is, it may be found useful in the realisation of the object at which we aim.

When we employ ourselves in scrutinising the stupendous chaos of phenomena with which we find ourselves surrounded, we cannot fail to perceive that each generically different existence is endowed with peculiar qualities or attributes, which mark out the distinction between *it* and every other species of object; that some phenomenal specificity differentiates existences, and indicates the point of dissimilitude between them; and that each object is possessed of the power of appropriating that—and that only with safety to itself—which will develop and mature the individuality of its nature. The " law of vitality" in plants and animals, is the *primordium* from which their developing powers arise. Each germ in either of these classes has impressed in its very constitution the power to be that *one* thing, and nothing else. It may be, in plants, that the soil is unfitted to yield the proper nutriment in proper quantities; that the atmosphere is ungenial, and the sunbeams scanty. This will produce a stunted, dwarfed, and deformed specimen of the plant, but it will not alter the radical and constitutional qualities with which it was originally endowed. It may be, in animals, that the climate is insalutary, the food-elements insufficiently produced, and extraneous circumstances unpropitious. This will not change the inherent attributes of its nature, though it will impede and injure its develop-

* Essay, Chap. I.

ment. So it is with man. There is a differentiating element—the mind—within him; and this mind is endowed with a specificality of nature no less essential and constitutional, no less definite, precise, and determinate, than those which appertain to surrounding objectivities. Upon this *uniqueness of structure*—if we dare use the expression—depends the peculiarity of product for which he is remarkable—thought. As

> " From the root
> Springs lighter the green stalk, from thence the leaves
> More airy, last the bright consummate flower,"

so thought, belief, science, and action, are developed from the intelligential germ. We do not wish to be understood here as asserting that ideas are either innate or connate. No! Man is born with *mind*, not with *thought*. This mind possesses a potential capacity of receiving impressions, and thence eliminating ideas. This capacity exists in an infant at birth, undeveloped and inactive, but competent of being impressed, excited, and developed in accordance with the laws of its being. From this it will be seen, that not ideas, but the power of idea-eduction, is innate, and that the thoughts which are excited within the mind are regulated by the opportunity afforded it for exercise and cultivation, and the necessary laws and modes of operation under which, by its very constitution, it is compelled to contemplate all external objectivities and internal operations.

" Man," says Emerson, " is that noble endogenous plant which grows like the palm, from within outward;" and again, " Man is endogenous, and education is his unfolding." This is the theory of mental evolution. Consciousness is the germinal which, by its indwelling energy, operates upon the impressions of which sensation informs it, and thus gradually builds up within itself the edifice of knowledge. The senses are but the nutriment-seeking filaments by which the mind strives to acquire materials fitted for building up its intellectual being, and evolving that ideal of Nature which we call—Science.

Consciousness is to the mind what *nervility* is to the body—the general informant, or rather recipient, of impressions. It is that singular power which the mind possesses of knowing all that passes on within it, or exerts itself upon it, by which the whole series of sensations, ideas, emotions, volitions, and actions, which operate in or upon the human intellection, is revealed and held up to view. It is not one single faculty or exertion of mind, but that by which the mind becomes privy to the phenomena of the mentality. This may be proved from the fact, that when men are earnestly excited, they lose all consciousness, and are hurried on by the irresistible power of the activities of the mind; while it is not until the excitement subsides, and calmness returns, that consciousness is capable of re-exerting itself. "We no more feel or know it (*i. e.*, a recent mental emotion) than we feel the feet, or the hand, or the brain of our body. The new deed is yet a part of life, remaining, for a time, immersed in our unconscious life. In some contemplative hour it detaches itself from the life like ripe fruit, to become a thought of the mind." * "The series of states in which the mind exists, from moment to moment, is all that can be known of the mind; and it cannot, *at the same moment*, exist in *two different states*, one of consciousness, and one of some other feeling wholly distinguishable from it." † Were we discoursing on the laws of mental growth, we should feel ourselves justified in dwelling longer upon the peculiar nature of consciousness. All that we, however, require to prove is, that the mind must grow from an internal principle, not from external accretion; must put forth its own energy to select, separate, and absorb, in order that it may afterwards re-combine, synthetise, and change. Knowledge is not an accumulation of facts and particulars, but these facts and particulars entering into and being absorbed by the mind, originate the ideas of law, truth, and duty. If this be accepted as truth, our task is easy; for Consciousness will then be proved to be the ultimate *criterion* of truth to each individual of the human race. And how can it be otherwise? Can we overstep the limits of our nature? Can we have any ideas which have not entered into the mind? Or can we have any ideas in the mind of which consciousness does not take cognisance? If not, then consciousness must be able to give us information of all that passes in the mind. By watching its operations, we may gain a knowledge of its laws, and of the power of those faculties which we are called upon continually to exert. That there *are* such laws, may be seen in the fact, that by no possible educative agency can the mind be brought to believe that the toothache is the beating of a drum, that an elephant could grow on a rose-bush, or that a triangle is a circle. No, there are necessary laws—modes of operation under which the mind is necessarily compelled to contemplate external objectivities—as truly impressed upon the constitution of the mind, as the "laws of vitality" are upon the infant animal, or the germinating plant; and it is only by the power of introversion, or self-seeing, which consciousness enables us to exercise, that we can gain a knowledge of the forms of thinking, and the principles on which our intelligential activities exert themselves.

* Emerson's Oration before the A. B. K. Society. † Brown's "Physiology of the Mind."

The human consciousness gains knowledge from two diverse sources; the one direct, unintervented, immediate, giving us information regarding the mental operations in their intuitional capacity; the other, indirect, intervented, and mediate, teaching us, by inference, of exciting objectivities. The one occupies itself in regard to all that passes on in the mind, explains the operation of its powers, the method of its excitement, the results of the impressions made on it, and the general workings of the understanding. The other employs itself in watching the impinging, the tangentiation of objects upon the mentality, strives to look beyond the circle of its finity, from the effect, thought, it wishes to glean information regarding the thought-excitant, and, by inference, attempts to detect the *outlying* impressibilities which produce such wondrous results upon the mind. These twin-powers of consciousness must proceed in accordance with the conditions of the human intellect, without which thought cannot be evolved. These conditions are called laws: law, in this sense, meaning the uniform *modus operandi* which has been impressed upon mind by its Author. This distinction between the intuitional and logical consciousness—the διανοια and the νους—it is of great importance to apprehend clearly; for every process of Reasoning takes for granted certain fundamental principles, without which no reasoning could proceed. It is the intuitional consciousness which reveals these to men. Not that the ideas are innate, but that the mind is so framed that, when once called into action, these ideas must as necessarily and inevitably arise within it, as the acorn, when placed in proper circumstances, must become an oak. "Truth, in the intuitional sense, is *being*—being manifesting itself to the human mind—being gazed upon immediately by the eye of the soul." * It cannot, therefore, admit of demonstration. Like the axioms of mathematical science, intuitional truths are the results of simple and internal knowledge, which, although primarily excited to action by external objects, precede all acquired information. Their extraordinary clearness, not their obscurity, renders them incapable of proof. Their self-evidence is not a defect, but a perfection. Upon these alone can we rely, as absolutely and irrefragably inconvertible. They are so inwovened and intertextured with the mind, that no development of thought can be educed without calling them into being.

Having premised this on the question of General Consciousness, we shall now be in a condition, without prejudice to that great fact, to render our explanation of "the Nature and Sources of Evidence" more

* Morell's "Philosophy of Religion."

simple and easy, by considering the several great streams from which Consciousness gains its knowledge, as separate sources of evidence, each contributing its own individual sort of information and certitude to the mind, under the following heads:—Intuition, Sensation, Memory, Analogy, Testimony, Probability, Induction. We will, however, defer the consideration of these items for another chapter.

CHAPTER VII.

JUDGMENT.—NATURE AND KINDS OF EVIDENCE.

"What I find to be truth shall be welcome to me, let it sound as it may. I will *know:* and should this be impossible, this much at least will I know, that it is not possible. Even to this result will I submit, should it present itself to me as truth."— FICHTE.

THE human mind has two different spheres of speculative inquiry— the one, the inner intellectual world revealed by Intuition—the other, the outer material universe made known to it by Sensation. In the former, by a self-seeing power peculiar to the human mentality, we gain evidence of all the feelings, volitions, states, and affections of the mind. In the latter, the senses are the *media* through which proof of the external world is gained. In both of these fields of investigation it is necessary that the mind should learn to determine regarding the validity of the evidence of its beliefs. The obvious tendency, however, of the philosophic spirit of the present age is towards the External, and the sense-shown, rather than the multiplex revealments of thought and affection which Intuition brings before the mental vision—it concentrates itself more upon the upbuilding of positive science, the acquirement of a mastery over nature, and the attainment of a knowledge of the laws of the material world, than upon what is generally regarded as the shadowy speculations of a fanciful, vain, and unsubstantial science, a science which treats of the mind alone, and requires the continued exercise of thought-introversion. Man has purchased his superiority in physical science, in invention and discovery, in sense-gratification, at the price of the relinquishment of the intuitional sphere of knowledge-attainment,—the loss of one-half of his mental empire. And thus, while positive science has risen like a giant-built pyramid, mental philosophy has been allowed to crumble into ruins, by neglect; yet, when we calmly reflect that truth is not granted to those who merely desire to become possessed of it, but to those who earnestly strive for its attainment; that it cannot be gained but by the full and consentaneous exertion of *all* the mental powers, we shall see the advantage of that department of inquiry, whose method and means of speculation raise up the faculties of the soul into strength, and which, in the very act of self-analysis, enables us to improve the whole inward world of our thoughts and affections, and gain an immense treasury of facts upon the most momentous subjects on which the human mind can exert itself.

We have, in the following pages, to show how the mind operates in the acquisition of knowledge, by considering, as briefly as possible, the various kinds of evidence of which we made mention in our last chapter: viz., Intuition, Sensation, Memory, Analogy, Testimony, Probability, and Induction. Before doing so, however, we may premise, that although Logic is founded on the laws and principles of the human mind, it does not undertake to say "why" they exist, or to explain the "wherefore" of our confidence being so trustingly placed in them. It undertakes to describe the fundamental principles of thought, but all it can assert as to their origin is, that they are interwoven with our mental constitution; *why* they are so is beyond our ken. Who can tell why attraction exists in matter? why some chemical substances possess an affinity for others? or, why life exerts itself in opposition to chemical and mechanical laws? These are "fundamental facts" to which our knowledge cannot extend. The *why* is known alone to the Eternal.

INTUITION is that power which the mind possesses of *looking at* itself, by which it becomes acquainted with its own existence, modes of operation, and powers of thought. When the intellect is excited to any course of action, this self-perceptive power enables it to discern its own state or condition under the excitement, and it thus becomes acquainted with the threefold fact—of its own being, the method of its own working and counter-working, and the ability of its several faculties: by this means we gain a knowledge of the constitution of the mind, of its powers of sensibility, understanding, and volition—of the agency of imagination, and the workings of our passions, emotions, and desires. By this self-introspective faculty we become impressed with an irresistible certainty that we perform the various functions of physical and mental life; that we suffer and act, think and remember, feel and reason. Intuition reveals to us the basis and groundwork of all thought. No process of reasoning is needful to convince us of those primary truths which it makes known. So soon as the mind becomes impressed it becomes sensible of the impression; and this sensibility is the constitutional fact which makes the intuitional revealments of our nature peculiarly self-evident. Of that which we see and feel passing within us we cannot rationally doubt; and as we have always the means of experimentalising upon the operations of our own mind, upon our powers of perception and will, upon our feelings of pleasure and pain, upon our ideas of unity or plurality, power or inefficacy, cause and effect, there seems no reasonable inlet to doubt concerning the truths of our mental intuitions. If, for instance, I assert that all men are sensible to appeals made to their sympathies in behalf of the wretched and oppressed, or, that all men are convinced of their own existence, I express in words—in the one case, a moral, in the other, a mental intuition—that which *I feel* within myself as Truth. If any one denies the truth of either of these propositions, all I can do is to collect examples of the actions of others, for these are the product of their thoughts, and maintain that these prove that the general intuitions of men agree with mine; and if these fail to satisfy, I must come to the conclusion, that the person whom I address either mistakes his own consciousness, or that his mind is differently constituted from mine: no arguments can avail when men's intuitions, if they ever do so, differ. We do not, however, maintain that all individual intuitions are absolute truth. We admit that one person's mind may be ruled by sense, another's by imagination, and that of a third by intellect, and that education and circumstances have much power in distorting the appearance of those objectivities which are placed before the mental eye. Yet it is evident, that if the general intuitions of humanity, as manifested by their words and actions, are similar, we have good grounds for receiving *them* as facts of consciousness. This, however, does not annul the general law of mentality, that the individual intuitions of men's minds are Truth to the persons in whose minds they arise. These are *to them* irrefragable and valid grounds of conviction. No certainty of demonstration can gainsay *these* soul-sprung verities; *to them* they are irresistible and inoppugnable. The hypochondriac and the monomaniac are impregnable to all reasoning, for they have the evidence of Consciousness that they are right. How, then, are we to decide what Truth is? This is the dilemma in which men find themselves. To the individual his experiences are true. Each person's Experience differs. What then is Truth? We can only answer, that in our present state the *absolute* truth is unattainable regarding everything except *our own* Experience; but when that experience coincides with the general experience of our "fellow co-heirs of mortality," we may warrantably conclude that we are in possession of the Truth. This, we suppose, is what is meant by the truism of an appeal to "Common Sense." This appeal to "Common Sense," however, is not necessary to decide *all* truth, but only to decide upon those grand primal truths which grow up in each soul as constitutionally as flowers spring from their seeds— what Jacobi calls "those certain, immediate, simple, and positive principles of Judgment which do not derive their authority from any process of reasoning, but rather preside over all reasoning." We believe, with Fichte, that "every seeming truth, born of thought alone, and not ultimately resting on Intuition, is false and spurious." We may, therefore, conclude this department of evidence by saying, that Intuition informs us by the mere act of thought-introversion of the *laws* or *forms* of thought, not of the *matter;* of all that relates to the powers, processes, and states of mind,—not of the truth, but of the facts which excite and impress it. The following appear to us a few of the chief Truths which Intuition reveals :—1st, A belief in *our own* existence as sentient and intellectual beings. 2nd, A firm faith in the evidence of our own senses. 3rd, A confiding reliance on the uniformity of the operations of Nature.—If we are asked for proof, we can only ask in return, Who was ever deemed sane that doubted them ?

SENSATION, as we very fully explained in a previous chapter, is the result of a preadapted relation between the organs of sense and the external world. When this result passes onwards to, and impresses itself upon the mind, Perception ensues. Of course, we include the conjoint actions of these two powers under this head of evidence. Each sensational organ conveys its own peculiar series of impressions to the mind, and originates its own peculiar succession of ideas in it—hence, each of the five senses constitutes one of the avenues by which a knowledge of the outward material universe is communicated to the intellection, and one of the causative agents by which the faculties of the soul are excited to activity. Mind is the germ, the senses the nutriment-bringers, thought the fruit. Hence, Sensation is the only inlet to Knowledge, though not the only factor in the production of it. The mind has a definite constitution upon which Sensation operates, and which it develops. All the faculties of the mind exist in it *potentially;* but they require to be excited to action by Sensation. This may be proved by the case of the blind, the deaf-mutes, &c., whose minds necessarily lie dormant for lack of the excitation of sensations,—Laura Bridgman and James Mitchell, for example.* Mind possesses certain properties; so

---

* See Dickens' account of Laura Bridgman, in "American Notes for General Circulation," and Dugald Stewart's of James Mitchell, in "Some Account of a Boy Born Blind and Deaf," Edinburgh, 1812.

do the objectivities around us: when the one is placed in communication with the other, ideas are as necessarily and inevitably produced, as an acid and an alkali combined will produce a precipitate; and as certainly as arsenite of potash mingled with sulphate of copper yields an apple-green precipitate, so certainly will the view of an external object produce the special and peculiar idea of that object. On this certainty of specific idea-production the ground of our reliance on Sensation is placed. "Thought succeeds thought, idea follows idea incessantly. If our senses are awake, we are constantly receiving sensations of the eye, the ear, the touch, and so forth, but not Sensations alone; after sensations, ideas are perpetually excited of sensations formerly received; after these ideas, other ideas; and during the whole course of our lives, a series of these two states of Consciousness is constantly going on;"* and yet, during the whole of these successions of sensations, if the sensational organs are healthy, we never find any two essentially different objects impressing the mind in a similar manner so as to produce the same objective ideas in the mind. This sentence requires explanation to divest it of a slight degree of ambiguity which we know not how otherwise to obviate. The sight of an overhanging mountain, and the view of a flash of forked lightning, are two essentially different objects which impress the mind in a similar manner, viz., producing the idea of fear and sublimity; but they do not impress it so as to produce the same objective idea—*i.e.*, the lightning can by no healthy power of sensation be thought a mountain, and *vice versâ*. From this specificality of idea-production we are led to rely on the accuracy of our sense-derived information, and so long as each object continues to convey exactly the same *one* objective sensation, we need not doubt the fact of its external existence; for we have no reasonable motive to doubt until we know what it is to be deceived.

It is most true, as some will be ready to suggest, that our sensations often inform us of appearances which cannot be substantiated by an appeal to the reality of things, such as the results of vision through a light-refracting medium; the effect of distance in diminishing the apparent magnitude of objects; or, to take individual instances, the deceptive appearances of a stick in the water; the difference between the real and apparent magnitude of the stars, &c. In the first place, we may observe that in all these cases the senses inform us correctly as to the *fact* of their existence: the only difference being in the *circumstantialities* of the fact. In the second place, as it is the senses which enable us to correct the erroneous impressions which they primarily gave us, they

* Mill's "Analysis of the Human Mind," p. 52.

are honest faculties after all, although not quite so attentive to their observations as they might be. Having thus the means of detecting the true from the false, and the power of discovering the general laws which prevent us from receiving accurate sensations in certain given cases, we have proof sufficient that Nature is not one huge deception, and that, in general, the " evidence of the senses " is worthy of the dependence usually placed in it. Perhaps it is worthy of remark in this place, that with regard to form, size, distance, and motion, sight and touch may each be our informants, and hence may be reciprocally employed to correct each other, while with regard to odour, taste, colour, and sound, we have no other evidence than is afforded us by that one sensational organ which has been appropriated to the reception of each of these species of sensation.

There are some philosophers who believe in " necessary truths;" for our part, we believe that all truths are " necessary," with this difference —that there are some truths which are absolute, *i.e.*, whose truth cannot possibly change, while others are mutable and contingent. Of the former sort are the primary facts of science. The sun moves on its axis, the earth revolves round the sun—two and two make four—the whole is greater than its part—two straight lines cannot enclose a space —vitality resists, to a certain extent, the laws of chemistry and mechanics, &c. Of the latter kind are the facts of history, of political geography, of every day life, some of the propositions of moral, mental, and political science; the tenets of criticism,, and the incidental conversations of men, &c.—as, Queen Victoria reigns—Malta is a British possession—the weather is unsettled—all men naturally act from selfish motives—every one enjoys poetry—stocks are up to-day, &c. The former, however, are equally with the latter the dictates of experience, and are no other way distinguishable from them than by their greater invariability. The little boy who desires a piece of bread has no innate or necessary idea of the truth of the whole being greater than its part, but he readily perceives by experience that the whole loaf from which his piece is cut is greater than the part which he receives; and it is no more an innate or necessary truth, anterior to experience, that two and two make four, than that the wires of a voltaic battery, if immersed, without communication with each other, into a cup of water, will decompose that water—the hydrogen being separated at the negative, and the oxygen at the positive pole—only that the latter is farther removed from our experience, and less frequently observed by us. Sensations as sensations are true, although they are not always the absolute truth of things; *e.g.*, I leave my house, which may be about sixty feet in height; as I depart, it gradually lessens to the view; does it really diminish as I withdraw? I cannot believe it, for when I return it is of the original size. I hence form the idea that distance diminishes the apparent magnitudes of bodies, and by applying this idea to the other objects which lie at a distance from me, I find it correct, nay, that it holds good through the whole range of creation; and it is from the perception of this fact that men are able to measure "these mighty spheres that gem infinity" with the same, if not greater, accuracy than the corn-field opposite my cottage.

MEMORY is that peculiar power of retentiveness by which ideas, feelings, volitions, &c., are kept as possessions in the mind, so that they may be recalled and reviewed by it, without reference to their originating causes. When our thoughts recur involuntarily, it is called Remembrance; when they are brought back by an effort of the will, it is denominated Recollection.

Memory, when properly exercised, supplies the Reason not only with materials, but also the means of constructing accurate judgments— it prepares for the use of the thought-powers a correct *fac-simile* of Experience, and is hence a principal source of the mind's *data* in reasoning.

It records and preserves the impressions conveyed through the organs of Sensation and Consciousness. Sensation merely concerns itself with what is immediately present. Memory, seizing upon those impressions—which would otherwise be evanescent—daguerreotypes them for ever for the use of the mind, and thus enables us to employ our past Experience as a guide to the present and a light to the future. The Logician, when he is desirous of discriminating, classifying, arranging, and operating upon his ideas, must, in a great measure, rely upon memory for his materials; and the accuracy of his inferences materially depends on the correctness of his former sensations, and the fidelity with which memory retains them.

Intuitions and sensations might pass and re-pass in uninterrupted successions through the mind, yet, were man destitute of memory or retentiveness, there could be no permanency in his knowledge, no generalised expressions of facts, no sure and stable basis of experience. The mind would resemble a *camera obscura*, which now receives an image, and immediately it is effaced by the introduction of another; and when the whole series of which it is susceptible has been pictured on it, the whole disappear, and there is no power of recalling them, except by the operations of the same causes which originated the picture-world we saw. Intuitions and sensations inform us of our present feelings, &c. Memory refers to those that are past. The former thought-powers tell us what we *do* feel, think, or will: the latter, what we *have* felt, thought, or willed, or by which we *have* been impressed. Any one who has engaged in self-retrospection, who has looked backward into the past experiences which Memory has laid up for him in her vast fact-treasury, will find little difficulty in admitting that Memory is one of the chief "sources of evidence." It is not, of course, so worthy of credit as Intuition or Sensation, for they have their facts present to the mind, whereas Memory can only recal former ideas to the mental view. Memory, too, is the criterion by which we judge the future: as we have found the operations of Nature, so do we still expect to find them. We do not require an innate *knowledge* of the proposition, "Like causes will produce like effects," to make us believe that the future will resemble the past. For instance, a child who has once tasted sugar, and appreciated its sweetness, does not make use of this learned phrase mentally: sweetness is the child's experience of sugar, and it can know nothing else except its experience; it therefore confidently expects the same result on a repetition of its former experience. Men do not hesitate to confide in the intimations of Memory; nay, they cannot do it; it is part of their personality. Without the evidence which this faculty yields, whence could the idea of our personal identity arise? Intuition and Sensation give us information of the impressions received in a succession of *points* of time. Memory colligates each present sensation with all that is past, conjoining them in the idea of Self; and this colligation of past and present constitutes our personality; and, in conjunction with consciousness, originates the notion of *egoism*. Why Memory should be thought so trustworthy, we have already said we cannot explain. It is one of the forms or laws of thought; farther than this we know nothing.

ANALOGY is a term employed to denote that peculiar feeling which is originated in the mind when it perceives a resemblance or similarity between objects as to their circumstances, relations, or effects, when the objects are dissimilar; or *vice versâ*, a resemblance of objects when their circumstances, &c., are incoincident. When one system of events, relations, or appearances, is observed and known, and another series of circumstances resembling them, but less known, occurs, and we reason that the causes are the same in each, we are said to reason analogically. Upon our ideas of similarity the force of analogy depends; and the more striking the resemblance, the more reliance do we place in the truth of analogical reasoning: instances of the value of analogy as a "source of evidence," and a ground for reasoning, may be gleaned from every page of the history of the sciences. Newton's discovery of gravitation; Franklin's discoveries in electricity; and the discovery of Neptune, &c., will readily occur to the reader's memory. "Let science bear witness," said the poet Campbell, "how many of her brightest discoveries have been struck out by the collision of analogy, and by original minds bringing one part of their vast information to consult and co-operate with another. For a single study is apt to tinge the spirit with a single colour, whilst expansive knowledge irradiates it, from many studies, with the many-coloured hues of thought, till they kindle by their assemblage, and blend and melt into the white light of inspiration. Newton made history and astronomy illustrate each other, and Richter and Dalton brought mathematics to bear upon chemistry, till science may now be said to be able to weigh at once an atom and a planet." When we know that certain phenomena result from certain causes, and perceive that similar phenomena result from unknown or undiscovered causes, we are led to infer that the causes are alike; or when we know the facts in one case resemble, in great part, the facts observed in another, we naturally conclude that the whole circumstances coincide. The greater the coincidence, the stronger the proof; the less the similarity, the less probability is there of its truth. Arguments from analogy should be used with caution. Unless the resemblance be very striking, and the conclusion can afterwards be subjected to experiment, it can never rise to certainty, but must ever remain in the " dim inane " of conjecture. One great use of analogy is to disarm prejudice by showing that the opinions which we intend to introduce are no more liable to objection than others whose truth is already unquestioned. The best instances of the uses of analogy are to be found in Butler's " Analogy of Religion," and Archbishop Whately's " Historic Doubts relative to Napoleon Bonaparte."

TESTIMONY is, in general, the evidence which other persons give on any point—the relation of the experience of others. Our belief in Testimony is founded on the reliance which we place in the general honesty of men. History, geography, biography, many of the facts of science and literature, and all our information regarding the general occurrences of human life, the actions of men, the state of business, morality, religion, &c., must all be believed in on Testimony. Our courts of law, our " commissions of inquiry," &c., recognise Testimony as a " source of evidence." Did the virtuous sentiments and moral affections of men possess the supremacy which they ought, were their intellectual powers able to keep in check the depraved propensities of their nature, Testimony would be as infallible a criterion of truth as personal experience. But this, unfortunately, is not the case; and hence we are admonished by every-day occurrences to look with a jealous eye on the affirmations of men, lest sinister motives influence them, and give them a fancied interest in practising deceit. We are thus necessitated to guard against being imposed on by deceptive testimony, and to use every precaution in acquiring a knowledge of the laws which are to be observed in judging regarding it.

Man, in his most perfect state, naturally desires to speak truly. It is difficult to speak falsely, and at the same time to steer clear of all probability of discovery. Truth is easily told. But it is long before the mind can acquire that incrustation of habit which enables it to utter falsehoods with the easy indifference of truth. The necessity of truthfulness is so impressed upon the minds of men, that they have, with one consent, agreed to brand the possessor of " lying lips " with every mark of ignominy. Despite, however, of this, we daily experience the need of some general rules for the purpose of guiding us in our judgment concerning testimonial proof.

Each individual, endowed with the average powers of humanity, has the capacity to understand the general physical and moral occurrences which take place around him; but as there are peculiar studies which fit men more readily for observations regarding particular phenomena, it is obvious, that the better the individual is acquainted with the peculiar phenomena concerning which he affirms anything, the greater is the validity of his testimony. But, considering that an average endowment of " common sense " capacitates us to judge with sufficient accuracy regarding the facts of ordinary cases, the sincerity or disinterestedness of the party is what is most liable to doubt, so that the greater the honesty of an individual in the common affairs of life, and the less his interest can be influenced by the point at issue, the more trustworthy is the testimony which he offers; and *vice versâ* misrepresentation can only proceed from two causes, inadequacy of observation, or intention to deceive. Want of general intelligence will produce the one; the love of falsehood, the hope of benefit, or the fear of injury, will occasion the other. If one or both of these causes can be reasonably supposed to be operating, or to have operated on the mind of the attestor, his evidence must be considered invalidated in a ratio with the probability of his disingenuousness.

When the honesty and ability of any set of witnesses is presumable, it is quite evident that the greater their number, the more infallibly trustworthy will be the proof. Nay, even when the number alone is gained, there is great probability of the truth of their statements, provided there may have been no collusion amongst them; for even though each may be more likely to speak falsely than truthfully, yet it is much more improbable that they should all lie alike, than that the circumstances should not have occurred. The time, too, which may have intervened between the event and the deposition, ought also to be taken into account; for the strongest memory is liable to forgetfulness by the lapse of time. The constant impression of new ideas on the mind tends to diminish the certainty with which old ones are retained. In matters of *fact*, honesty is the only requisite; in matters of *opinion*, whether relating to literature, morality, religion, or science, ability must be superadded. Great as may be the certainty attainable by Testimony, it is, however, less worthy of reliance than our own experience. It may be almost laid down as a law, that the greater the accordance of the evidence with experience, the more likely is it to be true. Not that our experience always is to be the criterion, for that would be to make the likelihood of the truth of facts be diminished in a ratio with our ignorance. When the testimony fulfils the above requirements, it may, in general, be considered worthy of belief, even although it transcend experience. Bruce, the Abyssinian traveller, was doubted, because his relations transcended our experience; subsequent inquiry, however, established their accuracy. From the above remarks it will be seen that in judging of Testimony, the four following things, with regard to the attestors, are to be observed :—

1st. The capacity of the witnesses to make observations, and give evidence. 2nd. Their character. 3rd. Their number. 4th. The time elapsed since the occurrence of which they speak. Regarding the facts concerning which they make attestation, we more readily place reliance if they have been, 1, possible; 2, patent to observation; 3, well known; 4, operative in the production or modification of future events.

PROBABILITY refers to the likelihood of an occurrence. The more numerous the causes which operate for and against the production of a certainty, the more difficult it is to discover the probability. When, however, the causes are ascertainable, they may be balanced, and the probability computed. If certain similar effects proceed from an unknown cause, and the majority of the effects are traced to one cause, it is probable the whole are the product of that cause. The uncertainty does not depend upon the absence of *a* cause, but from our want of knowledge of *the* cause. The grounds of probability are, 1st, The accordance of the circumstance with our knowledge or experience; 2nd, The reliability of testimony. Anything may be called improbable, if the chance of its occurrence is less than $\frac{1}{2}$ (one-half). If one premise be probable, and another certain, the conclusion will only be probable. If both premises be probable, the conclusion is not necessarily probable, but depends upon the probability of each premise. Supposing the premises of an argument to possess much more than one-half ($\frac{1}{2}$) of probability, the conclusion will not be in every case probable; for to state the case in its strongest light against ourselves, let each premise have seven-tenths of probability, the conclusion will be improbable; thus, $\frac{7}{10} \times \frac{7}{10} = \frac{49}{100}$. This uncertainty would increase with the improbability of each premise added.

CHAPTER VIII.

JUDGMENT.—NATURE AND KINDS OF EVIDENCE.

"Science consists of general propositions inferred from particular facts or from less general propositions, by Induction; and it is our object to discern the nature and laws of Induction in this sense."—WHEWELL.

INDUCTION is the term now universally employed to designate that systematic observation of any series of phenomena by which we are enabled, after careful verification, to deduce general inferences from the facts of experience. As a source of evidence, it depends upon the intuitional principles which the operations of the external universe develop in the mind. In looking upon Nature with an intelligent eye —in observing her processes—and carefully examining the reports which the sensational organs bring to the percipient faculties, men naturally perceive that of all that mighty mass of individualisms from which the mind receives impressions, many influence it in a similar manner. This leads the mind to observe the resemblances and dissimilarities of objects, to investigate their coherence, coexistence, and derivation; and thus the work of unification begins. As facts multiply their impressions on the mind, similar and concomitant series of phenomena are remarked and classified, and by this means gain prominency in the intellect; generalisation perceives the essential *oneness* of nature which coexist in many of them, apparently diverse and incoincident though they be; experimentalisation is employed— the law of their colligation begins to dawn on the mind—and is, at last, evolved from the vast multitude of special facts in which it lay latent.

Then "the memory disburdens itself of its cumbrous catalogue of particulars, and carries centuries of observation in a single formula."

The whole universe—that vast amplitude in which we dwell, and which affords so much scope for the exercise of our curiosity, research, and investigation—presents itself to us, primarily, as an immense concourse of objectivities in almost continual fluxion and change ; despite, however, of this multiplicity and mutability, a wondrous sameness of appearances, uniformity of procedure, and coincidence of phenomena, are evident to the intelligent eye. It is in the careful inspection of these that Induction employs itself—"Human knowledge does not consist in the bare collection or enumeration of facts ; this alone would be of little service, were we not to attempt the classification of them, and to educe from such classification general laws and principles. The knowledge which consists in individual truths could never be either extensive or definite, for the multiplicity which then must crowd in upon the mind only tends to confound and perplex it, while the memory, overburdened with particulars, is not able to retain a hundredth part of the materials which are collected. To prevent this, the power of generalisation comes to our aid, by which the individual facts are so classified under their proper conceptions, that they may at the same time be more easily retained, and their several relations to all other branches of knowledge accurately defined. The colligation and classification of facts, then, we may regard as the two first steps which are to be taken in the attainment of truth." * From the position which he occupies in this terrestrial compartment of the Temple of Creation —from his dependence upon the mutations to which nature is subject, for health, life, sustenance, and comfort—and from the special constitution of his intellectual powers, man has an irresistible tendency to exert himself in the study and pursuit of the truth of things—has a direct interest in becoming acquainted with the antecedences, concomitants, and consequents of the several states and conditions of objects—and finds it absolutely necessary to learn the modes of the occurrence and recurrence of the various and diversified contingencies which take place around him. Hence it is that Philosophy has always been an object of pursuit. Hence it has resulted that the process of Induction has had so many charms for the intellectual of the human race.—In this brief chapter we purpose to furnish the reader with a succinct outline of the Inductive Method, chiefly as it is propounded in the works of Lord-Chancellor Bacon, and the "Logic" of John Stuart Mill.

* Morell's "Hist. Spec. Phil.," Vol. I. p. 34.

The universe, whether mental or material, is a vast storehouse of facts. The great duty and interest of man, with regard to it, is to discover the Truth, to learn the cause or causes of each effect, and the effects of each cause. For this purpose he must, by assiduous and careful study, become acquainted with the arrangement, connection, and systematisation which reign in Nature. The objects which Induction renders necessary are primarily the two following:—1st, The investigation of facts preparatory to the formation of a general law. 2nd, The inferring of a general law from the facts thus investigated. To fulfil these requirements efficiently, three processes are needful.

I. To observe with attention and accuracy the great variety of objects of which the universe is composed, and to gain a knowledge of their several properties and qualities.

II. To group these various and multiplex objectivities, or series of phenomena, according to their several relations, coincidences, and properties, and arrange them, in conformity with their importance, into ordinate and subordinate classes.

III. To note the successions in which phenomena occur, the order of the events which result from them, for the purpose of discovering the bond of causation by which they are colligated into an endlessly-ramified chain of inter-related antecedence, coexistence, and consequence.

To perform these processes aright will require the earnest application of the whole of our percipient faculties, for "man, the servant and interpreter of Nature, does and knows so far as he has, either in fact or thought, observed the order of Nature : more he can neither understand nor perform." * In such circumstances it becomes of importance to know in what manner this investigative process may be most accurately performed. Now, "there are two ways of searching after and discovering truth : the one, from sense and particulars, flies upwards to the most general axioms, and from these principles, and their never-questioned truth, judges of and discovers intermediate axioms. The other, from sense and particulars, collects axioms ascending in a continuous and gradual manner, so that the most general axioms are arrived at in the last stage." † It is the latter of these methods with

---

* Homo Naturæ minister et interpres, tantum facit et intelligit, quantum de Naturæ ordinere vel mente observaverit; neo amplius scit aut potest.—"*Novum Organum*." *Liber Primis.—Aphorismus I.*

† Duæ viæ sunt atque esse possunt ad inquirendum et inveniendum veritatem. Altera a sensu et particularibus advolat ad axiomata maximè generalia, atque ex iis principiis eorumque mimota veritate judicat et invenit axiomata media; atque hæc via in usu est. Altera a sensu et particularibus excitat axiomata, ascendendo continentur

which we are at present concerned. By the conducting of investigations according to this—the Inductive—method, we gain a knowledge of external existences and their properties, the causes which are operative among them, the changes they undergo, and the effects which the exertion of these properties produce on other objects. In the former case, we acquire information of, and are warranted in making propositions concerning, the existence and properties of the objects only. In the latter, we perceive the reciprocal causative agency which bodies are capable of exerting upon each other. In the prosecution of these different departments of inquiry, Induction proceeds in a systematic manner, and guides its studies by a definite plan, which it will now be our duty to explain.

When we are desirous of elucidating the truth regarding any series of phenomena, the first step which we should take in the prosecution of our design, should be to write down the *data* upon which our speculations are to be founded. These will consist of a complete catalogue, or, at least, an extensive enumeration of the facts of experience in the order of their occurrence, and in all their modifications of manifestation. Great caution and care must be exercised in ascertaining the accuracy of the facts, or the validity of the proof on which we rest our confidence of their correctness. Experiments should be made, and accurately noted; doubtful incidents, while not actually thrown aside and discarded as valueless, should yet have their uncertainty estimated and allowed for. This narrative, carefully revised, all extraneous or unnecessary matter expunged, and the facts it contains properly arranged, form the materials of philosophy, and the elements of the superstructure of science. This Natural History of any given class of phenomena being prepared, we are now to proceed, by a judicious comparison of the collated facts, to discover the *form* or essence of these appearances; —that which is convertible with the quality for which the object is noticed, and which exists wherever that quality is found: for this purpose we are to consider which of all the qualities possessed by these diverse bodies must be excluded from any participation in the *form* or essence. In pursuance of this inquiry we must discard all those properties which are in the several objects merely accidental and essentially dissimilar; this will considerably widen our generalisation, but will materially limit the bounds of our investigation, in so far as we shall have ascertained that in these certain discarded qualities the *form* need not be sought. We next consider whether we can abstract any other

et gradatim, ut ultimo loco perveniatur ad maximè generalia; quæ via vera est sed intenta.—"*Novum Organum.*" *Liber Primus.—Aphorismus XIX.*

of the coinciding properties of the objects of our inquiry, and thus demarcate and set aside what is diverse and multiple, from that which is invariable in its nature: the multiplex and variable constitute the qualities, the unical and immutable constitute the *form*;—that property of which, if things were destitute, they would cease to be what they are.

The observations which occur in the foregoing paragraphs may be succinctly comprised in the three following laws, viz. :—

1st. Since nothing exists isolatedly in nature, it is necessary that we should multiply our observations and vary them by experiment, in order that we may succeed in perceiving the precise and actual constituents of any given phenomena, *i. e.*, so to disentangle the accessory from the essential, the purely accidental from the express essence, as shall enable us to perceive—distinct from the thousands of accompanying properties of any phenomena—the determining cause or condition of its existence.

2nd. Not only must we clearly and precisely perceive the point or points of coincidence and essentiality, but we must, at the same time, and by the same means, acquire an accurate knowledge of the points of differentiation and accidental attribution.

By these two laws we are able to classify, in ascending progression, individuals into species, and species into genera, and *vice versâ*, descendingly.

3rd. We must diligently and particularly observe whether the properties which we perceive in individual phenomena manifest themselves in different proportions in different circumstances, and whether these proportions differ according to any general rule or rules, and if so, what this rule or these rules are.

After the exclusions of which we have spoken in the previous paragraph have been made, it may so happen that some few properties may remain, in the possession of which the whole series of objects may coincide. Should this be the case, one or other of these remanent properties must be *assumed* as the cause, and, if possible, by experimentalisation or otherwise, examined as to its power of accounting for the phenomena concerning which we are prosecuting our inquiries; and this process must be repeated with each, until we discover that *one* individual property—on which alone the production of the events or appearances depends; for the motto of Inductive science is—" *Prudens interrogatio est dimidium scientiæ*." * This, however, can only be accomplished by that careful and orderly classification of " instances," of

* " Prudent questioning is the half of science."

which we shall describe the method immediately after the few following parenthetical sentences.

Subordinate to this investigation of *forms*, and frequently conducing much to the discovery of them, are the inquiries into the latent process (*latens processus*), and the latent schematism (*latens schematismus*). The former of these signifies that succession of events which occurs intermediate to the application of any change-causing instrumentality and the operation of the change, *e. g.*, the processes which intervene betwixt the application of a match, the explosion of a train of gun-powder, and the blasting of a quarry-rock, or the striking of the strings of a guitar and the impinging of its sounds upon the ear. The syringe-match, by which the doctrine of latent heat is so fully proven, presents a favourable instance of such inquiries reduced to experiment. The latter refers to that secret or hidden structure of bodies on which any of their properties depend, *e. g.*, the internal structure of plants. The investigations of chemistry regarding the component elements of bodies, and the consequences deducible from them, especially in that depart-ment which illustrates the doctrine of "*definite or multiple propor-tions*," afford many examples of the advantage of inquiring concerning the latent schematism.

But to have done with parentheses, and to revert to the process which we were describing in the paragraph antecedent to that which we have just penned, we shall find, in the prosecution of our inquiries regarding the various facts of which we wish to know the *rationale*, that there is a very great dissimilarity in their value, so far as the result at which we aim is concerned. Some contain the quality in a simple, others in a compound state. Some exhibit less of it, others more. Some are easy of interpretation, others difficult of solution. Some flash instantaneous conviction on the mind, others gain radiance by juxtaposition and comparison, and by their combinedly converging to the establishment of one law. This consideration led the illustrious Lord Bacon to adopt and propose a classification of the instances in which any phenomenal speciality occurred, according to their value, under the designation of prerogative instances (*prerogativæ instan-tiarum*), or those cases which ought to possess the chief claim to our regard in endeavouring to interpret any series of facts. His intention in this department of his *opus magnum* is to describe what are the most necessary or essential particulars with which we should concern our-selves in any investigation, or what instances in any series of phe-nomena which Nature presents to our observation, should be most especially regarded and attended to, in our attempts to discover the law by which their coherency and concatenation are secured in the vast system of the universe. Of these he enumerates twenty-seven sorts. Were we to name, define, and illustrate the whole of these, our readers will easily perceive that we should run the risk of becoming tediously prolix. We will only, therefore, mention a few of the most important of them, as specimens of the *modus operandi* which he proposes :—

I. *Instantiæ solitariæ*—solitary instances. These are of two classes: 1st. Those in which the objects differ in all qualities except one. 2nd. Those in which the objects agree in all points but one; thus, were the inquiry concerning electricity—A hare's skin and a piece of rough glass, both excited by a metal, would both become positivised, and would form *solitariæ instantiæ* of the first sort; while two pieces of quite dry ribbon, the one white and the other black, excited by a similar agency, would be instances of the latter kind.

II. *Instantiæ migrantes*—varying instances. Those properties of bodies which are observed changing from a greater to a less degree; as, objects undergoing the process of electrical excitation, &c.

III. *Instantiæ ostentivæ*—forth-showing instances. Those facts or objectivities which display the quality in question in its highest degree. A voltaic battery would be an *instantiæ ostentivæ* in electricity, and a barometer in pneumatics.

IV. *Instantiæ conformes* — analogous instances. Occurrences or things between which analogies and resemblances may be traced in some individual points, however divergent in others; thus, a *camera obscura* is an analogous instance to the *eye*, and the waterworks of a city, to the *heart*.

V. *Instantiæ comitatu atque hostiles*—companion and inimical instances. Qualities which invariably accompany each other, as heat and flame; and those which are unceasingly dissimilar and never discovered in conjunction or alliance, and which thus appear to be at war with each other, as malleability and transparency; the positive and negative poles of electricity.

VI. *Instantiæ cruciæ*—crucial instances. Those in which we, as it were, by experiment, apply the thumb-screw to nature, and compel her to confess her secrets; or, perhaps, those instances which point out the true path, as the ancient crosses did when two divergent roads occurred, for it will bear either interpretation, and is used, we believe, in both senses. Franklin's experiments in electricity would be instances of the former sort. Newton's discovery of gravitation was an instance of the latter sort, settling for ever the true theory of astronomy, and deciding demonstratively the superior truthfulness of the Copernican system over that of the Ptolemaic.*

With regard to such methods, "it has always appeared to us, we must confess, that the help which the classification of instances, under their titles of prerogative, affords to inductions, however just such classification may be in itself, is yet more apparent than real. The force of the instance must be felt in the mind before it can be referred to its place in the system; and before it can be either referred or appreciated, it must be known; and when it *is* appreciated, we are ready enough to weave our web of induction without greatly troubling ourselves whence it derives the weight we acknowledge it to have in our decisions. . . . . No doubt such instances as these are highly instructive, but the difficulty . . . . is to find such, not to perceive their force when found." †

Coinciding, as we do, in the just remarks of the great natural philosopher above quoted we had intended to remark on the inefficiency of induction *alone* to discover truth and to revert to the proof of the assertion made in a former chapter, that "induction is one of the modes in which Judgment operates." As, however, a future opportunity will present itself for that, when we are treating on "Syllogism," it may suffice just now to indicate our opinion that Induction is an investigative process, the results of which are propositions; these propositions become premises, and the sources of the *data* from which our conclusions are inferred. Should our Induction be false, our conclusion is nullified; and if our conclusion lead to the contradiction of any sufficiently established known truth, or the admission of an absurdity, our induction is incorrect. Facts carefully collected and considered give rise to hypotheses. These hypotheses are subjected to investigation; and if the phenomena which are being inquired into arrange themselves naturally and uncontradictorily in the manner which the

---

* We may here state that, besides the "Opera Francisi de Verulamio," we have been materially assisted in this abridgement by the following works, to which we may at once refer our readers for further information on the topic now before them :—Playfair's "Dissertation on the Progress of Physical Science," Stewart's "Dissertation on the Progress of Metaphysical, Ethical, and Political Philosophy," in the "Encyclopædia Britannica "—Hoppus's "Account of Bacon's Novum Organum," Craik's "Bacon: his Writings and his Philosophy," Napier's Essay on "Bacon," in the Edinburgh Philosophical Transactions, Deleyre's "Analyse de la Philosophie de Bacon," Macaulay's "Bacon," Ed. Rev., July, 1837, and paper "Bacon," in "Le Dictionaire des Sciences Philosophiques," &c. &c.

† Sir John Herschell's "Discourses on the Study of Natural Philosophy," in Lardner's Cyclopædia, art. 192.

substration had *à priori* fixed upon, the hypothesis is considered proved, and takes the rank of Theory : *e. g.*—Phrenology was first originated by the observation of a few facts; a hypothetical explanation was adopted; this hypothesis is in process of verification,—when that is done (if it can be done),* it will become a science, for then theory will be found to be in accordance with natural phenomena. A mere knowledge of facts is cumulative in a ratio with the existence and experience of man; we are not so destitute of facts as principles—principles which the master-minds of our species are alone fitted to discover and apply—principles which genius alone can elucidate from the dry catalogue of age-accumulated facts, and which are only discoverable by the "far-darting glance" of the mighty in intellect among men.

This appears to us all that is necessary for a brief analysis of the Baconian Method of Induction. This method has, however, been reduced with masterly ability to more generalised formularies, by J. S. Mill. We will now go on to give a very concise summary of these.

The four laws of Inductive Inquiry of this able author, are the Method of Agreement, the Method of Difference, the Method of Residues, and the Method of Concomitant Variations. ("Logic," b. III. c. viii.)

PRELIMINARY AXIOMS.—(1st.) "Whatever circumstance can be excluded, without prejudice to the phenomenon, or can be absent notwithstanding its presence, is not connected with it in the way of causation." (2nd.) "The unessential circumstances being thus eliminated, if only one remains, that one is the cause of which we are in search : if more than one, they either are, or contain among them, the cause; and so, *mutatis mutandis*, of the effect." (3rd.) "Whatever antecedent cannot be excluded without preventing the phenomenon, is the cause, part of the cause, or a condition, of that phenomenon." (4th.) "Whatever consequent can be excluded, with no other difference in the antecedents than the absence of a particular one, is the effect of that one." (5th.) "Those antecedents and consequents which are mutually present and mutually absent are causes (or effects) to each other, or are connected with each other by causation." (6th.) "Anything on whose modifications, the modifications of an effect are invariably consequent, must be the cause (or connected with the cause) of that effect." A cause "is the sum total of the conditions positive and negative taken together—the whole of the contingencies of every description—which being realised, the consequent follows."

* See, for a debate on this topic, "British Controversialist," vol. i.

G

I. METHOD OF AGREEMENT. When we compare different instances in which the fact concerning which our inquiries are made, or our investigation is undertaken, with each other, and invariably find that the same phenomenon results from the same specific circumstantialities, we are irresistibly compelled to believe, that, in these circumstances, the law of causation may be found; *e. g.*, Arsenite of potash, when compounded with sulphate of copper, invariably produces an apple-green precipitate, and when steel-filings are cast into a mixture of oil of vitriol and water, the steel-filings dissolve, and a sulphurous fume is emitted. When we have seen these experiments, resulting in the same manner in frequent repetitions, we are led to conclude that, in the combination of the respective bodies experimentalised upon, the causative agency exists. The *canon* of this method is this: "If two or more instances of the phenomenon under investigation have only one circumstance in common, the circumstance in which alone all the instances agree is the cause (or effect) of the phenomenon."

II. METHOD OF DIFFERENCE. "Instead of comparing different instances of a phenomenon, to discover in what they agree, this method compares an instance of its occurrence with an instance of its non-occurrence, to discover in what they differ." When we compare instances in which the observed fact happens with instances which coincide in every particular except the one which we seek to investigate, we are warranted in concluding that in that exceptional particular the cause (or effect) resides—*e. g.*, A stick of sealing-wax, unexcited, coincides with one in all points similar to itself: let now the one be frictionised, and a change will have occurred, and new manifestations will be given forth. We are here perfectly entitled to ascribe the causative agency to the friction, so far at least as the manifestations are concerned, and *vice versâ*, that the manifestations were the result of the excitation. The following is the formulary of this method: "If an instance in which the phenomenon under investigation occurs, and an instance in which it does not occur have every circumstance except the one in common, that one occurring only in the former, the circumstance in which they alone differ is the effect, or cause, or a necessary part of the cause, of the phenomenon."

III. METHOD OF RESIDUES. When we know all the antecedents of any effect, and some part of the causation-antecedents, we may conclude, with confidence, that the remaining antecedents are the causative agents in the production of the remainder of the effect.

A consideration of the centrifugal and centripetal forces will afford an illustration. The formula is thus expressed: "Subduct from any phenomenon such part as is known, by previous induction, to be the effect of certain antecedents, and the residue of the phenomenon is the effect of the remaining antecedents."

IV. METHOD OF CONCOMITANT VARIATIONS. This has a very close resemblance to Bacon's *instantiæ migrantes*; it refers to those natural agents whose phenomena we can observe, but which so intimately co-exist and interblend themselves with other objectivities, that we are unable to isolate or individualise them—*e. g.*, Heat is a quality so generally interfused through material bodies that we cannot abstract it entirely from them, neither can we so experiment upon it that we may separate and disconnect it from those things in which it inherently abides. To know, then, the laws by which its operations are guided, we must observe what series of phenomena increase as its power becomes greater, and what effects diminish in a ratio with its decrement, and thus we are guided to judge of its phenomena-educing properties. The law for investigating such subjects is thus given : " Whatever phenomenon varies in any manner, whenever another phenomenon varies in some particular manner, is either a cause or an effect of that phenomenon, or is connected with it by some fact of causation."

CHAPTER IX.

JUDGMENT.—IDOLS OF THE INTELLECT.

"This great and dangerous impostor, PREJUDICE, who dressing up falsehood in the likeness of truth, and so dexterously hoodwinking men's minds as to keep them in the dark, with a belief that *they* are more in the light than any that do not see with *their* eyes."—LOCKE.

> "Our senses narrow, and our reason frail,
> Life short, and Truth a gem which loves the deep,
> And all things weighed in Custom's falsest scale—
> Opinion and Omnipotence."—BYRON.

THE "Idols of the Intellect" is the somewhat fantastic, though, withal, appropriate and illustrative term by which Lord Bacon designates those errors, prepossessions, and prejudices to which man is liable in his investigations, and which, to use his own words, *Sunt* *abneganda et renuncienda, et intellectus ab iis omnino liberandus atque expurgandus.** In this chapter we intend to accept his classification of these *Idola*, and to describe, illustrate, and explain the method in which they most commonly operate; by so doing, our readers will learn from us the obstacles and hindrances which may cause them to turn aside from the highway of intellectual success, and how they may be overcome. Without some attention to this department of logical instruction, it is impossible to proceed aright in the work of Truth-acquirement. Unless we know the impediments in our way, our own tendency to enter into the "devious labyrinths of Error," and take due precautions to remove the one and avoid the other, we shall only return jaded, fatigued, and disappointed,—the object of our exertions unaccomplished, and our search vain, unfit to exert our minds with confidence, accuracy, acumen, and rapidity. Of these Error-Sources, Dr. Thomas Brown truly observes, " the temple which he purified was not that of Nature itself; but the temple of the Mind; in *its* innermost sanctuaries were all the Idols which he overthrew; and it was not till these were removed that Truth would deign to unveil herself."

Erroneous judgments are called Prejudices. A prejudice is an opinion formed without due examination of the premises on which it rests—the reception of a proposition as Truth, without a proper degree of verification—a bias of the mind resting on no stable foundation. The dispositions of the mind from which these arise, as well as these prejudices themselves, are both included in the Baconian term—Idols. Of these there are four classes, respectively denominated *Idola Tribus*, *Idola Specus*, *Idola Fori*, and *Idola Theatri*, each of which we will now notice as rapidly as possible, in the order in which they are here mentioned.

IDOLA TRIBUS—the Idols of the Tribe—are so denominated because they are common to humanity at large, are not confined to any mere sectional portion of the *Tribe*, but are universally diffused throughout it. They arise not from any peculiarity of circumstances, but from the circumscribed nature and variety of our minds, or from the power which imagination, passion, prepossession, or attachment has to warp the Judgment or cloud the Truth-percipient faculties. As created beings we have bounds set to our capacities, and limits assigned us which we cannot overstep. We are, as it were, the inhabitants of an island set in the midst of Truth's limitless sea. From this island we have no means of departure. We may employ any instrumentality we can to extend

---

* Must be solemnly abjured and renounced, and the intellect wholly freed and purified therefrom.

our visual range along the boundless continuity with which we are surrounded, but cannot emigrate on any voyage of discovery, however important or momentous; hence phenomena, and phenomena alone, are all of which we can attain a knowledge. Noumena we cannot perceive. Yet limited as the mind from its very nature is, such is the overweening vanity or folly of our race that more time has been spent, more ingenuity exerted, and more labour expended in searching for the undiscoverable, than in the scrutiny of what is utile and knowable. Some of these Error-sources are the noblest and grandest endowments with which our race is blest; but their unguarded and unrestrained exercise becomes fraught with many evil consequences. It is to be hoped, however, as men improve in a knowledge of their own Nature, these Idols will have fewer worshippers at their shrines, and that men will soon be led to abjure and renounce an idolatry so injurious to themselves and so pernicious to their race. "To be forewarned is to be forearmed;" therefore should our readers peruse these pages with a self-examining eye, saying, Have I bent my knee in Idolatry like this?

The chief place in the description of these Idola is due to *the spirit of systematisation*. We have formerly explained how the mind proceeds to classify the many myriads of phenomena which it observes. The advantage and beneficiality of this capacity cannot be doubted; but this, like all other human endowments, is liable to be abused. Men frequently deceive themselves by supposing that greater harmony is found in the variety of events, than there is warranty, in the truth of things, for believing. They seek to arrange the facts which they perceive, according to their preconceptions, and, in their haste to prove their suppositions true, wrench phenomena from their true classification, and by loose analogies endeavour to connect things in themselves essentially dissimilar. Hence it is that hypotheses are so often looked on with suspicious eye. Not that hypotheses are, *per se*, unworthy of regard; but because of their prejudicial effect upon the mind, by unfitting it for looking unbiassedly upon the phenomena of Nature. Hence did the ancient Philosophers, on perceiving that the heavenly bodies returned again into their orbitual paths, suppose that they revolved in *perfect circles*. Hence the great prominence given in olden times to the numbers 3 and 7. Hence, too, much of the false reasoning of the Ancients, of which the following specimen will, we think, more than amply suffice :—"There are four quarters of the world and four cardinal winds, consequently there are four Gospels in the Church as there are four pillars that support it and four breaths of life that render it immortal."[*] Rash and superficial generalisation and classification have been retarding causes of human progress in every generation. Systems of philosophy are constructed on insufficient *bases*, and before the labour of investigation has been sufficiently performed; and when men, by farther and more extended observation, see that it has become necessary to unlearn the philosophy of their ancestors, there is usually a period of fierce contention between the conservatists and the progressionists. This remark has been frequently verified in the history of science. This Error-source retards the march of Truth-acquirement in two different ways; 1st, By the rash, hasty, and precipitate manner in which it adopts general truths and constructs orderly systematisms, before the complement of the facts to be considered has been filled up; and 2nd, When these systematisms, be they creeds or scientific formularies, have been accepted, there is a general indisposition in the minds of men to admit any new truths into the already, as they think, completed circle, or the subversion of any stone in the fabric which had cost them so much labour to upbuild. Examples of this twofold operative power may be found in the axioms of physical science bequeathed to us by Aristotle, the Ptolemaic system of Astronomy, and the Vortices of Descartes, the persecution of Galileo, the reception of Jenner's Theory of Vaccination, and history of the science of Geology. Instead of too readily following the *spirit of systematisation* we should strive to learn how the finger of Truth is pointed, wait patiently on her instructions, and follow only where she leads. So shall we accurately learn the mysteries of the universe—not by mere mental exercitations, but by observation—not according to human suppositions, but in accordance with the Divine Idea which superintended its creation.

Our *Prepossessions* have a great influence in imposing upon the Judgment. These incline us to a great tenacity of opinion. Having imbibed our ideas on the most important topics of thought in early life from the lips of those whom we revered and whose memory we gratefully cherish, our attachment to *them* is transferred to their opinions, and we can scarcely believe that they can have been mingled with error. Self-love, too, complacently, yet slily, insinuates that it would be greatly derogatory to ourselves to be found in Error. Thus urged on by veneration, attachment, and self-esteem, we cannot permit ourselves to doubt of the truth of our opinions, and repel every attack upon the principles in which we have been educated, as an insult to the memory of those whom we respect, as well as derogatory to our own consistency and judgment; as if the tenacious and unhesitating adhesion to an idea

* Irenæus, lib. iii., cap. ii.

could, by some strange alchemy, transmute Falsehood into Truth. Another of our prepossessions we may mention as singularly pervertive of correct thought, namely, National partiality. This prevails to a great extent amongst mankind; so much so, that there are few nations which would yield the palm of precedency to another, either in literature, science, or the arts. The Jews, the Greeks, the Romans, the Persians, and the Carthaginians, all entertained inveterate prepossessions regarding their own superiority; and the recent jealousies existing between ourselves and the French and German nations fully illustrate the perniciously blinding effect which such partialities exert within the mind.

Imagination is apt to become enamoured with whatever excites it, or raises the emotions of wonder, amazement, sublimity, or beauty. A well-drawn analogy or brilliant figure of speech is often more convincing than an argument. The comparison of ideas is an irksome and tedious labour; and when one has but the tact of casting

> "O'er erring deeds and thoughts a heavenly hue
> Of words,"

the multitude of men will welcome him with the warmest expressions of applause; for their imaginations are easily captivated, let their reason be ever so rusty. We employ fancy, too, in filling up the deficiencies which we find in our knowledge, and giving it that rounded completeness in which the mind delights.

Restless activity is another retarding cause of human progress. For

> "There is a fire
> And motion of the soul, which will not dwell
> In its own narrow being, but *aspire*
> *Beyond the fitting medium of desire;*
> And, but once kindled, quenchless evermore,
> Preys upon high adventure, nor can tire
> Of aught but rest."

This aspirative tendency in the human soul, although it is undoubtedly an exceedingly valuable and most noble endowment, yet often tempts us to strive after the unattainable. The incomprehensible, the mysterious, the infinite, have strange charms for the mental powers. They cannot confess their impotence and incapacity to search into "the deep things" of Nature. Time, space, infinity, eternity, perfectibility, &c., they weary themselves with striving to investigate. Is it not lamentable to think that men will thus waste their time, ingenuity, and mental energy, in frivolous and inutile speculations, to a knowledge of which they can never attain, because they lie beyond the bounds of their cognition, and transcend their perceptive faculties? Why should we make inquiries into the nature of substance, spirit, and other *noumenal* essences, rather than into those things which are appreciable by our intellectual powers, and which are not only comprehensible but may become practically useful?

Will and Passion likewise affect the decisions of the Judgment, and obscure the light of rationality. "The human intellect is not a pure light, but receives a tincture from will and passion, and frames the sciences accordingly. What men desire to be true they believe; 'the wish is father to the thought;' therefore they reject difficulties through impatience of inquiry, moderate things because they limit their hopes, the deeper things of Nature through superstitious awe, the light of experience through pride and haughtiness, paradox on account of the opinions of the mob; and thus, in innumerable ways, and often imperceptibly, the affections tinge and colour the understanding." * When passion guides or self-interest sways, how difficult it is to hold the balance with an equal hand! How often do they rather eject from the mind every idea of candour, consistency, or justice. Impartiality is rarely to be expected when the will is biassed, and when passion prompts to the formation of an opinion, or the performance of an action; and most men will be found to be more willing to forsake the worship of Truth than stand singly in her defence against the multitude.

The fallaciousness and incompetency of the Senses impair our capacity of rightly deciding on many matters. They occupy themselves with the externals and superficialities of things, and seldom seek, except at the earnest promptings of the mind, to examine things in their contexture, organic properties, or powers of change. Sometimes they are neglectful of impressions made on them, at other times they bring in fallacious accounts of their experience. Sensations sometimes acquire a supremacy over the mind, and suffer it not to receive as Truth that for which no evidence is capable of being given to *them*. Thus spiritual phenomena are passed by unnoticed and unchronicled, while sensuous impressions are readily observed, registered, and recollected. All this is highly prejudicial to the impartial exertion of the Judgment, and leads it into many errors. Too frequently has a soulless and dehumanizing Materialism resulted from this sense dominance. We ought carefully to cultivate the neutrality of our sensation-powers, and perpetually to guard against that action and reaction of mind and sense which tends so much to the obscuration of our views of the supersensual.

Such, then, is a brief exposition of the *Idola Tribus*—those sources of

* "Novum Organum," lib. i., aph. xlix.

erroneous judgments to which our race is subject. Difficult and arduous as the task may be of emancipating ourselves from thraldom to their sway, or of abjuring the worship of these Idols, it is nevertheless our duty to make the attempt boldly, resolutely, and determinately; otherwise our investigations can neither be attended with pleasure nor crowned with success.

IDOLA SPECUS—Idols of the Cave. We have not only the publicly worshipped Idol-gods of our Tribe, but we have each one his own Lars and Penates—household gods at whose shrine we privately burn incense and offer homage. These Error-sources have their origin in the peculiar mental and corporeal constitution, habits, studies, and position of each individual. Some of these deserve to be particularly pointed out, in order that caution may be used regarding them.

Particular Studies unbalance the Judgment. One idea or set of ideas gains a pervadency in our minds, and we look upon the universe as if all its phenomena might be explained by the light which that idea or series of ideas gives. We seek in all other departments of knowledge, that peculiar kind of proof which our favourite science yields. Thus a mathematician will strive to reduce Moral Philosophy to a *formulæ* as rigid and demonstrative as the science of his delight; and may even go so far as to ask, gravely, what proposition "Paradise Lost" is meant to prove. Hence Descartes having applied his "Theory of Vortices" to the heavenly luminaries, constructed upon the same Theory a chemico-mechanical system of Medicine, which received much favour, for some time, on the Continent.

Difference of Mental Capacity also exerts itself prejudicially to the furtherance of the empire of Truth. Some minds are analytic, others synthetic. Some have greater readiness in observing differences, others, resemblances. Both are alike liable to error; the one by too great subtility of division, the other by supposing a too comprehensive range of conjunctive phenomena. Each extreme is alike to be avoided; and the mind should, as far as possible, be trained in the direction of its deficiency.

A too great reverence for Times is likewise one of those sources of prejudice which mightily impair our powers of accurate discrimination. One man, enamoured with the "days of old" and the "wisdom of our ancestors," considers nothing can be worthy of notice on which the rust of antiquity does not lie thick, and trembles at the very thought of innovation. Another, whose eye opens more widely to futurity, looks with disgust on all things characterized by ancientness of days, and earnestly desires that all old things would pass away, and make room for the glorious epoch of which he fondly dreams. Each of these is in Error. Man *is* progressive, and antiquity cannot satisfy him; but he is progressive by gradations, and is unable to suit himself to any sudden and unexpected change precipitately brought about.

Procrastination is another fruitful source of self-deception. We are very solicitous of ease, or we have peculiar fancies in which we are very fond of indulging. For the gratification of these whims and this love of passivity we too often neglect the improvement of the most important periods of life, and leave an accumulated heap of duties unperformed. Man, however, has such an aptitude for acknowledging the accuracy of this truth, and yet casting the practical consideration of it aside, that *we* need not hope to impress minds which have grown callous by often renewed and broken resolutions "to be up and doing."

Great care should be taken to preserve the neutrality of the mind; and if we be conscious of any of these Idol-gods dwelling in ourselves, *now* is the time for vigorous exertion for their rejection. Lest each man's "seducing familiar spirit" should gain supremacy, let *now* "contemplative Wisdom proceed to dislodge and chase away the *Idols of the Cave*."

Idola Fori—Idols of the Forum. "These," says Lord Bacon, "are the most troublesome of all." They are those which arise out of our intercourse with society, and chiefly proceed from the words or terms which we employ in the interchange of thought. The principal sorts of these result from the use of words which convey no real meaning to the mind, or whose signification is so indefinite that it is enlarged or circumscribed according to the mind which employs them. "Words," he again says, "are for the most part accommodated to the vulgar, and they define things by bounds which are most obvious to common minds; and when a more acute understanding or more accurate observation would enlarge these boundaries, and arrange them more in accordance with nature, *words cry out and forbid*." We may instance the words Liberty and Necessity, Taste, Beauty, and Education, as of the description meant. We are, however, happily released from the necessity of lengthening this department of our subject with any additional remarks, having already treated so fully upon the need of attention to the signification of words in a previous chapter.*

Idola Theatri. The Idols of the Theatre are the last class of Error-sources to which we are *now* to direct attention. These may be comprehended under the three following heads:—Partizanship, Fashion,

* Chapter iii. See this subject, also, more fully treated in Chapter xvii., "Concerning Fallacies,"

and Authority. *Political and Religious Rivalries* have been most prolific generators of evil. Whenever men allow themselves to get superstitiously attached to a party or a creed, their minds become blinded to the virtues and good qualities of those who differ from them. Discernment and candour are driven from their breasts, and a mole-eyed partiality usurps their place. It would be endless to attempt an enumeration of the monster evils of which this prejudice has been the occasion. History contains a crime-stained record of them on too many of its pages. Too frequently is a malignancy of soul and bitterness of heart, most alien to the spirit in which Truth should be sought, engendered by it. We take a one-sided view of every measure introduced by our opponents, and accuse them of the basest and most dishonourable motives; the heart is corrupted, Jealousy aroused, Envy—venomous Envy—fostered and bred; and thus the Judgment is fatally misled. We need only point to our elections, and the doings of bitter sectarians at all times and in all places, to show the fearfully ensanguined Idol to whose car these parties have yoked themselves, and the necessity there is for greater impartiality in the discussion of each other's views.* How much happier would it be for our race were we each to examine opinions honestly and candidly! Then Superstition would not "flourish like a green bay tree." Quackery would not immolate its myriads of deluded votaries. Party Zeal would not close our eyes to the perception of Truth and steel our hearts to the feelings of humanity, nor would National or Positional Jealousies "cry havoc, and let slip the dogs of war," or the heart-torturing vultures of Envy; but Truth, like a beneficent goddess, would scatter the seeds of Peace, contentment, happiness, prosperity, and love, throughout her subject universe.

Fashion is also a greatly prevalent mind-seducing and Judgment-perverting agency. Nothing is exempt from it. Dress, Amusements, Language, Social Customs, Opinions, Art, Science, Studies, Law, Religion, all succumb to its authority, and own its sway. The Reason of man is exceedingly ductile, and easily moulds itself to suit any prevailing *modishness*. It may not be wrong, in indifferent things, to follow the usual customs of society—the practice of the *beau-monde-ists* or the *bon-ton-ites;* but it is a most unjustifiable weakness to sacrifice our convictions on any vital point to the mere influence of the *mode* of the world. Men have often been likened to sheep, who unhesitatingly follow the bell-wether; and there is too much truth in the comparison. Hence originate the *cant* of parties, sects, classes, and coteries, formu-

---

* May we not justly hail the establishment and success of the " British Controversialist" as an omen of good, from its possession of this very much-desiderated quality?

laries of address, prudery, affectation, and costume *à la mode*. It is exceedingly necessary to cultivate so much independence of spirit as shall enable us to withstand the influence of Fashion whenever it advances beyond the foibles of men, and seeks to interfere with the unbiassed exercise of their intellectual faculties.

Authority differs little from Fashion except that the latter is the practice or opinion of the majority of that class to which we belong, while the former is the opinion or example of eminent individuals in the various walks of life. The reliance upon Authority is a prejudice so far as it is an unreasoning assent yielded to a point which we have not sufficiently examined for ourselves. It exercised a most disastrous effect upon the progress of mankind for many ages. Such was the domination of the scholastic philosophy over the minds of men for centuries. The distrust of authority and the investigation of Nature were the first steps in the march of modern intellect. Let, then, the opinions of every Theorist be candidly examined; let his arguments, not his authority, be the agency of our conviction of his accuracy. Daring and superior minds may build stately temples of philosophy; but if they be "mere pleasure domes, of rare device," without any of the real and stable materials of Nature, let them be rejected.

Thus we have rapidly, but, we hope, intelligibly, described and illustrated the Idols of the Intellect; nor let it be thought a thing contemptible that we thus perform the office of a compilator or an abridgee; for independently of the full confidence which we repose on the sagacity of our readers to perceive that we are not the mere retailers of the thoughts and words of other men, there is the important consideration that truths which have long lain imprisoned in several massive tomes, written in a dead language, are apt to be neglected, and to have their usefulness impaired, nor can they be brought readily enough into the service of the thoughtful, though, in the ordinary acceptation of the term, unlearned student. It is therefore a good service done to humanity to bring these great thoughts out of their prison-house, and set them free to yield instruction to the masses. Besides, old truths are sometimes despised in their other-land or antiquated dress, which if revivified under a modern form would strike upon the mind with all the force of newly discovered truths, and by mere novelty of statement and the modernisation of the exposition would be valued and appreciated more than they possibly could be in their "olden garb." But as our chapter has greatly exceeded our original intention, we will merely add a few rules to aid in the avoidance of error, and with these finish that department of our subject which relates to "Judgment."

1st.—Avoid hasty decisions. In every proposition presented for your assent, inquire whether the words accurately represent the thoughts—whether your ideas on the subject are distinct—whether there is any biassing motive latent in your mind. Thoroughly examine the evidence—then decide.

2nd.—If, after having used every precaution mentioned in the former rule, you find your ideas obscure, or the evidence deceptive, suspend your Judgment until these shall have been obviated.

3rd.—Never expect a greater degree, nor a different kind, of evidence, than that which the proposition admits, or the circumstances demand.

4th.—We ought not to deny what is evident because we cannot comprehend what is obscure.

5th.—Whatever we clearly and distinctly perceive, as contained in our idea of any objectivity—if due precautions have been employed in forming our ideas—may be, potentially, affirmed of that objectivity.

CHAPTER X.

RATIOCINATION.

" Every man is born to search for Truth, and to make free his nature from confusion and doubt."—MENDELSSOHN.

" *The writer* professes no more than to lay down, candidly and freely, his own conjectures concerning a subject lying somewhat in the dark, without any other design than an unbiassed inquiry after Truth."—LOCKE.

" The laws of our rational faculty, like those of every other natural agency, are only learned by seeing the agent at work."—MILL.

LOGIC depends, for its first principles, upon an investigation of the *laws of thought*, and hence a knowledge of " Mental Philosophy," in so far as it informs us of these laws, is substratory to an accurate and well-founded science of Ratiocination. As Mr. Hallam justly remarks, "every logical method is built upon the common faculties of human nature, which have been exercised since the Creation in discerning, better or worse, truth from falsehood, and inferring the unknown from the known." Logic is not, therefore, an enactatory science : it does not, with merely imperious and despotic *dicta*, utter its tyrannical behests, saying, Thus, and thus only, shalt thou do : it is not, as it has been represented, a mere system of mental enchainment, which enables the mind, like a mill horse, to go round and round, in continual progression but no advancement. It does not immure the mind in a dungeon of cumbrous and unnatural forms, and thus restrain the free-thoughted from pursuing their course of investigation. It is not a wily net of fine woven subtilties and cunning, to cast over the mental activities and impede their growth and onward motion—to retard alike their development and progression. It is not a mere curious specimen of perverted, though ingenious, human invention, having no foundation or warranty in the *facts* of the mentality. On the contrary, it explains the natural method of the operations of the human mind while engaged in the investigation; it is a system of law which has been carefully gleaned from a painstaking and persevering study of the intellect in its activity. It is strictly an inductive science: the whole superstructure is upbuilt upon that foundation which affords the highest evidence of any truth or series of truths— *conscious observation.* It is a verbalised picture of the invariable *forms* of active thought as it develops itself in accordance with the laws of the human mind, and is thus well calculated to assist men in the task of truth-investigation, both by warning them of the sources of Error, and by instructing them in the most accurate and infallible, because the most natural, forms of Ratiocination. It "does not tell us how to make syllogisms, but how we do syllogise when we do not violate the laws of our mind as much as we should violate the laws of our body, if we tried to walk upon our heads instead of upon our feet." * The great *desiderata* for the construction of such a system of Logic, which would be at once plain in its teachings and trustworthy in its *formulæ,* are an exact and determinate knowledge of the capacities of the intellection, " the limitations and conditions to which our minds themselves are subject," the process of idea-formation, and the laws which govern the evolution of thought. Could these be obtained, the whole of Logic might be reduced to a few axioms, from which would flow, with mathematical certainty, the whole of the formularies and processes of Ratiocination. Should we be successful, however, in indicating the *method* in which such a science might be constructed, we shall, for the present, be content, as we shall thus enable the intelligent student to extend his confidence in logical *axiomata* in proportion as he improves in his acquaintance with the modes of the mental operations. We dare not presume to assert that we shall succeed in completely developing the *rationale* of the mental processes by which men acquire certitude and confidence ; but our readers will generously pardon us should *we* not altogether succeed in proving to their entire satisfaction, that the teachings of Logic are the natural results of the action of those laws which

* " Moral and Metaphysical Philosophy"—Ancient. Rev. F. D. Maurice. " Encyclopædia Metropolitana," New Edit., p. 171.

are inwoven with, while they limit and circumscribe, the mind: nor impute to the science the incapacity of its professed teacher.

Facts are the products of law;—the individual manifestations and results of the great governing agencies or operative properties with which the Creator has endowed every specifically different existence in the universe. If, therefore, we carefully examine any series of manifested facts, and colligate them into assimilatory classes, we shall acquire a knowledge of the laws on which these facts depend for their development, and discover the modes in which these laws regulate and control their evolution. Let it, however, be noted here, that the word *law* is used to signify—what we think it should always be understood as meaning—not an essential and self-efficient power; but an expression of the general fact from which all the particular facts proceed as results: the cause, principle, or propension, by which, from a derived, though invariably-acting, tendency, individual facts are educed. If, then, by an attentive surveyance of any series of distinct, individuated facts, we can attain to a knowledge of the general fact on which their manifestations proximately depend, and, by our acquaintance with this fact, can reproduce other similar products, by placing them under the same proximately-efficient agency, such intelligence must of necessity be highly conducive to human happiness and intellectual advancement. In no department can these inquiries be followed by such manifold benefits as in the acquisition of a knowledge of the principles of thought-development; for it is by the exercise of the human thought-powers that each new truth is gained,—each new invention elaborated,—each new principle eliminated,—and each new discovery disentangled from the ravelled skein of our ideas. On these truths, inventions, principles, and discoveries—and, consequently, on that by which they are educed and perfectioned—the world's prosperity, advancement, and happiness are contingent. And seeing it is of so great moment, we can offer no other apology, nor do we think any other is required, for occupying attention somewhat lengthily upon the *facts* of the reasoning process, for the purpose of attempting to discover an answer to that all-important inquiry,—What are the laws of Ratiocination?

The advantage of such an investigation will be readily seen from the fact, that man is only capable of gaining information because he is endowed with knowledge-acquiring faculties; that he can only *know* in a ratio with the original power of these faculties and the subsequent exercise which he gives them; and that he will know more accurately and truly the more perfectly these mental capacities are employed in accordance with the laws of their action; as it is evident, that the fewer the impediments and hindrances offered to the realization of knowledge, the more easily will it be acquired; and that the more accurate our acquaintance with the laws of thought, the more fitted shall we be to remove or overcome the obstacles which impair or retard the due exertion of the mental functions.

But here let us interject a remark on the distinction which we think ought to obtain between the *manner* and the *matter* of thought. The former is thought in its subjectivity—in the method in which it evolves itself in the mind—in its action circumscribed by the laws of the intellection—in its obediency to the *forms* of the mentality. The latter is thought in its objectivity—in its phenomenal appearance to the mind: but as each phenomenal existence is symbolised either in or to the mind, by a word or words, it follows that, in a logical sense, this verbalised expression may be considered congruent with, and representative of, the phenomenal manifestations; and hence the *matter of thought* may, in certain cases, be regarded as thought in its manifestation in language—in its word-symbolisation. The former relates to the general operations of the intellectual faculties, irrespective of the investiture which ideas receive from words—the signs of thought; the latter refers to the attainment of true and accurate notions, and with the attempt to translate these inner and mind-contained conceptions into words. By abstracting our attention, as far as possible, from the words and even the ideas upon which our thought-powers are exercised—*i.e.*, the *matter* of thought, and fixing our minds carefully upon the operative processes which they perform—*i.e.*, the *manner* of thought, we may find that the *manner* may very probably be unical, while the *matter* may be indefinitely multiplex. Not so easily, perhaps, may this be observed, as, in looking upon machinery in action, we shall find the lever, the axle, the pulley and wheel, all engaged in the invariable fulfilment of their laws, however diverse may be the processes of manufacture, locomotion, &c., in which they are employed, and however complex may be the combinations into which they are formed. Yet, we believe, as surely and invariably will the several mental powers, if carefully and attentively surveyed in operation, be found to fulfil definite and peculiar laws. We will endeavour to prove that this is a fact; and, if it be found so, we shall, perhaps the more readily, be enabled to discover what is the law of the Ratiocinative faculty.

We advance this, then, as a fact in Mental Philosophy;—that Experience is the basis of all human knowledge; that without *that*, as an excitant, no idea can possibly exist in the mind, unless, indeed, by immediate and direct inspiration; that unless our Consciousness be impressed through the channels of our Sensational organisms, and Reflection be excited in us by these impressions, we can have no knowledge. By this, we do not mean that we can *not* know anything except that which we have experienced, but that we can have no knowledge which is not excited by, derived from, and founded upon our experience, either by congruency, resemblance, causative agency, or some other definitive relationship. For it is evident that knowledge must have an object—must have reference to some definitive existence. Knowledge necessarily implies a power which *knows* and an *object* known. Without Experience, either of our own, or that of some one else, the mind cannot become cognizant of the existence, and can acquire no knowledge of objectivities. Experience we here employ to signify the results of any one or more of those mental processes formerly detailed, illustrated, and explained, under the head " Nature and Kinds of Evidence." The truth of the assertion, that Experience is the basis or groundwork of knowledge, is assailed, and even denied, by those sects of philosophers whose systems of psychology are founded upon the assumptions of " innate ideas," "fundamental verities," &c., and may be supposed, on that account, to require some considerable amount of proof. For our own part, we believe that the mind is naturally adapted to eliminate Truth from the phenomena of Nature, and is so constituted, that, by the mere evolution of its faculties in accordance with the laws which govern them, it is capable of acquiring certitude and confidence. It is true that there are few topics upon which we can assert our opinions with perfect and irrefragable reliance; nay, that on many subjects the utmost amount of evidence which we can receive, rises only to probability. But this, be it remembered, originates in our relative imperfection; is a necessity of our derivative being, and does not at all impugn the capacities of our intellection, *so far* as these capacities extend. We find, then—to return to our proof of the Experience-origin of our Knowledge—that human knowledge increases only with the cumulativeness of human Experience; that practice results in relative perfection; and that untrained reasoners argue best on those topics with which their experience renders them most familiar; that knowledge and truth are only gradually and progressively communicable to the mind; *they* originate in the formation of elementary conceptions, one fact or idea being upbuilt upon the other: that the advances of the mind are made in successive stages, and that every advance depends upon what has already been accomplished. The law of progression is interwoven with the texture of the mentality; as well might the bright flower-denizens of the garden start into sudden and unnurtured growth and luxuriancy of bloom, as any truth or series of truths spring up in a mind unprepared by experience to develop it. It is from this cause, too, that any thing or event which takes place contrary to or diverse from our experience, *e.g.*, an earthquake or a fierce summer hail-shower, paralyses us with terror, strikes us with alarm and surprise, or otherwise interrupts the train of our ideas. Hence, too, men acquire by habit, which is the result of experience, a belief in the uniformity of the operations of Nature, and calculate upon the occurrence or recurrence of events as they have previously witnessed them, with the most unshaken confidence. We think a great deal of the misunderstanding upon this subject results from the neglect of the distinction which we hope we have in the preceding paragraph pointed out with sufficient clearness, between the *manner* and the *matter* of thought. By a slight confusion of ideas, as it appears to us, those who believe in the *innateness* or *fundamentality* of some truths, and their consequent priority and superiority to experience, apply that necessity which is to be found in their *matter, i. e.*, the nature of the thing inquired into, to the *manner, i. e.*, the formulæ of thought, and thus assign a different origin to certain truths, not from any real appreciable mental distinction in the manner in which our thought-powers operate, but in the superior universality of the possession of certain attributes by the objectivities presented to them.* To illustrate this, we will quote the following paragraph from Coleridge, which, if we mistake not (for we have not the work now at hand for reference), appeared in the "Friend:"—"A man having seen a million of moss-roses, red, concludes, from his own experience and that of others, that all moss-roses are red. That is a maxim with him—the greatest amount of his knowledge on the subject. But it is only true until some gardener has produced a white moss-rose; after which, the maxim is good for nothing. Again: suppose Adam watching the sun sinking under the western horizon for the first time: he is seized with gloom and terror, relieved by scarce a ray of hope that he will ever see the glorious light again. The next evening, when it declines, his hopes are stronger, but still mixed with fear; and even at the end of a thousand years, all that a man can feel is a hope and an expectation so strong as to preclude anxiety. Now compare this, in its highest

---

* "A wide difference must be made between two kinds of truths; one which relates simply to the nature of things and their unchangeable essence, independently of their existence; the other which relates to things existing, and especially to human accidents and events, which may or may not be, when we inquire about the future, but which cannot be otherwise when we inquire about the past."—"*Port Royal Logic,*" Part IV., chap. xiii., p. 352.

degree, with the assurance which you have that the two sides of any triangle are greater than the third. This demonstrated of one triangle, is seen to be eternally true of all imaginable triangles. This is a truth at once perceived by the intuitive reason, independently of experience. It is, and must be so, multiply and vary the shapes and sizes of triangles as you may." No one will deny, we think, that this is strongly and vigorously expressed, and that it is an accurate statement of the distinction sought to be made betwixt innate ideas or fundamental truths, and experience-deduced verities; so that we cannot be charged with couching our lance at a weak or a self-made opponent, with whatever presumption we may be taunted for daring the tourney with a foe so lordly. Well then, will the reader peruse the passage a second time, reflecting, as he reads, upon the almost infinite variety of change-causing influences which may be exerted on a moss-rose; the equally innumerous, invisible, awful, and mysterious forces which might be employed to cloud the sun, or close the eye of man for ever; and the comparatively few, simple, and obvious properties which the triangle possesses; while we gently whisper in his ear, that this so-called intuitive perception, gained independently of experience, is, in Euclid's " Elements," tolerably lengthily demonstrated by reference to formerly acquired, though more elementary, experiences—viz., other propositions and definitions. Is not all this sufficient to prove that the complexity of the one kind of ideas, and the simplicity of the other, is the real cause of the comparatively intuitive perception made by our idea-formative faculties? Indeed, the real causes of the superiorly rapid and perfect progress of the mathematical, and many of the physical, sciences, are the greater simplicity of the experience on which they are founded—the greater purity in which the elements may be procured—the greater facilities which they possess for experimentation—and the regular and gradational nature of the superstructure which is thus able to be raised. So that we think we are quite warranted in asserting that it is in the nature of the things that the additional certitude is found, not in a different *manner* of thought-education. It is undeniable that prince, peasant, child, and philosopher, all alike judge of the unknown, and the future, by the familiar, the experienced, and the past. Hence the necessity, the use, and the agreeability of pictures, diagrams, models, experiments, &c., and those figures of speech, metaphor, simile, personification, and analogy: they yield to the mind a sort of substitute for experience: they serve to introduce the idea into the mind, and, when the elementary ideas are gained, both knowledge and progress are possible. Every new item of experience impresses itself on our Consciousness, and, being registered in the mentality, becomes the originator of an idea, or is connected by some relationship, discoverable by the generalizing faculty, with some idea previously educed and formed from some item of prior experience. There are two chief and distinct sources of Experience—internal feelings and external impressions : our internal feelings comprise all our appetites, passions, sympathies, mental capacities, &c.,—all that is included in the signification of that multi-continent though little pronoun *I;* our external impressions are those varied and multiplied revealments of the objectivities of the outward world which we receive through our senses. The former of these are immediately cognoscible by the mentality, the latter are, to a certain extent, mediately and inferentially manifested to the intellection ; but both impress themselves on our Consciousness, and thus originate thought. The former, however, are characterized by self-evidence ; for we really cannot suppose that our own internal mental operations are deceptive ; the latter are inductively arrived at, and so are less evident. Beyond these sources, however, *we* know no other method of acquiring knowledge ; and, consequently, we believe that Experience is the basis of knowledge ; and that to human beings, Consciousness is the only ultimate criterion of certitude.

But "Experience," says Dr. Whewell, "must always consist of a limited number of observations. And however numerous these may be, they can show nothing with regard to the infinite number of cases in which the experiment has not been made. Experience being thus unable to prove a fact to be universal, is, as will readily be seen, still more incapable of proving a fact to be necessary." * * * * "She contemplates external objects, but she cannot detect any internal bond which indissolubly connects the future with the past,—the possible with the real. To learn a proposition by Experience, and to see it to be necessarily true, are two altogether different processes of thought." * * * * "Experience cannot bestow that universality which she herself cannot have, and that necessity of which she has no comprehension." * * * * "It will then appear, that when the mind collects from observation truths of a wide and comprehensive kind, which approach to the simplicity and universality of the truths of pure science, she gives them this character by throwing upon them the light of her own fundamental experience." * These are strong sentences, and pithily expressed, and *appear* to have a good deal of truth in them. Let the reader, however, notice, in the first place, the sort of admission, that simplicity has somewhat to do with the formation of necessary

---

* Whewell's "Philosophy of the Inductive Sciences," pp. 59, 60.

truths, and compare it with the explanation we have formerly given. Again : let him reflect that men *know* their experience, and can *know* nothing else ; *that* is irresistible : now, if the attributes of any object be so simple and so easily perceived, as, being once seen, all its properties are known, and these properties be unalterable, our experience is quite sufficient to account for the necessity and universality of our belief regarding it ; for if *all* our experience has been uniform, regarding any series of objects,—if no one exceptional instance has been met with, how is it possible that we can look upon the revelations of our own experience but as necessary truths ? When each future experience is confirmatory of our first, how can we doubt the facts which that experience has made known ? Is it not plain, then, that the "necessity" and "universality" of our belief results from this :—that this is our experience ; that we cannot possibly transcend *that* experience ; and that, consequently, we must believe in what our experience has enabled us to *know* regarding any series of objects, until at least that experience be changed by the occurrence of a new experience. We cannot possibly believe in that which Experience, in some shape or other, has never presented to our minds ; and whatever has been so presented, we must believe to be "necessary" and "universal," simply because that is the sum-total of what we *know* concerning it. Take a simple illustration from every-day life.—An infant, whose only definite idea of objects is of their nutrient properties, is found continually to apply all objects, indiscriminately, to its mouth, until, gradually, experience corrects the erroneous induction. When it grows up, until it has become more capable of noticing, we see it act on the same system, if it has been agreeably impressed by any of the objectivities, with the properties of which it is acquainted, *e. g.*, sugar or honey : it so trustingly reposes in the truth,—the necessary and universal truth, of its experience, that parents frequently conceal the most nauseous and ill-tasted drugs in these naturally pleasant-tasted objects, and it takes them unsuspectingly ; and thus, too early, is often taught its first lesson in doubt and scepticism, by the very being to whom the evolution of its moral nature has been entrusted.

So much, then, having been advanced in proof of the assertion that Experience is the ground-work of Knowledge, let us next inquire how this affects the subject under consideration. We have, in former chapters shown, at sufficient length, how it is that the mind becomes acquainted with the properties of objects ; and that it can really and truly acquire no acquaintance with anything else, and, consequently, that the sum-total of our knowledge is, in reality, of qualities only, and not of things.   Now, each item of our experience, whether internally perceived or externally originated, must come under the influence of the faculty of Generalization, whose peculiar province it is to reduce the vast multiplicity of objects which call it into activity, into distinct classes, characterized by some peculiar and definite quality, or collection of qualities ; to which classes the mind applies generic names, applicable not only to the whole of any one class, but also to each individual comprehended or comprehendible in that class.   This process is thus the great means by which propositions are capable of being made by the "Judgment;" for, names being applied by the mind to classes of objects possessed of certain attributes, the Judgment has only to settle whether the object in question displays the same properties, and it is immediately entitled to be ranged under that class whose peculiar properties it exhibits.   The Judgment can only decide upon the agreement, or incongruency, of objects whose relations flash the conviction of their identity upon the mind by a mere juxtapositional view.   When this cannot be effected, however, the process becomes more intricate and involved—the mind seeks the aid of an intermediate idea, and Ratiocination commences.   Correctly and carefully considered, however, it will be found that the process of generalization actually involves the whole *law of Ratiocination*, inductive and deductive ; for, as Reasoning consists of a series of propositions, and each proposition must be an affirmation or a negation of the existence of some quality, property, or relation, as belonging to some particular objectivity or collection of objectivities, it is evident that the generalizing faculty, in its operations, is, in reality, the instinctive operation of the Ratiocinative power.   All Reasoning is employed for the purpose of discovering—1st. From the *known* qualities, &c., of *known* objectivities, the *unknown* qualities, &c., of *known* existences ; or—2nd. From certain *known* and *manifested* qualities, &c., the *unknown* existences in which they inhere ; *e. g.* :—

> 1st. All planets revolve, in certain specific periods and in definite orbits, round the sun :
>
> Neptune is a planet ;
>
> Therefore, Neptune revolves, in a certain specific period, and in a definite orbit, round the sun.

> Again :
>
> All bodies which, in every possible position in which they can be viewed, project a circular shadow, are spherical :
>
> The earth, in every position in which it can be viewed, projects a circular shadow ;

Therefore, the earth is a spherical body.

2nd. Neptune revolves, in a certain specific period, and in a definite orbit, round the sun:

All bodies which do so are called Planets;

Therefore, Neptune is a Planet.

Again:

The earth projects a circular shadow in whatever position it can be viewed:

Those bodies which, in every possible position in which they can be viewed, project a circular shadow, are spherical;

Therefore the earth is a spherical body.

Let us now very briefly trace the operation of the generalizing faculty. When it, for the first time, receives the impression of any one new objectivity, it is impressed by that objectivity, in virtue of its possessing certain attributes. When a second time an object is presented to it, possessed of precisely the same general attributes, it has no hesitation in ranking the latter object in the same class and under the same idea as that which first impressed its perceptivity; and if a name has been assigned to the former, the same designation will be readily applied to the latter; or if no cognomen has as yet been attached to the idea-originating object, the same name will certainly be applied to both; because, as we formerly explained, the mind designates not the *objects* which excite ideas in it, but the *ideas* which these have originated; so that, however multiplex the objects may be which are comprehended in any class, the idea which represents that class in the mind is unical. The conception of a class having been originated in the mind then, the idea will stand thus: the object + its attributes—or rather, certain attributes + an inferred object;—the name being but the communication-sign of the conception. Let us now suppose a new object presented to the mind, and, the classificatory office of generalization being begun, the object will be arranged in its class somewhat after the following fashion :—The mind will discern, by its attributes, that it has an affinity to some particular class; the peculiarities of this class will then be called up in the mind, and the newly-presented object will be affirmed or denied of that class. This *form* of the mind, then—this law of its operation, when verbally expressed or represented in words, constitutes a syllogism; and from this very fact of the mentality, we find that the syllogism is an accurate verbalized representation of the process through which the mind passes while engaged in the act of Ratiocination ; and that the general *formula* of that act is, *that whenever two (or more) objects agree or disagree in any relation, quality, property, circum-*

*stance, attribute, &c., with one and the same third, they agree or dis-
agree with each other in so far as such relation, quality, property, circumstance, attribute, &c., is concerned.*

We cannot at present proceed farther in the development of this topic. We will return to it in our next chapter. Permit us, however, in this place merely to indicate two important points which, if our idea be correct, will be established. 1st.—That the old antagonism of induction and deduction will be destroyed; for they will both be shown to be necessary to the production of a valid syllogism, or act of Reasoning:—induction as the initiatory power,—that which gathers up and registers the qualities, &c., of objects; deduction as the continuatory power, by which additions are made to our knowledge. 2nd.—That either of these processes is defective when singly employed: but that this arises from the necessary and relative imperfection of our nature as derivative beings, and is, therefore, no valid argument for their disuse, but rather that we ought the more carefully to cultivate our powers, so that all defects not naturally inherent in us may be uprooted, removed, or vanquished. For it is by arduous, well-regulated, and continuous cultivation alone that man can attain that modicum of relative perfection which it is granted him to acquire. Truth is not a boon freely granted to those who merely desire its possession, but a reward bestowed upon the continuous and uninterrupted exertion of our mental powers. To those alone who resolutely practise thought-introversion, will the multiplex feelings, emotions, capacities, and processes of the intellection, become clearly and accurately defined; but to the negligent inquirer, they will emit no elucidatory spark. Hence, if we wish to gain authentic knowledge regarding the inherent powers and capacities of our nature, we must labour assiduously in their eduction, and attentively consider the manner in which they exercise themselves. The results of this labour will be—increased mental power, readiness of perception, intellectual acumen, higher capacities of enjoyment and progression, and loftier views of the nobility of our thinking part. "There is," as Carlyle says, "a perennial nobleness and even sacredness in work." This is pre-eminently true of mental toil—of intellectual exertion. Wherefore let us labour earnestly, manfully, hopefully, and think with Tennyson as we do so :—

> "Not in vain the distance beckons. Forward! forward! let us range;
> Let the great world spin for ever down the ringing grooves of change.
> Through the shadow of the globe, we sweep into the younger day;
> Better fifty years of Europe, than a cycle of Cathay."

CHAPTER XI.

RATIOCINATION.—THE INVESTIGATION AND DISCOVERY OF TRUTH.

"Science is nothing but the finding of analogy—identity in the most remote parts. The ambitious student sits down before each refractory fact, one after another; reduces all strange constitutions, all new powers, to their class and their law; and goes on for ever to animate the last fibre of organization—the outskirts of Nature—by insight."— EMERSON.

MAN is naturally filled with a yearning desire—an invincible aspiration—a quenchless curiosity, which continually prompts him to unwearied exertion, in order that he may

> " Perceive
> The reason and the science of his being,
> And the relations, with the universe,
> Of all things actual and possible."

This God-implanted impulse finds perpetual exercise in the contemplation and investigation of those myriads of co-existent objectivities which he perceives around him in the universe. All that is beautiful, sublime, mysterious, varied, and utile, afford unceasing allurements to human curiosity, and yield incessant occupation to his mental powers. The brilliant, sun-diffused lustrousness which mantles the rosy cheek of morn—the exquisitely tinged flowers which bloom beneath the summer's care—the steep-sided hill, where " the stiff grass amid the heath-plant waves "—

> " *Here* the shadowy main,
> Dim-tinted—*there* the mighty majesty
> Of that huge amphitheatre of rich
> And elmy fields,"

—the ripe harvest-clad landscape—the shadow-yielding forestry—the lake reposing calmly in the bosom of the vale—" the river rushing o'er its pebbled bed," reflecting back the sunbeams' golden gifts—the clouds —the quiet dells—the rock-engirt and wave-washed shore—

> " Heaven's ebon vault,
> Studded with stars unutterably bright,
> Through which the moon's unclouded grandeur rolls,"

—the boiling geyser—the irruptive blaze of the fire-vomiting volcano —the lightning, those " dread arrows of the clouds "—the poison-breath of the simoon—the fury-blast of the hurricane—the wide tempestweltered ocean—the upheaving earthquake—all natural phenomena—all animal and vegetable existence—all normal and abnormal states of mind, incite the curiosity and the research of man. It is impossible that he can look unmoved on these Creation-phenomena, nor ask himself those immensely significant questions, Whence? When? How? and Why? Truly, it is from scenes and circumstances like these that man drinks in his

> " Intellectual life,
> All sweet sensations, all ennobling thoughts,
> All adoration of the God in Nature,
> All lovely and all honourable things,
> Whatever makes his mortal spirit feel
> The joy and greatness of his future being!"

On the eduction of these self-communings depends the mental progress of humanity.—It is not until these ideas spring into being in the human soul that the full glory of his intellectual life can be felt. The universe is the nutrition-agency by which the mental germ is quickened into activity, and the blossomry of thought is produced. As this mind-life and thought-fruition advances, savagery and superstition are changed, even as the embattled mists that throng around the uprising sun are converted into "clouds of feathery gold shaded with deepest purple." There is a purifying and ennobling influence in intellectuality; hence it is that we have faith in the beneficiality of educative exertion, even when it is extended beyond the boundaries which were wont to limit its diffusion; and hence it is that we have endeavoured to give instruction in "The Art of Reasoning," beyond the precincts of collegiate halls, and have sought to open up the well-springs of knowledege to all classes of men who earnestly desire to drink of their mind-improving waters.

We have now arrived at that point in our prelections at which we may intelligibly and profitably describe "the method and order of truth-investigation," and, by a few examples culled from those bright pages which chronicle the conquests of science, demonstrate that it may be said of Logic—"The art itself is Nature."

I. The Law of Observational Activity.

Observation is the origin of all knowledge,—the primal external agency by which the germ of mentality is nourished into growth. The senses are the agents through which observation acquires a knowledge of external objects; and the perceptions thus attained are the crude materials which enter the mind as *facts*, and are subsequently ripened into *Truth*. Facts are the single stones of which the edifice of Science is upbuilt;—of small value scattered and isolated, but collectively of great and essential service in the erection of the temple of Truth. By observation, facts receive an entrance into the mind, and thus become the objects upon which Memory, Judgment, and Reason, exercise themselves; in which process truth is evolved, and certitude attained. We cannot open our eyes to the perception of the light, expand our ear to receive the undulations of the air, or place our senses in any relation to those stimuli which excite them to action, without being impressed by the objectivities around, and thus we may, in one sense, be said to observe. This, however, is not the observation of which we speak. We mean the observation in which the developing thought-powers engage themselves when the shadows of great thoughts loom hazily around the horizon of the mind—when the soul first begins to be awakened to the pleasures of intellectual exertion, and seeks to penetrate the secrets of that world of mysterious beauty and grandeur of which it finds itself a denizen. The observation on which we are remarking does not content itself with merely noticing the phenomena which present themselves to our sensational ken; but it goes after, it searches for, and seeks to place itself in relation with, other phenomena lying beyond, though capable of tangentiating upon, that circle. Observation is to look upon Creation with a thoughtful eye; is to exercise discrimination and discernment; is carefully to note the purposes, functions, qualities, and differences of objects, and thus to take the initiatory step in that series of mental processes which enables us to perceive the elements, operations, results, and causes of things,—originates science,—and effectuates the acquirement of Truth.

II. The Law of Suppositional Explanation.

Hypothesis succeeds Observation, and is a new exertion of the mental powers. It postulates the accuracy of the investigations in which observation is employed, and from this early step in Truth-search, strives to rise " higher still, and higher." It accepts from observation its account of the phenomenal facts which it had gathered;—receives these as the *data* of its speculations, and then asks under what generic formula the law which regulates their interdependency may be expressed; and thus seeks to account for the causation of phenomena, and makes a guess at what may reasonably be considered as a solution of the causality of the facts of observation. It proceeds upon the ground that where certain determinate conditions exist, certain determinate causative agencies have preceded, and certain determinative results will follow them; and from the few, and perhaps ill-arranged, facts with which observation furnishes it, strive to deduce some probable truth. For this purpose it *subpones* or *underlays* an hypothesis or imaginary explanation of the causes which superinduce any given series of phenomenal manifestations. The operation to be performed in the formation of an hypothesis is this;—given a series of phenomena, concerning which we know of no efficient producing cause, to assign the probable causality of that series. This is evidently a tentative process—a calculation of likelihoods and probabilities, which is not to be accepted as Truth, but merely taken as a helper or guide in our investigations of Truth. The grand object of Hypothesis is to discover a conception which will bind together in our mentality the coherences, derivations, and relations of phenomena. This, of course, must be formed by the facts of observation suggesting to, or originating in, the mind an idea which may account for them; this idea, of course, implying that something corresponding to it exists in the phenomenal series. Hypothesis is an incipient theory—a gratuitous assumption, by which we are enabled to collate, classify, and generalise phenomena. There is a widely prevalent prejudice in the present age against hypotheses and theories. We need not say that we do not share in it; we consider the framing of hypotheses a prefectly legitimate operation of the intellectual faculties. For it is quite evident that by discursive or general observation, facts can only be accumulated, as it were, in unorganised heaps—in unsystematised groups, or chaotisms; but the elements of many sciences—the rudiments of many truths, may exist in these facts. How, then, are either sciences or truths to be elicited from these conglomerated individual facts;—how are they to be disentangled from the ravelment in which they are amassed, and be woven into a web of celestial dye?   Clearly by searching among them in order to discover a probable sequency and subordination, which may be afterwards subjected to verification. This the mind, in framing hypotheses, does:— it organises the facts of observation—arranges the unsystematised chaotisms into analogous groups—collocates the individualities of the masses according to certain relations and congruencies which it supposes it perceives among them;—it adjusts and classifies sensational impressions into certain sequences—endeavours to imagine what the order of these phenomenal manifestations may be—strives to estimate their probable collateralities and successions—which is first, which middlemost or intermediate, and which final; and thus the understanding gives them a supposititious *oneness*, and the mind is able to look upon these groups of multiplex facts—the *data* of science and the elements of truth—as sequent and systematic wholes. Some such mental process as this, therefore, we consider as distinctly necessary in all our researches; for unless some such definite idea as this affords us—

some fixed notion of what we are in search of—be carried along with us in our induction, we shall be apt to accumulate not only false, but superfluous, experiences; and thus be retarded in our progress, or bewildered in our search. This *a priori*, though observation-suggested conception, which we endeavour to substantiate by Induction, is the lamp which we bear along with us, to enable us the more certainly to thread the labyrinth of discovery. We place this hypothetical conception before us, and then "interrogate" each objectivity of the class we meet, as to how far it lends support to it; upon the response of these oracles depends the fate of our hypothesis. This is the prescient questioning (*prudens interrogatio*), which Bacon says is the one-half of science (*est dimidium scientiæ*). Whence, then, so great zeal for the "Inductive Philosophy" as to decry all hypothetical opinions? Whence this narrow-minded "Positivism" which calls so loudly for "rigid induction, and nothing else?" Whence this disparagement of the grandly conceptive thought-powers of our nature? *Dux atque imperator vitæ mortalium animus est;* [*] why then should we seek to limit its power, or circumscribe the range of its activities? Bacon recalled men's minds from verbal disputations to an attention to facts; but he did not thereby assert that we were to neglect that "magic light" with which the soul illumines Nature. We are inclined to believe with Coleridge, that Bacon demands as the motive for, and guide of, all truth-search "the intellectual or mental initiative," which is only to be found in Hypothesis. It would be strange were these sticklers for "rigid induction" to find that their "great master" was in the field against them. And we think he is so:—we think that he fully appreciated the need and value of hypothesis, and did not limit his philosophy to a mere barren catalogue of facts. We can only at present cite as evidence his aphorisms on "Inchoate interpretation, or the first vintage," his tables "on Heat," and the following very significant extract from his "Distributio Operis:"—"*Etenim experimentorum longè major est subtilitas quàm sensûs ipsius, licet instrumentis exquisitis adjuti (de iis loquimur experimentis quæ ad intentionem ejus quod quæritur perité et secundum artem excogitata et apposita sunt)."* [†] Do not these fully substantiate our opinion that Bacon did not object to Hypothesis when duly subordinated to subsequent verification by the

---

[*] "The soul is the leader and commander of the lives of men."

[†] "For the delicacy of investigation attainable by experiments, is much greater than is possible by the senses, although aided by the most perfect instruments (we speak of those experiments which are judiciously and ingeniously devised and employed, *in accordance with the intention which presides over the investigation*)."— "*Distributio Operis,*" *pars prima,* paragraph 9.

inductive process? What mere cant is it, then—this zealous clamour for "rigid induction"? Who has ever gained Truth by the *mere* collocation of numberless items of observation, and brought not forth from the resources of his own inner nature the colligating conception —the idea which forms the *substration* on which the mind rests as the expression of an ultimate fact in nature? Is there nothing more required in the investigation of phenomena than the mere sensational powers exercised in classifying objectivities? or is there an exertion of Reason—a mental eduction *subponed* beneath the facts which observation yields? For our own parts, we believe that there are two elements in Knowledge—the facts of phenomenal manifestation, and the inner conceptive power which reduces these facts to law, and presents them to the intellect, no longer isolated, loose, detached, and unconnected, but conjoined, colligated, and subordinated—their dependencies determined, and their relations methodised. It is from considerations such as these that we advance the assertion, that Hypothesis is a perfectly legitimate exertion of the intellection, and holds its place in the series of mental operations on which Truth-investigation depends. It must be distinctly recollected, however, that being but an assumed explanation of the phenomena, it is only a tentative process,— one which must be put to the proof, and be tested in every possible manner. "Hypotheses are susceptible of the highest degree of evidence when two conditions are fulfilled—when the given Hypothesis explains many phenomena, and contradicts none—and when every other Hypothesis is inconsistent with some of the phenomena." *

III. The Law of Inductive Verification.

Induction is the testing operation through which all hypothetical opinions must be made to pass. The method in which this process is performed has been already fully explained; † and here it is our intention merely to mention it briefly, as forming one of that grand series of mental states upon which the investigation of Truth depends, and from which its discovery results. Induction is systematized observation—an experiment or series of experiments, to prove or disprove an hypothesis. It re-observes the facts on which the Hypothesis is founded;—endeavours to extend its views to facts beyond those which have been already presented to the mind. Sometimes, to aid its investigation, it strives to invent in miniature a model of the phenomena which it discovers, and seeks, by various experiments, to test the accuracy of the reports concerning external objects or internal states which perceptivity brings to the mind. Having thus, by a

---

* G. L. Le Sage's "Teleology."   † See Chapter VIII.

careful and patient survey of apparent facts, in every possible light and position in which the mental faculties can be made to view them, ascertained their actuality, it accumulates and classifies them,—compares them with the supposititious account which the Hypothesis had given,—refers them to their proximate causes, and then, by specifying and generalizing these causes, subsequently arrives at a knowledge of the simple law from which all these phenomenal manifestations ultimately result. If this law and that enounced in the Hypothesis, coincide, we have attained a Truth. If this truth be arrived at by an accurate and sufficiently generalized Induction, we may from it deduce new truths, foresee the occurrence and recurrence of certain yet un-manifested facts, and make them a part of one system; and, in the words of Dr. Whewell, "it must, one would think, strike all persons in proportion to their thoughtfulness, that when nature thus does our bidding, she acknowledges that we have learnt her true language. If we can predict new facts which we have not seen, as well as explain those which we have seen, it must be because our explanation is not a mere *formula* of observed facts, but a truth of a deeper kind." By Observation we received the spontaneous and immethodical results of externalities operating on our senses, or the unregulated intimations of our Consciousness; but in Induction, Volition is exercised, and by an effort of our Will, the phenomena, whether of mind or matter, are detained for the inspection of the Intellect. By this energy of the Will, the Attention is aroused, the knowledge-attaining faculties are quickened, and have their powers intensified. The passivity or inertia of the mind is overcome, and activity or motivity is conveyed to the cognitive capacities. In the one case, the sensational powers are free and purposeless,—in the other, regulated and subordinated to a men-tally-originated design. In Observation, even although the activities be exercised, the mental efforts are comparatively valueless, because undirected and aimless; but in Induction, no exertion of the intellect is uselessly consumed; for it informs us either of the truth or falsehood of our preconceptions. In the former process, we *find* facts—in the latter, we "*go out and compel them to come in.*" The object of Induction is verification—is the establishment of some definite formula, law, or conception, under which the mind may accurately survey a series of phenomena. If our previous observation has been limited, injudicious, or erroneous, the hypothesis which we have built upon that observation will be inconformable to truth. When, therefore, the facts and the hypothesis are compared, the incorrectness will be discovered, and a new hypothesis will be rendered necessary.

IV. The Law of Contemplative Survey.

Theory is an ordinated account of the facts which accurate Inductive Observation has ascertained. It is the result of Intellectual Observation or reflective penetration. Theory is educed by the accurate survey of facts, in order to discern the law or laws by which they are governed, and under which they act,—the mind, abstracting the attention from the facts, and fixing it upon the law or laws by which their action is produced,—succeeds in dissevering in the intellection,—*i. e.*, contemplatively, not in reality,—the experience or facts from the law or laws of their *modus operandi*, and by expressing this in a definite formula enables the mentality to contemplate the *method* of fact-evolution disjoined from the *manner* of fact-existence; in other words, Theory ordinates experience, and then the mind can reflect upon the expression of this ordination independently of the experience from which the formula of ordination was eliminated. Theory is an organised view of the mutual relations which subsist in any series of phenomena. By it the antecedents, causative agency, and consequents of a train of facts, are determined; and the *linealities* of phenomena are sundered, in the mind's eye, from their *collateralities*. Every true theory is the expression of a *fact* in Nature,—bears reference to, and gives a solution of, the law or laws of what metaphysicians term the *forms* of phenomenal manifestations.

Before proceeding to illustrate the preceding reasoning by an appeal to the facts of science, we may be permitted to make the following brief recapitulation :—Observation collects examples, instances; and may inform us of facts, though it cannot unaidedly communicate any knowledge of truths. Hypothesis strives to classify the results of Observation under some general (supposititious) law; when this law is postulated, systematized observation,—*i. e.*, Induction—is called into action, to compare the results which would flow from this (imaginary) law, with the actual processes of Nature. If these agree, the Hypothesis is correct, and becomes Theory, *i. e.*, the means by which the mind may contemplatively survey any series of facts, and from the laws discovered as ruling amongst these, can deduce new facts or infer new truths. Observation, Hypothesis, Induction, and Theory, form one continuous system of mental operations, every one of which must be called into action before we can ascertain any new truth, or acquire any acquaintance with those laws which enable us to colligate the facts of Nature into systematized groups, the unition-bonds of which we can perceive.

We have already more than hinted our belief that the history of

Science fully confirms the opinions advanced in the foregoing portion of this chapter, and we purpose to devote the remainder of our space to a brief attempt to prove that the "investigation of truth," whether in Science or in Art, has proceeded according to the plan sketched out in this article, and that the "discovery of truth" has uniformly resulted from the pursuance of the method hereintofore described. For this the following succinctly-detailed examples may suffice :—

Franklin *observed* the similarity between the spark elicited from an electrical machine, and that exhibited while the lightning's flash spread its broad glare along the arched sky; he *supposed* that they were identical — reduced his *hypothesis* to experiment ; floated his kite through the black surcharged heavens—brought down the electric fluid from the gloomy cloud—and by this *Induction*, proved the truth of his hypothesis, and enlarged, if he did not remodel, the *Theory* of Electric Science.

Senefelder *observed* that a certain kind of compact granular lime-stone had the property of imbibing grease, and *knew* that grease and water have an antipathy to each other. He supposed that were a drawing or writing made on a piece of paper with an ink of a greasy nature,—*e. g.*, one composed of wax, soap, and lampblack,—placed on a stone—and then washed over with water, the stone would imbibe the greasy matter of the drawing or writing, while the wet part of the stone would resist amalgamation with the ink employed. This was an *Hypothesis*. He reduced this supposition to experiment—a process of *Induction*,—and eminent success was the result. Thus was " Lithography" discovered. The expression of the principles upon which this art is founded, constitutes the *Theory* of it, and from this Theory the farther results of Chromo-lithography and Anastatic printing have subsequently been deduced.

On the first day of the year 1801, Ceres, one of a group of small planets called the Asteroids, was discovered by Piazzi of Palermo, and subsequent investigation has increased their number to fourteen. Let us inquire how this series of planetary bodies was discovered, and compare the process by which this was accomplished, with the mode of investigation and discovery of which we have been treating. The Baron de Zach *observed* that all the known planets, except those of Mars and Jupiter, revolved in orbits possessed of a definite ratio to each other, which nearly corresponded to double distances ; but that between the two abovementioned there was a great gap—an abyssmal infinitude—with no known planet occupying it. He *assumed* that Nature was uniform in her operations, and that if a planet were found in that, so far as hitherto known, untenanted immensity, the law would be completely realized, and the whole series of the orbits of the planets would be brought into definite proportions to each other. This idea led to the *hypothesis*, that a planet did actually exist, and he calculated the orbit which it should occupy fifteen years prior to the known existence of any planet in that part of the sky. In consequence of this idea, a convention of astronomers was held at Lilienthal, in 1800, who determined to map out the heavens into twenty-four zones, and by taking up one each, to search for the supposititious planet. A short time after they commenced the search, Piazzi observed Ceres moving in its hitherto unnoticed pathway, and Bode's law became an astronomical *Theory*.

From this law, discovered by Bode, a knowledge of the "law of perturbations," and the observation of the irregularities of Uranus, Mr. Adams made the *hypothesis*, that beyond the infinitude occupied by this supposed sentinel-planet, another starry wanderer had his home. To resolve this by *Induction* was, however, a difficult task;—nevertheless, with an ardour and exactness which struck the scientific world with surprise, the difficult inverse problem he had set himself was solved, and in October, 1845, he was able to say, "Look at a given point in the infinity of the celestial vault, at a given time, and a star, unseen as yet by mortal eye, will present itself to view :—that planet causes the irregularities of Uranus." The Astronomer-Royal of Britain did not make use of the *data* of discovery which Mr. Adams put into his hands, but the same, or, at least, a similar hypothesis had entered into the mind of a French mathematician—Leverrier—a similar process of computation was gone through, and the results were presented to M. Galle, of Berlin, informing him of the position the planet would occupy on the 23rd of September, 1846 : on that day the given space was explored, and a new planet—Neptune—was revealed to man.

Had we space, we might detail a thousand others; but the above will be sufficient to prove that the opinions contained in the previous portion of this chapter are correct, and that Observation, Hypothesis, Induction, and Theory, form the links of a chain of mental operations which are needful in "the investigation and discovery of Truth."

CHAPTER XII.

RATIOCINATION.—THE DOCTRINE OF THE SYLLOGISM.

"I pretend to no sagacity capable of striking out uncommon discoveries: my dependence must rest solely upon my care and vigilance, which keep me constantly upon the watch for such sparks of light as occur from time to time, spontaneously. I shall present the reader with nothing but what he may have had in his view before:—I pretend only to remind him of things that may have slipped his memory, or to point out to him objects that may have escaped his notice."—TUCKER.

"Le raisonnement consiste à déduire, à inférer, à tirer un jugement d'autres jugemens déja connus."*—MARSAIS.

IN proposing to fill the present chapter with an attempt to expound "the doctrine of the Syllogism," we know that we shall have a large amount of prejudice and misapprehension to encounter. It has become so fashionable of late to treat the defenders of "the syllogistic mode of reasoning," as some people call it, with ridicule, that we can scarcely expect to be exempted from a share of the same dignified and convincing method of argumentation. There is such an air of superior wisdom supposed to be evinced in decrying old-world notions—in rejecting as "foolishness" that which for so long a time has been esteemed by "the world's grey fathers" as the true philosophy of thought—in possessing the capacity of perceiving the "triviality" of "the quips, the cranks, and learned quillets" which prevailed during the lengthy reign of Scholasticism—in being able to detect the blundering irrelation which subsists between the *true* "Art of Reasoning" and the "syllogistic mode"—and in being competent to resist having the mind warped, and the strength of the intellectual faculties restrained, by the absurd dialectism of the stout Stagyrite, whose vain and futile "invention" held the mental powers of man so long in thrall,—that we do not wonder at the existence of a wide-spread antagonism to and a sturdy contempt of the Aristotelic Logic. If, however, we have been successful—as we hope we have—in convincing our readers of the inexpediency and error of offering worship at the secret shrines of the "Idols of the Intellect," we confidently expect that they will peruse this chapter with the same attention, impartiality, and critical thoughtfulness as they have bestowed upon its predecessors. We are perfectly cognizant of the fact, that the great names—names endeared to every student of the "philosophy of mind"—of Locke, Reid, Campbell,

* "Reasoning consists in deducing, inferring, or drawing one conclusion from others already known."

Stewart, &c., may be cited against our opinion. We do not wish, however, to be influenced in our decisions by the wisdom of the past alone; nor to entrust our intellectual guidance to any set of men, however highly endowed with the heaven-gift of genius. We do not wish to rest our belief of any great philosophic truth merely upon the basis of the greatest collection of great names which may be quoted in support of it. Much as we revere the mighty masters in the science of human thought, we revere Truth more; hence it is that we most earnestly desire to employ our own reasoning powers in the impartial and unbiassed investigation of the evidence adduced in favour of any opinion, and thus, as far as in us lies, by a careful balancing and assaying of arguments, to acquire, if possible, the most accurate ideas upon any topic which may occupy our minds. Man's real position upon this earth is that of a *Truth-seeker ;*—not always, however, does he, or can he, become a *Truth-finder.* This may partly result from the limitations of his nature, but far more frequently does it result from the adoption of erroneous methods of search; and more frequently still, from the neglect of all method whatever. Our object, in this article, is not to advance *a* mode of truth investigation, but to attempt to unfold and explain what is *the* method which the mind itself, by the very constitution of its nature, is necessitated to employ. In so doing, we have no intention of being the apologists of Error in any of its multiform disguises; but we do wish to retain any truth, by whomsoever elaborated, which may be useful to man, and which is capable of aiding him in the work of intellectual culture. Let it not be imagined, however, that we place our thoughts on this subject before our readers merely for the purpose of their being unthinkingly assented to by them, but rather that they may read and judge for themselves as to the accuracy of the reasoning which we bring before them. We wish to write didactically, not dogmatically. Believing, as we do, that "the grand and, indeed, only characteristic of truth is its capability of enduring the test of universal experience, and coming unchanged out of every possible form of fair discussion," *—we cannot fear that our investigation will result in evil. No one of our readers, we hope, will rashly and unphilosophically prejudge the matter, and decide upon the erroneousness of our opinions before he has carefully read the proofs we offer, and subjected them to a fair, candid, and unbiassed criticism; and in all their meditations on this subject, let them hold in remembrance the oft-repeated maxim of Locke, that "Reason must be our last guide and judge in everything." If, after such a course of thought,

* Herschell's " Discourse on Natural Philosophy," art. 6.

the opinions to be hereinafter advanced shall appear to be accordant with, and agreeable to, the process of mental action which self-consciousness makes known, let them be accepted as true; but if they seem incoincident with, and inconformable to, the operations which by the revelations of consciousness are perceived going on in the mind while employed in the act of reasoning, let them be counted erroneous. By this means, they may be subjected to experiment, and made amenable to the laws of a strict and rigorous induction. Such criticism we do not fear to invite. We have no intention of homologating all that Aristotle and the Schoolmen have written on this subject, or of defending the verbal subtleties and useless logomachies by which the latter-mentioned parties gained such distinguished honours and eminence-denoting titles; but we do seriously believe that, as a philosophical exposition of the *form* of the mental act called Reasoning, "the doctrine of the Syllogism" is not only a tenable account, but is, besides, really and truly explanatory of the necessary and essential laws by which the mind is governed in the performance of that operation; and this view of the matter we will now hasten to lay before you.

Let us, then, clearly and distinctly understand on what basis the Syllogistic Logic rests—on what fundamental truths it reposes—why it results from them as a *formal* science,—one which derives its being from the essentialities of the mental constitution itself. Every science exists under conditions—is built upon the subsumptions that there are laws which determine the facts upon which its inquiries are expended, and that if we could look upon these facts in the light of these laws, an orderly, harmonious, and consistent whole would be presented to our view. Hence it is of primary importance in the study of any science, to gain an accurate, definite, and precise acquaintance with its laws. Then it is that facts—the inarticulate, but truth-continent language of Nature—become expressive! Then it is that the mysterious hieroglyphics written with a Divine finger on the fair page of creation cease to be meaningless—become translatable—become words of wisdom, oracular in their multi-significance! The light of law reflected on the mind from the objectivities which surround it, reveals their unition-bonds, causative agencies, qualities, relationships, &c.; and the immense multiplicity of truth-rays which emanate from them are, by one grand master-thought, converged into a mental unity. The $\phi\tilde{\omega}\varsigma$ $\nu o\epsilon\rho o\nu$—the light of the understanding—being thus kindled, flashes forth its illuminating radiance in all directions. From this consideration, it will appear obvious that if we desire to appreciate the full power of any science,—to afford a complete and satisfactory account of the *rationale* of the phenomena of which it is cognizant, we must look upon these phenomena in the light which the laws of that science emit, and watch the harmonizing effects which these produce on the whole of the objectivities which come within the range of its influence. It is only by such a method of study that we can acquire accurate notions of the nature, purposes, capabilities, &c., of any science;—any isolated and external point must give incorrect and inadequate ideas of its efficiency. It is from this central—this light-forth-giving point that we wish you to look upon the phenomena with which Logic concerns itself.

Language is the exponent of thought, and ideas are the exponibles upon which it operates. But it is only as we are impressed by objectivities that we can perceive them—only as they reveal themselves to our minds can we know them; so that if we attend not to the *forms* of our thought-powers—the manner in which our intellect operates under the rules and conditions which limit it—how can we expect that we can fully comprehend the art of thinking—the philosophy of thought? Now, between Logic and Language there obtains this great distinction:—that the former exerts itself to unfold and elucidate the *manner* of thought—to describe *how* we think; the latter employs itself in explaining the *matter* of thought—in making known *what* we think. By Language, men aim at the transference of their ideas in the speediest and most intelligible manner. The great object, therefore, which they keep in view, is to express so much of their mental operations as will make the matter of thought perfectly understood, and no more. The general intellectual endowments and characteristics of all men—however much they may differ in power—differ but slightly in their nature; and consequently, the process of thought-evolution is nearly similar in all; it is not necessary, then, that the whole of the mental operations which are gone through by one mind should be verbally unfolded to another. It is in general quite sufficient that a similar train of thought is excited in the other's mind, and then the whole process will be instinctively gone on with by him; "for," to use the significant language of Hobbes, "thought is quick." It is on this account that common language abounds in elisions—that men leave many of the steps of their mental on-goings without explicit utterance, well knowing that they must be performed implicitly by the thinker, as they are the mere results of the excitation of the intellectual capacities of our nature. This elisive method of communication is eminently fitted for ordinary intercourse, because then the only object before the mind is to convey to others the matter concerning which the thinking powers were employing themselves—is to add its share to the general fund of remark upon business, instruction, &c., according as the circumstances demand; but it is quite evident that if we wish to attain a knowledge of the *modus operandi* of the thought-powers, in all its exactitude and methodicality, we must not rely upon that which is merely the adventitious dress or outward covering of our thoughts, but must look beneath the surfacism of verbalized expression—fix our mental eye upon the internal workings of the intellectual faculties, and by careful scrutiny and watchful investigation, become acquainted with the laws which regulate their action, and the manner in which thought-germination proceeds. When this is performed with accuracy and care, a formal science will be educed, which will be as invariable as the constitution of the human mind, and as incapable of being in error in its principles of evolution as the intellectual faculties are unable to overstep the limits which in the Creator's wisdom have been assigned to them.

We do not, by any means, assert that an analysis so accurate, searching, keen, and clear, has ever yet been made; least of all, do we wish to insinuate that we have accomplished, or are capable of accomplishing, so great and important a task. "The investigations thus proposed have obviously many analogies to a voyage of discovery. In these, no individual is completely successful; but the enterprise of many adventurers is required; while the observations of each may be useful to all who follow; and even the errors and failures of some may put others on the right track. In taking the present course, accordingly, I have endeavoured to avail myself of the experience of those who have pursued different courses, both when it follows and when it departs from theirs; and have thus recorded my observations for the benefit of others, who may hereafter be more successful, and who may derive useful suggestions from my very mistakes. For even when the main object of a voyage is missed, valuable discoveries may still be made. The Pole, perhaps, may never be reached, yet every advance towards it is an important achievement. The course now taken, I am persuaded, lies in the right direction, and, if skilfully followed, is likely to lead so far into the surrounding regions as to give more correct ideas of their general aspect, and of their bearings upon the point which is ultimately in view."*

Returning, however, from this digression, we may observe, that the difference between the purposes of ordinary discourse—viz., the expression of *the matter of thought*, and the end which Logic seeks to attain —viz., a knowledge of *the manner of thought*, being so distinct, an

* Cairns on "Moral Freedom," Preface, p. ix.

equal distinctness must be pursued in the mode of investigation. We cannot, it would seem, confide in the utterances of vocal speech, nor in the idea-symbolisation of writing, as full, clear, and accurate expositions of the operations of the mentality; for this would be to confound the casual and variable *forms of expression* with the necessary and invariable *forms of thought*—would be to hold language as a complete and perfect representative of the processes of thought, notwithstanding its clear want of any scientific elaboration. But we cannot, surely, accept the method of explaining *what* we think, as identical with the scientific exposition of *how* we think! It is necessary, therefore, for us to abstract our attention, as much as possible, from the forms of thought-expression, and rivet it upon the forms of thought-evolution; or, if this be impossible without the aid of words, we must be allowed to include and express in the verbal symbols we employ, all that may be found in the thinking process. In this attempt to translate into visible or audible signs the procedure of the mind, however, we must carefully abstain from allowing any one of those elisions, which ordinary discourse allows, to be omitted in our verbal representation, as it is quite evident that the whole scientific value of the knowledge thus attained will depend upon its being complete and perfect in its analysis.

Before proceeding to attempt to give an analysis of the reasoning process, however, it has occurred to us that it will be necessary to premise the following observation—viz., that all objectivities may be arranged into three great classes, according to the kind of impression which they make upon the mind. 1st—Those which are perfectly simple, or which make a unical impression on our Perceptivity; concerning these, no erroneous opinions can be formed, except through a defect in the inlets of knowledge; 2nd—Those which are always united and inseparable, and *vice versâ*, which are never united and always separate; it is with these that the Mathematical and Physical sciences chiefly concern themselves, and from which, what are usually denominated "necessary truths" are educed; 3rd—Those which may exist either separately or unitedly, or whose conjunctions and disjunctions are contingent; these are the kinds of phenomena in the investigation of which Morals, Politics, and Sociology are principally engaged. In Chapter V. we detailed the principal classes of relations which objects bear to each other; referring to it, therefore, for what farther information may be required on this topic, we proceed to remark that it appears from the above general, though rude, classification of objectivities, that the laws of Mathematics, and the mathematico-physical sciences, are much more easy of discovery than those of the sciences which refer to the moral, civil, or social state of man ; and this arises not only from the greater facility which they afford to experimentation, but also from the greater invariability of the conjunctions and disjunctions which obtains in the former as compared with the latter ; so that we may be prepared to find a less degree of certainty in any reasoning concerning the latter than we do in the former.*

Ratiocination is the synthesis of two judgments, or the comparison of two distinct—*i. e.*, diverse—ideas, through the intermediatcy of another *known* or hypothetical idea.   The verbal expression of such an act of the mentality is called a Syllogism.   The whole process is founded upon the mind's power of perceiving identity and diversity. It is the comparison by the intellect of idea with idea ; but there are, and must necessarily be, many ideas whose relations cannot be observed at a mere glance by the comparing faculty, in which case it will be found requisite that some intermediate and known idea should be placed before the mind, in order that a more ready perception of their agreement or disagreement may be attained.   This fact may be illustrated thus :—suppose the proprietor of two fields to be desirous of discovering the relation of equality or inequality which they bear to each other, it would be necessary, in order to accomplish his purpose, to fix upon some definite mode of comparison—say the adoption of some known dimension-sign, as a yard, which could be applied to each—the relation which each field bore to this dimension-sign would be readily gained, and thus the relation in which they stood to each other would be easily comprehended.   Exactly so is it with Logic,—so much so, that this might be called a practical syllogism.

The whole of these cognate operations which are necessary in an act

---

* Xenophon, in his " *Memorabilia*," makes Socrates point out the distinction between the two latter classes in these words—for the sake of unlearned readers, and to save space, we give only a translation :—

"Ippias answered and said, ' Do you still say the same things which you said when I heard you many years since ?'   And Socrates spoke : ' Does it appear strange to you to say the same thing of the same things ?   Perhaps it would appear more singular to you not to say the same thing of the same things.'   And Ippias said : ' I would strive to say something new always.'   And Socrates spoke : ' If then any person should inquire of you concerning the size and appearance of Socrates, would you try to say one thing to-day, and another thing another day ?   And if any one were to ask you how much twice five were, would you endeavour one day to say one thing, and another thing on another day ?'   And Ippias said : ' As to these things, I, as you do, should say the same things at all times ; but as to what is good and what is right, I think I could find something to say which could neither be contradicted by thee nor by any one else.' "—" *Mem.*" iv. 4, 13.

of reasoning, appear to be the result of a power of comparative survey possessed by the mind, the complexity and difficulty of the process increasing as the intellect pushes its inquiries farther. In Perceptivity we find the comparison of the qualities of one object with those of another, in order to arrange them into classes;—in Judgment, the comparison of one class of objectivities with another, conjoined with the assertion of their congruence or inconformability;—in Ratiocination, the comparison of two Judgments, in order to discover *their* relation or irrelation, and an assertion which embodies this mental decision. Each one of these forms of the intellect educes a new idea, and each idea differs in complexity from the one which preceded it;—*e.g.*, Perceptivity, comparing a number of the heavenly bodies, finds that they agree in the possession of a certain quality, and forms of them a class of objects under the name Planets. Judgment, continuing the process, farther compares the idea expressed in the words, " all planets," and " revolve round the sun,"—and predicates their agreement in the proposition, " all planets revolve round the sun." Again: a newly-discovered body appears in the heavens—Judgment is called on to exercise its functions: it compares the ideas which the words " Neptune " and " planet " express, and asserts their congruency thus;—" Neptune is a planet." Furnished with these materials, Ratiocination arranges them for further comparison, and proceeds in this manner :—

All planets revolve round the sun:
Neptune is a planet;
Therefore it revolves round the sun.

There are contained in this syllogism three, and only three, terms—viz., " Planet," " revolve round the sun," and " Neptune ;" and three, and only three, propositions. It is the same with all valid Syllogisms ; for the two ideas concerning the relation or irrelation of which the mind is as yet *formally* undecided, are both compared with another idea which bears a known or hypothetical relation to each. In one proposition, therefore, there is contained an assertion of the congruency or incoincidence of the known or hypothetical idea with one of the doubtful ones ; the other asserts the same concerning that idea and the other doubtful one; and then there is the conclusion, in which the mind, now freed from doubt, asserts the agreement or disagreement between them. These three propositions, when definitely related and consecutively disposed, constitute a Syllogism, which may be defined as *a verbal representation of that act of the mind by which we ascertain that two ideas stand to each other in a certain relation of agreement or*

*disagreement, through the knowledge that they stand in that same rela-
tion to a third.*   We subjoin the following instances:—

"It is beneath the glowing rays of a tropical sun," says Humboldt,
  "that the noblest forms of vegetation are developed :"
The Banian tree is one of the noblest forms of vegetation ;
Therefore, the Banian tree is developed beneath the rays of a tropical
  sun.

The Fine Arts soften the manners of men :
Poetry is one of the Fine Arts ;
Therefore, Poetry softens the manners of men.

The radii of the same, or of equal circles, are equal :
The lines A B, B C, and C A, are the radii of the same, or of equal
  circles ;
Therefore, they are equal.

An equilateral triangle is a figure that has three
  equal sides :
The lines A B, B C, and C A, constitute a figure
  with three equal sides ;
Therefore, the figure composed of A B, B C, and
  C A, is an equilateral triangle.

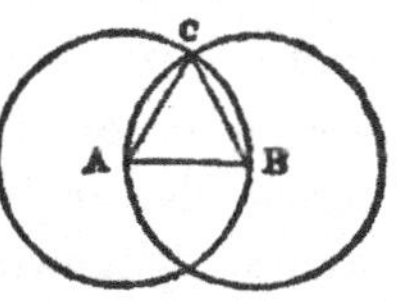

The first two assertions are technically denominated the *premises*, and
the last the *conclusion*.   The premise which contains the larger assertion is called the *major premise*, and that which contains the less assertion the *minor premise*.

From the mere consideration of what argumentation is, it must
appear obvious that these three parts are involved in every act of it.
There is, first, the thing to be proved ; second, the medium of proof ;
third, the conclusion.   It is true that in ordinary discourse, reasonings
and arguments are stated much more briefly, and frequently in such a
manner that it is difficult to discriminate these various parts ; but we
shall find, that if we wish to test the soundness of any argument, the
best method of procedure is to decompose it into these three elementary
propositions, so that we may clearly see the general principle—*i. e.*,
major premise ; the assertion of relation or irrelation—*i. e.*, the minor
premise ; and the conclusion or inference.   The mind is thus put in the
best possible position for guarding against the admission of error ;
because it can now examine the argument both in the whole and in its
several parts ; and thus, as in chemistry, when an analysis is performed,
adulteration is more easily detected than otherwise.   For example, let

the following argument be presented to the mind :—"He is dishonest, and should be shunned."   Shall we not much more clearly perceive the truth or falsehood which it contains by giving it the full mental development ?—viz.,

> Every dishonest person should be shunned :
> He is a dishonest person ;
> Therefore, he should be shunned.

Or, if a fallacy is sought to be palmed upon us—*e. g.*, this employed, in substance, by Locke,[*] "Innate ideas cannot be enumerated, and, consequently, cannot exist "—shall we not more readily discover the error when we place the whole argument at full length before the mind? Let us see.

> Things which cannot be numbered do not exist :
> Innate ideas cannot be numbered ;
> Therefore, they cannot exist.

Here the lurking fallacy is unearthed ; for who will seriously maintain that the innumerability of any series of objects—the stars, for instance —is a proof of their non-existence.   We think that this will make much clearer the assertion which we advanced before, that though human language does not explicitly exponentiate the whole of the mental evolutions, yet implicitly they are always performed ; for were this not the case, it would be impossible to antedate the reasoning, in the manner we have done above, to some foregone proposition.

To add still another stone to the evidence-building we are engaged in erecting, let us revert to what we established in our last chapter—viz., That there are three distinct and different steps in " the investigation and discovery of Truth."   Observation, which is an act of the Perceptivity ; Hypothesis, which is the result of the presentation of facts to the mind, on the perception of which the faculties of knowledge-acquirement instinctively spring into activity, and form a product, which product our readers will now perceive is equivalent to a major premise or a general principle-enunciative ; and Induction, the elaborative faculty, which *leads in* this, that, and the other fact, to be compared with the effects deducible from the (suppositious) law, and thus enables the mind, by a clear process of verification, to evolve from the particular and the contingent, a knowledge of the necessary and essential. Besides this, too, when the verificatory comparison is completed, and the Theory of any series of facts has been settled, the law which contains an expression of that Theory becomes the major premise, by which

* " Essay concerning Human Understanding," book i., chap. ii.

farther discoveries are progressed with. As the morning sun, when it arises, first dawns faintly, and illuminates with a dim light a few prominent objects, but gradually diffuses a greater and greater quantity of radiance, till "all is light" within the horizon of our ken;—so it is with Truth :—When it first arises in our mind we cannot have universal experience of its certitude; but we can unfold in our intellect what consequences are deducible from it; and when we have gained a knowledge of these, we can try their re-applicability to the actually existing facts as they present themselves. If these deductions, when subjected to verification, are not confirmed by realities, we must retrace the steps taken. Error has certainly crept into our mind :—either the judgment has been rashly formed—the particulars adopted for experiment have not been rightly included in the subject—or our comparison of the fact with the major premise has been illogically proceeded with. In either case the argumentation is invalidated.

Were man destitute of the power of Ratiocination, there could be no transference of the knowledge gained by Induction, from one series of objectivities to those of a class possessed of identical properties—no carrying forward of already attained experience as applicable to our guidance in the future. Of the continual catalogizing of facts, what good would result ? Would not the mind become overwhelmed with their innumerability ? Would not its burden be greater than it could bear ? But when we bind a number of facts together in the unition-bond of one common idea, or one general law, the mind does not so readily faint and fail. Then the separate and individual facts are ordinated and *sub*ordinated by one grand general conception—some master thought—which gives them unity, and makes them all mere parts of one integral idea. But how is this done ? Recall to your memory the distinction formerly asserted to obtain between the intuitional and the logical consciousness,* and it will be plain. The Intuitional Consciousness, by the juxtaposition and comparison of the objectivities presented to it, strives to evolve some conception which may colligate the seemingly diverse and detached phenomena which tangentiate upon it, into the unicality of law ;—a law which when adequately received by the mentality, gives it the power of anticipating and foretelling the consequent, on the perception of the antecedent ; and from a knowledge of the cause to infer the effect it will produce. This conception must be suggested to the mental powers by the excitation of certain facts ; and before it can be accepted as true, its re-applicability to these facts must be made evident. This latter exercise is the work of the Logical Con-

* Chapter VI.

sciousness. It unfolds the conception, brings under it the various facts, and endeavours to verify the accuracy of the idea or law, by the comparison of the effects deducible from the ideal-law, and those manifested by the actual existences with which that law concerns itself. The Intuitional Consciousness endeavours to integralise and impart unicality to our knowledge ;—the Logical Consciousness strives, by Induction, to certiorate it. The former, by grouping phenomena together in new points of view, attempts to generalize the ideas which they excite, and thus produce in the mind a generic formula under which they may all be classed ;—the latter seeks to re-apply this formula *to* the objectivities of that class ;—measures, as it were, their capacity of being contained within it ; and thus, by the mutual action and reaction of the Hypothetical and the Real upon each other, the sciences attain perfection. In the first dawn of light upon the mind, an " Hypothesis merely performs the function of an unknown quantity in Algebra, and is assumed for the purpose of submitting the phenomena to a scientific calculus ;" but when the Hypothesis, by reference to the facts, is proven to be correct, and thus becomes a scientific truth, we can apply it to a thousand other facts of which we previously knew nothing :—we can clear away many errors which hung like cobwebs in the chambers of the mind, and can march on "from strength unto strength," in gaining a fuller, a higher, and more complete development of Truth. Thus we see it is possible to discover, or at least to make an approximation towards the discovery, of the central point of a circle of truth, while we may not be capable of finding out the whole of the facts *outlying* that centre, yet *inlying* the circumference—*e. g.*, Nicholas Copernicus (born A.D. 1473, at Thorn, in Prussia) taught that the sun was the centre of our system, and that the planets moved round him in elliptical orbits proportioned to their size and distance, long before the discovery of the Asteroids, Uranus, and Neptune—nay, prior to the grand discoveries made by the illustrious Newton. This, it will be found, is the usual course of *ratiocinative* speculation ; and if it be so, why this contempt of the Syllogism ? why this attempt to underrate its efficacy ? One would almost imagine some men were proud of being divested of their mind's most dear and glorious privilege. No general truth can be acquired—no process of reasoning can be prosecuted—no scientific discovery can be properly carried out, without the use of reasoning ; and that reasoning, as invariably as the laws of the mentality operate, may be reduced to Syllogisms ; and then only can its real significance and worth be fairly expressed to the mind.

Ratiocination, however, it must be recollected, undertakes to inform us *how to reason*, and not *how to know*. Knowledge and Reasoning are each distinct; for it is only when we have attained Knowledge—either real or imaginary—that we can begin the process of Reasoning. Knowledge supplies the *matter* on which Ratiocination is to operate; and a Syllogism is a correct expression of the *manner* in which, from Induction-derived facts, we can deduce other facts, which as yet *outlie* our Experience, and which gives us the means of accurately applying the test of Induction to Hypothetical opinions. This is not, of course, the *whole* process of Truth-acquirement; but it must be admitted to form an important and an essential part of it. Is it, then, a valid argument against Syllogistic Logic—in fact, there is *no other*—that it assists only in a part of the process of Truth-acquirement, and is consequently useless, and unworthy of study?—Because it is not the means of obtaining clear, definite, and precise ideas upon all knowledge and all mysteries, is it therefore to be discarded as valueless? Is any other science contemned because it cannot do more than it pretends? Of Logic it may be said, that it is looked at askance because it is misunderstood—because it cannot perform impossibilities—because it will not do more than it purposes—because it is not a complete organon, by which, all other sciences apart—unaided and alone—it cannot enter into the *penetralia* of Nature's temple, and compel the oracle to give forth utterances. In a future chapter we will show the absurdity of this,—explain the real use of the science,—describe the processes of "Formal Logic," and thence—our student will learn the truth of what we have stated above, and that

> " The head and front of *its* offending
> Hath this extent—no more."

We have then, we consider, said sufficient to prove that the Syllogistic Logic is not—as Dr. Campbell, Professor Stewart, &c., have termed it—a "vain invention," but the true and veritable type of all reasoning;—that it presents a full, clear, and accurate analysis of that process;—that it is an indispensable agent in the "investigation and discovery of Truth;"—and that it really is not

> " Vain wisdom all, and false philosophy."

CHAPTER XIII.

RATIOCINATION.—FORMAL LOGIC.

᾽ " Γίνεται δε τεχνη ὅταν ἐκ πολλαν τῆς ἐμπειρίας εννοηματαν καθολου μια γένηται περι εμοίαν ὑποληψις."[a]—Αριστοτέλης.

THE CATEGORIES.—The mind, in the formation of notions or conceptions, is subject to laws, which are independent of, and superior to, the appearances which Sensation makes known to it, and to which these appearances must conform. To these general conceptions, or necessary mental laws, all particular and individual conceptions must be referred, and under these they must be ranged; for the mind has limitations and methods of action from which it cannot free itself. These general conceptions are denominated the Categories, and are the highest predicates, or *summa genera*, one or other of which is capable of being truthfully affirmed of every "object able to be named." Some notion of the method in which they originate in the mind may be formed from the following observations :—All the impressions made on the human mind must proceed either from *substances* or their *attributes :* but attributes may be either essential or circumstantial. Essential attributes are those without which objects could not exist or become comprehensible. Circumstantial attributes are such as are incidental or casual, and are of minor importance as compared with those which are essential. The Categories may be thus defined :—I. Substance, that which is in itself— which can be thought of *per se—i. e.*, by itself—that in which attributes inhere ;—II. Quantity—the how much, the how great, and the as much as—or Number, Magnitude, and Time. Number is either concrete or discrete. Of Magnitude there are three species—viz., line, surface, and solid. Time is either successive or permanent ;—III. Quality—that which describes the kind or sort of which a thing is ; of this there are four species—1st, Habit, or that adventitious quality which is acquired by the influence of custom or frequent repetition— as Virtue, Vice, the Power of Writing, &c. ; 2nd, Natural Power, or that which inheres in the kind of being—as Reason, Will, &c. ; 3rd, Patible Quality—that which can be superinduced in or on a subject— as sounds, colours, hardness, softness, &c.; 4th, Shape, that which determines the exterior of quantity ;—IV. Relation, or the ordination

---

[a] " Art begins when, from many experiences, one general conception is originated which will be reapplicable to all similar things."—ARISTOTLE.

or subordination which one idea bears to another,—the prior idea
is called the relative, the latter the correlative —as prince, subject;
master, servant; parent, child;—V. Action—the production of an
effect—as to anger;—VI. Passion—the endurance of an action—as
to be angered;—VII. The Where, the place in which a substance
is, to which it is going, or from which it is coming—as In Paris,
To Rome, From Athens;—VIII. The When, or *the point of time*
as distinguished from the time mentioned in II., which is time *how
long*, or duration. The *When* is denoted thus; to-morrow, a month
ago, on the 1st of May: the *how long* thus;—an hour, a day, a year, a
century, &c.;—IX. Position in Space. This does not refer to the *where*,
as VII., but to the *how*—as sitting, standing, oblique;—X. Habit or
Dress—that which is put upon another,—Attire, as in the poet—

> " Why look you there! see how it steals away!
> My father, in his *Habit* as he lived!
> Look, where he goes, even now out at the portal." *

The II., III., IV., and V. are essential attributes—the VI., VII., VIII.,
IX., and X. are circumstantial. The teachings of this paragraph may
perhaps be more impressively represented to the mind by the subjoined
Table, in which the order of arrangement may be readily seen at one
view, viz.:—

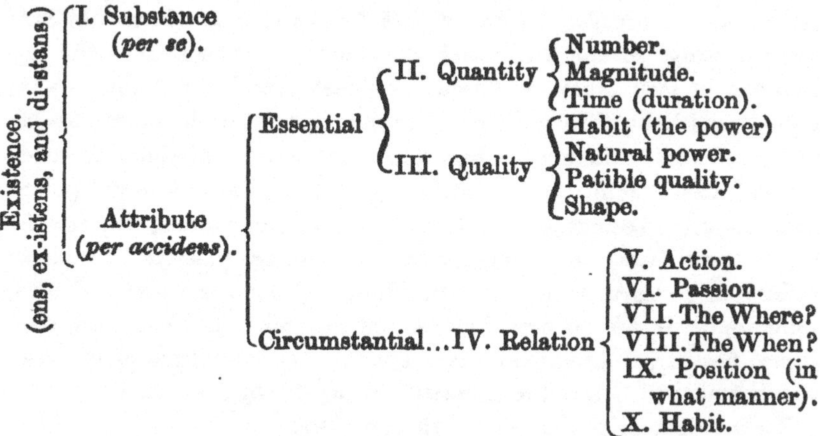

The following Latin Distich may assist some of our readers to
remember the Categories :—

> " Summa decem Substantia, Quantum, Quale, Relatio,
> Actio, Passio, Ubi, Quando, Situs, Habitus."✝

---

* " Hamlet," Act iii., scene 3.

✝ The above lines may be thus translated, viz.:—" The summa genera are ten—Substance, Quantity, Quality, Relation, Action, Passion, Where, When, Position, and Habit."

From these Categories the sciences are evolved! for under these every art or science, and every object of human thought is comprehended. Substance is the basis of History, whether Natural or Civil; Quantity, of Mathematics; Quality and Quantity conjoined, of Optics and Medicine; Relation, of Ethics; Action and Quantity, of Astronomy, Music, and Mechanics; Passion and Action, of Electricity; the Where, of Geography; the When, of Chronology; Position and Quality, of Sculpture; Habit and Position, of Painting; and other arts and sciences similarly. Now when any one thinks upon this attempt to classify, arrange, and systematize the objects of knowledge, imperfect and unsuited to the scientific wants of our own age, as it undoubtedly is, he cannot but be struck with the masterly character of that mind which could thus map out the several elements of knowledge. And though it has been compared to a classification "of animals into men, quadrupeds, horses, asses, and ponies;" yet it would be difficult to point to any attempt at classification which has been more successful, or is more complete, whether it be that of Locke, Hume, Kant, Hegel, Brown, or Cousin.* No one can be blind to the importance of such an arrangement and orderly disposition of the objectivities of thought: it marks an era in thinking; for when the mind begins to apprehend not only objects, but their relations and attributes, it is easy to see that the elements of a μεθοδος—a *transit-path* from the idea of one object to the knowledge of another, have been attained. Prior to this, the conceptions of men must have been somewhat chaotically mingled—"an undistinguishable throng;" but after this, distinction becomes possible, and methodical thinking has begun to acquire the indispensable condition of practicability. The strivings of the human thought-powers seem about to become successful in subduing surrounding objectivities to its own laws, and thus making Reasoning possible. Such an endeavour to learn the laws of the ideative powers is worthy of being signalized. It, for the first time, shows that all is not confused, transitory, fleeting, and immethodical; but that there are fixed mental laws which limit and reduce the apparent infinity of objects.

To the Catagories succeed the theory of the

PREDICABLES.—The logical predicables constitute a fivefold division of the *relations* which Common Names bear to each other, with reference to what they denote in the particular subject about which discourse is held, and may be thus defined:—Genus, the similar part of the essential qualities of objects; the coinciding and agreeing attributes of

---

* See an important article on this subject, entitled, "The Conditions of the Thinkable," in Sir Wm. Hamilton's "Discussions," p. 577.

specifically differing external existences : Species, the essential attributes of any particular object—that which constitutes it what it *is* : Difference, that attribute which essentially distinguishes one object from another : Property, any other essential, inherent attribute, except the differentiating one : Accident, any attribute not essentially involved in our idea of an object, and which may exist or not, without materially altering our idea of its nature. Thus, when we assert that Man is a rational animal who can speak, *Animal* expresses the Genus ; *Rational Animal*, the Species ; *Rational*, the Difference ; *can speak*, the Property ; and were we to say of any one man that he is *tall, ignorant, fair complexioned*, or named *John*, these words would respectively express the Accidents of his nature. Were we, however, to say that an animal is an organised being, endowed with the power of voluntary motion, *Being* would indicate the Genus ; *Organised Being*, the Species ; *Organised*, the Difference ; *Voluntary Motion*, the Property ; and furry, feathered, &c., would, if added, constitute the Accidents. Thus we see that Predicables are merely *relative* divisions, which we can use according to the purport of our discourse. They imply no necessary difference in the words we use, but merely the relative signification of our words as regards the subject with which our present predication is concerned.

These may be tabularly arranged thus, viz. :—

Genus (γενος).
Differentia (διαφορα). } Species (ειδος.) { Proprium (ιδιόν).
{ Accidens (συμβεβηκος).

"It is to be remarked of these distinctions, that they express, not what the predicate is in its own meaning, but what relation it bears to the subject of which it happens, on the particular occasion, to be predicated. There are not some names which are exclusively *genera*, and others which are exclusively *differentiæ*; but the same name is referred to one or another Predicable according to the subject of which it is predicated on the particular occasion. *Animal*, for instance, is a genus with respect to *man* or *John*; a species with respect to *Substance* or *Being*. *Rectangular* is one of the *differentiæ* of a geometrical square ; it is merely one of the *accidentia* of the table at which I am writing. The words Genus, Species, &c., are therefore relative terms ; they are names applied to certain predicates, to express the relation between them and some given subject ; a regulation grounded, as we shall see, not on what the predicate *connotes*, but on the class which it *denotes*, and on the place which, in some given classification, that class occupies relatively to the particular subject."*

It ought, however, to be mentioned, that the above-given exposition

* J. S. Mill's "System of Logic," Book I., chap. vii., par. 2, p. 134.

of the predicables, although that which is commonly received, is not precisely the Aristotelic doctrine; it is, however, legitimately founded upon what he taught in the first Book of "The Topics." This classification was expounded by Porphyry, the chief of the Neo-platonic School, who was born in or near Tyre about A.D. 232, and died about 312, in his work on "The Categories which now form the introduction to the 'Organon' of Aristotle."

A brief outline of the scheme elaborated by "the mighty Stagyrite" may, not inappropriately, be given here, in order that our readers may see the points of difference between the two classifications. Every proposition asserts regarding a subject one of the four following predicables, viz. :—

I. Genus (γενος); II. Property (ἰδιόν); III. Definition (ὅρος); IV. Accident (συμβεβηκος).

These may be arranged tabularly thus, viz. :—

PREDICABLES	Capable of becoming Subjects—convertible	Definition. Property.
	Incapable of becoming Subjects entire—inconvertible	Genus. Accident.

It will be seen that in this classification *Differentia* holds no place. It, like the Genus, *may* be predicated of many things which differ in species, and hence its absence from the Aristotelic *Predicabilia* has been accounted for thus:—"The Species may be regarded as composed, not of the marks of the Genus and the difference, so well as of those of two concurrent or communicant genera: for the difference is but a genus which, from its overlapping part of another, is used as a distinctive mark of that part which it overlaps. If (for an easy example) in analysing our notion of the red-flowering currant—Ribes Sanguineum —we regard 'currant' as the *genus*, and 'red-flowering' as the *difference*, we may also regard 'red-flowering' as a wide *genus*, wider, in fact, than 'currant,' and therefore we may say that our notion of the plant is formed from the concurrence of two genera. Let A be the class of 'red-flowering' things, B the class 'currant;' then X the part of each which is in the other will be our notion of 'red-flowering currant.' " *

It must of course have been observed that the *Genus* is a more abstract form of thought than the Species, and hence that the genus *has* the greater *extension*, and the species the greater *comprehension*.†

* Thomson's "Laws of Thought," Part II., par. 60, p. 147.
† See for an explanation of these terms p. 137.

Genera are either *summa* (highest) or *subalterna* (subalternate);
Species are either *subalternæ* (subalternate) or *infimæ* (lowest).

A Genus Summum, or highest genus, is the highest class in a scale of classification; one which is not treated as a *species;* having, in the given classification, no genus above it.

A Genus Subalternum, successive or inferior genus, is one which is alternately a species in subordination to a genus summum and a genus to subordinate species.

A Species Subalterna, successive or inferior species, is one which, while comprehended under a genus, is itself divisible into other species.

Subalternate genera and species are interchangeable names.

A Species Infima, or lowest species, sometimes called species proper, indicates the earliest step in classification, and contains individuals only; it is not divisible into other species, but is the lowest subdivision, in the given classification, of which a genus is capable.

When a *genus* is divided into species they are called *co-ordinate* or *cognate species:* to indicate that they are not subordinate to each other.

The *genus* of which they are cognate species is called *Proximate;* that to which they are related as their genus summum is called *Remote.*

The following rules regulate reasoning from genera and species, viz.:

1st. Whatever may be asserted of the genus may be asserted also of the species.

2nd. That which cannot be asserted of the genus cannot be received as an adequate statement of all that is implied in the species.

3rd. Whenever an assertion is made involving the whole of the qualities contained in the species, the qualities contained in the genus must be mentioned.

4th. Whatever is true of the whole genus is not necessarily the whole of the truth regarding the species.

Differentia is either generic or specific; generic difference is that which constitutes subalternate species; specific difference is that which constitutes infimæ species.

The peculiar characteristics which distinguish the individuals contained in infimæ species constitutes the numerical difference.

Proprium is of two kinds—viz., *generic* or *specific;* generic, when it necessarily accompanies or results from the essential quality implied in the *summum* or *subalternate genera;* specific, when it is implied in the essence of the species infima.

A generic proprium is predicable, not only of species, but also of the various individuals comprehended in a species; specific property is only predicable of the individuals of a species. The following law relates to the *proprium*—viz., *Wherever a differentia exists, therein is implied the existence of a species and a specific property.*

Accidens is of two kinds—viz., separable and inseparable; separable, when it can be regarded as absent in the individual; inseparable, when the individual cannot be conceived of in its entirety without thinking of it.

It is evident that the *Predicabilia* are an analysis of the process of thought implied in Generalization, and that the aforementioned categories may be denominated the "*summa genera*" of things *thought of as objective.*

The processes implied in the formation of ideas may be thus exhibited—viz., Sensation + Reflection = Perception + Memory + Abstraction + Generalization = Ideation. The several steps and processes which result in the excitation of the latter power have been excellently summed up as follow—viz., "1. The nature of every higher notion is found in the lower; consequently, 2. The name of the higher may always be applied to the lower. Thus, Man may be called an animal because the marks of life and sensation, which distinguish animals, are found in him. 3. The higher notion (genus) includes the lower notion (species) with other species, and is consequently of wider *extension* than it. But the species implies more *marks*—has a fuller definition—than the genus; and is said, therefore, to be of deeper *intension* [*i. e.*, of greater comprehension] than it. 4. That set of marks which distinguishes any species from the other species in the same genus is called its specific difference. 5. The whole nature of a species is ascertained, and its definition given, when the properties of the genus and those which make the specific difference are brought together. 6. We ascend from lower conceptions to higher by throwing away specific differences, *i. e.*, by Abstraction. We descend to lower ones by resuming the marks we have thrown away, *i. e.*, by Determination. 7. In a system of subordinate genera each must contain the individuals included in the lowest. 8. Co-ordinate species cannot contain the same individuals. 9. The conception of an object consists of the aggregate of its marks, with the notion of existence superadded. 10. Singular objects [*i. e.*, individuals] are invariably referred to and viewed through general conceptions. 11. A conception is complete and adequate when it can be resolved at pleasure into its implied marks by definition, and into its contained species by Division." *

Of the signs of Ideas, *i. e.*, Terms. Words are signs invented

---

* Thomson's "Laws of Thought," Part I., par. 66, p. 140.

by the mind, and employed by the general agreement and consent of men, to indicate the results of Ideation, *i.e.*, to name, and by this means be enabled to communicate, their thoughts.* Words are, therefore, the signs of ideas. A Term is the logical name of such words as express ideas, thought of *objectively, i. e.*, such words as are capable of becoming either the subjects or predicates of a logical proposition. In other and more correct phraseology, *A Logical term is a significant word which does not express relation or time.*

Logical Terms are variously divided into singular, or proper, and common; abstract and concrete; univocal and equivocal; absolute and relative; definite and indefinite; positive and privative; compatible and incompatible, &c.

A Singular Term denotes only one object of thought; as, this universe, that poem, a soldier, Queen Victoria, &c.

A Proper Term represents only one object of thought by a name appropriated, in the same sense, only to that individual idea; as, Cæsar, Aristotle, &c.

A Common Term applies, in the same sense, to each and every one of a class of objects ; as, man, city, empire, &c.

Every proper term is also a singular term, although the reverse does not hold; a common term may be made singular by prefixing a limitative word.

An Abstract Term is the name of an attribute regarded apart from the subjects in which it is usually found; *i. e.*, as an individual substance, *pro tempore, e. g.*, rotundity, prudence, length, &c.

A Concrete Term is the name of a quality regarded as existing in some object of thought and implying that object; as, round, prudent, long, &c.

A Univocal Term has only one signification to whatever object of thought it may be applied; as, sagacity, man, &c.

An Equivocal Term is one which has various significations, according to the object of thought to which it is applied; as, sting, review, post, &c.

These are sometimes called Analogous terms from having one meaning, with various modifications and applications resulting from our perception of analogies or other associations.

* The question of "the Origin of Language," in its full extent, is one upon which it would be injudicious in us to insist here. A full view of the opinions of the author of this work upon that topic may be found in his Articles on Rhetoric contributed to " The British Controversialist" in the early part of 1852. A debate upon the same topic—though in *that* the present writer took no part—appeared in the pages of the same magazine in the latter portion of 1851. To these we refer our readers for farther information.

Absolute Terms are such as have a complete or independent meaning—a meaning wholly contained within itself; as, London, Alexander, &c.

A Relative Term is one which, besides *denoting* its own object, *connotes* another idea called its correlative; as, master, which *connotes* servant; teacher, pupil, &c.

A Definite Term is one to which a negative particle is *not* prefixed.

An Indefinite Term is one to which a negative particle is prefixed.

The division of Terms into *definite* and *indefinite* is the foundation of the Dichotomous or Bifurcate system of division—that, namely, which employs a positive affirmation in one of the condividends and a corresponding negation in the other; *e.g.*, sentient and non-sentient; corporeal and incorporeal; animate and inanimate, &c.[*]

A Positive Term is one in which a quality is spoken of as being possessed, at present, by an object of thought; as, a *thoughtful* man, *pleasant* society, &c.

A Privative Term is one which expresses an object considered as not employing one of its capacities—*i. e.*, being, as it were, for the time deprived of it; as, a man not speaking, a horse motionless, &c.

Compatible Terms are such as may be predicated of one and the same object at one and the same time; as, a house *small*, but *elegant;* a work *popular*, and *undeserving* of its popularity, &c.

Incompatible Terms are either Contradictory or Contrary. "Two marks, which stand to each other as positive and privative, like *wise* and *unwise*, are called *Contradictory*, because it would be a contradiction in terms to assign them at the same time to the same object. Two marks are called *Contrary* when it is known *a posteriori*, by experience, and not *a priori*, by the very form of the expression, that they cannot belong to the same object; as, *wise* and *wicked, warm* and *frozen*."

Proper Terms are called *Non-connotative*. All concrete Common Terms are called connotative; they denote a subject and imply an attribute.

We may add a few sentences in explanation of two words employed in reference to terms which are to be found in all logical treatises, and which has occurred in the preceding and will frequently recur in the subsequent portions of this work, viz.—Extension and Comprehension;—by the former is meant, the aggregate of all the individuals of which a term may be affirmed or denied; while by the latter is signified the aggregate of all the simple ideas which unitedly make up the complex idea which the term denotes. They are both significant of aggregates; but in the former the parts are *individuals*, and taken separately; and in the latter the parts are *ideas*, and taken collectively—*e. g.*, the term "dog" may be applied to

* See this system fully explained in Bentham's Works, Vol. VIII.

every individual of the species of animal of which that word is the name-sign—as, mastiffs, greyhounds, beagles, terriers, foxhounds, &c.; and this is the *extension* of the term. Again: the same term may be considered as including in its signification the ideas of life, sensation, voluntary motion, four-footedness, &c., which constitute the properties of that kind of creature; and these united ideas are the *comprehension* of the term. Hence results the logical rule, *the greater the extension the less the comprehension of a term, and the greater the comprehension of a term, the less the extension of it*—*e.g.*, the term "animal" has a greater extension than the term "man," because it can be predicated of man, bird, beast, &c.; but the term "man" has a greater comprehension, for it contains not only all the ideas included in the word "animal," but also those of speech-power, risibility, moral perception, progressiveness, rationality, &c., which belong to that "paragon of animals"—man. So if we take the Series—Being, Material Being, Animal, Mammal, Man, European, Englishman, Londoner, John Smith; John Smith, Clothier; John Smith, Clothier, Charing Cross;—we shall find that each is greater in extension, and less in comprehension, than its sequent.

DIVISION.—Division, in its literal signification, means the separating into its component parts of any really existing whole. This is *Physical Division*, which is always employed upon integral wholes, the constituents of which are integrants or parts of a whole; it consists in the partition or subdivision of individuals into portions. Logical, Metaphysical, or Ideal Division, however, is employed in a secondary or figurative sense to denote the distinct enumeration of all the species included in a genus, descending regularly and systematically from the summum genus of the given class through the proximate, *i. e.*, subalternate genera and species, until all the co-ordinate species of which the idea of the genus is made up, be exhaustively exhibited; *e. g.*, If we take the term "*Tree*," and say it is composed of *root, trunk, leaves, branches, seed-vessels,* &c., we employ Physical Division; again, if we take the term "Tree" and divide it into *endogenous, exogenous,* and *acrogenous,* we employ a Logical Division, as we should do, also, if we divided it into *oak, elm, ash, birch,* &c.

The rules of Division are as follow, viz. :—

1st. We should divide our subject according to the design we have in view.

2nd. We should begin with the highest genus and proceed regularly through the intermediate and subalternate genera and species as far as is necessary.

3rd. All the constituent species must make up the idea implied in the genus.

4th. The several constituent species of each *genus* should exclude each other.

5th. We must be careful to keep in mind *the principle of division* with which we set out.

6th. We ought not to subdivide unnecessarily.

7th. Whatever may be affirmed of the whole genus may be affirmed of each of its contained species.

PROPOSITIONS.—Having now so far expounded the doctrine of Terms, we must now proceed to explain those combinations of terms which imply the operation of the faculty of Judgment, *i. e.*, Propositions. Language, we have already remarked, is articulate sound made significant by the agreement of those who employ it. It is of two kinds, Predicative and Non-Predicative. Predicative speech constitutes Propositions. Definitions of the chief distinctions of propositions have already been given.* Propositions are now, however, to be considered in a new point of view—viz., that which in logical phrase is denominated "the Affections of Proposition." These are of two kinds—1st, Absolute; 2nd, Relative. The Absolute Affections of Propositions are Quantity and Quality. The Relative ones are Subalternation, Opposition, and Conversion.

Quantity.—Quantity is the determination of the extension of the subject of a proposition; it is either universality or particularity. Propositions with regard to quantity are therefore Universal or Particular. A Universal Proposition is one the subject of which is distributed— *e.g.*, taken in its entire extension. If it be a Universal name, the universality will require to be indicated by some sign—as, "all, every, none;" but if it be a proper name, no such mark is required, because being applicable to one individual only, it must always be taken in its entire extension. A Particular Proposition is one whose subject is not distributed—*i. e.*, is not taken in its entire extension. The subject must be a universal name; and to show that it is taken particularly, it has usually a mark of particularity placed before it—as, "some, many, a few," &c. When it has not this mark its quantity is *indefinite*.

Quality.—Quality is denotative of the kind of predication made in the proposition: it is either affirmative or negative; and with regard to their quality, propositions are so called. An Affirmative Proposition is one in which the predicate contains the entire extension of the subject of the proposition. This will happen when the entire comprehension

* See *ante*, Chapter V.

of the predicate is included in the entire comprehension of the subject. A Negative Proposition is one in which the entire extension of the subject is excluded from the predicate. This will occur when there is one idea or more contained in the entire comprehension of the predicate than is contained in the entire comprehension of the subject.

The absolute affections of PROPOSITIONS are, therefore, two, viz.—

QUANTITY, *as to which they are*
- Universal—in which the whole *subject* is asserted to agree or disagree with the *Predicate*.
- Particular—in which a part only of the *subject* is asserted to agree or disagree with the *Predicate*.

QUALITY, *as to which they are*
- Affirmative—in which the predicate is asserted *to agree* with the subject.
- Negative—in which the predicate is asserted *not to agree* with the subject.

The four properties of propositions thus educed from Quantity and Quality are, for the sake of brevity and ease of remembrance, denoted by the four vowels, A, E, I, O,—which are employed respectively thus: —A, Universal Affirmative; E, Universal Negative; I, Particular Affirmative; O, Particular Negative; and the following monastic couplet has been constructed as a mnemonic aid :—

> " Asserit A, negat E, sed universaliter ambæ;
> Asserit I, negat O, sed particulariter ambo." *

The following table will show the different relations of Quantity and Quality in propositions :—

Kinds of Propositions.	*Subjects.*	*Predicates.*	*Examples.*
A, Universal Affirmative.	Universal.	Particular.	Every oak is a tree.
E, Universal Negative.	Universal.	Universal.	No horned animal is carnivorous.
I, Particular Affirmative.	Particular.	Particular.	Some men are just.
O, Particular Negative.	Particular.	Universal.	Some flowers are not fragrant.

If this table be attentively considered, the correctness of the following rules regarding Quantity and Quality will become evident :—

1st. All *universal,* but no *particular,* propositions distribute—*i. e.,* take in its entire extension, the *subject.*

---

* A asserts, E denies, but both are universal;
I asserts, O denies, but both are particular.

2nd. All negative, but no affirmative, propositions distribute the *predicate*.

3rd. Anything whatever affirmed or denied respecting any term distributed, may with equal truth be affirmed or denied of anything contained in the entire extension of that term; for, as in the extension of a term *every* individual is included of which that term may be predicated, that which may be predicated of *all* must necessarily be capable of being predicated of each—*e. g.*, Let it be affirmed that " animals have the power of voluntary motion ;" that affirmation must be equally true of Lion, Man, John Smith, or Pompey (a dog).

Subalternation.—Subalternation is the deduction of a particular proposition from a universal one, without the transposition of its terms—*e. g.*, All human laws are imperfect : *ergo*, some human laws are imperfect.   The universal proposition is technically called the *subalternant ;* the particular one educed, the *subalternate*.   There are two rules of subalternation which require particular attention—viz.,

1st. The truth of the universal implies the truth of the particular, and the falsehood of the particular the falsehood of the universal.

2nd. The truth of the particular does not imply the truth of the universal, nor the falsehood of the universal the falsehood of the particular.   Hence,

3rd. From a true subalternant a false subalternate cannot follow; but a false subalternant may give a true subalternate.

Subalternation enables us from A to deduce I, as, A, All plants grow —I, Some plant grows ; and from E to infer O, as, E, No thief is trustworthy—O, Some thieves are not trustworthy.

Opposition.—Opposition is the disagreement, either in Quantity or Quality, or in Quality alone, of propositions having the same subjects and predicates.   It is of three kinds—Contradiction, Contrariety, and Sub-contrariety.

Contradiction is opposition both in *Quantity* and *Quality* in propositions whose subjects and predicates are the same—between universal affirmatives and particular negatives, and universal negatives and particular affirmatives—*i. e.*, between A and O, E and I—*e. g.*, A, Every oak is a tree—O, Some oaks are not trees ; E, No horned animal is carnivorous—I, Some horned animals are carnivorous.   Two contradictory propositions can never be both true or both false.   One is always true, and the other false ; it follows as a consequence, therefore, that if the one be true, the other is false, and if the one be false the other is true.

Contrariety is opposition in *Quality* alone—between universal affirmatives and universal negatives, having the same subjects and predicates—*e.g.*, A, All planets revolve round the sun—E, No planets revolve round the sun. Contrary propositions may both of them be false, but cannot both be true. From the *truth* of the one, the *falsity* of the other may be inferred; but the *falsity* of the one is *no datum* for the *truth* of the other.

Sub-contrariety is opposition in *Quality* alone—between particular affirmatives and particular negatives, having the same subjects and predicates—*e.g.*, I, Some men are just—O, Some men are not just. In sub-contrary propositions both may be true, but both cannot be false. From this it is evident that from the *falsity* of one, the *truth* of the other is deducible; but from the *truth* of the one, the *falsity* of the other cannot be inferred. The correctness of the one does not imply the incorrectness of the other. In opposite propositions, the following rule holds good—viz., *In necessary matters—i.e., what cannot be otherwise—all affirmations are true, and all negatives false; in impossible matters—i.e., what cannot be—all negatives are true, and all affirmatives are false; in contingent matters—i.e., what may or may not be—all universals are false, and all particulars true.*

An attentive study of the following scheme, which we have copied from Whateley's "Logic," will readily illustrate the truth of what is asserted in the above paragraph on "Opposition:"—

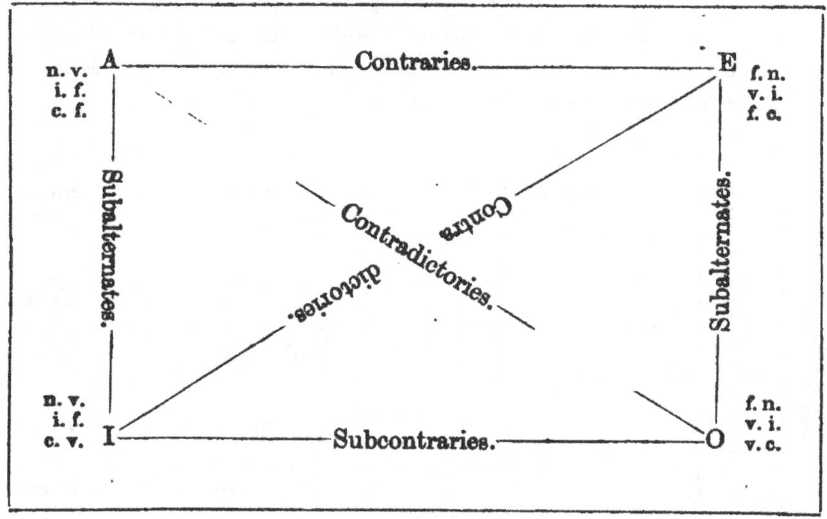

The letters *n, i, c,* signify, respectively, necessary, impossible, and contingent matter; and *v, f—verum,* true—and *falsum,* false.

Perhaps, however, the following table, copied from "A Syllabus of

"Logic," by Thomas Solly, Esq., may be more readily understood; at least, it may serve as a key to the easy comprehension of that which precedes it:—

Opposition.

Contradictory.

		If one is	the other is
Between A and O		True	False.
		False	True.
Between E and I		True	False.
		False	True.

Contrary.

		If one is	the other is
Between A and E		True	False.
		False	Contingent.

Sub-Contrary.

		If one is	the other is
Between I and O		False	True.
		True	Contingent.

Subalternation.

Between A and I:

If A is	True	then I is	True.
	False		Contingent.
If I is	True	then A is	Contingent.
	False		False.

Between E and O:

If E is	True	then O is	True.
	False		Contingent.
If O is	True	then E is	Contingent.
	False		False.

We shall subjoin another scheme in which the doctrine of "Opposition" has been very clearly elaborated. It is extracted from Munro's "Manual of Logic:"—

Opposition.

Subalternate.

Between A and I:

	A	I
N, True		True.
I, False		False.
C, False		True.

Between E and O:

	E	O
N, False		False.
I, True		True.
C, False		True.

Contrary.

Between A and E:

	A	E
N, True		False.
I, False		True.
C, False		False.

Sub-Contrary.

Between I and O:

	I	O
N, True		False.
I, False		True.
C, True		True.

Opposition. Contradictory.

Between A and O . . . .

	A		O
N, True	. . . .		False.
I, False	. . . .		True.
C, False	. . . .		True.

Between E and I . . . .

	E		I
N, False	. . . .		True.
I, True	. . . .		False.
C, False	. . . .		True.

Conversion.—Conversion is the inference of one proposition from another, by the transposition of the subject into the place of the predicate, and of the predicate into the place of the subject, in such a manner as to preserve both the truth and the Quality of the proposition. The transposed proposition is called the *convertend* or *exposita*, the inferred one is denominated the *converse*. No Conversion is permitted *except the truth of the converse is implied in the truth of the convertend*. Then it is called *Illative* Conversion.

Illative Conversion is of three kinds—Simple, Accidental, and Contrapositional.

Simple conversion takes place when the quantity and quality of the *convertend* are preserved in the *converse*, so that if the one is universal or particular, affirmative or negative, the other is so likewise. This can only occur when the subject and predicate of a proposition are co-extensive, *i.e.*, when both are *distributed*. All universal negatives or particular affirmatives admit of conversion, and yet preserve the truth—*e.g.*, E, no horned animal is carnivorous; No carnivorous animal is horned. I, Some statesmen are Protestants; Some Protestants are statesmen.

Accidental conversion, otherwise called conversion *per accidens*, or by limitation, occurs when after the transposition of the terms the quality of the *convertend* is preserved while the quantity is limited or lessened in the converse. In such conversion, the affirmation or negation remains unchanged, but a universal *convertend* is *converted* into a particular *converse*. Universal affirmatives and negatives allow of accidental conversion by the use of subalternation. The converse always becomes particular—*e.g.*, A, Every oak is a tree, is changed, firstly, by subalternation, into I, Some oaks are trees, and then by conversion *per accidens*, Some trees are oaks; and E, No horned animal is carnivorous, by subalternation becomes, No carnivorous animal is horned, whence O, Some carnivorous animals are not horned.

Contrapositional conversion, or conversion by negation.—This takes place when the terms are transposed, and the *contradictory of the predicate* is put for the *subject*, and the *quality* of the proposition is changed. Particular negatives and universal affirmatives admit of such conversion. In particular negatives the quality is changed by transposing the negation-sign from the copula to the predicate, and then employing simple conversion—*e.g.*, O, Some stars are not planets, becomes I, Some things not planets are stars. In universal affirmatives the terms are transposed, the negation-sign is attached to the new subject, and thus forms its contradictory—a universal negative; the converse will then be exactly equipollent to the convertend—*e.g.*, A, All men are fallible, becomes, E, All infallible beings are not men, which bears an exact equipollency to E, None but fallible beings are men. This Mnemonicism has been constructed as an aid to the mind in recollecting the laws of conversion—

> "Simpliciter E, I, convertitur; E, A, per accid;
> A, O, per contra; sic fit conversio tota." *

CHAPTER XIV.

RATIOCINATION.—FORMAL LOGIC.

"It will be readily acknowledged that many of the maxims of the School Logic are founded in Truth and Nature, and have so long obtained universal approbation, that they are now become proverbial in philosophy."—BEATTIE.

"The scholar of the first ages received into him the world around; brooded thereon; gave it the new arrangement of his own mind, and uttered it again. It came into him —life; it went out from him—truth. * * * It was dead fact; now it is quick thought. * * * In proportion to the completeness of the distillation, so will the purity and imperishableness of the product be. But none is quite perfect."—EMERSON.

SYLLOGISMS.—A syllogism is an enunciation, in which, from certain admitted propositions, a necessary conclusion is drawn distinct from them, yet employing the same idea. Or a syllogism is such a combination of two judgments, *i. e.*, propositions, as shall necessitate a third as their consequence. When a doubt is entertained on any topic, it becomes, before we can proceed to solve it, a question. To resolve this doubt, and determine the question, we must proceed to compare the ideas contained in the question with some other idea to which they each bear a similar and mutual relation. When this is done correctly, the doubt will be cleared away, and, in the conclusion, the question

---

* E, I, are converted simply; E, A, per accidens; A, O, by contraposition; in these ways all conversion is done.

will be answered. There are, thus, in every process of argumentation, three parts;—1st, The thing concerning which the question is asked; 2nd, The question asked concerning it; 3rd, The mutually agreeing common term with which they are compared. These are denominated respectively the *minor, major,* and *middle* terms; and the sentence in which the *first* and *third* are compared together is called the *minor premiss;* that in which the *second* and *third* are compared, the *major premiss;* and the one which contains the comparison of the *first* and *second,* the conclusion; *e. g.,* question, Does the moon shine by her own light?

       (*Middle Term.*)   (*Major Term.*)
No body which changes its phases | shines by its own light; (*Major Premiss.*)

  (*Minor Term.*)   (*Middle Term.*)
  The moon | is a body that changes its phases ; (*Minor Premiss*).
    (*Minor Term.*)   (*Major Term.*)
  Therefore, the moon | does not | shine by its own light; *Conclusion.*

The terms and premisses may be thus distinguished, viz.:—1st. The *predicate* of the conclusion is the *major* term; and the premiss in which it is contained, is the major premiss. 2nd. The *subject* of the conclusion is the *minor* term; and the premiss in which it is contained, the *minor* premiss. 3rd. That term which is common to both premisses is the *middle* term.

FIGURE is the technical term employed to designate the classification of syllogisms according to the various positions the *middle term* is able to occupy. This position, it is evident, can only be varied fourfold, as it can only be, I., The subject of the major proposition, and the predicate of the minor; II., The predicate in both; III., The subject in both; IV., The predicate of the major, and the subject of the minor, proposition. These, then, respectively, as numbered, constitute the *four* syllogistic figures: thus exhibitable, viz.:—

I. M P	II. P M	III. M P	IV. P M
S M	S M	M S	M S
S P	S P	S P	S P

Where S = Subject, P = Predicate, and M = Middle term.

MOOD is also a technicalism. It expresses those *modifications* or changes which take place in syllogisms, in consequence of their differences in quantity or quality. Now, as there are four different kinds of propositions, marked by the symbols A, E, I, O, and as each one of these four kinds may form any one of the three propositions, which unitedly form a syllogism, from a merely arithmetical view, it would appear that there would be sixty-four moods, as all the possible methods of combining them by threes amount to that number (4+4+4=64). This is only true numerically, however; for fifty-four of these either violate the rules which govern the formation of syllogisms, or are either unnecessarily intricate, irregular, and involved, or useless, and have, in consequence thereof, been discarded. Some of the remaining ten, again, are employed only in certain figures, as they contravene some one or more of the rules of the other figures. This causes certain other retrenchments; so that, in all the figures and moods together, the valid forms of syllogism amount only to *nineteen*.

The undershown table will exhibit at one view the position of the terms in each of these figures, and the moods validly employable in them :—

Fig. I.   *Moods.*

	1	2	3	4
Middle, Major	A	E	A	E
Minor, *Middle*	A	A	I	I
Minor, Major	A	E	I	O

Fig. II.   *Moods.*

	1	2	3	4
Major, *Middle*	E	A	E	A
Minor, *Middle*	A	E	I	O
Minor, Major	E	E	O	O

Fig. III.   *Moods.*

	1	2	3	4	5	6
Middle, Major.	A	I	A	E	O	E
Middle, Minor.	A	A	I	A	A	I
Minor, Major ..	I	I	I	O	O	O

Fig. IV.   *Moods.*

	1	2	3	4	5
Major, *Middle* ...	A	A	I	E	E
Middle, Minor ...	A	E	A	A	I
Minor, Major	I	E	I	O	O

These, it will be seen, give 4+4+6+5=19. But as E, I, O, is valid in all the moods; E, A, E, common to the first and second; A, I, I, common to the first and third; A, A, I,—I, A, I, and E, A, O, common to the third and fourth; and A, E, E, common to the second and fourth,—the whole sum of the valid and strictly useful moods is *ten*.

The following monastic, doggerel quintet, has been composed, in order, among other purposes, to show the various kinds of propositions entering into each valid syllogism, and the moods which belong to each figure. The other mysteries which it contains will be explained hereafter. Meanwhile, we may intimate that the following words bear the translation which we place after them, viz., *dato primae*, give ye to the first; *secundae*, to the second; *tertia habet*, the third has; *quarta insuper addit*, moreover, the fourth adds.

The words untranslated show the number of the moods, and the italicised vowels in them the order and kind of the propositions :—

Fig. I.   B*a*rb*a*r*a*, C*e*l*a*r*e*nt, D*a*r*ii*, F*e*r*io* dato primae;

Fig. II.   C*e*s*a*r*e*, C*a*m*e*str*e*s, F*e*st*i*n*o*, B*a*r*o*k*o*, secundae;

Fig. III. { Tertia *Darapti, Disimis, Datisi, Felapton,*
{ *Bokardo, Ferison,* habet : Quarta insuper addit,

Fig. IV. Bramantip, *Camenes, Dimaris, Fesapo, Fresison.*

The dictum on which the *rationale* of the syllogism is founded, is, that " whatever is predicable or predicated concerning any term distributed, whether affirmatively or negatively, is predicable, or may be predicated in the same sense, concerning any or everything contained under that distributed term." " Whatever is true of a class is true of everything which can be shown to be a member of that class." The following axioms, too, are worthy of being remembered, namely,—1st. If two things agree, in the same sense, with one and the same third, they agree with one another, in that sense. 2nd. If, of two things, one agrees, and the other disagrees, in the same sense, with one and the same third, they disagree, in that sense, with each other. 3rd. If, of two things, neither agrees with one and the same third, in the same sense, no inference is deducible. 4th. Particular terms are contained in universals, but universals are not contained in particulars. 5th. The aggregation of all the particular terms contained in a universal, is equal to that universal. From these axioms are deduced the following general rules, by which the validity of syllogisms is to be judged. The syllogism which violates *any one* of them cannot be accepted as *formally* true. It is in consequence of their not fulfilling the requirements of these rules that the great number of moods before mentioned have been rejected.

I. The middle term must be distributed, *i.e.,* taken in its entire extension, at least once in the premisses, else the conclusion will be illegitimate. When the middle term is undistributed, it stands only in an ambiguous and equivocal relation to the other terms, and is thus virtually equivalent to two middle terms, the other terms not being compared with one and the same third, but with different parts of the same whole. The first axiom is thus contravened, *e.g.,* from the premisses, *coal is a mineral, granite is a mineral,* it is not at all inferrible that *coal is granite.*

II. No term should be distributed in the conclusion which was not distributed in, at least, one of the premisses. The neglect of this rule would produce an *illicit process* either of the *major* or *minor term.* It would be equivalent to the introduction of a fourth term. It would violate the fourth axiom, by considering a universal as contained in a particular, *e.g., All men educated in universities are intelligent. Artizans are not educated in universities,* will not at all warrant the conclusion, *Artizans are not intelligent.*

"If the *major* or *minor* terms are undistributed in the premisses the predicate and subject must be respectively undistributed in the conclusion. When this rule is violated in a Syllogism whose *major* term is undistributed in the major premiss, but whose *predicate* is distributed in the *conclusion*, the resulting fallacy is called *an illicit process of the major*. When the *minor* term is undistributed in the minor premiss, and the *subject* is distributed in the *conclusion*, the resulting fallacy is called *an illicit process of the minor*." *

Hence, 1st. If the *predicate* of the conclusion is distributed, the major term must be distributed in the major premiss.

2nd. If the *subject* of the conclusion is distributed, the minor term must be distributed in the minor premiss.

III. From two negative premisses no conclusion is deducible. This is a mere repetition of the third axiom; the premisses do not assert any agreement, they only state the fact of the disagreement of their terms with the middle, and, consequently, nothing can be determined regarding the agreement or disagreement of these terms between themselves, *e.g.*, though I assert *Syrius is not a planet*, *Procyon is not a planet*, these dicta prove nothing.

IV. From two affirmative premisses a negative conclusion cannot follow; for, if there be but one middle term, both terms agree with it, and cannot therefore disagree by axiom first.

V. One negative premiss necessitates a negative conclusion. In a negative premiss, the middle term disagrees with the other term, it follows from rule III. that the other premiss must be affirmative, *i.e.*, it must express the agreement of the middle term with the other term, by axiom second, then, they must disagree, and the expression of that disagreement constitutes the conclusion negative.

VI. From two particular premisses nothing can be inferred. For, if they are both affirmative, the middle term will be undistributed, which contravenes rule I. If the one is negative, and the other affirmative, the conclusion must, by rule V., be negative, but the predicate of the negative conclusion must be universal; if it be so, there is no distributed middle term, and rule I. is again violated. By rule V. they cannot both be negative.

VII. If either of the premisses be particular, the conclusion will be particular. If they are both affirmative, to draw a universal conclusion would give an *illicit process*, for a term would be taken distributedly in the conclusion which was undistributed in one of the premisses in opposition to rule II. If one be affirmative, and the other negative,

<hr>

* Solly's " Syllabus of Logic," p. 82.

there will be two particular terms in the premisses, namely, the *predicate* of the *affirmative*, and the *subject* of the *negative proposition*, the *predicate* of the *conclusion* will consequently be *universal* and the *subject particular*, and hence would result a *particular conclusion*.

These rules are also expressed in the following lines, namely,

"Distribuas medium ; nec quartus terminus adsit;
Utraque nec praemissa negans, nec particularis,
Sectetur partem conclusio deteriorem ;
Et non distribuat, nisi cum praemissa, negatve."*

The following are examples of all the Valid Syllogisms as they appear in each Figure and Mood.

FIGURE I.

BAR- *All persons possessed of irresponsible power* are incapable of bearing opposition, or the assertion of the self-rights of others :
BA-   All autocrats are *possessed of irresponsible power ;*
RA.   Therefore, all autocrats are incapable of bearing opposition, or the assertion of the self-rights of others.

CE-   *No delinquency* deserves free pardon :
LA-   All forgery is *delinquency ;*
RENT. Therefore, no forgery deserves free pardon.

DA- *All things productive of social amelioration* deserve attention :
RI- Some sanitary measures are *productive of social amelioration ;*
I.   Therefore, some sanitary measures deserve attention.

FE- *Nothing which impedes commerce* can be ultimately advantageous to the revenue :
RI- Some taxes on exports *impede commerce ;*
O.   Therefore, some taxes on exports cannot be ultimately advantageous to the revenue.

FIGURE II.

CES- No vicious conduct is *praiseworthy :*
A-   All instances of generous devotion are *praiseworthy ;*
RE.   Therefore, no instance of generous devotion is vicious conduct.

CAM- All virtuous actions are *lastingly beneficial :*
ES-   No act of deception is *lastingly beneficial ;*
TRES. Therefore, no act of deception is a virtuous action.

FES- Nothing is right which will *ultimately produce evil :*
TI-   Some kinds of company-keeping will *ultimately produce evil ;*
NO.   Therefore, some kinds of company-keeping are not right.

BA-   All the truly noble are *virtuous :*
ROK- Some who are called noble are not *virtuous ;*
O.   Some who are called noble are not truly so.

---

* Thou shalt distribute the middle, nor let four terms be present:
And neither may both premisses be negative or particular ;
The conclusion must always follow the weaker part,
And it shall not distribute or deny unless when (one of) the premisses do so.

FIGURE III.

DA- *All kinds of lightning* are attracted by trees, water, metallic substances, &c.:
RAP- *All kinds of lightning* are dangerous;
TI.   Some dangerous things are attracted by trees, water, metallic substances, &c.

DIS- *Some things which increase the difficulty of gaining foreign articles* cause
         smuggling:
AM- *All things which increase the difficulty of gaining foreign articles* are high
         import duties;
IS.   Therefore, some high import duties cause smuggling.

DA- *All taxes not proportioned to the condition of those who pay them* are unjust:
TIS- *Some of the taxes which are not proportioned to the condition of those paying
         them* are the window tax, the advertisement tax, the income tax, &c.;
I.   Therefore, the window tax, the advertisement tax, the income tax, &c., are unjust.

FE- *No branch of science can be made* absolutely perfect:
LAP- *All branches of science* are worthy of diligent culture;
TON. Some things worthy of diligent culture cannot be made absolutely perfect.

BOK- *Some truly noble-minded men* are not philosophers:
AR- *All truly noble-minded men* are worthy of admiration;
DO.   Some who are worthy of admiration are not philosophers.

FE- *No wise man pursues that,* in the attainment of which he thinks he will be
         unsuccessful:
RIS- *Some wise men* pursue fame;
ON.   Some who pursue fame think they will not be unsuccessful in gaining it.

FIGURE IV.

BRAM- All the wonderful operations of Nature are *continually in action:*
AN-   *All things that are continually in action* do not surprise us;
TIP.   Some things that do not surprise us are the wonderful operations of Nature.

CAM- All miracles are *things of rare occurrence:*
E-   *No things of rare occurrence* make a slight impression on the mind;
NES. None of the things which make a slight impression on the mind are miracles.

DIM- Some taxes on the necessaries of life are *oppressive:*
A-   *All that is oppressive* ought to be repealed;
RIS.   Some taxes on the necessaries of life ought to be repealed.

FES- No immoral acts are *permitted as amusements:*
A-   *All that is permitted as amusements* is calculated to inspire joy;
PO.   Some things calculated to inspire joy are not immoral acts.

FRES- No acts of injustice are *legitimate means of enrichment:*
IS-   *Some legitimate means of enrichment* fail;
ON.   Some things fail that are not acts of injustice.

It cannot have escaped the notice of any one who has attentively studied the examples of syllogisms which we have given, that those of the first figure are more natural in their form, possess the power of placing the truth most obviously before the mind, and that they yield conclusions of all the four sorts, namely, affirmative, negative, universal, and particular. The syllogisms of the first figure gain this completeness of comparison, this clearness, immediatcy, and directness, from their strict accordancy with the Aristotelic *dictum*. It is, on this account, looked upon as the perfect mood, while all others are esteemed imperfect ones. The principles on which the other figures depend, however, are quite conformable to the dictum, as well as to the principles, of *common sense*. They are these:—Fig. 2. If any quality, property, or attribute, is universally predicable of any certain class of objects, any object which does not, or class of objects which do not, possess that quality, &c., cannot possibly belong to that class; or, if a quality, &c., is universally predicable, as not existing in any member of any class, any object which does, or class of objects which do, possess that quality, &c., is manifestly predicable as not belonging to that class; hence, all the conclusions of the second figure are negative. Fig. 3. If two qualities, properties, or attributes, belong to the same class, or the same part of a class, they *may coexist* in the same class, or part of a class; but, if one of the two qualities, &c., belong to the same class, or the same part of a class, and the other be excluded from that class, or part of a class, they do not invariably coexist in the same class, and hence the conclusion of the third figure must be particular. Fig. 4. If a whole class, or any part of it, be contained in another, and that other in a third, the first class must contain some members of that third; again, if a whole class, or any part of it, is excluded from another which is wholly or partly contained in a third, the first is in part excluded from that third; but, on the contrary, if one class is universally contained in another from which a third is completely excluded, that third is wholly excluded from the first; hence, in the fourth figure, we cannot have a universal affirmative conclusion. To obviate these imperfections, a method has been contrived by which the imperfect moods of these three figures may be changed into the perfect moods of the first, by certain alterations in the terms or propositions of which the syllogisms consist; this is designated REDUCTION OF SYLLOGISMS. The imperfect mood to be reduced is the *Reducend;* that to which it is reducible, the *Reduct;* and the object of the operation is so to alter the forms of the syllogisms, declared to be legitimate in the several moods of the second, third, and fourth figures, as to produce equally valid ones in the first, either preserving the same conclusion, or producing one which, by conversion, will become its equivalent, or contradictory. Reduction is of two kinds, Direct and Indirect.

Direct or Ostensible Reduction is employed, when, from the transposition or conversion of the premisses contained in a syllogism of the imperfect mood, we gain one which yields the same conclusion in a perfect mood, or else one from which the same conclusion is immediately inferrible by conversion.

Indirect Reduction, or, *Reductio ad impossibile vel ad absurdum*, is used when, by taking the contradictory of the conclusion, and one of the premises, we deduce a conclusion which contradicts the other premises—when we do not prove that the conclusion of the Reducend is true, but that it cannot be false, or that an absurdity would be the result of supposing it untrue. In a prior page, we gave a few doggerel verses, some portion of the mysteries of which we then explained, and promised to elucidate the others at another time. That period has come; and we now remark, that these lines are so constructed as to indicate the method of procedure which each mood requires for its *reduction*. The initial letters—B, C, D, F—point out to which mood of the first figure—Barbara, Celarent, Darii, Ferio, respectively—the given moods may be altered; *M*, signifies *mutandis praemissis*, i.e., the premisses being transposed; *S*, indicates that the proposition symbolized by the vowel preceding it should be converted simply; *P*, that the conversion should be *per accidens*, or, by limitation; *K*, intimates that indirect reduction is to be employed: the use of contra-positional conversion, however, will render indirect reduction unnecessary. The following mnemonic lines are the key to the former quintet :—

> "Barbara, demonstrat B ; Celarent, C, reducit;
> D, redit ad Darii ; F, redit ad Ferio ;
> S, vult simpliciter verti ; P, vero per accid ;
> M, vult transponi ; K, per impossibile duci."*

Examples of Reduction, and a Table, by which all the forms of valid syllogisms of the second, third, and fourth figures are shown to be reducible to others of the first, and how this may be done is explained.

Cesare.	*Celarent.*
No sensualist is *truly happy* :	*No truly happy man* is a sensualist :
All really wise men are *truly happy* ;	All really wise men are *truly happy* ;
Therefore, no sensualist is a really wise man.	Therefore, no sensualist is a really wise man.

* B, points out Barbara; Celarent reduces C ;
D, yields to Darii ; F, to Ferio ;
S, wishes simple, but P, accidental conversion ;
M, desires transposition ; K, indirect reduction.

<table>
<tr><td colspan="2">Darapti.</td><td colspan="2">Darii.</td></tr>
</table>

All good men are happy:	*All good men* are happy:
All good men resist their evil desires ;	Some who resist their evil desires are *good men ;*
Some who resist evil desires are happy.	Some who resist their evil desires are happy.

The following Table will show at a glance the various kinds of reduction in each mood, and the method of its accomplishment :—

	Reducens.	*Reducts.*	*Method of Accomplishment.*
Fig. II.	Cesare	Celarent	Convert major premiss simply.
	Camestres	Celarent	Transpose the premisses ; convert the minor and conclusion simply.
	Festino	Ferio	Convert the major premiss simply.
	Baroko	Barbara	Reduce indirectly, or convert by contraposition.
Fig. III.	Darapti	Darii	Convert minor premiss *per accidens.*
	Disamis	Darii	Transpose the premisses ; convert the major and conclusion simply.
	Datisi	Darii	Convert the minor premiss simply.
	Felapton	Ferio	Convert the minor premiss *per accidens.*
	Ferison	Ferio	Convert the minor premiss simply.
	Bokardo	Barbara	Reduce indirectly, or by contraposition.
Fig. IV.	Bramantip	Barbara	Transpose premisses ; convert conclusion *per accidens.*
	Camenes	Celarent	Transpose premisses ; convert conclusion simply.
	Dimaris	Darii	Transpose premisses ; convert conclusion simply.
	Fesapo	Ferio	Convert the major premiss simply, the minor *per accidens.*
	Fresison	Ferio	Convert the major and minor premisses simply.

The following are the Syllogisms capable of being relegated to Fig. I. by *Reductio ad impossibile* :—

Fig. II.	Fig. III.	Fig. IV.
Cesare to Ferio.	Darapti to Celarent.	Bramantip to Celarent.
Camestres to Darii.	Felapton to Barbara.	Camenes to Darii.
Festino to Celarent.	Disamis to Celarent.	Dimaris to Celarent.
Baroko to Barbara.	Datisi to Ferio.	Fesapo to Barbara or Celarent.
	Bokardo to Barbara.	Fresison to Darii or Celarent.
	Ferison to Darii.	

TABLE OF ALL THE CATEGORICAL SYLLOGISMS

(Showing those which are VALID in each mood, and those which are *not*, with the reason).

Name of Mood.	Form of Mood.		Figure I.	Figure II.	Fig. III.	Figure IV.
	Sub.	Pred.	M. P. S. M. S. P.	P. M. S. M. S. P.	M. P. M. S. S. P.	P. M. M. S. S. P.
A, A, A	D D D	U U U	VALID.	Undistrib. Middle.	Illicit Minor.	Illicit Minor.
A, A, I	D D U	U U U	*Valid,** but useless.	Undistrib. Middle.	VALID.	VALID.
A, I, I	D U U	U U U	VALID.	Undistrib. Middle.	VALID.	Undistrib. Middle.
I, A, I	U D U	U U U	Undistrib. Middle.	Undistrib. Middle.	VALID.	VALID.
A, E, E	D D D	U D D	Illicit Major.	VALID.	Illicit Major.	VALID.
A, E, O	D D U	U D D	Illicit Major.	*Valid,** but useless.	Illicit Major.	*Valid,** but useless.
A, O, O	D U U	U D D	Illicit Major.	VALID.	Illicit Major.	Undistrib. Middle.
E, A, E	D D D	U D U D	VALID.	VALID.	Illicit Minor.	Illicit Minor.
E, A, O	D D U	U D U D	*Valid,** but useless.	*Valid,** but useless.	VALID.	VALID.
E, I, O	D U U	U D U D	VALID.	VALID.	VALID.	VALID.
O, A, O	U D U	D U D	Undistrib. Middle.	Illicit Major.	VALID.	Illicit Major.

* Useless because they give a *particular* conclusion, though their premisses warrant a *universal* one.

CHAPTER XV.

RATIOCINATION.—THE USES OF THE SYLLOGISM.

"Those in whom the faculty of Reason is predominant, and who most skilfully dispose their thoughts with a view to render them clear and intelligible, are always the best able to persuade others of the truth of what they lay down."—DESCARTES.

WHEN we perform the act of self-introspection with diligence and carefulness, and endeavour, through the intimations of Consciousness, to ascertain the precise nature of the mode in which the thought-powers operate during the period in which the Ratiocinative faculty is active, we shall perceive—despite of the amazing swiftness and subtlety of the electricity of thought—if we dare use that expression to shadow forth and typify the mysterious nature of the mentality—that our Reason is capable of exerting itself in two diverse manners, and may almost be said to be possessed of two distinct powers; the one, that by which new truths are primarily apprehended—by which the *suggestions* of experience are soonest appreciated—by which the revealments of sensation and consciousness are generalised into hypotheses—and the first faint dawnings of new and hitherto unthought-of ideas are earliest comprehended;—the other, that by which those truths which experience has suggested are eliminated, developed, and verified—by which the whole series of consequences involved in the adoption of any opinion are fully and adequately presented to the mind, and by which the accuracy or erroneousness of our mental generalisations and hypothetical conceptions is brought before the intellect in such a manner as shall lead to their being accepted or rejected. This two-fold capacity of the mentality is recognised by the philosophers of many different schools;—the former is the Intellect—Νοῦς—of Plato; the pure Reason—*Reine Vernunft*—of Kant; and the Spontaneity—*Spontanéité*—of Cousin;—while the latter is the Logical power—Διανοια; the Understanding—*Verstand;* and the Reflectivity—*Réflection*—of the same parties respectively. The one, Kant, defines as the faculty of forming primary notions—*Vermögen der Urtheile;* the other, as the faculty of drawing conclusions—*i.e.,* syllogizing, *Vermögen der Schlusse.* Coleridge, too, if our memory serves us correctly, somewhere distinguishes these two powers by the names, *vis rationalis* and *vis regulatrix;*—the Reason, or that which comprehends, generalizes, co-ordinates, and hypothesizes; and the Understanding, or that which regulates, unfolds, and subordinates all the impressions which the mind receives, according to the necessary laws of thought. The former is that faculty which first, dimly and obscurely it may be, gains a glimpse of those laws "in which endless discoveries are contained implicitly, and to which, as they afterwards arise, they may be referred in endless succession;" the latter is that power by which these primary ideas are brought forth into definitude, by which the dim-seen notions of the spontaneous Intellection are made distinct and clear, and by which all the remote consequences of any law are progressively and gradually eliminated. Nor is it by philosophers alone that these powers are recognised as distinct. Universal experience has herein confirmed the teachings of philosophy; for it has led men in every age to look upon those who were endowed with the power of throwing the light of Reason upon the secrets of Nature as possessed of a superior capacity to that which appertains to common mortals. It carefully distinguishes between "the far-darting glance" of Genius, whose eye is illuminated by "the light which never was on land and shore," and the mere acuteness and versatility of Talent. We all know that the primal desideratum in discovery is the attainment of accurate guiding conceptions, and that it is much easier to understand and even expound the *rationale* of any new discovery or invention, than to work out in our own minds the elementary conceptions from which discoveries result. Have we not all often wondered at the simplicity and commonness of the circumstances which constituted to the minds of scientific men the points of origination for some of their most renowned Genius-achievements? These ideas seem to arise in the mind by a special activity resulting from its peculiar constitution and previous habits, and by a certain capacity of looking at the objects of experience in new points of view; and thus it is that we are continually called upon to see "obscurities in science, which appeared impenetrable, suddenly dispelled, and the most barren and unpromising fields of inquiry converted, as if by inspiration, into rich and inexhaustible mines of knowledge and power, by a simple change in the point of vision, or by merely bringing to bear on them some principle which it never occurred before to try." These considerations are sufficient, we conceive, to warrant us in arriving at the conclusion, that the Ratiocinative faculty is duplex in its mode of acting. But in order that our meaning may be rendered more intelligible, and that we may reduce our observations from the abstract to the concrete, it may be advisable to present our readers with an illustration. This we will do by a slight reference to the grand discovery of the immortal Newton. The fall of bodies to the earth, which experience continually revealed to him, or if you will have the old traditionary story,—the fall of an apple from a tree in his garden at Woolthorpe—suggested to his mind the law of Gravitation.   Thus far, the act was one of mental spontaneity,—an exercise of the pure Reason; but no sooner had this suggestion been given to the mind,—no sooner had this thought-germ been planted in the Intellect, than with the characteristic ardour of an original mind, he called into action the faculty of Reflectivity,—the Logical power, in order to try the truth or falsehood of the hypothesis.   The truth of the law then became, in logical phrase, the question, to prove which a middle term required to be sought.   Confining our attention merely to the astronomical relation, we may state that *a priori* calculations were made upon each of the then known planets in succession, for the purpose of ascertaining the amount of their several deflections, on the assumption that the law was true; that the results of these calculations were then compared with the amount of deflection which actual experiment made known, and that a nearly perfect coincidence between them was immediately observed.   There was then no longer any room for doubt.   The law was true.

To state the matter in the most general terms, as a direct hypothetical Syllogism, the undershown may, perhaps, suffice :—

> If it be true that " the gravitating forces of bodies are to each other, *directly as their masses*, and *inversely as the squares of their distances*," then the sun, and all the bodies which revolve round him, should act and react on each other, in accordance with this rule.

> But the planets—*i.e.*, all the bodies (comets excepted) which revolve round the sun, act and react upon him and upon each other, in accordance with this rule
> (as per the coincidence of the *a priori* calculations which I made, and the inductive observations which I carefully executed);

> Therefore, it is true, that " the gravitating forces of bodies are to each other, *directly as their masses*, and *inversely as the squares of their distances*." *   [The rationale of this argument will be found in Chapters xi. and xvi.]

* While remarking on this subject in the text, it occurred to us that it would be useful for our young readers were we to subjoin the following sentence or two from an Oration on the Life and Genius of Sir Isaac Newton, by Thomas Cooper.   Speaking of the discovery of the law of Gravitation, he says, " None of you, I trust, will join in the foolish attempt to depreciate the mind of this illustrious discoverer, by that senseless remark, 'It was all accident.'   Accident! why, had not hundreds of men seen apples fall, and eaten them, too, and yet had never thought of this doctrine of Gravitation?

Accepting, then, as true, this analysis of the Reason, which establishes a two-fold capacity in the thought-powers, we shall find that there is also a corresponding duplex distinction in the operations which it performs;—I. The mind is possessed of the power of discovering new truths; II. The intellectual faculties are capable of developing the truths which we have discovered, or which we imagine we have discovered, by analyzing what is necessarily included in them, but which we have failed to recognise as involved in their adoption, either through incapacity all at once to discover the latent qualities and relations which appertain to the objects with which the mind becomes conversant, and to perceive the whole series of consequences which result from any opinion which we accept, or through the assumption of opinions as true, by education, reading, conversation, &c., before they have been legitimately wrought out by our own intellectual powers.

Having, then, arrived at this point, we will now proceed to investigate "the Uses of the Syllogism" in their relation to the two peculiar capacities which we believe belong to the Ratiocinative power; and for this purpose we shall inquire—

I.—What is the "Use of the Syllogism" in the discovery of new truths?

We have had occasion to mention, in a former chapter, and, if we mistake not, to prove, that all our knowledge is Experience-originated, and that however much we may exert our imagination and intellect combined, we are quite incapable of transcending that Experience. It is true that we can, by the aid of Reason, arrive at a knowledge of the necessary and inevitable occurrence of many things before they actually do occur, and that by the wondrous powers of Imagination we may picture forth scenes of far more than earthly beauty, and a succession of events of bliss and joy greater far than mortal ever experienced; but still the *data* upon which Reason acts, and from which Imagination culls, are given in Experience, and we only employ the known, as in Algebraic Equations, for an index and exponent by which we may discover the unknown. This idea has been most accurately expressed by an eminent writer thus;—"Philosophy being strictly confined to

---

Be assured that no grand truth has ever fallen 'by accident' into a man's mouth when he happened to yawn. No! no! It is not to the listless and indolent that Nature's revelations are made. The mind must be prepared to perceive it; it must yearn after a discovery of Nature's secrets; it must be girt up and grappling with the difficulty. I tell you, young men, again, it is the Searcher—and the Searcher alone—who finds the gold of Truth; it is the Worker—and the Worker alone—who discovers that 'Open sesame' which is to unlock the opulent secrets of the universe."

experience, often embraces in its definitions only what lies within that sphere; and when it refers to anything beyond, it still connects what is *beyond* with what is *within*.   Nay, in tracing out existences, it often comes to one which is the last of those experienced, but which indicates another set not directly experienced, lying, as it were, on the boundary line between them.   In such a case, what thus lies upon the line is taken as an indication or exponent of what is not experienced.   When a definition is given of the latter, accordingly, it is either confined to the former, or derives from that its principal materials; that is, the exponent is either substituted for what it indicates, or is employed as the best means of characterizing it.   In short, what is only indicated, is best known by its relations to what is experienced, as being most closely connected with it." *

It will follow from the above statement, that every absolutely new truth must be furnished to the mind by experience, and that by no possible exercise of our mentality can we attain to any such truth if it be not suggested by, and implicitly contained in, our experience.   Such an assertion, some of our readers will be ready to exclaim, is tantamount to a complete surrender of the opinion that the Syllogism is of any use in the discovery of new truths.   But a little reflection is all that is necessary to rectify this rash conclusion.   It must be borne in mind, that we cannot know objects *per se*—*i.e.*, as they are *in themselves;* that *noumena* are beyond our perceptive-ken;   and that phenomena alone are capable of impressing our minds.   It is somewhat difficult for us to believe this, because we feel that we can produce no change unless through some instrumentality, and then assume that no change can be produced on ourselves unless through some instrumentality likewise, and thence infer that we are affected by noumena or objectivities, when in reality the phenomena or qualities of objects are all that can ever impress us.   Seeing, then, that we can only know the properties of objects, and that the mind names its *ideas*, and not the *objects* which originate these ideas, it will immediately appear that it is an inevitable necessity of the intellect to generalize its experience;   for if we can know objects only through their properties, our only idea of these objects must be that of particular and special collections of properties. Now we must, perforce, think of objects as we have experienced them. If, then, every absolutely new truth can only enter the mind through experience, it must be evident that the proposition in which it is contained can only be *experience-expressed*.   But we are liable to collect erroneous experience, as well as to apply an idea too hastily to

* Cairns on "Moral Freedom," p. 231.

the explanation of our new experiences; as in the case of the North American Indians, who, having obtained a quantity of gunpowder, rashly concluded that its grains were the seeds of a plant, and sowed it upon one of their extensive prairies, in the hope of reaping a rich harvest of the "thunder" of the pale faces. We have not space to particularize regarding the possibility of erroneous conceptions; however, we may be allowed to submit the following observations which may somewhat assist our readers in elaborating the point for themselves:—1st, All new truths of experience may be expressed in, or contained under, one or other of the propositions of relation—viz., Existence, Coevality, Succession, Causation, Similarity, Diversity, Quantity, Quality, &c.; 2nd, That we can only know the properties and relations of objects, the changes they undergo, and the effects which they are able to produce; 3rd, That we know all the causes concurring to the production of an effect, if all of them appear to our experience; some, if only some affect us; none, if we have not observed any; and *vice versa*, we know all the effects capable of resulting from a cause if, the cause being known, we have perceived them all, and some and none upon the conditions before stated; 4th, That all propositions of Causation relate to—1st, Single causes capable of producing specific single effects, and *vice versa*, certain single specific effects producible by certain single causes; 2nd, Certain several causes combined, or capable of being combined, in order to the production of one species of effect, and *vice versa*, one species of effect produced or producible by the combined agency of several causes; 3rd, One definite cause capable of producing several different effects, and *vice versa*, several different effects produced or producible by one definite cause. It will be seen from the above remarks that there are many possibilities of error arising from the too hasty acceptance and generalization of the suggestions of Experience. We may instance the supposing of an accidental property, quality, relation, &c., to be an essential one; the mistaking of the number of causes concurring to the production of an effect, &c. How, then, are the erroneous conceptions, the rash generalizations, and the immature hypotheses resulting from the suggestions of experience operating upon the mental Spontaneity to be corrected? How are we to rectify the *ideas* of the Reason? What "compensating balance" can we employ to bring the Intellect and the realities of things into correspondence and coincidence? Plainly, as we imagine, thus:—by stating the Reason-educed idea, law, or discovery, to the mentality as a question to which the mind by its own natural laws will impart its formal character; announce the middle term, which will be sufficient to prove the point; this middle term must then be referred to Experience, to be proven,—in other words, Induction must be employed to ascertain whether the actual facts of the case will bear out and substantiate that which the mind, by its own formal processes, demands as the condition of verification. If the Induction be rigidly performed, and the requirements of the Reflectivity or logical process be accurately fulfilled, the mind can no longer hesitate in accepting the product of the Intellect as true and real. Such, we consider, is an approximation to the accurate analysis of the process of the Ratiocinative faculty in Truth-discovery. We do not say that this is always explicitly *et totidem verbis* stated in the mind; it is sufficient for our purpose that it is an implicit condition to the adoption by the mentality of any generalization, hypothesis, or theory whatever, as the expression of one of those truths of science on which it can repose as a guiding principle in all its future dealings with the objectivities with which it is concerned. If this be not an expression of the general fact of Consciousness, how do we account for the rejection by the mind of those numerous fanciful yet baseless theories which flash as frequently and as transiently as summer lightning through the avenues of thought? How comes it that we find that all the great discoveries for which our era is conspicuous, have flitted like fairy visions before the wide-open eyes of the geniuses of other times, and that yet the day of their realization was so long delayed? Does it not seem that the mind, although capable of catching up the shadowy suggestions of experience, and "nourishing a youth sublime with the *fairy* tales of science," yet feels that a process of verification is necessary previous to their being rendered worthy of belief? Were some such intellectual act not performed, we should be believing in truths without any processes which lead to them, and acting on principles destitute of known basis or foundation; and if such a process be performed, in what other manner can it be than in that which we have stated? We know of no other. To the question proposed, we answer, that "the use of the Syllogism in the discovery of new truths" is to verify and certiorate them to the mentality, by indicating the amount of inductive evidence which by the forms of the thought-powers is necessary to the complete demonstration of the point or points at issue.

II.—What are "the Uses of the Syllogism" in the development of those truths which we have discovered, or which we have had suggested by Experience to the Intellect?

"There is as great a difference between the seeds of thought and their perfect development as between the oak and the acorn. The mind is ever thinking; and new thoughts not only add to our stock of

knowledge, but in some measure alter its appearance." *   Although the
Reason possesses, as we have seen, the power of having suggested to it,
and thus implanted in it, the seminal reasons of things—λογοι σπερμα-
τικοι, yet the young seedling must be nourished into growth, and trained
into shape, by the aid of experience :—the vital and vivifying power,
indeed, resides in the mind, but experience is the condition and means
of its development.   From this consideration it would seem that it is
not enough that the germs of thought should have been excited to
active and living manifestation, but that a farther process is necessary
—namely, evolution.   It is concerning the share which the syllogism
exerts in this process that our present inquiries are begun.   In order
to set this in a clear light, we may again refer to the aforementioned
fact, that all our knowledge consists in an acquaintance with the properties, qualities, relations, &c., of bodies, and may farther mention,
that of these there are, as it appears to us, two great classes, which
may be characterized respectively as *manifest* and *latent ;*—under the
former are to be ranked those properties, qualities, relations, &c., which
present themselves most obviously, conspicuously, and ordinarily to
the survey of the mind ; and under the latter, those which require a
keener insight, and a more close and scrutinizing inspection.   It must
be evident to every one that the mechanical philosopher, and the
chemist, look upon matter with a far different purpose from that of
ordinary observers ; that the physician and anatomist gaze and experiment upon the human frame in a manner obviously distinct from that
of unprofessional persons ; that the astronomer views the heavenly
bodies with an eye far more acute, and a mind differently biassed from
that of those unlearned in the science ; and that the psychologist fixes
his mind with a greater degree of analytic skill, and with a nicer discrimination, as well as more defined presiding intention than that
employed by men unmindful of such pursuits.   In each and all of
these cases, as well as in many others, the main difference consists in
the fact, that the one party engages his mind only with the manifest,
the other with the latent properties, &c., of the several objects of
investigation.   Manifest properties are, generally speaking, those which
differentiate bodies, while latent qualities are those which lead to their
identification and colligation ; the latter constitute the generic and
specific properties, &c., of objects, while the former consist of the dif-
ferential and the accidental.   Although a knowledge of the manifest
relations of bodies is more easily attained, that of their latent qualities
is of greater importance ; for, on account of the vast multiplicity of

* Douglas's " Philosophy of Mind," p. 173.

objects with which we are surrounded, unless we were endowed with a capacity of discovering these similarities in things, we could never apply our knowledge—even supposing we could obtain it—to any useful purpose, or put it to any advantageous use.

The operations of mind by which latent qualities, relations, &c., are discovered, are these:—1st, It observes the similar qualities which exist in different objects, and then sets them down as common attributes; 2nd, It examines these common qualities, in order that it may discover their peculiar properties, or those which are necessarily and invariably found to accompany them; 3rd, It institutes comparisons between several common attributes, that it may discover their resemblance to each other, and it then considers these as more general common qualities; 4th, It classifies and colligates together the objects which possess these common properties. It is by such exercises that the latent qualities of bodies are rendered cognoscible by the Intellect. Ideas of one species of property, when compared, suggest ideas of other relations, and these again of others still farther removed from common observation; and thus by the placing of objects before the mind in a variety of positions, throwing upon them a great number of different lights, and employing new and enlarged modes of analysis and comparison, most interesting discoveries are frequently made, most unexpected relations are often revealed, and new truths are frequently presented to the mentality. It is by more extensive analysis, more accurate comparison, and stricter attention to the requirements of experimental evidence, that Chemistry has elicited such a useful as well as curious store of knowledge from objects which have been obtruding themselves on the notice of man from the earliest periods of time. It is by the same means that Astronomy is now capable of looking upon the star-studded scroll which gentle evening unrolls to his gaze, and reading therefrom so many lessons of Wisdom. We might proceed thus through the whole circle of the sciences, showing that inquiries regarding the latent properties of objects have constantly been found to produce beneficial results, and to enlarge the sphere of human knowledge. But our rapidly-filling pages warn us to be more brief in noticing the query contained at the head of these observations. This our readers will not be slow to perceive we have been answering, when they consider that the Manifest relations of objectivities imply and suggest their latent properties and relations, and that we are irresistibly led to attribute the same properties to those bodies which impress their similarity most strongly on the mind. Hence our confidence in reasoning from analogy! Hence the appropriateness of similes, metaphors, and allegories!   Now, whenever experience has suggested a new truth, or what we imagine to be a new truth, to the mind, by conjoining with the idea of a Manifest relation the invariable possession of a latent quality, the mind strives to develop this thought, to compare it with experience, and to *induce* under it the greatest possible number of objects or classes of objects.   In the development of thought, therefore, syllogism directs us what is the proper form the evidence should take to prove the premises; and the premises being once proven, it is evident we may infer from these premises many other truths implicitly contained, though not formally enunciated, in them, and in this light at least the doctrine of J. S. Mill is correct—"that the force of the syllogism consists in *an inductive assertion with an interpretation added to it.*"   But there is obviously another important use of the syllogism—namely, unfolding to the mind the consequences of those general truths which have been received by men as the general laws of science, and teaching their peculiar applications, either singly or in combination.   Such are the laws of Gravitation, Motion, and of the six simple Mechanical Powers, of Multiple Proportions in Chemistry, the rules of Grammar, Logic, Rhetoric, Criticism, &c. Indeed, it may be said that as all complex machines, however intricate and involved may be their structure, consist but of combinations of the six simple mechanical powers; so does all reasoning, however complex, resolve itself into terms, propositions, and syllogisms.   We could have wished to follow this subject into more explicit detail, but we have perhaps said enough to set the mind of the reader in the way of elaborating the topic farther for himself.   In our next chapter we will treat of Informal Syllogisms, which will lead to some further illustration and exemplification of "the Uses of the Syllogistic Logic."   Meanwhile, our readers will permit us to exhort them to follow out in their own minds the ideas presented to them; this they will doubtless find advantageous to their general mental culture; for there is no saying more correct than that

"Truth springeth out of Truth."

CHAPTER XVI.

RATIOCINATION.—INFORMAL SYLLOGISMS.

" To understand the theory of that which is the appropriate occupation of men in general, and to learn to do that well *which every one* will *and* must *do, well or ill, may surely be considered as an essential part of a liberal education."*—WHATELEY.

HITHERTO our attention has been chiefly confined to the consideration of pure categorical syllogisms, or such as in all points fulfil the laws of the thought-process, in its rigid adherence to the formalisms of the mentality. But as the mind, in its present condition, cannot always acquire knowledge of a kind so definite and certain as such reasoning demands, and is not at all times capable of attaining so accurate an acquaintance with surrounding objectivities and their relations as is requisite in processes of such a precise and strictly formal character as those which we have previously described, it would seem necessary that it should possess the power of adapting the method of its intelligential acts to the circumstances which call forth its powers, and thus be rendered capable of reasoning with ease, accuracy, and dispatch, upon the almost innumerable probabilities which are daily and hourly exciting the thought-agencies of men. It will be seen as we proceed that this is really the case, and that while the same code of general laws still hold their undivided jurisdiction over the operations of the ratiocinative faculty, some slight practical variations are permitted to suit the various purposes of the Intellect when engaged in its investigations. These we purpose in our present chapter to explain under the general designation of " Informal Syllogisms."

I.—A Hypothetical Syllogism is, as its name imports, one whose conclusion rests upon the truth or falsehood of some fact—the accuracy or inaccuracy of some prior inference, or the occurrence or non-occurrence of some event;—one whose conclusion does not flow from absolute and positive premisses, but is limited in its validity by the contingency or conditionality of some other fact, occurrence, or opinion, which is expressed in the hypothetical proposition which forms its major premiss. It is, however, to be remarked that the mere fact of the major premiss of a syllogism being a hypothetical proposition does not necessarily and *per se* entitle that syllogism to be considered hypothetical. A proposition may be, and indeed often is, strictly categorical, even although both premisses be hypothetical. If the contingency be carried forward into the conclusion, and reappear there, the hypothesis is considered as a part of one of the terms, and is thus rendered strictly categorical in form; but when the reasoning *rests* upon the hypothesis, when *that* is the pivot upon which the question turns, and when the conditional premiss bears in itself an illative force, and the inference arising from the conjunction of the premisses yields a categorical—*i. e.*, a positively and directly assertive conclusion, the syllogism is correctly denominated hypothetical. The following examples will illustrate the distinction between categorical and hypothetical syllogisms, while the latter will exemplify what is meant in the aforegiven definition :—

Example I.—CATEGORICAL.

BAR- If men are not holy they cannot be happy :

BA- If men are hypocrites they are not holy ;

RA- If men are hypocrites they cannot be happy.

Example II.—HYPOTHETICAL.

If all men do not admire the same objects, Taste cannot be uniform :

But "one mind perceives deformity, where another is sensible of Beauty" *—*i. e.*, all men do not admire the same objects ;

Therefore, Taste cannot be uniform.

Of Hypothetical Syllogisms there are obviously four moods—1st, That in which the antecedent is affirmed, and the consequent is accepted in the conclusion; 2nd, That in which the antecedent is denied, and the consequent is rejected; 3rd, That in which the consequent is denied, and the rejection of the antecedent follows; 4th, That in which the consequent is established, and the antecedent is held as proved. Of these, however, the 1st and 3rd alone are admissible; for in mood 2nd, the denial of the antecedent will not disprove the truth of the consequent, because that may follow from other antecedents; nor in mood 4th will the proof of the consequent establish the accuracy of the antedent, as other antecedents may produce the same consequents. There are then only two admissible moods—Direct and Indirect; these are scholastically denominated *modus ponens* and *modus tollens*.

1st.—Direct hypothetical syllogisms proceed on the principle that if the antecedent be granted or proved, the consequent results from it by illation. It consists of a hypothetical major premiss, which affirms the conjunction of two things conditionally—a categorical minor, which

---

* Hume's "Essays," vol. i., essay 22.

affirms the hypothetical antecedent—and a conclusion in which the consequent is considered established—*e. g.*,

> If it be true that the eclipses of the satellites of Jupiter occur sixteen minutes later when the earth is in that part of her orbit which is at the greatest distance from that planet, than they do when it is in the nearest position with regard to it, it will follow that light must travel at the rate of ninety-five millions of miles in eight minutes :
>
> But it is true that these eclipses do occur so much later in the given position ;
>
> Therefore light travels at the rate of ninety-five millions of miles in eight minutes—*i. e.*, about two hundred thousand miles in a second.

2nd.—Indirect hypothetical syllogisms proceed on the principle, that if the consequent can be denied, the antecedent, in so far as the implied condition is concerned, is false. It consists of a hypothetical major premiss, which contains a conjunctive affirmation, a categorical negative minor, and a conclusion in which the hypothesis is positively rejected —*e. g.*,

> If the mind be possessed of no moral perceptivity, the slave who quietly weeps over his bondage, and the hero who boldly gives his blood for his country, will produce the same impression on it :
>
> But they do not produce the same impression on the mind ;
>
> Therefore, the mind is possessed of moral perceptivity.

II.—A Disjunctive Syllogism is one whose major premiss is a disjunctive proposition. The principle upon which such syllogisms are considered valid is, that *only some* of the asserted things can be true, and that if these be affirmed, the rest may be denied ; or if the rest be denied, these may be affirmed. The accuracy of such reasoning, however, will depend upon the completeness of the enumeration made in the major premiss, and the distinctness of the parts asserted as disjunct ; for if one of the disjunct parts can be affirmed of any of those from which it is asserted to be disjoined, the argumentation is invalid. Such syllogisms admit of great variety, according as the members of the major premiss are more or less numerous. When the major premiss consists of two members only, the minor asserts the one and the conclusion denies the other ; or the minor denies the one and the conclusion affirms the other—*e. g.*,

> It is either true that ignorance is useful, or that knowledge is so :
>
> But it is not true that ignorance is useful ;
>
> Therefore, knowledge is so.

When the major premiss consists of more than two members, the minor
affirms one or more to be true, and the conclusion negatives the remaining terms ; or the minor denies one or more of the terms, and the conclusion affirms the truth or predicability of the other—*e. g.*,

> The angle B A C must either be equal to, or greater or less than,
>   the angle E D F:
> But it is neither equal to, nor less than, it ;
> Therefore, the angle B A C is greater than the angle E D F.*

III.—Dilemma is a species of argument which is in some sort a compound of the two kinds of reasoning just described.   It might therefore
be defined as a hypothetical, disjunctive syllogism.   The Dilemma is so
framed that the denial of the consequent or consequents, negatives the
antecedent ; and the admission of the consequent or consequents,
renders the antecedent predicable.   In arguments of this kind, two or
more suppositions are placed before the mind in such a manner that
whichever term be accepted, a conclusion favourable to the reasoner's
point may be inferred.   In the major premiss, it is asserted that some
one or more of the antecedents must be true, and that some one or more
of the consequents is false ; the minor affirms or denies, as the case
may demand ; and the conclusion states the inference affirmatively or
negatively, according to the *quality* of the minor.   Of this kind of argumentation there are two species, Direct and Indirect.

A Direct Dilemma may either be simple or complex.

1st.—A Direct Simple dilemma is one whose major premiss contains
several antecedents, any one of which may be considered capable of
producing the single consequent which is attributed to their agency,
whose minor affirms the antecedents in a disjunctive proposition, and
whose conclusion affirms the consequent categorically.   "This kind of
argument was urged by the opponents of Don Carlos, the pretender to
the Spanish throne, which he claimed as heir-male, against his niece
the queen, by virtue of the Salic law excluding females, which was
established (contrary to the ancient Spanish usage) by a former king of
Spain, and was repealed by king Ferdinand.   They say,

> "If a king of Spain has a right to alter the law of succession, Carlos
>   has no claim, and if no king of Spain has that right, Carlos has
>   no claim :
> But a king of Spain has, or has not, that right ;
> Therefore, (on either supposition) Carlos has no claim." †

---

* "Euclid," book i., prop. 25.
† Whateley's "Easy Lessons on Reasoning," p. 104.

> "Three courses are before us—to go backward, to stand still, or to
>   go forward:
> We cannot go backward—we cannot stand still;
> We must, therefore, go forward."

A Direct Complex dilemma is one in which the major premiss affirms
that several distinct antecedents have each different and determinate
consequents; the minor asserts these antecedents in a disjunctive proposition; and the conclusion determines that some one of these several
consequents must be true—*e. g.*,

> "We must either gratify our vicious propensities, or resist them:
> To gratify them will involve us in sin and misery; to resist them
>   requires the exercise of self-denial;
> Therefore, we must either be subject to misery, if we gratify our
>   passions; or submit to self-denial if we restrain them."

2nd.—An Indirect dilemma is one which has a major premiss which
contains an affirmation regarding one antecedent and several consequents, or several antecedents and one or more consequents; a minor
which denies the consequent or consequents; and a conclusion which
denies the antecedent or antecedents—*e. g.*,

> If men were prudent, they would act morally for their own good;
>   if benevolent, for the good of others:
> Many men will not act morally, either for their own good, or that
>   of others;
> Such men are, therefore, neither prudent, nor benevolent.

In all accurately constructed dilemma-arguments, the *one* part of the
minor premiss may be capable of being denied, but both or all should
never be capable of being negatived; on this account it is that we speak
of offering any one either horn of the dilemma. It is when we have
thus shut up an opponent, that he can neither accept nor reject all the
parts, but is left to choose either one he pleases, and is, despite of
that, unable to escape, he is said in common phrase to be " caught."
Although the word dilemma is now used as a synonym for what Sam
Slick denominates "bein' in a fix," yet we think that the names of
trilemma, quartilemma, &c., ought to be adopted, according to the
number of antecedents and consequents which the major premiss contains.

IV.—Enthymeme is a syllogism in which one of the premisses is, for
the sake of brevity, suppressed. It appears at first sight to consist of
two propositions only; but upon a closer inspection we may easily per-

ceive that the reasoning is imperfect—*e. g.*, the sentence, "*possunt quia posse videntur*"—they are able because they think they are able—seems as it were, of itself, quite complete; but it will not appear so if any one denies that every one is able to do what he thinks he is capable of doing. The full reasoning comprehended in the sentence of Virgil, may be thus syllogized :—

> Every one is able to do whatever he thinks himself capable of doing :
> They think that they are able ;
> Therefore, they are capable of doing it.

An enthymeme, it will now be seen, consists of a premiss and a conclusion, the former of which receives the name of antecedent, the latter being denominated the consequent; while there is, besides, contained in it a reference to another premiss, which, from the certainty that it will be supplied by the hearer, is retained ἐν θυμῷ—in the mind. Such syllogisms as these may be rendered formal by the insertion of the omitted premiss. To determine which is omitted, however, is sometimes difficult, and may be effected in a different manner, according as the omitted member be one of a categorical or hypothetical syllogism. If the syllogism be categorical, the enthymeme will contain *three* terms, one of which will occur twice; by doing which it is known to be an extreme, the term found in conjunction with it in the consequent will be the other extreme, and the remaining one the middle term ; hence results the following rules :—1st. If the *subject* of the *consequent* appear in the *antecedent*, it is the major premiss that is omitted ; if in the *predicate*, it is the minor. 2nd. If neither *subject* nor *predicate* of the *consequent* be found in the *antecedent*, it is the major premiss that is omitted, and the syllogism is either hypothetical or disjunctive— *e. g.*, the enthymeme, "Sensualists cannot realise their wishes ; for it is impossible to enjoy perpetual gratification without satiety," is thus rendered formal and categorical :—

> CAM-   Sensualists wish *to enjoy perpetual gratification without satiety :*
> ES-   It is impossible to enjoy perpetual gratification without satiety ;
> TRES.   Therefore, it is impossible for sensualists to realise their wishes.

Again : the enthymeme, "In the infancy of society, penal laws must have been extremely severe; as the more barbarous the people, the stronger must be the bonds to restrain them," * may thus be restored to its categorical form :—

BAR- *The more barbarous* the people, the stronger must be the bonds to restrain them—*i. e.*, penal laws :
BA- In the infancy of society, men were *more barbarous than now;*
RA. Therefore, in the infancy of society, penal laws must have been extremely severe.

Again : " Man is accountable ; therefore, he is possessed of power to do good or ill," † may thus be syllogized :—

If Man is accountable, he must be possessed of power to do good or ill :
But he is accountable ;
Therefore, he must be possessed of power to do good or ill.

V.—Epichirēma is a syllogism to one or both of the premisses of which the proof is annexed. Taking the last example, it will become an Epichirēma by proving the major term thus :—

If Man is accountable, he must be possessed of power to do good or ill ; for to call a person to account, to approve or disapprove of his conduct who had no power to do good or evil, is absurd :
Man is accountable ;
Therefore, he is possessed of the power of doing good or ill.

This is a very common method of argumentation in public addresses; each premiss is separately and lengthily proved : the multiplicity of things brought forward often confuses the mind of the listener, and he is frequently led to yield the assent of his reason to a conclusion of much wider and more extensive application than the given premisses really justify. Cicero's *pro Milone* is an elaborate epichirema. The major premiss is, " Self-defence is lawful." This he proves from a consideration of the general principles of justice, from the usages of many nations, the natural instinct of man, and by the examples of illustrious men. The minor premiss is, " Milo acted in self-defence :" this is proved by the fact, that Clodius lay in wait to slay him, and that he had arms and guards with him, while Milo was almost unprovided with any ; and he then concludes that " What he did in self-defence was lawful "—viz., his killing of Clodius.

* Tytler's "Elements of History," p. 14.
† Reid's " Essays on the Active Powers of the Mind," essay i., chap. vii.

VI.—Sorites. This species of argument is only an abbreviated series of syllogisms arranged in such a manner that the predicate of each prior one becomes the subject of its successor, and so on in regular progression, until in the conclusion the subject of the first premiss is affirmed or denied of the predicate of the last. In such a series as this the strength of the conclusion is only equivalent to that of the weakest link in the chain of reasoning. It is obvious that such a series of concatenated syllogisms may be carried on to any extent, so long as the purpose of the speaker requires it, and the chain is preserved unbroken. In the listener, however, it requires diligent attention, as the introduction of one premiss of a doubtful nature will vitiate the whole process of argumentation in which it is employed. The following is a specimen of a sorites :—

> Happiness is the result of obedience to the Divine laws :
> Obedience to the Divine laws constitutes virtuous conduct :
> Virtuous conduct is the subordination of the inferior to the superior
> portions of our nature :
> This cannot be done without the practice of self-control ;
> Happiness, therefore, is the result of the practice of self-control.

The following are the rules which govern Sorites :—viz., 1st, The last premiss alone can be negative ; 2nd, The first premiss alone can be particular ; 3rd, If the first premiss be particular, and the last negative, the conclusion must be particular or negative.

If we are desirous of ascertaining the validity of a chain of reasoning such as this, it can easily be done by decomposing the series into the several syllogisms of which it consists. In doing this, we must consider the *second proposition* of the Sorites the *major premiss*, and the *first proposition the minor*—*e.g.*,

> BAR- Obedience to the Divine laws constitutes virtuous conduct :
> BA-   Happiness is the result of obedience to the Divine laws ;
> RA.   Therefore, happiness is the result of virtuous conduct.

The conclusion of the first syllogism is then to be considered as the *minor premiss* of the second syllogism, and the next proposition the *major*—*e.g.*,

> BAR- Virtuous conduct is the subordination of the inferior to the
> superior portions of our nature :
> BA-   Happiness is the result of virtuous conduct ;
> RA.   Therefore, happiness is the result of the subordination of
> the inferior to the superior portions of our nature.

The same rule now holds good through the whole series, and must be carefully followed—*e.g.*,

BAR- The inferior portions of our nature cannot be subordinated to the superior without the practice of self-control:

BA- Happiness is the result of the subordination of the inferior to the superior portions of our nature;

RA. Therefore happiness is the result of the practice of self-control.

VII.—A Prosyllogism consists of two syllogisms so joined together, that the conclusion of the prior forms one of the premisses of the posterior, and is thus nearly related to the Sorites. The Soliloquy of Juno—

"Pallas ne exurere classem
Argivûm atque ipsos, potuit submergere ponti; &c.
*   *   *   *
Ast ego, quæ Divum incedo regina, Jovisque
Et soror et conjux, una cum gente tot annos
Bella gero; et quisquam numen Junonis adoret:
Præteræ, aut supplex aris imponat honorem!"*

may be exhibited, so far as the reasoning process is concerned, in a prosyllogism, thus:—

Whoever is greater than Minerva ought to be able to do more:
I, the sister and wife of Jupiter, am greater than she;
Therefore, I ought to be able to do more.
But Minerva was able to avenge her wrongs;
Therefore, I ought to be more capable of avenging mine.

VIII.—Analogy, or Parity of Reasoning, is a species of argumentation of which there are a considerable number of varieties. It consists in tracing those general, although, it may be, imperfect resemblances which exist among differing and distinct existences, and from the similitudes observable in them, inferring the proportional similarity of their causes, or the comparative sameness of their effects. As the coincidences and similarities of properties perceptible in the objectivities which impress the mind differ materially in their degrees, it will be obvious that there is in the common affairs of life a very wide range for the practical exercise of this description of reasoning. It will therefore be of great service if we can find some general expression of the laws which

* "Was not Pallas able to burn the fleet of the Greeks, and to overwhelm them in the sea? But I, who am the queen of the gods—both the wife and the sister of Jupiter —carry on war with one nation so many years, and shall any one yet worship the divinity of Juno, or suppliantly place an oblation on my altar."—"*Æneid*," book i.

hold good in Analogical arguments to which we can refer as settled points in the employment of any such methods of ratiocination. As an attempt to supply this want, we may be allowed to observe—1st, The lowest degree of belief ought in general to be attached to those arguments from Analogy, in which *one* circumstance alone is similar, and *all others* are dissimilar. 2nd, The highest degree of belief, short of absolute conviction, ought to be conceded to those arguments in which *all* the circumstances, except *one*, resemble each other. 3rd, The lowest degree of similarity may show that a thing is *possible*. 4th, The highest degree of resemblance demonstrates the extreme probability of the accuracy of the reasoning. 5th, The degree of belief ought to be strictly proportioned to the ratio between the agreeing and the disagreeing elements contained in the objects brought forward as analogous. The chief precautions to be observed in reasoning from Analogy are these—1st, Never reason from supposititious resemblances; see that the similarity is real, not nominal. 2nd, Never demand or yield assent to any conclusion which is not warranted by the degree of resemblance which the objects bear to each other. 3rd, When actual and well-ascertained facts are opposed to our Analogy, so far as to involve the point at issue in our reasoning, we may generally consider our Analogy as incompetent.

Analogical reasoning seems to depend for its validity upon the natural and inherent tendency which operates in the minds of men to rely upon Experience. This may be couched in many varied phrases, and these phrases may be accounted "fundamental truths," "primary verities," &c., as is the fashion in some metaphysical schools: but whether we say, "the future will resemble the past;" "approximate causes will produce proportional effects;" "similars produce similars;" or, "our past experience is the guide of our future actions," &c., we conceive the meaning is equally the same, and is equally convincing regarding the imperative necessity of watchfulness as to the teachings of that world-renowned taskmaster, Experience. The supposition or postulation of the truth of Experience may be considered as the major premiss, and the other terms may be thus formally reduced to syllogisms —viz.,

Wherever similar general causes operate, similar general effects will most probably result:
Similar general causes operate in the earth and the planets;
Therefore, similar-general effects will most probably result in both.

But Life, Vegetation, &c., are the results of these laws on earth;

Therefore, Life, Vegetation, &c., may most probably be found in the planets.*

Nearly allied to this kind of argument is that which Aristotle denominated Oratorical Induction, but which is now more generally designated Reasoning by Example. The general principle on which this species of ratiocination proceeds is, that any two causes or effects which are in each point precisely similar, must produce, or have been produced by, precisely similar causes or effects—*e.g.*, The loss of its colonies ruined Holland; therefore, a similar loss will ruin England. Such arguments as these are, of course, invalidated by proving that there is a disparity or dissimilarity in the cases.

The most general statement of the law of "Reasoning by Analogy" is the following, viz., The same attributes may be predicated of distinct but similar objects, if *they* can be proven to be the results of the points of resemblance in things, and not of the points of difference.

IX.—Induction is another species of reasoning depending upon the principle of resemblance for its validity. Of the processes by which such ratiocination is conducted we have treated so fully in a previous chapter,† that our remarks at present must be brief. Induction consists in attributing the properties which are to be found in each part of a whole to that whole. It maintains that what is true of each one of the parts is also true of the whole. It collects, classifies, and groups together families, as it were, of particular facts; observes with care and precision the particular attributes which they all, in common, possess; and from these eliminates a greater fact or law. In this method of argument, we reason from specials to generals—from individuals to a generic whole. It will be seen from this, that it is of the highest importance that we should use the utmost caution and vigilance in discriminating between the accidental and essential qualities of objects.

Induction is either Perfect or Imperfect: Perfect when all the parts of a whole are enumerated; Imperfect when all the parts of the whole either are not, or cannot be so. It is seldom, however, that man can attain to a knowledge of the whole of the individuals contained in any class of objectivities, and hence we are generally constrained to rest satisfied with a limited enumeration, depending upon analogy for the accuracy of the reasoning founded upon the observed particulars. Induction seems to be the appropriate method of leading the several facts of which we become cognizant into the judgment-hall of the mentality, therein to have their relation to human concerns decided

* For other remarks on this topic, see Chapter VII.

† Chapter VIII.

upon; and that general propositions and axioms may be evolved from them, in order, that they may supply to the mind "the forth-flowing fonts of future experiments." "This is the *principle* of an indefinite, not to say infinite, *progression;* but this progression, which is truly Method, requires not only the proper choice of an initiative, but also the following it out through all its ramifications. It requires, in short, a constant wakefulness of mind, so that if we wander but in a single instance from our path, we cannot reach the goal, but by retracing our steps to the point of divergency, and thence beginning our progress anew. Thus a ship beating off and on an unknown coast, often takes, in nautical phrase, 'a new departure;' and thus it is necessary often to recur to that regulating process which the French language so happily expresses by the word *s'orienter—i.e.*, to find out the east for ourselves, and so put to rights our faulty reckoning."*

CHAPTER XVII.

RATIOCINATION.—CONCERNING FALLACIES.

"Although a masculine good sense will generally escape, in practice, from merely logical perplexities (that is, will cut the knot, for all immediate results of practice, which it cannot untie), yet errors 'in the first intention' come round upon us in subsequent stages, unless they are met by their proper and commensurate solutions. *Logic must be freed by Logic:* a false dialectical appearance of truth must be put down by the fullest exposure of the absolute and hidden truth; since, also, it will continually happen that a plausible sophism, which had been summarily crushed, for the moment, by a strong appeal to general good sense, upon the absurd consequences arising, will infallibly return upon us when no such startling consequences are at hand."—THOMAS DE QUINCEY.

"To err is human," is a maxim which has become so trite and commonplace, that its utterance no longer strikes upon the Intellect as the expression of a sad and lamentable fact,—one which ought to be deplored and mourned over,—but, above all, if possible, amended. Instead of awakening such feelings, however, it is now too frequently quoted as a ready, convenient, and indisputable excuse for many of the vagaries, reprehensibilities, inadvertencies, follies, and even crimes of men; and is thus too often made—although in a widely different sense—like Charity—to cover "a multitude of sins." We act improperly in so doing. Error ought to be regarded as a disease of the

* Coleridge "On Method," p. 18.

mentality, and every remedial agency which human ingenuity can discover—and in the case of Religion and Morals, which Divine grace has seen fit to impart—ought to be employed, in order that our intelligential nature may be, as far as possible, restored to that state in which it may be capable of performing its proper functions unimpairedly. And, although we may not yet have attained to a complete and accurate diagnosis of each individual mind-malady,—although we may not be able to distinguish definitely between those which are *pathognomonic* and those which are *adjunct*; yet if we can at all discover the causes, indications, and method of cure, of any one or more of these mental infirmities, we shall do well to strive earnestly to do so. Now, one of the chief uses of Philosophy is to effect this;—is to make us acquainted with the nature of our mental constitution, so that we may "discover the powers thereof, how far they reach, to what things they are in any degree proportionate, and where they fail us." It teaches us to "anatomize the thoughts and purposes of men;" and thus to gain a knowledge of "our being's end and aim;" and having attained this knowledge, surely it becomes us to apply it, practically, to the remedying of those defects which are observable in the mode of our thought-processes. Philosophy habituates the mind to close, vigorous, accurate, and comprehensive mental exertion; to a ready perception of the truth or fallacy of any given series of propositions. We do, indeed, readily grant that such an investigation

> " Quale per incertam Lunam sub luce maligna
> Est iter in silvis ; ubi coelum condidit umbra
> Jupiter, et rebus nox abstulit atra colorem ;" *

and yet no one who understands

> " How use doth breed a habit in a man;"

can doubt the efficacy of training the mind in the detection of errors ; of cultivating the truth-percipient faculties ; and of diligently educating the thought-powers, so that they may with equal readiness discern what ought to produce immediate and infallible conviction in the mind, and what ought to lead to doubt, or to total disbelief; and by these means be enabled to distinguish between the specious apparency of the sophist's guileful words, the illogical deductions of the untrained or biassed mind, and the sterling gold, fresh from the mintage of heavenly Truth.

* " Is even as a pathway through the woods, under the scanty light of the uncertain moon, when Jupiter has covered the sky with a cloud, and gloomy night has abstracted the colour from things."—*Virgil's* " *Æneid*," book vi., 270.

Of the sources of Error, we have already spoken at considerable length, in our chapter on the " Idols of the Intellect ;" it now remains for us to show how fatally these errors may operate for evil in our ratiocinative processes, and to explain, in as comprehensive and succinct a manner as possible, in what way we may best avoid falling into error in our own reasonings, or most easily and certainly detect the fallacious reasonings of others. Referring to the chapter above mentioned for a more complete exposition of these Error-sources, we shall merely re-sketch, in outline, the principal topics of thought which will serve to render this chapter intelligible by itself, and then proceed to fulfil the chief object which we have in view in its composition—viz., to give the reader some information " concerning fallacies."

There are a few words continually occurring in debate, and which we shall require to use in this chapter, which it may be well to notice and define—viz., Truth, Error, Falsity, Falsehood, Fallacy, and Sophism.

Truth is the expression of our ideas in such a manner as to give an accurate detail of the objects, circumstances, &c., concerning which we are conversing. Although, from defect in position, opportunity, organization, &c., what appears Truth to one man does not appear so to all ; yet there must be some *criteria* for distinguishing between absolute and relative Truth.   Of such a nature we suppose the following enumeration to be :—1st, Absolute Truth must refer to objects, circumstances, &c., which actually exist, or have occurred ; 2nd, Our ideas must have been excited by these very objects, circumstances, &c. ; 3rd, That the same objects, circumstances, &c., would produce the self-same ideas in any similarly constituted individual of our race, supposing, in each case, the physical and mental structure to be free from gross defects ; 4th, That the comparison of the ideas educed in similar minds, by the same objects, circumstances, &c., is the only test at which we can arrive for the detection of error, or the discovery of Truth.   This latter sentence seems to throw us into the hands of the *common sense* philosophers.   It may be remarked here, that although the belief of each individual may be true *to him*, it by no means follows that that is absolute truth ; so that belief is not altogether synonymous with Truth ; for men in different ages have believed opposite things ; and men of the present day differ in some things, " wide as the poles asunder," in their matters of belief—*e. g.*, The Ptolemaic and Copernican systems of Astronomy, the Brahminic and Christian faiths, and the philosophies of Hegel and Comte.

" All Error," says Cousin, " is only an incomplete view of the Truth."

This we do not hold as a correct definition;—we think that Error con-sists of two parts—1st, An *incomplete* view of the Truth; and, 2nd, The formation of opinions *different* from the truth—*e.g.*, The Judaic religion was " an incomplete view of the truth;" the Ptolemaic system of Astronomy was " different from the truth."

Falsity signifies the verbal expression of an error, when that error is believed by the person who utters it, and when, consequently, there is no intention to deceive.

A Falsehood is the verbal expression of some known error, with intention to deceive. Thoughts can only be communicated to others through the medium of words; words, therefore, become the images of thought; but a representation is only true so far as a resemblance exists between it and the thing represented; in like manner, a thought expressed is only true so far as the words accord with that idea; and if the inaccordancy arises intentionally, it is then justly stigmatized and reprobated as a falsehood.

A Fallacy is the verbal expression of a thought, with an apparent, though not a real, correctness;—it may either be accompanied or not with an intention to deceive.

A Sophism is a fallacy uttered with the intention to deceive: one expressly framed in a deceptive way.

It is obvious, from the above explanations of the meanings of terms, that the chief sources of error, either in ourselves or others, are of two kinds—viz., 1st, Intellectual; 2nd, Volitionary.

1st. Intellectual. " The human intellect is like an unequal mirror to the rays of things, which mixes its own nature with the nature of things, and thus distorts and perverts them" *—*i.e.*, Consciousness being a mere state of the percipient faculties excited in us by the action of objectivities, which, inferentially, we believe to be external to us, can only inform us of the fact of its own excitation, but cannot, by any possibility, acquaint us with the appearance of things, *per se*. We can only know the *non ego*—*i.e.*, what is beyond, and impresses conscious-ness, by its influence upon the *ego*—*i.e.*, Consciousness. We can only ascertain, with certainty, the change in the subject—*i.e.*, our mind; we cannot acquire an absolute knowledge of the object—*i.e.*, the exter-nality which affects our mind. To us, *the without* is only known by the fact that it produces certain effects on *the within*; and it by no means follows that the cause resembles the effect which it produces,—

---

* " Estque intellectus humanus instar speculi inæqualis ad radios rerum, qui suam naturam naturæ rerum immiscet, eamque distorquet et inficit."—*Bacon's " Novum Organon,"* lib. i., aph. xii.

how different, for instance, is the fire, from the pain of the burn which it occasions!—so that our knowledge being merely relative, we can attain to no absolute knowledge of the essences or quintessences of things. We cannot isolate ourselves, and place ourselves beyond the reach of consciousness, because it is only *through* our consciousness that knowledge is attainable. A full acquaintance with our own intellectual incapacity will be of much service to us, by restraining us from entering upon inquiries of which we are unable to attain any certain or irrefragable solution; for "when we know our own strength, we shall the better know what to undertake with hope of success; and when we shall have well surveyed the *powers* of our minds, and made some estimate of what we may expect from them, we shall not be inclined either to sit still, and not set our thoughts on work at all, in despair of knowing anything; or on the other side, to question everything, and disclaim all knowledge, because some things are not to be understood." *

But it is not only from the incapacity of the Intellect, the oneness of medium through which all knowledge is presented to the mind, or the fact, that all our ideas are the result of impressions on, or rather changes in, the *ego*—that we suffer. Were this the only Error-source, it would be, comparatively, but a small matter; for as we *must* rely upon the intimations of Consciousness, our Experience would necessarily and inevitably be true *to us*, altogether independent of the reality or seemingness of external objects. We suffer much more from inaccuracy of observation, rashness in generalization, and carelessness or precipitancy in inference, than from the circumscribed nature of our mental faculties. Indeed, precipitation and inattention are most inimical to correctness of thought; for, Bacon truly observes, that "a syllogism consists of propositions, propositions of words, and words are the signs of ideas; therefore, if our ideas themselves, which are the basis of all reasoning, are confused, and too hastily formed, nothing that is built upon them can be stable." † We must not, however, in these remarks, be understood as homologating all the deductions which sophistical minds have drawn, or may draw, from the admittedly grave errors into which men may fall by neglecting the due precautions necessary for preparing the mind to perceive and acknowledge Truth.

. * Locke's "Essay concerning the Human Understanding," book i., chap. i., sect. 7.

+ " Syllogismus ex propositionibus constat, propositiones ex verbis, verba notionum tesseræ sunt, Itaque, si notiones ipsæ (id quo basis rei est) confusæ sint et temere a rebus abstractæ nihil in iis quæ superstruuntur est firmitudinis."—*Bacon's "Novum Organon,"* lib. i., aph. xiv.

All that we desire to do is, to warn our readers against acquiring that habit of mind which "gains remote conclusions with a jump,"—that over-active impetuosity of mind which so surely indicates the mental characteristic of inconsiderateness. Nor do we wish to lend any encouragement whatever to the opposite tendency, of inert passivity of intellect. When the mind thus lazily adopts opinions, unjustified by facts, and fails to exert itself for the attainment of accurate ideas and information, nothing can be expected but that obscurity and confusion should reign paramount in the mind, and that incorrect reasoning will, in all probability, be allowed to pass undetected. The mind should be somewhat like a continental country—the passport system ought to be in active operation, and no idea should be allowed ingress or egress until, upon due examination, it is found to be what it represents itself. We cannot too frequently or too earnestly recommend the sedulous cultivation of habits of accurate observation, careful reflection, and the attainment of a power of sifting particulars, as some of the primary requisites of the intellect zealously bent on Truth-acquisition. Among Intellectual Error-sources may be reckoned—1st, Those which arise from the circumscribed nature of the human mind; 2nd, Carelessness in investigation; 3rd, Precipitancy in making inferences; 4th, The want of opportunity to form accurate opinions, or to acquire correct information; 5th, The tendency of the mind to give too great prominence to professional or favourite pursuits; 6th, The different views which may be taken of the same event by persons of different idiosyncrasies; 7th, One-ideadness; 8th, The readiness with which we judge of things according to their external appearance; 9th, Fanciful associations of ideas; 10th, The natural bent of the mind; 11th, Narrowness of mind; 12th, Deficiencies in memory, or the perceptive powers; and others of a similar kind.

II.—Volitionary. The will being the agent of the emotions, desires, affections, and passions, as well as of the intellect, it is frequently led into error by the impetuousness or insinuative power of some one or more of these; and as each power of the mentality exerts an influence upon the others, the errors of one faculty may be communicated to the whole mind. When the will acts according to the desire of any one or more of the emotional feelings, and causes the intellect to swerve from the execution of its duty, we denominate the result a prejudice—*i. e.*, a premature, illegitimate, and unfairly-arrived at judgment. It is exceedingly difficult to keep the mind passionless and unbiassed;—to preserve "the mind's eye" always clear, pure, and unimpaired;—and to maintain the intellect in its lofty supremacy :—so free from being flattered by self-love, allured by fancied interests, or excited by personal hatreds, as to prevent it from believing that it perceives the truth, accuracy, or justice of all that it wishes to think or do. This opinion has been eloquently expressed by Jean Paul Richter, when he remarks, that " passion, contemplated through the medium of the imagination, is like a ray of light transmitted through a prism,—we can calmly, and with undazzled eye, study its complicated nature, and analyze its variety of tints ; but passion brought home to us in its reality, through our own feelings and experience, is like the same ray transmitted through a lens —blinding, burning, consuming whatever it falls upon." But the greater any danger is, the more care ought we to employ, in order to avoid it ; so that the very imminence of this liability to stray from truth and right, ought to nerve us up to manly and energetic endeavours to preserve ourselves from being led into error,—" caught up in the Mahlströme of party strife, sectarian contention, love of self, envy of others, or yield ourselves up to any other of the almost innumerable passion-exciting, desire-creating, or emotion-producing influences, which ' whirl us into error.' " Among Volitionary Error-sources may be enumerated those resulting from—1st, Prepossessions ; 2nd, Selfishness ; 3rd, National vanity ; 4th, Partizanship ; 5th, The predominance of imagination ; 6th, The various passions and affections of the mind ; 7th, The tendency of the mind to run to extremes ; 8th, Procrastination ; 9th, Love of Times ; 10th, Fashion ; 11th, Authority ; 12th, Depravity of mind, and some other similar " fallacies of the feelings," &c.

It is not our design, either in the foregoing or succeeding pages, to expose the weaknesses and imperfections of the human mind, or to signalize the Error-sources through which it most frequently and easily receives fallacious reasonings, for the purpose of teaching our readers " the art of imposing upon men,"—of making " the worse appear the better reason." We do not wish to bring their skill and intelligence into play for such an ignominious purpose. We do not desire to sharpen their mental powers in order that they may attain the mind-subtlety of Hudibras :—

> " He was in Logic a great critic,
> Profoundly skilled in analytic ;
> He could distinguish and divide
> A hair 'twixt south and south-west side,—
> On either which he would dispute,
> Confute, change hands, and still confute ;

> For he a rope of sand could twist
> As tough as learned Sorbonist;
> And weave fine cobwebs, fit for skull
> That's empty when the moon is full."

Or even the mental legerdemain of Goldsmith's Schoolmaster, of whom it is said, that

> " Even though vanquished, he could argue still."

No ; our aim is higher ; it is to show the mind its own weaknesses, in order that it may guard against being deceived, and, by spreading amongst our readers a knowledge of the most common fallacies, render them less likely to be imposed upon by the artifices of the rhetorician or the spurious syllogisms of the sophist. To point out the avenues through which error is most likely to approach, is, in our opinion, the best means of enabling the mind to adopt precautions against its entrance, and to capacitate it for building up defences against the attacks or encroachments of designing men. But it is not to be supposed that every fallacy or sophism will be so easily discovered, or so readily detected, as those which are quoted in the following pages may appear to be ; for it is much easier to detect an error when the very passage in which it occurs is placed before you ; and as these are generally freed from any extraneous matter, with which sophistical discourse is frequently much diluted, they seem much simpler than they really are. Another reason is, that the examples in any didactic book are commonly as far removed from abstruseness as possible, in order to illustrate the principle as clearly as possible to minds which are, comparatively speaking, unpractised in such pursuits.

A Fallacy has been most felicitously defined by Archbishop Whately, as " any unsound mode of arguing, which appears to demand our conviction, and to be decisive of the question in hand, when, in fairness, it is not so." These Fallacies have been variously classified and arranged, from the days of Aristotle downwards. It is our intention to present, in synoptic tables, the systems of classification adopted by Aristotle, Mill, and Whately : and afterwards to present such an abstract of the teachings of these logicians as, we think, will be useful and agreeable to our readers.

The Aristotelic classification considers Fallacies as composed of two great classes—1st, Those in which the error is contained in the form of the expression [*in dictione*] ; 2nd, Those in which it is contained in something distinct from the form of the expression [*extra dictionem*].

Of the first class there are six varieties; of the second, seven; as may be seen in the following table :—

In the Expression.	Distinct from the Expression.
1. Equivocation.	1. Accident.
2. Amphibology.	2. From what is true in particular circumstances, to infer as if from an absolute truth.
3. Composition.	3. Ignorance of the point in dispute.
4. Division.	4. Assigning a false cause.
5. Accent or Prosody.	5. Deducing a conclusion which does not follow.
6. Figure of speech.	6. Begging the question.
	7. Many interrogations, as if admitting but one answer.

The fallacies of the first class may be refuted by showing the law of syllogism with whose requirements they do not accord. Most commonly, the transgression lies in an *undistributed middle*, or an *illicit process* of the *major* or *minor* term. Those of the second class cannot be so readily detected, as they require a knowledge not only of the expression, but also of the matter of discourse. This, however, will be farther explained when we proceed to treat of them individually. J. S. Mill's synoptic table of fallacies is exceedingly exhaustive, as it contains not only those which may occur in reasoning, but all those to which we are liable in judgment.

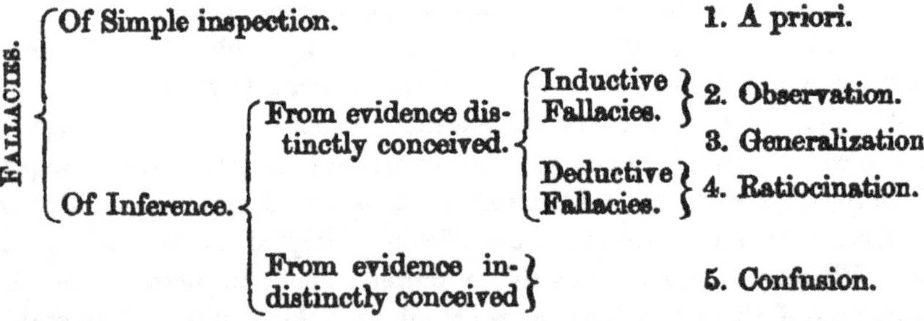

Archbishop Whately's tabular view of fallacies is, like everything else in his admirable treatise, distinguished for lucidity of arrangement and clearness of exposition.

FALLACIES.

Logical, or Formal.
(*i.e.*, when the fault is strictly in the very process of reasoning: the conclusion *not following* from the premisses.)

- **Purely Logical.**
  (*i.e.*, where the fallaciousness is apparent from the mere *form of the expression*.)

  Undistributed Middle. Illicit Process, &c.

- **Semi-Logical.**
  (The middle term being ambiguous in sense.)

  - **In itself.**
    - Accidentally.
    - From some connection between the different senses.
      - Resemblance. Analogy. Cause and Effect.
  - **From the context.**
    - Fallacy of division and composition.
    - Fallacy of accident.

Non-Logical, or Material.
(*i.e.*, when the conclusion *does fellow* from the premisses.)

- **Premisses unduly assumed.**
  - (*Petitio principii*) Premisses depending on the conclusion.
    - Circle.
    - Assuming a proposition not the very same as the question, but unfairly implied in it.
  - Premisses false, or unsupported.

- **Conclusion irrelevant,** *ignoratio elenchus.*
  - Fallacies of objections.
  - Fallacy of shifting ground
    - To something wholly irrelevant.
    - From premisses to premisses alternately.
  - Fallacy of using complex and general terms.
  - Fallacy of appeals to the passions; *ad hominem, ad verecundiam,*&c.

In the belief that in our former chapters we have, at some length, explained the origin and causes of the errors into which the mind is liable to be led, in the exercise of perceptivity, judgment, and generalization—*i. e.*, the 1st, 2nd, and 3rd classes of fallacies mentioned in the synoptic table of J. S. Mill, and cautioned our readers to guard against and avoid them; and assuming that the tabular scheme of fallacies which we extract from Archbishop Whately's able treatise on "Logic," contains an accurate and extensive classification of the various ramifications into which the fallacies, classes 4th and 5th of Mr. Mill's table, expand themselves,—we will proceed, in the first place, to give an exposition of those fallacies which are contained under the words "Purely Logical," in the first division of the scheme referred to.

PURELY LOGICAL FALLACIES.—Of Purely Logical fallacies there are three varieties—viz., 1st. Those resulting from an *undistributed middle*. In such apparent syllogisms, the middle term is undistributed in such a manner, as that the major term is compared with one part of the term, and the minor with another part; and the two terms are thus in contravention of the two first axioms (page 147),—neither asserted to agree or disagree "in the *same sense* with one and the *same third;*" but, on the contrary, are declared invalid by axiom 3, which asserts, that "if of two things, neither agrees with one and the same third, in the same sense, no inference is deducible;" as well as by Rule I., which directs that "the middle term must be distributed—*i. e.*, taken in its entire extension, at least, once in the premisses, else the conclusion will be illegitimate." The following are examples of this fallacy :—

> All good men are beloved by their associates :
> This man is beloved by his associates ;
> Therefore, he is a good man.

> All beautiful things are useful :
> Cranes, levers, pulleys, ploughs, &c., are useful ;
> Therefore, they are beautiful things.

2nd. Those which have an *illicit process* in their terms. In apparent syllogisms of this sort, one of the middle terms "is distributed in the conclusion, which was not distributed in, at least, one of the premisses," and thus transgresses Rule II., and thus directly violates the *dictum* upon which syllogistic reasoning proceeds,—as it distinctly requires that any affirmation or negation made regarding any term, must be made regarding something *contained under* that term ;—if, then, an affirmation or negation be made concerning something *excluded from* that term, the reasoning is obviously invalidated; as may be observed on reading the following examples :—

> Money contributes to national prosperity :
> Grain, imported from foreign countries, is not money ;
> Therefore, such grain does not contribute to national prosperity.

> Nations which do reciprocate our Free-trade measures, ought to be
>   permitted to import their grain, &c., duty free :
> Several countries do not reciprocate our Free-trade measures ;
> Therefore, those nations ought not to be permitted to import their
>   grain, &c., duty free.

3rd. Those from which, having *negative premisses*, an *affirmative conclusion* is deduced, and *vice versâ*.   These apparent syllogisms infringe Rules III. and IV., as well as Axiom 3 :—

> All native industry ought to be carefully protected :
> All the labours of our artizans, agriculturalists, authors, &c., constitute our native industry ;
> Therefore, none of the labours of foreign artizans, agriculturalists, authors, &c., ought to be protected.

> All men should purchase in the cheapest market :
> The cheapest market is where the best goods are got for least money ;
> Therefore, no man should purchase anywhere but where the best goods are got for the least money.

It is quite evident that, however seemingly true the conclusions to these apparent syllogisms, the premisses are quite invalid as reasons or grounds of action; as there is no inferentiality implied in the construction, they have no illative power.

We intended to devote much more space to the illustration of those fallacies; but we fear that the length of this chapter may make it fatiguing to our readers, and we will conclude our remarks with two rules, by which, if properly attended to, Purely Logical fallacies may be easily detected.

1st. In every accurately constructed syllogism, or just process of argumentation, one of the premisses must show that a certain conclusion results from some certain assertion; and the other must make it appear quite evident that the conditions of the former premiss are fulfilled, and thus that the conclusion is justly inferrible—*e.g.*,

> The formal enunciation of vague, commonplace generalities from
>   the pulpit, cannot warm the heart, or excite repentance in the
>   soul :

Many preachers enunciate vague, commonplace generalities in a
formal manner;
Therefore, many preachers cannot warm the heart, or excite re-
pentance in the soul.

2nd. As the premisses of every syllogism which is constructed in
accordance with the *dictum*, axioms, and rules, contain the middle term
twice; so that middle term must, in each premiss, bear precisely the
same signification. Thus, it will not do to use the following syllogism :—

No man who is destitute of character ought to be trusted :
This man is destitute of character;
Therefore, he ought not to be trusted;

if, in the major premiss, we employ the word character to denote all
those peculiar moral qualities which constitute an amiable and trustworthy person, and, in the minor, make the same word expressive of
those strongly-marked peculiarities which render a man remarkable.
Many persons construct their reasonings in this Jesuitical manner, and
try to calm their consciences when they do feel a qualm from that too-
little heeded monitor, by the mental reservation, that they did not mean
to express by the term, that particular shade of signification which it
ostensibly bore. There are so many minute and delicate gradations in
the signification of words, in every language,—but more particularly in
our own, that it is not an easy matter, at all times, to detect the
" cunningly devised deceits" which men, in the course of argumentation,
too frequently employ.

We will finish the topic " Ratiocination" in our next chapter, which
will contain an analytic view of the Semi-logical and Non-logical fallacies. Till then, we must say with the old play—

"I pray you, gentle sirs, commend me to your love."

CHAPTER XVIII.

RATIOCINATION.—CONCERNING FALLACIES.

"An amendment of the general habits of thought is, in most of the departments of knowledge, as important as even the discovery of new Truths."—Sir James Mackintosh.

"Prejudices, I should think, would be a sort of property, which, like paving stones in a man's pocket, it would be kind to free him from as soon as possible."—G. P. R. James.

"When we wish to see an object distinctly through a glass, we take care to wipe the glass free from all specks and dust." So ought we also to do with the mind. We ought to exercise the utmost vigilance and caution in the removal of every hindrance to the attainment of accuracy of mental perception,—every obstacle and impediment to the acquisition of truth. To do this effectually, we must consider it an all-paramount object in mental culture to become acquainted with the most common violations of the necessary laws of thought which the mind is liable to commit, and to gain a knowledge of the most usual fallacies—those specious apparently-legitimate syllogisms that

> "Keep the word of promise to the *ear*
> But break it to the *heart*,"—

which men are in the habit of employing. These will generally be found to abound in equivocal terms. Like the heathen oracles of old, they are double-meaning and indefinite. To sophistical reasoning the defects of language are a great assistance; for it is copious in seemingly synonymous terms, and phrases of nearly-allied signification. The taste which men have acquired for Rhetorical ornaments, and the custom, which our luxuriousness of ear has rendered necessary, of varying the terms and diction of our discourse, is another aid, if not sometimes an actual temptation, to the palming off of an elegantly-expressed ambiguity or sophism for the unadulterated ore of truth; thus reasoning *with* words instead of *by* them. Our own language, indeed, from its multiplex derivative sources, its copious verbology, its abundance of apparent parallelisms of expression, and its luxuriant variability of phrase, is peculiarily available for the concealment of Sophisms, and the utterance, in specious language, of errors in thought. Sophisms, like eastern serpents, are most frequently found hidden beneath the fairest flowers. Now as "Error is only effectually to be confounded by searching deep, and tracing it to its source,"[*] it becomes us, as rational creatures, to study well the error-liabilities of our nature. And let it not be thought, when comparing the high aims now enunciated, with the exemplifications contained in these brief chapters, that the whole purpose of the science is to teach men to expend their "ingenuity and industry" upon the λογοί ἀκανθωδεις—the thorny subtleties of a vain and sterile science, either upon *mere words*, or upon *nugæ difficiles* (laborious trifles), which have never yielded, and are never likely to yield, any substantial benefit to mankind, for there can be little doubt that, however apparently simple the examples given may be, if the principles be fairly illustrated by them, any party who thoroughly studies the subject will find that these principles are applicable to the detection of all errors of a similar nature, however much they may differ in the comparative importance of their several subjects. It is thus, indeed, that all sciences are taught; their principles are illustrated by references to the most simple specimens within reach of the mind of the author. To exemplify them by reference to the highest departments of truth, with which they concerned themselves, would exhibit the grossest pedantry, as well as the utmost injudiciousness.

Having proceeded thus far with our preamble, we have thought it advisable to check our wayward course, and with due regard to the impatience of our readers, we shall now set about the fulfilment of the promise made in the preceding chapter, viz., to present "an analytic view of the Semi-Logical and Non-Logical Fallacies."

In the purely Logical Fallacies, spoken of formerly, the erroneousness of the reasoning is quite evident, from the mere form of the expression ; in other words, from their direct violation of the laws of all true reasoning. The Fallacies of which we are now about to discourse, differ from these considerably. They *appear* to conform to the requirements of the reasoning faculty, and do not bear broadly on their front the evidence of their deceptiveness : hence they are much more likely to escape detection than the class of which we have already treated. "Now, here it is," say the opponents of Logic, "that the vanity of the Study appears most prominently ; for here it leaves the greatest difficulty untouched." With all due deference to those high authorities—those worshippers of Ego—who, with a wave of the hand, and a toss of the head, would consign the most perfect, finished, positive, and practical science which has been bequeathed to us by the genius of ancient time, to "the tomb of all the Capulets,"—we most humbly and respectfully depone—1st, That any accusation brought against a science to the effect that it does

* Sir J. Herschell's "Discourse on the Study of Natural Philosophy," p. 9.

not perform more than it professes to accomplish, is clearly irrelevant. 2nd, That to charge any *single* science with worthlessness, because it cannot efficiently perform that which it would require *all the sciences combined* to effectuate, is decidedly unfair. 3rd, That first to misapprehend the purpose and province of a science and then to charge that science with the consequences arising out of that misapprehension is a sheer case of "*petitio principii*." 4th, That they completely ignore the indirect aid which Logical science gives for the detection of such Fallacies—(*a*) by training the intellect to accuracy of though; (*b*) by pointing out the invariable *modus operandi* of the reasoning faculty; (*c*) by teaching us where the fallacy is most probably to be found, and (*d*) by informing us on what principles to condemn the fallacious argument when discovered. 5th, That if Logic is not "*the* Science of Reasoning," one of three things must follow—(*a*) there is no Science of Reasoning; (*b*) the Science of Reasoning is "part and parcel" of some other science; or (*c*) the Science of Reasoning is yet undiscovered. Are they prepared to maintain any one of these *theses?* They may answer by accusing us of being among those whom the Greek satirist contemptuously called ἔμποροι λήρου, λόγων ὑποκριτῆρες—traffickers in trifles, arbiters of verbalities; but this is scarcely argument, and until argument can be produced they will, perhaps, excuse our demanding *that* prior to conviction.

SEMILOGICAL FALLACIES are such as have a *middle term* of an ambiguous signification. In the purely Logical Fallacies the major and minor terms are compared with *different* parts of *the same middle term*, but in those now under review, the extremes are, in reality, compared with *two* different *middle* terms, in consequence of the variability of meaning alternately attached to the middle term—*i. e.*, in its being, while apparently the same word, employed in *two* diverse significations. This ambiguity may appear in many different forms, some of which we state below, viz. :—

I.—The ambiguity may originate in *the term itself*, and may thus produce, 1st, the fallacy of *equivocation*, and 2nd, the fallacy of *figure of speech*. The former signifies the employment of a middle term in such a manner that, in connection with each of the extremes, it may be understood in a different sense—*e. g.*,

> Whatever is capable of receiving a double meaning cannot have proceeded from a perfect moral being:
> The Bible contains many passages capable of receiving a double meaning;
> Therefore, the Bible cannot have proceeded from a perfect moral being;

in which the words "double meaning," in the major proposition, signify equivocal or ambiguous, and in the minor, a primary and secondary signification.   There are many words in our language capable of this *duplicity*—in both of its significations—of import : *e. g.*—*apparent*, meaning plain, visible, and seeming, not real ; *charge*, command, accusation ; *grateful*, thankful, or pleasant, agreeable ; *nervous*, weak in the nerves, or energetic ; *prefer*, to make choice of, or to promote, &c., &c.* The latter imports the use of a *middle term*, which is *paronymous* (*i. e.*, connected by grammatical affinity, as noun, adjective, or verb, &c., or derived from the same root), with one of the extremes, as if it were coincident in signification, or synonymous with it—*e. g.*,

> He who is well-known as a designing character ought never to be trusted :
> All engravers are professional designers ;
> Therefore, engravers ought never to be trusted.

It was a fallacy of this kind which a popular orator is reported to have employed for the disparagement of a rival, who was at the time suffering from ill health, when he said, " The gentleman has said he cannot venture himself in such an atmosphere, but this is the atmosphere in which I delight to breathe ;" where a metaphorical sense of the term atmosphere is adroitly substituted for the literal signification,—and yet this is said to have created a divertissement in his favour.

II.—The ambiguity may proceed from the different *applications* of which the word is susceptible. The difference of *application* may result, 1st, from accident ; 2nd, from neglecting to distinguish between the " first and second intention " of the terms ; 3rd, from a resemblance or analogy between the things spoken of, or the words employed to designate them ; 4th, from the same name being adopted as the sign of correlated things—*i. e.*, such as are connected in *time* or *place; as wholes* and *parts, cause* and *effect,* &c.   Indeed, " The mixture of those things by speech which by nature are divided" (and the separation of those things by speech which by nature are conjoined) " is the mother of all error."   As an example of the first species of the fallacies contained in this class, we quote the following from an old work in our possession, to which, as it wants the title-page, we cannot more particularly refer :—

> Nothing is better than heaven :
> A penny is better than nothing ;
> Therefore, a penny is better than heaven.

* See Trench "On the Study of Words," lect. iv. ; "A Selection of English Synonyms," edited by Archbishop Whately; and Whately's "Elements of Logic" (ninth edition), appendix i.

Here in the major proposition *nothing* is used in a *positive* sense; in the minor, however, it denotes a *negation*, and hence the signification in each is diverse.

Of the 2nd sort we consider it necessary to remark that words in the hands of the sophist are exceedingly flexible, and that a very slight divergency is frequently quite enough for his purpose; now to aid the reasoner in the detection of such fallacies, Logicians request us to note that words are, in general, changeable in their meaning as far as they possess (*a*) an etymological import, (*b*) a vague and general signification, and (*c*) a special and applied sense. The etymological signification of a word is that which it bears in the original language to which it can be traced,—*e.g.*, *thing* means all that we are able to *think* about. The general signification is that which includes and comprehends all the special senses of a term, and is what Logicians denominated the "first intention,"—*e.g.*, the word *line* signifies "extension in length," and consequently includes and comprehends within it, all the particular significations which it receives in Mathematics, Geography, Perspective, Military tactics, Angling, &c., and in common conversation. The special signification of a term is that limited and circumscribed sense in which it is employed in some one branch of knowledge, or in accordance with some professional technicality or conversational usage; this corresponds with what Logicians call the "second intention;"—*e.g.*, the word *physician*, which in its general sense ought to signify "one acquainted with *the Laws of Nature*"—νόμοι φυσεως,—is in a special sense employed to denote "one acquainted with *the Laws of Nature*, so far as they relate to health and disease." It was a fallacy of this kind which was employed during the rebellion of 1745, by the use of the word "pretender," which, in its general sense, means a claimant, and in its special signification, a *false* claimant. The following syllogism will be found invalid, if in the major we understand the word in a special, and in the minor in its general signification.

> Those who have aided or abetted a pretender ought to be
>   punished :
> Prince Charles is a pretender to the British throne ;
> Therefore, those who have aided or abetted him ought to be
>   punished.

Regarding the 3rd species of class 2, we may observe that there is a tendency in the mind to speak analogically, and to apply the same terms to objects or attributes which *resemble* each other ; thus we employ the words *sweet* and *beautiful* to characterize sights and sounds, while in reality, *sweet* is only applicable to *tastes*, and *beautiful* only to *sights*; so *acute*, which is originally applicable to *a cutting* instrument, is applied as a characterizing adjective to angles, sounds, tastes, sensations, and mental capacities, &c.; and thus we talk of "*ploughing* the deep," "*skimming* the surface," "*fathoming* a subject," "*overturning* an argument," "*weighing* an assertion," "*hunting* up a figure," "*pursuing* a topic," "*defeating* an object," "*crushing* an opponent," &c. In all these and similar cases, Logicians call the *primary* signification proper, and the secondary one *improper;* and it is necessary in all cases to observe that the *same sense* is always applied to the *same term* throughout the whole of the *same* piece of argumentation; thus the following apparent syllogism is invalid, because enthusiasm in the major signifies *zeal*, and in the minor, that *wild insanity* which was displayed ἐν θυσία in the sacrifices of the ancients.

> All who worship the God of the christians truly, must be filled with enthusiasm:
> But all enthusiasm is madness;
> Therefore, all who worship the God of the christians truly, must be filled with madness.

The following rules, if attended to carefully, may assist us in avoiding fallacies of this kind—viz., 1st. By whatever name any object has or may be once designated, by that name and no other let it always hereafter be called. 2nd. Whatever be the object in the designation of which any given word has been or may be employed, do not employ that same word as the designative of any other object;—or thus, in rhyme—

> To the same nature the same nomenclature:
> The same nomenclature to the same nature.

. Numerous errors originate in that sort of ambiguous terms, contained in class 4th. As instances of the *kind* of indefinite terms which constitute this class, we may mention *heat*, which signifies not only the quality of *producing* certain impressions in us, but also the *impressions* themselves;—sensation, which denotes both the faculty of mind which is capable of being impressed, by any external object, through the senses, and each effect pleasurable, painful, or indifferent which reaches the mentality through the operation of any cause external to that mind; when we employ that figure of speech denominated *Synecdoche*, in which the whole is spoken of as a part, or a part as the whole; we are liable to become the dupes either of our own inattention, or of the wiles of the Sophist—*e.g.*, the following syllogism is fallacious, because it does not allow for the figure of speech contained in the passage to which it refers :—

> If the Scriptures command us to do that which is absurd, they
>   cannot be divinely inspired :
> But they command us " to preach the gospel to *every creature*,"—
>   *i. e.*, to insects, fishes, birds, and animals, which is absurd ;
> Therefore, the Scriptures cannot be divinely inspired.

The specific which Logic recommends as a preservative against being imposed upon by any one of the fallacies contained in either of the two classes of which we have now spoken, is to demand a definition of the suspected term or its applications *in so far as regards the argument at issue*, and then to show the incongruency of signification which has been admitted into the apparent syllogism.

III.—This class contains those fallacies which may arise from the artful manner in which the question is placed before the mind of the hearer ; and thus it comprises the fallacy of many interrogations. It is a very convenient circumstance for the sophist that the mind of man is exceedingly desirous of Rhetorical ornamentation, and of being pleasurably stimulated by figures of speech and the *curiosa felicitas* of diction ; hence the beauties of style are highly valued, and knowing that while the mind is acquiring pleasure, the acuteness of the intellect is less actively displayed, the sophist, very naturally, cultivates the " art of pleasing " with much assiduity, and adapts his style to the purpose in view. *Erotesis*, or interrogation, by enabling him to conceal the duplex signification which he wishes to have attached to any particular phrase, becomes one of his favourite means of stultifying the mind. It admits of two varieties—1st. That in which the terms are so arranged as to involve more than one question, each of which requires a different answer, while it in appearance requires only one—*e. g.*, Ought we to act according to expediency ?—meaning either ought we ever to act according to expediency ? or is expediency a proper rule of action ? 2nd. That in which the question is put in such a way as to leave the *extent* of the question indefinite—*e. g.*, Do not children owe subordination to their parents ? meaning either subordination *in all things* or in *those only* which are *just*. This species of fallacy is avoided by showing the distinction between the questions, and answering them in turn.

IV.—This class is composed of those apparent-syllogisms which become ambiguous from the *context*, or from the arrangement of the words in a sentence. It comprises—1st, fallacies of ambiguous arrangement ; 2nd, fallacies of division ; 3rd, fallacies of composition ; 4th, fallacies of accident.

In case 1st of this class, the terms are so disposed that they may readily be understood in two senses. Some of the ancient heathen oracles affords excellent specimens of this sophistical artifice, *e. g.*, the response of the oracle of Apollo to Pyrrhus the King of Epirus,—" Aio te, Æacida, Romanos vincere posse," which may either signify, " I tell thee the Romans are able to conquer you," or, " I tell thee thou art able to conquer the Romans."   Our own Shakespeare has been successful in imparting a similar indefiniteness to one of his witch-prophecies, when he says,—

<blockquote>" The Duke yet lives that Henry shall depose ;"</blockquote>

which may mean either that the duke shall depose Henry, or that Henry shall depose the duke.   In the fallacies of the 2nd sort comprehended in this class, the middle term is used *collectively* in the *major premiss*, and *distributively* in the *minor—e. g.*,

> All the taxes levied upon the inhabitants of this country, per annum, amount to about £76,000,000.
> But this amount divided among 26,000,000 of inhabitants gives less than £3 per annum to each person ;
> Therefore, each person in this country is lightly taxed.

Here it may be shown that what is true of a *collective* whole, is not necessarily true of each individual unity ;—*e. g.*,

> *All* the apples on this tree are worth five shillings :
> This is an apple on that tree ;
> Therefore, it is worth five shillings.

The 3rd species of fallacy comprised in this class, is precisely the reverse of that which precedes it.   In the seeming syllogisms which it comprehends, the major premiss is employed in a distributive sense, and the minor in a collective one, thus assuming that what is true of *some* of the individuals of a class, is true also of *all* the individuals in that class ;—*e. g.*,

> Monopolies in the corn trade, the manufacture of certain kinds of goods, the selling of particular sorts of commodities, the granting of certain privileges, &c., &c., are beneficial to the several monopoly holders :
> But these monopoly holders constitute the whole community ;
> Therefore a system of monopolies is beneficial to the whole community.

Here it will require to be shown that the several monopolies are only beneficial when held *separately*, not when each individual or class has a peculiar monopoly of his or its own, and so in all other cases the fallacy lies in assuming that what is true of the *single* members of a class is true of all that class taken together.

Of the fallacy of accidents, case 4th, there are three varieties, viz., (*a*) When what is predicable of a thing simply, and absolutely, is assumed to be true in *particular circumstances;* (*b*) When what is true of a thing *under certain circumstances* is assumed to be true concerning it, *absolutely* and essentially; (*c*) When what is able to be predicated of a thing *under certain circumstances* is predicated of it in *other*, and these *differing circumstances.* These fallacies are to be controverted by showing the difference between the thing itself,—simply and absolutely considered,—and the concomitant circumstances with which it is surrounded in the given instance—*e. g.,*

> The true Church of Christ has existed since the days of the Apostles :
> The Protestant churches have not existed since the days of the Apostles ;
> Therefore no one of the Protestant churches can be the "true Church."

> Those who are over-credulous ought not to have their statements relied upon:
> The Ancient Historians were in many instances over-credulous ;
> Therefore they ought never to have their statements relied upon.

> It is the right of a Briton to be free: (*Meaning so long as he is obedient to the laws of his country :*)
> I am a Briton ; (*one who has transgressed the laws ;*)
> Therefore I ought to be free.

By showing the variable and partial uses of the terms employed, or the circumstantial difference implied, we extricate ourselves from the necessity of admitting the fallacious reasoning.

NON-LOGICAL OR MATERIAL FALLACIES are such as contain errors in the opinions assumed as premisses, or in the conclusion deduced, rather than in any readily-perceptible divergence from the syllogistic form. Of such Fallacies there are two species :—1st. Those in which the premisses are unduly assumed. 2nd. Those in which the conclusion is irrelevant, *i.e.*, not such as is demanded by the argument.

I. In the class whose premises are unduly assumed there are several nearly related but distinct species of Fallacies. 1st. Those which involve a *petitio principii, i.e.,* in which premisses are employed, either equivalent, in reality, to the conclusion, or necessarily involving it. 2nd. Those which are denominated by Aristotelians *non causa pro causa*, *i.e.*, assigning a reason which is either insufficient as evidence, not itself adequately proven, or not necessarily connected with the conclusion which is sought to be established by it. 3rd. *Reasoning in a Circle*, in which, in a series of arguments, the same facts or opinions are employed both as the *media of proof* by which the conclusion is to be established, and the conclusion which is supposed to be proven by them. There are many contrivances employed, and many disguises put on, by the Sophist, in order to avoid detection in the use of such seeming-arguments; sometimes terms are made use of which are widely different in appearance, but which, in reality, possess the same signification; sometimes by diffuse and wordy disquisition he is enabled to separate the premisses so far that the *real point* which *ought* to have been proven is lost sight of, and another *somewhat* like it is substituted in its place; at other times he introduces as a premiss an assertion which, along with something else, by which it is concealed, involves the conclusion.

1st. The following apparent argument is invalid, viz. :—

Induction is the only true science of Reasoning;
Syllogistic Logic is not Induction;
Therefore Syllogistic Logic is not the true science of Reasoning:

because in the premisses the point is already definitely assumed by the exclusion of all other sciences of Reasoning except Induction, *i.e.*, the major premiss distinctly involves the conclusion deduced from it. Now to reason on the assumption that certain opinions are accurate, which have not been proven, and are not at all likely to be granted in any discussion upon any topics between parties who properly understand the terms employed, is manifestly to lay a foundation upon broken reeds, while to attempt to prove an opinion by asserting that same opinion in different phraseology is obviously absurd.

2nd. As an example of the Fallacy *non causa pro causa* we might adduce the anecdote which is related of Charles II., and Milton, viz., Charles II. having seen Milton, who at this time had, in consequence of the strenuous exertions made by him in favour of popular liberty, become blind, thus accosted him:—"Think you not that the crime which you committed against my father must have been very great, seeing that Heaven has seen fit to punish it by such a severe loss as that which you have sustained?" "Nay, sire," Milton replied, "if my crime *on that account* may be adjudged great, how much greater must have been the criminality of your father, seeing that I have only lost my eyes, but he his head." As another example, we may subjoin a succinct account of "Ricardo's Theory of Rent." Ricardo asserts that the varying fertility of different soils is the *cause* of rent, and defines rent to be the difference between the produce of the same amount of capital on an inferiorly fertile soil, and that which is superior. Hence it will follow that were there no inferiority of productive power in different soils, there would be no rent. Syllogistically thus :—

> Whenever a cause is inoperative, the effect cannot result :
> The varying fertility of existing soils is the *cause* of rent ;
> Therefore were there no soils of differing fertility, there would be no rent.

Now it is quite obvious that this is a flagrant Fallacy—an instance of "*non causa pro causa*," for in point of fact the scarcity of fertile soil in comparison to the wants of mankind, and the consequent *competition* between parties for its possession, is that which causes rent to be offered and taken, and it is because the better sorts of land pay rent that the inferiorly productive soils are taken into cultivation.

3rd. Of "Reasoning in a Circle," we may subjoin the following instance, viz. :—

> The Scriptures being divinely inspired, whatever they declare to be true must be so :
> The Scriptures declare that God exists ;
> Therefore that God exists is true.

Here it is evident that the being of God is presupposed in the fact of the Scriptures being divinely inspired, and then we deduce the fact of God's existence from the declaration of that book which he is said to have inspired, thus assuming his existence, in the very act of *proving*,—which is absurd. The above class of Fallacies are generally couched in a phrase, which throws the mind out of its reckoning. Obscure diction, sly insinuations, cunning inuendos, artful twining together of words, hardihood of assertion, &c., are some of the means employed by the Sophist, either to ensnare or brow-beat his opponent. In order to prevent ourselves from being made his victims, we must call for explicit expression, clear unambiguous diction, plain statements, and the authorities on which they rest, and a collocation of words perfectly free from the possibility of having an uncertain meaning attached to them. At the same time we must show the defects of perspicuity or accuracy under which his phraseology labours—the inexactness of his statements, the want of connexion between the reason or cause assigned by him, and that which is the real one ; and otherwise use every available means to reform him, as well as to acquire truth for ourselves.

II. The class of Fallacies which are included in the characteristic of having *irrelevant conclusions* may be more lengthily defined as consisting of such specimens of reasoning as substitute for the conclusion which truly results from the premisses, or which the question at issue demands,—another essentially different, though related to it with various degrees of nearness or remoteness. Of such Fallacious methods of procedure there are several sorts, viz.—1st. Changing the point in dispute. 2nd. Reasoning from alternate premisses to alternate conclusions. 3rd. Proving only a part of the conclusion. 4th. Proving too much. 5th. The Fallacy of objections. 6th. The suppression of the truth.

1st. The Fallacies which are included under this head, viz., "Changing the point in dispute," are frequently very dexterously and covertly performed; this is materially assisted by a series of nicely rounded and sonorous periods, in which a series of pseudo-synonymes have been employed, all bearing some general relation to the signification of the real term—some slight connexion in apparent meaning to *the term* requiring, for the time being, to be shrouded in mist. In long, keenly-contested, and exciting debate, this Fallacy is very often employed, the losing party's egotism gains the ascendancy over his love of truth, and, by a wily stratagem which can only be adequately described by the use of the Vulgar Americanism "dodge," he manages to create such a "*sensation*" by a collocation of fine-spun sentences, that he is able to escape from his unlucky *locale* and gain a new vantage-ground. Thus, if in the present much-disputed Educational question a person should prove that it was necessary that all the people should be educated, instead of proving that the people, in general, were *not* educated, and should then proceed as if he had proven *that* to advance a claim for state-interference, he would be guilty of the fallacy of changing the point in dispute. Of course, if ingeniously and showily advanced, such a sophism might pass undiscovered; but the fallacy would not, on that account, be the less egregious.

2nd. The fallacies comprehended under the title "reasoning from alternate premisses to alternate conclusions," is of most frequent recurrence in oral debate or disquisition, although it may sometimes also be found in written works, but then it creates a prejudice against itself, by giving the work a loose, disjointed, and incoherent appearance; the web of thought seems loosely and carelessly woven. Thus a person may reason from the probable to the possible, and from that again to the probable; from justice to expediency, and back again to justice; from the particular to the universal, and thence to the particular again; from the abstract to the concrete, and revert to the abstract; from the absolute to the absolute and accidental conjoined, and thence recur to the absolute, and *vice versâ* in each case. It is by a fallacy of this description that slave-holding is sometimes sought to be justified, *viz.*:

It is expedient that slaves should be held: (*Here follow certain illustrations of the* (apparent) *truth of this proposition:*)
But true expediency must always accord with justice;
Therefore it is right and proper that slaves should be held.

3rd. "Proving only a part of the conclusion" is a very common fallacy with inexperienced thinkers, and is not unfrequently a useful instrument in the hand of the sophist. It is not always easy to keep before the mind's eye a clear and definite idea of the *extent* of proof required in order to establish a given proposition, and in the self-esteem of the auditors, the disingenuous speaker frequently finds a potent ally. He has only to address a few words of flattery to them on their general intelligence, to assert that the inference is perfectly clear, that any one of ordinary sagacity may readily and easily find proofs in everything around him, and that all who are not wilfully blind or virtually insane must arrive at the same conclusion as that at which he has arrived, and of which he might have convinced them more at length, by adducing other innumerable and irrefragable proofs, did he not feel that he would in so doing be guilty of at once insulting their judgment and wasting their highly valuable time. There is an admirable article entitled "Plenty more in the Cellar," in one of "Old Humphrey's" works, which is a clever *exposé* of this fallacy, but which from its length we are precluded from inserting. If it be wished to deny the professional skill of any party it will not do to give as a reason that the person became a bankrupt: such an argument would prove too little, as it would still require to be shown—which we opine could not—that success invariably attends professional skill, and that such skill may not be combined with deficiency in business habits, &c.

4th. This kind of fallacy is the reverse of the last mentioned. In it the speaker *proves too much* for the point which he wishes to establish, and consequently invalidates his argument. Of such fallacies the following is an instance. "In all demonstrative sciences," says Hume, "the rules are *certain* and *infallible*; but when we apply them, our *fallible* and *uncertain* faculties are very apt to depart from them and fall into error." He had forgot surely that the rules of the demon-strative sciences are discovered by our "*fallible* and *uncertain* faculties," and have no authority but that of human judgment. If they be infallible some human judgments are infallible. * * * He claims *infallibility* to certain decisions of the human faculties in order to prove that *all* their decisions are *fallible*."*

5th. "The fallacy of objections" is an exceedingly unfair method of reasoning, and despite of its frequency of use, is altogether inad-missible as a correct process of argumentation. It consists in a person's advancing a series of objections against an opinion, and requesting you to reject that opinion on account of the objections urged against it. Now this is not the proper way to put an argument; for it must be considered whether there are more or greater objections urgeable *against* that opinion, than *for* it; as well as whether there may not be *more* and *greater* objections against the opinion sought to be *substituted* for it. "But," the Sophist will say, when he is beaten out of this stronghold, "we do not wish you to accept of our opinion, we only wish you to judge impartially; we only wish you to remain unpledged to any one of the opinions so long as such objec-tions are capable of being urged against it." Such a mode of arguing involves a Fallacy, for it is a virtual call for a decision in his favour, while he *seems* only to request neutrality. "Not to resolve, is to resolve," says Bacon. Hence it follows that to remain neutral is to decide in favour of the Sophist's proposition. In all such argumen-tations the objections should be carefully balanced, accurately weighed, and the decision given to that opinion against which the fewest and least important objections can be produced; *e. g.*, if the argument for the "division of labour" be assailed by the objections that it degrades the character of the common artizan, and reduces the operator to an almost instinct-moved animal,—that it debilitates the body, and renders the habits enervated,—that it introduces an insipid uniformity into life, and produces a general torpor of the intellect, and the annihilation of every manly virtue, these objections must be compared with, not only,—Firstly, the advantages resulting from the division of labour, but also, Secondly, with the disadvantages connected with its aboli-tion. Some of the advantages are,—it increases the dexterity of the manipulative power of the artizan—concentrates his mind on the per-fection of his work—adds to the likelihood of invention—enables the work to be more expeditiously performed—multiplies the conveniences of life, and renders them, in consequence of their cheapness, more

* Reid's "Essays on the Human Mind," Essay vii. chap. vi.

readily attainable. Some of the disadvantages of its abolition are, —the impossibility of every man producing, making, bartering, doing, &c., everything for himself—the discomforts and semi-barbarism which would ensue from this—the differing tastes and capacities of men— the absolute necessity for some such division of labour for the maintenance of Government—the making of laws—the spread of education, and the cultivation of science, &c. Were we to remain undecided upon this question because of the objections urged against it, we could not adopt the division of labour, and consequently would, virtually, be giving a decision in the objector's favour.

6th. *Fallacies of the sort denominated suppressio veri* may be employed in a thousand different ways; they are all, however, characterized by the fact that they contain a skilful evasion of the *point* of an argument by an ellipsis of some essential term in it; or, when making an attack, by leaving out some qualifying word or phrase by which an erroneous impression may be created, and an unfair advantage gained—*e. g.*,

> The National Public School Association will not permit (*sectarian*) religion to be taught in schools :
> Any Association which advocates the abolition of (—?) religious education in schools, may justly be stigmatized as an infidel one ;
> Therefore the National Public School Association is an infidel body.

There are a few Latin technicalisms in common use among Logicians, which we think it may be advisable in this place briefly to explain, viz., *A priori*, — Reasoning from the cause to the effect. *A posteriori*, — Reasoning from the effect to the cause. *Argumentum a fortiori, aut ex magis probabili ad minus*, — An argument from one established conclusion to another which ought to be stronger, *e. g.*, If we ought even to love our enemies, how much more ought we to love our friends? *Argumentum ex concesso*,—Reasoning from the truth of a proposition on which it was agreed to give up the contested point. *Argumentum ad judicium*,—Reasoning by an appeal to common sense for a substantiation of the facts stated. *Argumentum ad ignorantiam*,—An argument derived from our opponent's ignorance. *Argumentum ad hominem*,—An argument founded upon the principles, belief, or opinion of our antagonists, whether these are right or wrong. *Argumentum ad fidem*, — An argument which is derived from our reliance upon testimony. *Argumentum ad verecundiam*,— An argument drawn from the modesty of our opponent by quoting an authority which he will be ashamed to have the egotism to disregard. *Argumentum ad populum aut passiones,*—An appeal to the prejudices, passions, or feelings of the mob. *Reductio ad absurdum,*—A proof of the truth of anything by showing the folly or absurdity of a contrary opinion. All the above mentioned kinds of arguments, although perfectly warrantable and admissible in particular circumstances, are generally fallacious when employed as *absolute* proofs. They may be employed in order to arouse attention, disarm prejudice, silence quibbling, produce carefulness in the expression of arguments, show the probability of a thing which is thought improbable, &c. But they ought seldom to be employed as positively and irrefragably demonstrating a general or absolute truth.

In concluding the present chapter, let us exhort each reader to labour diligently for the acquisition of accuracy of thought; freedom from self-delusion, or readiness to be deceived by Sophistries. Let not our labours in the composition of the present work be " the mere record of a vain endeavour " to aid the " good time coming ;" but may it in after days produce fruit in the keenness and closeness of the reasoning of those who have studied it. Let the instructions, which we flatter ourselves they contain, be carefully digested by their minds, and received into the thought-circulation of their mentality, that they may at all times be able to avoid the snares of the Sophist.

"There *are* certain ideas, or *forms of mental apprehension*, which may be applied to facts in such a manner as to bring into view *fundamental principles of science;* while the same facts, however arranged or reasoned about, so long as these *appropriate ideas* are not employed, cannot give rise to any exact or substantial knowledge."— WHEWELL.

"By Method, I understand a collection of certain and easy rules, of such a nature as to prevent any one, who shall have observed them with accuracy, from assuming, at any time, the untrue for the true, by which, no exértion of the mind being uselessly expended, but, on the contrary, science being gradually increased, a person may attain to a true knowledge of all those things of which his capacity permits the attainment."— DESCARTES.

"THE word METHOD (μεθοδος) being of Grecian origin * * * it is in the Greek language that we must seek for its primary and fundamental signification. Now, in Greek, it literally means a way, or path of transit. Hence the first idea of *method* is a *progressive transition* from one step in any course to another."* Accepting this account of the primal import of the term, and influenced by a maturer consideration as well as a deeper and more comprehensive study of the subject, we are now inclined to give the word Method a wider and more extensive significancy than that given to it in our introductory chapter. Our recent studies have enabled us to become more conversant than before with the chief metaphysical writers of Germany and France, especially Kant, Jacobi, Fichte, Schelling, and Hegel amongst the former; and Descartes, Buffier, Cousin, Jouffroy, Comte, &c., among the latter; while we have of late been necessitated to bestow a considerable degree of time and attention to a re-perusal of most of the metaphysical articles of Sir Wm. Hamilton, Thos. De Quincey, Dr. Ferrier, G. H. Lewes, &c., as well as the works of Bacon, Brown, Coleridge, Hallam, Whewell, Mill, Maurice, Morell, &c. In the course of these studies we have become so convinced of the great, nay, indispensable, importance of Method in the acquisition of knowledge, that we beg our readers to accept of the following amplified definition of that term—viz., *Method is the arrangement of our ideas, that is, the results of our perceptivity, judgment, and ratiocination in such a manner as shall best facilitate*

* Coleridge "On Method," p. 14, Ency. Metro., New Ed.

the acquisition, remembrance, and communication of knowledge. According to this definition, it will appear that Method consists of these three parts—viz.:—I. Those arrangements of ideas which relate to the facilitation of the acquisition of knowledge, including a theoretical and practical acquaintance with the rules of syllogistic logic, and the principles of philosophical investigation generally. II. Those arrangements of ideas which have reference to the storing up of knowledge in the memory, comprising an acquaintance with the laws of logical classification and division, together with an aptness in applying them; as well as a knowledge of those laws of mnemonics and of simple and relative suggestion which are discoverable by the study of the mind. III. Those arrangements of ideas which assist in the communication of knowledge, comprehending the classification, co-ordination, and succession of ideas, the laws of composition and criticism, &c., which are necessary for the interchange of information.

"All things in us, and about us, are a chaos, without Method; and so long as the mind is entirely passive, so long as there is an habitual submission of the understanding to mere events and images, as such, without any attempt to arrange and classify them, so long the chaos must continue. There may be transition, but there can never be progress—there may be sensation, but there cannot be thought; for the total absence of Method renders thinking impracticable, as we find that partial defects of Method proportionably render thinking a trouble and fatigue. But as soon as the mind becomes accustomed to contemplate, not *things* only, but likewise the *relations* of things, there is immediate need of some path, or way of transit, from one to another of the things related;—there must be some law of agreement or contrast between them—there must be some mode of comparison; in short, there must be Method. We may, therefore, assert that the *relations of things* form the prime objects, or, so to speak, the materials of Method, and that the contemplation of those relations is the indispensable condition of thinking methodically. Of these relations of things we distinguish two principal kinds. One of them is the relation by which we understand that a thing *must be;* the other, that by which we merely perceive that it *is.*" * The former is that which is to occupy our attention in the present chapter, the latter we shall briefly notice in our next.

Method is a collection of rules which, if we follow out legitimately, will realize a given end. A Method, however, will and must vary according to the end pursued. In our present chapter we shall assume

* Coleridge "On Method," p. 15.

that the attainment of true knowledge is the aim of the reader, and we shall arrange our remarks for the purpose of aiding him in the accomplishment of this praiseworthy and honourable design. In every investigative process about which our minds can be employed, there must be some definite and particular *points* which require elucidation, arrangement, and consecutive ordination, and that department of logical science which teaches the *modus operandi* of classification in such a manner as shall make each antecedent point tend to the explanation and ready comprehension of each and all of its sequents, is included under the term Method. Considered as effecting this object, the study of Method is all-important, for it is through such instructions as these that we are enabled to carry up every fact to successive platforms, and find in every fact a germ of expansion. True it is that this seems to demand a comprehensive eye and a well-balanced soul; but it must be recollected that strict discipline is necessary in order to acquire these, and that if we wait until we feel ourselves possessed of them we shall wait long indeed. Rather let us at once begin to culture our intellect to cope with the necessities and requirements of our being, and labour diligently for the attainment of that "philosophic habitude of soul" which the study of Method is calculated to superinduce. Method demands of us, as an initiative, that we should lay restraints upon our mental powers—that we should determine the channel in which the mind's activities should flow—and that we should aim at the concentration and subordination of the intellect. We must not be mere passive recipients of impressions—mere reservoirs of stagnating thought—mere changelings, whose minds are agitated into thought-ripples by every wind of circumstance that fans them—but men of steady, stubborn thought, who will not stand appalled at obstacles, but are determined to search diligently for truth "until we find it." If we be so, Method will be most willing to become our ally. It will teach us how to keep the object—*id quod jacet ob oculos*—at which we are aiming, continually before us, and so to change our position in regard to it as shall enable us to see the light falling upon it in the greatest number of directions. Thus only can true knowledge be obtained. "To try wrong guesses is apparently the only way to hit upon right ones. The character of the true philosopher is, not that he never conjectures hazardously, but that his conjectures are clearly conceived and brought into rigid contact with facts. He sees and compares distinctly the ideas and the things— the relations of his notions to each other and phenomena. Under these conditions it is not only excusable, but necessary for him, to snatch at every semblance of general rule, to try all promising forms of simplicity and symmetry,"* for "it must be obvious to the most superficial thinker, that discovery consists either in the detection of some concealed relation, some deep-seated affinity which baffles ordinary research, or in the discovery of some simple fact which is connected by slender ramifications with the subject to be investigated; but which, when once detected, carries us back by its divergence to all the phenomena which it embraces and explains."†

Some of the pre-requisites of Method—some of those essentials without which no Method can be philosophically excogitated, properly understood, or practically applied, may now be mentioned. We must possess an acquaintance with the nature of those powers whose operations we are desirous of directing, wherein they can serve us, and wherein they are likely to fail. We must know how our intellect may most easily be brought to perform its functions with accuracy, and what precautions are necessary in the reception of the reports of our senses. This requires a knowledge of the elementary powers of the mentality as well as of the laws which govern their operations. We must know how truth may be evolved from truth—how the variable and complicated may be reduced to sameness, simplicity, and unicality —how the mind must proceed in the "manipulation" of facts in order to educe the sciences and the arts. We must analyse the movements and doings of the mind, observe and experimentalize upon our own thoughts, and become practically conversant with the best methods of employing them. Hence results the necessity of studying the syllogistic logic, in order that we may learn the necessary laws by which conclusions may be legitimately and determinately deduced from given premisses. But we must do far more than this: we must bring the multifarious and insulated phenomena which surround us, within the grasp of generalized principles—we must read our experience attentively, and thence gain new premisses for new syllogisms; and when our own experience is too limited, we must enrich our minds with the experiences of others, or acquire an artificial experience by the employment of experimentation, and from all these sources gain the materials on which to syllogise in future. The qualities, attributes, relations, &c., of the objectivities around us must be carefully conned and observed, in order, if possible, to unicalize the divergent rays of things, and to concentrate their apparently aimless diffuseness into definite *foci*, that thus we may be able to generalize slowly, going from particular things to those that are more general, and from those to others of greater extent, and so on

* Whewell's "History of the Inductive Sciences," vol. I., p. 373.
† Brewster's "Life of Sir Isaac Newton," p. 336.

until we arrive at the universal laws of nature.* We must study the principles which pervade nature—the causes which operate in the production of effects—the modes of operation which natural objects follow —the sequences in which they advance, recede, or otherwise exert themselves—distinguish between concomitances or concurrent facts and those which exert a causative agency—learn the limits by which causes and effects are conjoined, and acquire a knowledge of the universal and immutable as contradistinguished from the transient and individual. We must discover the grand centres round which, as in an orbit, phenomena revolve—from which their utility and beneficiality are derived. Facts must be observed in their concrete form, their coincidences and similarities traced out, until from them extensive and abstract generalizations and *formulæ* are deduced, and then these elemental forms of reasoning must be re-pursued from the abstract and generalized to the concrete and particular. Every conception must be subjected to the rigid test of experiment, and the deliberate inquiry and plodding drudgery of induction and deduction must be undeviatingly pursued. In Method we must believe Milton, when he asserts that

> " ———— in the soul
> Are many faculties, which serve
> Reason as *chief*,"

and make every other faculty subordinate to it. The senses and reflection conjoined, may yield the elementary ideas, memory may store them up, judgment may arrange and classify them, but reason must co-ordinate, deduce, and infer. When we are

> " Voyaging through strange seas of thought alone"

she must direct the helm, consult the compass, and survey the chart. Unless such be the Method pursued by us in all our investigations, we may depend upon being named as belonging to that class whom the satirist stigmatizes as

> " By dint of experience improving in blunders."

Let us, by all means, avoid this, by examining calmly, observing carefully and minutely, experimenting perseveringly, analyzing accurately, and thinking methodically, ever looking upon each idea as the embryo of a new truth, which, like the favourably-planted acorn, may fructify, and grow, and reproduce; for "we know that a physical principle, when it becomes a scientific truth, has a thousand-fold application, of which we knew nothing before. . . . The moment a broad principle is educed and brought into the light of a scientific fact, we can at once apply it to every branch of human knowledge; we can clear away with

* Bacon's " *Nov. Org.*," Aphorisms-xix. and civ.

it a thousand errors or absurdities which cluster round the region of unphilosophical thinking; and by its suggestion can point the way to new developments of noblest truth."* It is from such generalization as this that knowledge derives all its value. "Without it our information would be reduced to scattered and unconnected facts, which, like separate filaments, would be utterly destitute of strength. If knowledge be power, it is because its threads are bound and twisted together in general theorems. And theory, so far from being inconsistent with practice, is practice itself, and that in the most extensive meaning of the term. The theorist differs, it is true, from the practical man; for the one is conversant with facts collectively, the other individually. The one is a wholesale dealer in experience, the other only retails it."†

It must have been observed from our preceding chapters, as well as from the opinions expressed in this one, that we are no exclusives—no bigoted and devoted followers of any schematist. In philosophical speculations we can aver that we are

" Nullius addictus jurare in verba magistri."

We believe that science has an *obverse* and a *reverse* side—that each fact is related on one side to *induction*, and on the other to *deduction*—that the mental energies of man must be regulated and trained, and must have their activity subordinated and determined by the study of the syllogistic *formulæ*, as well as invigorated and exercised, stimulated and quickened, enriched and fertilized by the practice of the laws of the Baconian Induction. We must not only know how to develop thought, but also how to acquire the elements from which thought is to be eliminated. Facts must form the food which we are mentally to digest, receive into the circulation of our Reason, and employ in life, business, study, and action. If to trace effects to their causes, to become acquainted with the Laws of Nature, and to learn the invariable sequences of phenomena, be the object of all science; and if facts be the manifestations of law—the effects of an intelligent *pre-coordination* of phenomena, then it can only be by the study of facts, that a knowledge of the laws on which facts depend, can be attained— that science can be rendered possible. But each fact must be looked at by the eye of Reason, in the light of common sense, and interpreted by the aid of phenomena of a kindred character, before its scientific value can be settled. We must institute a rigid and severe process of analy-

---

* Morell "On the Philosophical Tendencies of the Age," p. 167, 168.

† Dr. Dionysius Lardner's "Discourse on the Advantages of Natural Philosophy and Astronomy," 1829; p. 26.

zation, in order to ascertain all the ingredients which enter into the causation of any phenomenon, and separate it from all foreign or adventitious admixture : having done so, we can infer that all similar phenomena are the result of the same causative elements. Thus far Induction will bring us, but there is another process, no less necessary and imperative, viz., to take this general truth as a torch-light to farther discoveries,—to go forth and demand of phenomena whether they homologate the inference, whether they support the theory. Not only this, but the work of *prescience* is yet all to be done ; events have to be calculated and foretold ; and having thus acquired the law, man has now to go farther forward, has to conquer the realms of practice, and institute the arts ; these latter processes are the task of deductive philosophy. The Empiricist may scorn Theory and deal skilfully with isolated particulars,—the man of details may talk with apparent learnedness,—the practical man may pride himself · on his inductions of particulars ; but unless Theory be verified by deduction, science is but as

——" a tale
Told by an idiot, full of sound and fury,
Signifying nothing,"

and can never become what it ought to be, a vast classified collection of fruitful and immortal truths,—the mother of the arts and the ameliorator of life.

In farther prelecting on the present topic it may not be unadvisable to lay before our readers a few remarks on *the true method of science.* Science is systematized knowledge—knowledge co-ordinated by the eye of Reason in the light of law. True science consists not of mere orderly tabular or schematic arrangements of fact ; this is but the natural history,—the preparatory step to true science. Perceptivity furnishes the mentality with the conceptions. Judgment (in its function of induction) supplies the classification, by which the mind is placed in a position to apprehend the relations of things—whether obvious or latent. Ratiocination connects phenomena by a principle of causality by which new truths may be correctly evolved, and by which future phenomena may be calculated. Perceptivity gives the term, — Judgment, the proposition, — Ratiocination, the Syllogism. Science invariably begins with individualities, but if it terminated there, it would be empiricism and not Science. Not until we rise from specific phenomena to general laws can we be said, with truth, to have attained to a scientific view of realities. Thus alone can truths receive a scientific connective, and a true unition-bond. Science is not the educt of sense but of reason,—is not the result of mere perceptual activity but of mental, *i.e.*, rational idea-elimination. Sense is incapable of observing the *power* by which phenomena are evolved. Reason's well-trained and clear-visioned orb alone can gain a glimpse of that essential element in all philosophically-conducted speculation—a colligating conception. Gravity, Electricity, Magnetism, Time, Space, Force, &c., are not given in the sensational portion of man's nature, but in the ratiocinative part. Hence it follows that Induction is not the *logical*, but the *chronological* beginning of science. Nature is so adapted to the constitution of our minds that it is continually placing us in such circumstances as gradually " excite its vegetating and germinating powers to produce new fruits of thoughts, new conceptions, new imaginations and ideas," and these we must arrange and classify. Individualities must be separated into that which is *essential*, and that which is *accidental*. Science originates with the analytic powers, but cannot be completed without the aid of the Synthetic faculty. By Analysis we mean the resolving of a complex whole into its elementary parts, that power by which we are enabled to discriminate the essence of a thing from its accidents. By Synthesis we understand the placing together of a number of discriminated facts, in order to educe from them a definite truth. The former constitutes Induction, and proceeds upon the truth of the axiom that *whatever is true of all the constituent specificalities, is true likewise of the constituted generic idea.* The latter constitutes Deduction, and proceeds upon the reverse maxim, viz.,—*Whatever is true of the constituted generic idea, is true likewise of all the constituent specificalities*, or in other words, viz., those of the Aristotelic *dictum*,—" Whatever is predicable or predicated, concerning any term distributed, whether affirmatively, or negatively, is predicable, or may be predicated, in the same sense, concerning any or every thing contained under that distributed term." Induction, it will now be seen, investigates and assimilates a plurality of objectivities, and reduces them to a unical, all-inclusive idea. Deduction, on the contrary, begins with ideas unicalized,—possessed of a mental oneness,—and predicates unicality of attributes to each of the plurality of thoughts contained, or bound up together, in those generic ideas. The one examines the *physical* wholes of things, the other their *logical* wholes. What is true of a logical whole is true of each of its parts; what is true of a physical whole, however, is not so. The one collects the facts of phenomena, and strives therefrom to acquire a general idea or law, the other posits this idea or law, and endeavours to classify phenomena under it. The former receives and operates upon ideas in their greatest *comprehension*, the latter in their greatest *exten-sion.* "In fact, between the *deductive* method and the *inductive* method there is only this difference, that in the former we begin with the *major* and *minor* premisses, and *deduce* the *consequent;* whereas in the latter we begin with the *minor premiss* (the observed conditions) and the consequent (the attendant phenomena), and from these *infer* the *major premiss,*—that is, the law or generalized fact." * Thus it is evident that these methods are not antagonistic, but mutually aidant,—not rival, but co-operative systems,—the one is but the necessary com-plement of the other. To reason without having a solid substratum of facts is certainly folly, and is, of all things, the most likely to lead us to the formation of erroneous opinions. While, on the other hand, an unqualified and exclusive advocacy of the Inductive philosophy is quite unwarrantable, and seems justly obnoxious to the ridicule cast on it by Kant, viz., that such a method of philosophizing must be pur-sued, " under the vainglorious fancy of seeing farther and more surely, by means of mole eyes fixed upon the earth, than with eyes fitted to a being to whom God

' Os homini sublime dedit : cœlumque tueri

Jussit, et erectos ad sidera tollere vultus.' " +

" The Philosophy of Fact " is unattainable except through " The Philo-sophy of Thought,"—a knowledge of the laws of the mentality. To found reasoning upon facts, to collect, examine, and compare them, to deduce from them certain generalized rules for our direction regarding them, and to try the re-applicability of our rule to the given series of facts about which it concerns itself, is the only way to attain Truth. Unless used in this manner, the most extensive tabular collections of " Instantiæ " would serve us but poorly, and the seeds of experience would be infertile and unproductive. Our adoration of Baconism has reached its culminating point, and we are now beginning to see that it is by a judicious employment of Aristotelianism and Baconism com-bined, that science must attain its perfectionment.

Our readers have already had presented to them a brief but compre-hensive abstract of " Induction," ‡ and they ought now to be in a position to understand an explanation of those points in which it is deficient. As this topic has been frequently insisted on previously, we do not intend here to recapitulate the arguments formerly em-ployed, but are, at present, desirous of indicating four several and

---

* " The Theory of Human Progression," p. 506.

+ " —— gave a lofty countenance, and who was ordered to gaze on heaven, and raise his face uprightly to the stars."

‡ *Vide* Chapters VIII. and IX.

distinct defects, which we believe to be chargeable against the Baconian Philosophy, viz. :—

1st. Its *formulæ* presume that the topic under investigation is new, and the pathway hitherto completely unexplored,—pre-supposes us to have no experience already collected,—and admits of no deviation from its laws, whatever be our former acquaintance with the subject.

2nd. It assumes that every definite *effect* has its own definite and individual *cause*, and does not provide any *formulæ* for the evolution of those cases in which many *effects* flow from the same *cause*.

3rd. It assumes that every definite *cause* has its own definite and individual *effect*, and does not provide any *formulæ* for the evolution of those cases in which many *causes* combine to produce one *effect*.

4th. It furnishes us with no key to the explication of the neutralizing operation of different causes.

Did space permit, we could follow these classifications up with illustrative examples in proof of the positions taken, but viewing our rapidly diminishing space, we are warned to forbear : however, lest it should be supposed by any one that we are unprepared to substantiate the above charges, we may name the following instances in which Induction would be inefficacious were its formulæ strictly observed, viz., crime, an effect which proceeds from many causes ; extravagance, a cause which produces many effects ; and the equilibrium of forces wherein causes neutralize each other.

We intended in this chapter to give a summary view of the Methodology of the most famous of the continental philosophers. We perceive now that that would extend our work far beyond its due and proper limits, and however much tempted by inclination to go on, we think it will be most advisable to abstain for the present, and confine our remarks to the explanation of the Methods of the celebrated French philosophers, Descartes and Comte.

Réné Descartes Duperron was born at La Haye, in Tourrain, on the 31st of March, 1596 (at this time Bacon would be 35 years of age), of Breton parentage. His mother died a few days after his birth, and he himself was exceedingly sickly. At an early age he entered the college of the Jesuits at La Flêche, and therein studied the Classical Languages, Mathematics, Logic, Rhetoric, and Physics. Here he attained an idea of the almost complete darkness which overshrouded the tree of knowledge, and resolved to set himself, in his after life, the task of dispersing that darkness, and gaining some of the goodly fruit which grew upon that tree. The futility of the science of that day for practical purposes, and the incompetency of Philosophy to give fitting responses to the inquiries of an earnestly inquiring soul, yearning to behold, if possible, Truth face to face, was made woefully evident, and he determined to seek no other science than that which he could find in himself, or else in the great book of the world. He afterwards entered the army, and passed his life, for a time, in camps and travel; but at length, in the year 1629, when he was 33 years of age, he retired to Holland, and engaged in the execution of his youthful design. "He did not desire," he said, "to rebuild the town in which others dwelt, but to re-construct the dwelling-place of his own intellect. He might for this purpose employ old materials; but the plan must be new, and the ground must be thoroughly cleared." * Thus, for the first time, was the experiment which Bacon desiderated attempted, viz., "No one has yet been found of so constant and severe a mind, as to have determined and tasked himself utterly to abolish theories and common notions, and to apply his intellect, altogether smoothed and even, to particulars anew. Accordingly, that human reason which we have is a kind of medley and unsorted collection, from much trust and much accident, and the childish notions which we first imbibed; whereas, if one of mature age and sound senses, and a mind thoroughly cleared, should apply himself freshly to experiment and particulars, of him better things might be hoped." Proceeding upon this principle Descartes postulated a preliminary doubt, which may be best explained in his own language, viz., "In order to rid oneself of all prejudice it is only necessary to determine, not to affirm or deny anything of what we formerly affirmed or denied, until it has been carefully re-examined. But we are not, on this account, prohibited from retaining in our memory the whole of the notions themselves." † This doubt then, as a mere *pro tempore* suspension of the Judgment, was negative, not positive. He resolved, so far as concerned his philosophic inquiries, to consider all his former impressions as if they had never been,—to regard, as far as was practicable, his mind as a blank;—he doubted the existence of the world, of God, of Truth. Thought then was to re-conquer as much from the realms of doubt as it was able; stripping his mind of everything except his own existence, he postulated *that* as a certainty in the famous axiom, *Cogito ergo sum*, "I think, therefore I am," and then sought to establish some first principle from which another might be logically deduced, until by a direct, obvious, and rigidly sequentic train of reasoning he should attain a knowledge of all truth. Mighty labour!

* "Discourse on Method," part 1st.

† *Vide* "Lettre de M. Descartes à M. Clerselier," in Jules Simon's edition of "Œuvres de Descartes." Paris: Charpentier, 1851, p. 367.

Was it capable of accomplishment? At all events the *attempt* was praiseworthy. In order to its accomplishment a method was requisite,—rules required to be laid down. They were these :—

Rule I. Never accept anything as true which is not clearly known to be so; *i.e.*, carefully avoid rashness and prejudice, and comprise nothing within the proposition except what is so distinctly presented to the mind as entirely to preclude doubt.

Rule II. Divide each difficulty under examination into as many parts as possible, so that each part being more easily conceived may be more readily understood.

Rule III. Commence all investigations with the most simple and easily understood objects, and from these ascend gradually to the knowledge of the more complex.

Rule IV. Make enumerations so complete, and reviews so circumspect, as to insure that nothing essential to the attainment of the truth may be omitted.

Consciousness being thus postulated as the basis of all certitude, and these rules being laid down for the guidance of the mind, all that was necessary for the attainment of the primary elements of philosophy was to consult consciousness what ideas, impressed upon, or residing within it, were most clearly and distinctly cognoscible by it, and then this was to be considered as truth. Only to indicate the results of such a philosophy would occupy much space; we now merely mention a few. Having thought as a posited fact, we discover that our thoughts are limited, but that we have an idea of infinitude. Infinity of thought implies infinity of power, and perfection; for we observe that our power and perfectibility increase in exact ratio with the extension of our power of accurate thinking. Infinity of thought, power, and perfectibility, constitute our idea of God. But our mentality is impressed, we feel, by something different from itself. Things which differ in their properties are diverse in their nature, hence we not only infer the existence of matter, but also the essential distinction between *matter* and *mind.* That cannot be an essential portion of Deity which implies limitation in space or power. Matter, if self-existent, would limit him in space, and imply his powerlessness to create it; therefore matter is not self-existent, but created, and its creator is God. We have educed from the one posited fact—thought—the facts of God's existence—the existence of matter—the distinctness of matter and mind, and the necessary creation of the world. Such are a few of the results of this philosophy. Descartes, during his life, was persecuted as an Atheist. He died at Stockholm, whither he had been invited by Queen Christina, of Sweden, A.D. 1650.

M. Auguste Comte is an illustrious living philosopher, who, between the years 1830 and 1842 published a large and most valuable treatise, in 6 vols., 8vo, entitled "Cours de la philosophie positive," which has met with but scanty encouragement from the public, and yet bears evidence, in many parts, of profound thought, acute analytical skill, and a comprehensive range of mental vision. We are far from wishing to be understood as homolgating all his opinions, and yet we think there is so much of merit in his method that we would be glad if the brief and hurried glimpse which we can now take of the general scope of his writings should incite any of our readers to thirst for more information regarding his system—perchance incline them to seek the fountain-source itself. All that we can undertake just now is merely to notice *results*, not *processes;* starting apparently from the suggestion contained in Bacon's "*Novum Organum,*" aph. lxxx.—viz., that no effective progress in science could be made until the several sciences had been individually expanded, and the several facts contained in these sciences brought back again to a general philosophy. The problem which M. Comte sets himself, is the discovery of science possessed of the requisite *generality.* He found philosophy in a singularly unsettled state—one party denying that a general science was possible, and another asserting that general science was the great desideratum of the age. Positive science was thus, in his opinion, scarcely general enough; and general science was not sufficiently positive. To construct a science in which these defects would be avoided, he accepted as his mission. To do this, however, it was necessary to learn, if possible, the natural law of mental evolution. Looking at the method in which men have made advances in knowledge, he perceived that each science had a definite chronological course to fulfil, in which it passed through three distinct and successive stages—viz., 1st. Fetechism, or the mystical era, in which each effect is believed to proceed from the direct agency of supernatural beings, *e.g.,* the mythology of ancient nations. 2nd. The metaphysical era, in which men engage in vague and futile attempts to discover the causes and essences of things, *e.g.,* astrology and alchemy. 3rd. The positive era, in which, mind having advanced, men no longer believe in the mystic mythology of the early ages, or in the imaginary occult qualities, formalities, and quiddities of the metaphysical stage, but look upon creation as the result of a complex series of laws according to which all events begin, proceed, and terminate. Physical science, history, mental and moral philosophy, and sociology, equally confirm

this view of humanitarian progression.   In fixing our eye upon Science
we find it readily divisable into two grand genera—viz., the pure and
the mixed.   The pure sciences are those which are possessed of definite
and distinct laws, from which, independently of the existence of external
objectivities, might be deduced equally unambiguous results.   The
mixed sciences are those which result from the study of natural objects,
hence they are composed of mixed rules, *i.e.*, rules derived both from
induction and deduction.   There are six positive sciences, each differing
from its sequent in being less in *comprehension* and greater in *extension*
—viz., Mathematics, which concerns itself with the ideas of *number*,
quantity, and *extent ;*—Astronomy—which refers to the distances, sizes,
and forms of the solar orb and the planetary bodies; the orbits in
which they career, and the forces by which they are moved,—is, in
other words, the science of gravitation;—Physics, whose special consideration is expended upon the larger masses of matter, and in the
ascertaining of the laws relating to weight, electricity, light, caloric,
magnetism, and sonorousness;—Chemistry, which studies the laws
which regulate the molecular composition of bodies, and determines the
conditions which preside over their definitive combinations, *i.e.*, the
atomic affinities of unlike substances;—Biology, whose office it is to
explain the laws of life, from the lowliest vegetable to the loftiest
animal—describe the organic functions and faculties, and study the
whole physical, moral, and intellectual nature of man;—Sociology,
which looks upon society in order to discover the laws of social
evolution—the successive phases and changes which society presents
and undergoes—distinguishes between the transitory and unstable,
and the necessary and permanent.   This, he asserts, takes in all that is
knowable by the human intellect.   Such are the positive sciences and
their offices; any discovery made in one of the antecedents, creates the
possibility of progress in the sequents.   From the base upwards this is
applicable, but from the apex to the basement there is no descent of
improveability.   Thus we have given us the law in which progress is
possible, and are certified of the futility of any other course.   The
foregoing is but a brief and rapid glimpse of what we conceive to be
the *leading* idea of this great work.   Could we follow it out more
fully by illustration and explanation, our readers would see the vast
importance of the step which this great philosopher has taken.   Had
we space for the necessary *adversaria* which, as an antidote, it would
require, its value would be made more evident by shewing how sug-
gestive of thought it was, merely in the requisites necessary for limiting,
circumscribing, and correcting it, pruning its extravagances, correcting

its viciousness, and supplying its defects. Another opportunity, in a future work, must be taken for this; meanwhile we shall conclude this chapter with the following rules for the guidance of our students in making methodical inquiries :—

Rule I. It is necessary to *know* before we begin to *reason*.

Rule II. The subject of inquiry should be clearly and distinctly comprehended.

Rule III. The subject of inquiry should be carefully detached from any extraneous matter.

Rule IV. If the subject be compound, it should be separated into its component parts.

Rule V. Begin with the most simple, and proceed gradually to the consideration of the most complex object or objects.

Rule VI. Let no absolute or final step be taken unless sufficient evidence upon the point be attainable.

Rule VII. Be careful and cautious in the searching out of middle terms, in order that the path from the known to the unknown may be made gentle and easy.

Rule VIII. If it be necessary to reason upon things which are, as a whole, incapable of being otherwise than obscurely comprehended, proceed only so far as the way lies clear before you, while you employ every means in your power to dissipate the darkness which clouds the prospect.

Rule IX. The nature, kind, and degree of evidence necessary for the proof of any particular topic, must be accepted in any inquiry regarding that topic, and the logical processes which *that* necessitates must be faithfully and accurately performed.

CHAPTER XX.

ON METHOD.

"All's well that ends well."—SHAKSPERE.

"Hic labor extremus, longarum hæc meta viarum." [*]—VIRGIL.

"I must now quit a subject on which I have, perhaps, dwelt too long."—HALLAM.

"How much remains to be done for the improvement of that part of Logic whose province it is to fix the limits by which contiguous departments of study are defined and separated! and how many unsuspected affinities may be reasonably presumed to exist among sciences which, to our circumscribed views, appear, at present, the most alien from each other! The abstract Geometry of Appollonius and Archimedes was found, after an interval of two thousand years, to furnish a torch to the physical inquiries of Newton; while, in the further progress of Knowledge, the Etymology of Languages has been happily employed to fill up the chasms of Ancient History; and the conclusions of Comparative Anatomy to illustrate the theory of the earth. For my own part, even if the task were executed with the most complete success, I should be strongly inclined to think that its appropriate place would be as a branch of an article on Logic." [†]   Agreeing, as we do, with the opinions expressed in the foregoing extract, yet we feel, forcibly, the difficulty of executing the great design which it unfolds to the mind; indeed, the very multiplicity of topics which seem to us to be included in the signification of the word Method, introduces a sort of embarrassment into our mind which is likely to make this chapter the most *immethodical* of all those which have preceded it. We could have wished, had space permitted, to lay before our readers an abstract of the methods of various philosophers in a somewhat fuller form than we can now do, but as we have the hope of shortly returning to this subject,[‡] we shall content ourselves, for the present, with giving a tabulated outline of Bacon's classification of knowledge, as contained in his treatise "De Augmentis Scientiarum." We dare not now, however, do more than present the following brief *formula* of his Methodology, viz.—

---

[*] This is our final labour, this the termination of our lengthy journeyings.

[†] Stewart's "Preliminary Discourse on Metaphysical and Moral Science," Preface, p. 11.

[‡] In a series of articles on "European Philosophy," the "Prolegomena" to which has appeared in the pages of "The British Controversialist," vol. iii., which see. The author hopes to proceed with that topic regularly, in the same work, during the year 1854.

KNOWLEDGE.

Memory.		Imagination.	Reason.
History.		**Poesy.**	**Philosophy.**

Natural.	Civil.		
1. History of Creatures, or Nature in Action.	1. Literary.	1. Narrative or Heroic.	1. Divine, or Theology natural & revealed.
2. History of Marvels, or nature varying.	2. Ecclesiastic.	2. Representative or Dramatic.	2. Natural, or Science Speculative and Operative.
3. History of Arts, or Nature varied.	3. Civil.	3. Allusive and Parabolical	3. Human, or Anthropology & Sociology.
		4. Appendices—viz., Biographies, Orations, Letters, and Apophthegms.	

This classification has been slightly varied by D'Alembert, in his
"Encyclopedical tree of the arrangements of human knowledge," by the
extension of the province of Imagination, and placing it last in the
catalogue of primary intellectual powers; but we think this alteration
more refined than philosophical. Locke, also, has attempted the mighty
task of arranging, classifying, and co-ordinating human knowledge, in
the last chapter of his celebrated "Essay." This classification may be
tabulated as follows—viz.,

KNOWLEDGE.

Φυσικη. (*Physics.*)	Πρακτικη. (*Operative skill.*)	Σημειωτικη. (*Sign-knowledge.*)
1. Natural Philosophy.	1. Ethics.	1. Logic.
2. Mental Philosophy.	2. The Mechanical Arts.	2. Language.
3. Natural Theology.	3. The Fine Arts.	3. Rites, Ceremonies, Customs, Fashions, &c.

The Categories of Kant are next deserving of attention, as an attempt
to methodize "the laws of the Understanding." These constitute the
forms under some one of which the mind is necessitated to marshal each
individual object of thought, and they comprehend all the possible
judgments which the human mind is capable of forming. They may be
exhibited thus :—

LAWS OF THE UNDERSTANDING.

I. Quantity.	II. Quality.	III. Relation.	IV. Modality.
1. Unity.	1. Reality.	1. Substance and Attribute.	1. Possibility or Impossibility.
2. Plurality.	2. Negation.	2. Causality and Subsequency.	2. Existence or Non-existence.
3. Universality or Totality.	3. Limitation.	3. Action and Reaction.	3. Necessity or Contingency.

The *triadial* system of Hegel, as the representative of another and a differing Methodology, deserves mention. His general principle is, that everything has two contrary aspects in which it may be viewed, but that Truth, Reality, and Being, are the results of the idea educed in the mind by the identity—or becoming-united-into-one—of these diverse aspects. Everything is thus *triadial*. There are, firstly, the two contraries ; and secondly, the resultant of their identity ; thus—

First. *Thought unconditioned.*

I. Quality.	II. Quantity.	III. Measure.
1. Being unconditioned.	1. Pure quantity.	1. The Union or *realization* of quality, and quantity.
2. Existence or Being conditioned.	2. Divisible quantity.	
3. Existence realized.	3. Degree of quantity.	

Second. *Thought conditioned.*

I. Noumenon.	II. Phenomenon.	III. Reality.
1. Ideal Being.	1. Appearances.	1. Substance.
2. Essential Being.	2. Matter and Form, or appearances conditioned.	2. Causation.
3. Thing.	3. Relation, or *becomingness*.	3. Action.

Third. *Thought* identiated, *or realized.*

I. Idea (mental).	II. Object.	III. Idea (real).
1. Term.	1. Mechanicals.	1. Life.
2. Judgment.	2. Chemicals.	2. Intelligence.
3. Inference.	3. Final cause.	3. The absolute.

The system of Comte we have already explained, and may therefore pass on to the New Methodology, propounded in a most excellent work, recently published, under the title of "The Theory of Human Progression." The ideas of the author may be thus abridgedly expressed —viz.,—each science posits, or lays down, an idea—that regarding which it treats. The name of this idea is a substantive. Each science presents to the mind the three following parts—viz., 1st. Its substantive. 2nd. The *relation* between that and another substantive, *i.e.*, the proposition. 3rd. A new idea evolved from the consideration of the relation of that and another proposition, *i.e.*, the syllogism. Every science, therefore, consists of terms, propositions, and syllogisms. Classification is not science, but the preparation for science. Science is an educt of the mind. Ontology is, therefore, the fountain of science. Logic teaches the forms of the mental operations, gives out the laws of identity and equality, and is hence the primary science. The co-ordination of the sciences may be thus exhibited :—

I. Primary knowledge—necessary and universal.

II. Science.
- Ontologic.
- Logic. Formal Thought.
- Mathematic. Number, Quantity, Space.
- Dynamic. Force.
- Physic. Mechanic, Magnetic, Chemic, Electro-galvanic.
- Organic. Botanic, Zoologic.
- Anthropologic. Artistic, Economic, Socialistic, Politic.
- Theologic.

III. Philosophy.
- Critic. Knowledge.
- Dikaistic. Duty.
- Elpistic. Hope.

IV. Revelation. Theic.

These formulæ are not given here so much because they can convey much information to the mind, as to introduce our readers to a new field of thought. We may thus pique their curiosity, and lead them on to higher studies; and at the same time we offer no apology for inserting them, because we believe that a chapter on Method is the proper place in which to introduce a notice of every attempt to methodize and arrange the details of human knowledge. All that we regret is, that we cannot now more fully explain them, and that we have been compelled to do such injustice to their respective authors as to present the mere skeleton of their thoughts. But if a Cuvier, or an Owen, from a few scattered and fragmentary bones is capable of filling up the outline of the animal structure to which these bones belonged, so ought the student of mind also to be able to follow out the general scope and design of any philosophy from such skeletonic abstracts as those which we have now placed before him.

We are compelled to omit, however unwillingly, all mention of the works of Concio, Gaulier, Algezeri, Vico, Plocquet, Ventura, Chretien, and the Authors of the "Port Royal System of Logic," and shall now proceed, as briefly as may be, to the consideration of the remaining divisions of our subject.

The *second* part of Method is that which relates to the arrangement of the things able to named, *i.e.*, of knowledge. Of logical classification and division we have already spoken under the topics Categories, Predicables, Syllogisms, Fallacies, to which we beg to refer our readers.

We shall now proceed, most briefly, to explain the laws of simple and relative suggestion.

"Not every thought to every thought succeeds indifferently," says the acute Hobbes, and thus, for the first time, introduced the idea of *law* as regulating the succession of our thoughts. Hartley next endeavoured to analyze some of the complex thoughts which take up their residence in the mind, by reference to this "law of association," and thus to bring to the test of experiment the assertion which Hobbes has made in the third chapter of the "Leviathan,"—viz., that "in the wild ranging of the mind a man may oftimes perceive the way of it, and the dependence of one thought upon another." In this he, to some extent, succeeded. Upon this subject Dr. Reid remarks, that "we seem to treat the thoughts that present themselves to the fancy in crowds, as a great man treats the persons who attend his levee. They are all ambitious of his attention : he goes round the circle, bestowing a bow upon one, a smile upon another, asks a short question of a third, while a fourth is honoured with a particular conference ; and the greater part have no particular mark of attention, but go as they came. It is true he can give no mark of his attention to those who came not there, but he has a sufficient number for making a choice and distinction." Mr. James Mill, in his " Analysis of the Human Mind," set himself strenuously to the task of discovering by what connecting links our thoughts are recalled and reproduced, and gave out the following as the general associative law—viz., "*Our ideas spring up and exist in the order in which the sensations existed, of which they are the copy.*" This law branches out into the three following secondary laws—viz., 1st. Ideas of sensations which impress the mind simultaneously, reappear simultaneously. 2nd. Ideas of sensations which impress the mind successively, reappear successively. 3rd. Ideas of sensations are made to reappear by other sensations which have occurred either simultaneously with, or successively to, the sensations whose representatives they recall. The primary influences which operate in enabling the mind to recall its ideas, are—Resemblance, Contrast, Juxtaposition, and Consecutiveness. The circumstances which modify the recurrence of ideas are the following—viz., 1st. The duration of the original impression. 2nd. The greater or less similarity of impressions. 3rd. The greater or less frequency of recurrence. 4th. The recentness or remoteness of the date of the impressions. 5th. The greater or less accuracy of the original impressions. 6th. Original mental differences among men. 7th. Mental habits. The philosophy of the recurrence of simple ideas is denominated simple suggestion. Relative suggestion signifies the calling up of ideas regarding the *relations* of objects, ideas, attributes, &c., in contradistinction to the suggestion of simple conceptions. Relations are capable of a twofold division—viz., into Coexistent Relations, and Relations of Succession. Under the former are classed the relations of Coevality, Similarity, Quality, &c.; under the latter, Succession, Causa-

tion, Position, &c.* Dr. Thomas Brown made all reasoning consist of a series of Relative suggestions. He says, " Objects, and the relations of objects—these are all that reasoning involves, and these must always be involved in every reasoning." " One conception follows another conception, according to certain laws of suggestion, to which our Divine Author has adapted our mental constitution ; and by another set of laws, which the same Divine Author has established, certain feelings of relation arise from the consideration of the suggesting and suggested objects. This is all in which reasoning, as felt by us, truly consists. * * * Each subject of our thoughts suggests something which forms a part of it, or something which has to it a certain relation of proportion ; and the relation of comprehension in the one case, or of proportion in the other case, is felt accordingly at every step." †
The Philosophy of Suggestion has been most elegantly expressed by Samuel Rogers, in " The Pleasures of Memory," in the following lines :—

> " Lulled in the countless chambers of the brain,
> Our thoughts are linked by many a hidden chain ;
> Awake but one, and lo ! what myriads rise !
> Each stamps its image as the other flies.
>   *   *   *   *   *
> Each at thy call advances or retires,
> As Judgment dictates or the scene inspires.
> Each thrills the seat of sense, that sacred source,
> Whence the fine nerves direct their mazy course,
> And through the mind invisibly convey
> The subtle quick vibrations as they play."

The *third* part of Method concerns itself with the *communication* of knowledge, and refers either to *narrative* or *argumentative* discourse. It will readily appear from a consideration of what has been said above, that that method of communicating knowledge which most nearly corresponds to "the laws of suggestion" which are impressed upon the mind, is that which ought to be most uniformly employed. It will follow from this that in narrative discourses, the natural order is most to be preferred, and ought most frequently to be adopted, because it will be that which most accurately accords with the laws of the mind, and is consequently that which will be most easily comprehended by it; thus Civil History will generally follow the laws of succession in time, or causative agency ; Natural History those of similarity, quality, or position. In argumentative discourse, however,

* *Vide* Chapter IV.
† Brown " On the Philosophy of the Mind," lect. 49.

Q

there are two methods of arrangement, which severally, according to the purpose which we have in view, add weight and aptness to the evidence which we can produce. These are respectively denominated Analysis and Synthesis. These terms have already been fully defined,* and we shall therefore assume that their significations are sufficiently known by our readers to enable them to comprehend our future remarks. When we are desirous of exhibiting the mode in which we proceeded to examine a subject, and of detailing the results which followed from each step in our investigation, we must present our views in the analytical order. Thus we impart to another the several processes in which we engaged; we lead him along the pathway which we travelled; we point out to him the various objects which arrested our attention; we place him in a position to judge of the accuracy of our procedure, and are thus fully justified in appealing to him for his verdict upon the point at issue. But it is obvious that in every investigation which we may make, many false steps will be taken; many observations will have been made entirely foreign to our purpose; many hypotheses may have been thought of which subsequent observations may have led us to reject.† These, as contributing little or nothing to the illustration of the subject, it is not necessary to bring prominently into view, unless, indeed, some peculiar importance has been attached to such hypotheses either by the errors of former ages or the prevalence of such notions among the individuals constituting the auditory.—In such cases it is necessary to notice and refute them; but, in general, it is only necessary to bring forward the most extraordinary examples which prove the accuracy of an hypothesis, or those which are best adapted to illustrate, enforce, and establish the truth of the propositions sought to be established. Locke's "Essay on the Human Understanding," Hume's "Inquiry concerning the Principles of Morals," Butler's "Analogy," James Mill's "Analysis of the Human Mind," Brown's "Lectures on the Philosophy of Mind," Knight's "Principles of Taste," and Cairn's "Moral Freedom," contain the best specimens of Philosophical Analysis which have come under our notice, so far as we at present remember.

When we wish to convey information in the didactic style,—to explain any science or system of science to those who are unacquainted with such speculations,—to show the general principles which pervade nature, and the laws from which particulars flow,—we generally employ

---

* Chapter XIX.

† In proof of this see " Life of Kepler," or in default of this, Whewell's " History of the Inductive Sciences," book v.

the Synthetic method, and exhibit the general truths or comprehensive propositions in which are wrapped up, or involved, the rational explanations of individual facts. The question of the relative advantages of Synthesis and Analysis for the purposes of communication has been thus strongly put by Priestley. "Is it not much readier to take the right key at first, and open a number of locks, than to begin with examining the locks, and after trying several keys that will open one or two of them only, at last to produce that which will open them all ?"[*] Hartley's "Observations on Man," Godwin's "Political Justice," Kant's "Critique of Pure Reason," Comte's "Philosophie Positive," Buffier's "Premières Vérités," Stoddart's "Universal Grammar," and Whately's "Logic," contain some of the most valuable specimens of Synthetic argumentation which we can at present recollect.

"Neither of these two *Methods* should be too scrupulously pursued, either in the invention or communication of knowledge. It is enough if the order of nature be but observed in making the knowledge of things following depend on the knowledge of things which go before; oftentimes a mixed method will be found most effectual for these purposes; and indeed a wise and judicious prospect of our main end and design must regulate all method whatsoever."[†]

The following are the chief rules which ought to be attended to in the communication of knowledge :—

I. So dispose the materials of discourse that they will impinge upon and affect the most usual and the most influential laws of suggestion.

II. Explain the terms to be employed so clearly as to free them from any ambiguity.

III. State the question or subject of inquiry, and separate it distinctly from any adventitious circumstances.

IV. Enumerate carefully and exhaustively the several points which shall come under discussion as proofs of the point at issue.

V. Mention and consider these several points in such an order that the determination of one may lead, by an easy transition, to the proving of the others.

VI. All the arguments relating to one topic should be taken up while considering *that* topic, and ought not to be introduced at random.

VII. Objections should be honestly met, candidly dealt with, and never evaded.

VIII. Subordinate and doubtful points ought carefully to be distinguished from those which are essential.

---

[*] Priestley's Works, vol. xxiii., p. 287.
[†] Watts's "Logic," par. iv., chap. i., p. 166.

IX. Objections and difficulties should be carefully balanced; and if in equipoise, either suspend the judgment, or give the decision on the side of virtue, morality, justice, and religion.

We have purposely abstained from treating these points more fully, as they fall more completely under the province of "RHETORIC," and may at a future period, in a volume devoted to that subject, be more elaborately discoursed about; meanwhile,

> "My task is done:
>
> *   *   *   *
>
> The torch shall be extinguished which hath lit
> My midnight lamp;—and what is writ is writ;—
> WOULD IT WERE WORTHIER!"

APPENDIX.

A.

ON RECENT LOGICAL DEVELOPMENTS.

SECTION I.

THE three greatest names in Logical Science, at the present day, in Great Britain, are, unquestionably, Archbishop Whately, Sir William Hamilton, and John Stuart Mill; and the logical writings of these eminent individuals shall therefore form the chief topics of the present portion of this Appendix, although we shall precede our remarks on these authors by a cursory glance at the works of their predecessors in the present century.

In 1801 appeared "The Elements of the Philosophy of the Mind and of Moral Philosophy, to which is prefixed a Compendium of Logic," by Thomas Belsham. This work contains "the substance of a course of lectures which the author delivered to his pupils." The motto of the work is "Whatever is true cannot be injurious," and we find in the preface the following pithy and excellent sentence, "Truth is Victory," as well as this judicious observation of the utility of Logic—"The formality of Syllogistic reasoning is justly laid aside in modern composition; but the ability to define correctly, to think justly, to analyze a complex process of argumentation, to detect plausible sophistry, and to arrange ideas and reasonings in a clear and luminous method, will always be of use." "The use of Logic" he defines to be, "to guide and assist the intellectual powers in the investigation of truth, and the communication of it to others." He treats of it under the four heads Perception, Judgment, Reasoning, and Disposition. We recommend for perusal Sections II. and III. of Part III., wherein he demonstrates at length the validity of the several rules of Syllogism. The whole work is carefully compiled, the chief authorities being Watt, Locke, Duncan, and Priestley, but it is exceedingly bald and uninviting in style.

Dr. Richard Kirwan (1807) published an elementary Logic, which has been called "respectable" by Sir William Hamilton. Dugald Stewart and Dr. Thomas Brown held possession of the public favour for a considerable time, and their depreciatory remarks regarding Logic as a Science materially lessened the interest felt in its cultivation. Crackenthorpe, Saunderson, Wallis, Aldrich, and even Ketts, were beginning to be forgotten, when a quickening impulse was given to the study by the publication (1825) of Whately's "Elements." Straightway on the re-attraction of some popular attention to the study re-inaugurated by this work, there issued from the press a whole brood of *Logics*,—*e.g.*, "Outline of a New System of Logic, with a Critical Examination of Dr. Whately's 'Elements,'" by George Bentham, Esq., 1827 (nephew of Jeremy Bentham), in which he maintains opinions analogous to those entertained by his uncle in "Works," vol. iii., p. 285—295, and vol. viii., p. 213—293; "Introduction to Logic," by Rev. Samuel Hinds, in which Whately's Logic is avowedly abridged; "*Artis Logicæ Rudimenta*," Oxford, 1828, attributed to T. S. Hill; "Questions on Aldrich's Logic," Key to ditto, both Oxford, 1829; "An Examination of some Passages in Dr. Whately's 'Elements of Logic,'" by G. C. Lewis, Esq. (now editor of the "Edinburgh Review"), Oxford, 1829,—all having reference to, and being either laudatory of, or animadverting upon, this much and deservedly renowned work. This influence has not yet spent itself, as might be easily proved by reference to many recent publications on this subject: but of this more again. Whately defines "Logic, in the most extensive sense in which it has been thought advisable to employ the name," * * * "as the *Science* and also as the *Art* of Reasoning." "The process of Reasoning itself, *alone*, is the appropriate province of Logic." "Logic is *entirely conversant about language*." "It is the Art of employing language properly for the purpose of reasoning." This latter definition seems to be the one most properly to be regarded as expositive of the author's system. It seems, to us, to be very far from exhaustive of what a science and art of Logic should be. Although, therefore, the most reverend Archbishop is not here amenable to censure "for not having undertaken a work of a different kind and on a different subject" from that which he proposed to himself, it is yet competent to any one to show reasons why *his* seems to be, however slightly, an erroneous or inadequate view of the province of Logic; for, as he himself observes, "errors are the more carefully to be pointed out in proportion to the authority by which they are sanctioned." It may be objected, that the Archbishop's definition represents Logic as being only a kind of mental arithmetic, not conducted by figures, but by words; that it destroys the true correlation of thought and language, and implies that thought is a result of language rather than the converse, which is the true opinion. The learned Hallam, too, has said, "Nor do I deny that it is philosophically worth while to know that *all general reasoning by words* may be reduced into syllogism, as it is to know, that most of plane geometry may be resolved into the superposition of equal triangles; but to represent this *portion* of logical science as *the whole*, appears to me almost like teaching the scholar Euclid's axioms and the axiomatic theorem to which I have alluded, and calling this the science of geometry." We believe that the Whatelyan system of Logic is not only erroneous but inadequate, and erroneous because it is inadequate, inasmuch as he accepts language as the *representative* of thought, whereas it is only the *exponent* of it; whence he is unable to verify the verbally-expressed as the logically-implied. The most vicious portion of the Logic under review is that which treats of induction, and attempts to show that it is, "all in all," a syllogistic process, whereas it is, in our opinion, in the first instance, a preparatory process, and in the second, a tentative and proving procedure. The best portions of this work, so far as we are qualified to judge, are those which expound the philosophy of "propositions" and the method of detecting "fallacies." The whole work abounds in acute and valuable observations; and though this radical inconsistency seems to us fatal to its pretensions, as a full, complete, and accurate exposition of logical science, we unhesitatingly recommend its perusal to every earnest thinker, and advise the student to study its pages with care and attention.

Sir William Hamilton possesses perhaps the most acute and uniformly philosophical mind in the British dominions. He is, *facile princeps*, *the* British philosopher of the age. As a thinker he is world-famous. Although his philosophical writings are few—the chief, so far as we are aware, being the "notes" and "dissertations" of his edition of Reid's Works, and the articles on "Logic," "Perception," and "Modern Philosophy," republished in the "Discussions," with the exceedingly valuable philosophical appendices which that volume contains—he has been extensively influencive in the philosophical development of other minds, and there is now growing up around him a distinguished *school*, of which Thomson, Dove, Baynes, Macvicar, Ferrier, Veitch, M'Cosh, and Cairns are the best known. In Germany, France, and America, the principal countries in the world for the culture of thought, his name is mentioned with honour and respect. Yielding all respect due to his great name, we yet cannot acknowledge ourselves wholly convinced of the grand results deducible from the formal extension which Sir William Hamilton proposes. It is, however, to be premised that we have no complete exposition of the author's system proceeding from his own pen, the principal reliable sources of information being (*a*) "Logic," in the "Discussions," p. 116—174; (*b*) Appendix II. (Logical), p. 614—652*, in the same work; (*c*) T. S. Baynes, "On the New Analytic of Logical Forms;" (*d*) several scattered notes attached to Reid's "Brief Account of Aristotle's Logic," Hamilton's "Reid;" and hence that our views, which are gathered up from these several separate sources, may not be pertinent were we to read a regularly sequentive whole in exposition of this science constructed on the principles of this author. This we interject, *en passant*, as exonerative of possible misconceptions, and shall now proceed to indicate the chief points of this Logic.

Logic is the science of the laws of thought as thought. All predication is only the utterance of thought. All that thought implicitly contains ought to be, in Logic, explicitly displayed. This will give us all the strictly legitimate *forms* of thought, and will enable us to find all the principles which truly legitimate any form of thought—*i.e.*, the supreme canon or canons of all syllogistic reasoning. Thought operates upon concepts. Concepts are the ideas resulting from that general attribute, or those general attributes, in the possession of which a plurality of objects coincide. Concepts, being general ideas, are imperfect signs [marks] of objects. To find the full thought truly representative of an object, we must introduce all the concepts, in unity, under which, in any aspect, it can be thought. This necessitates predication. The concept (No. 2) of which concept (No. 1) is predicated, must, in its extension, either be greater, equal to, or less, than it. Hence arises the necessity for the thorough-going quantification of the predicate (No. 2), as well as of the subject (No. 1). Every predication becomes thus, in the mind of the thinker, an equation of two concepts, and hence, also, "Conversion" is in all cases clearly possible in one species—viz., Simple Conversion. Reasoning implies the discovery of the relations which subsist between partly or wholly differing concepts. Therefore, the one supreme canon of all Categorical Syllogisms is, "*what worse relation of subject and predicate subsists between either of two terms and a common third term, with which one, at least, is positively related; that relation subsists between the two terms themselves.*" It follows thence, that Figure is an unessential variation of a valid Syllogism, and that Reduction is useless; that the number of moods, validly accurate and admissable in each figure, is equalised, and that all *mediate* inference is one; and that the conjunctive and disjunctive forms of

Hypothetical reasoning are modes of immediate inference. It also results, from this thorough-going quantification of the predicate, that the syllogistic process is equally applicable to Induction and Deduction. This is, of course, but the merest skeleton of the system—the beautiful system of notation, the new mnemonics, the syllogistic rules, the acute exposures of ancient errors, the vast amount of erudition which his pages display, have all been passed unnoticed. But we think that upon the whole we have managed to indicate the processes by which from the germ-thought the results have been elaborated. The chief merit—and it is far from being a slight one—which we perceive in the new analytic, is that it brings forth into clearer light that which the ancient Logic aimed at effecting—viz., the means of securing, in all our reasoning processes, the just equation of thought with thought. The ancient "Conversions" and "Reductions" were means of doing this, resulting, as we apprehend, not from a deficiency of analysis, but from a superior analysis, inasmuch as, having tried every possible mode of formally expressing thought, they rejected those which failed in legitimating the illative equation of which they were in search. Their object was not to extend their system to all possible modes of predication, but to test all possible modes of predication, and to restrict the mind to the use of those alone which gave the due equation of thought which the Reason required. Their object was to exhibit an exhaustively concise list of all the possible methods of expressing thought which could yield, from their explicit form and their implicit signification, a knowledge of the true relations which one thought bears to another. It may be that their analysis was too rigid, and that they have rejected too much; if so, let it be revoked, but do not let it be unjustly said of them, "They were, in the main, right as far as they went; but they did not go far enough. Their investigation of the form of thought was arrested before it had attained the necessary completeness." So far as our present reading extends we are inclined to believe that the new analytic is chiefly a restoration and revocation of certain elements which the ancients, by a (perhaps too?) severe analysis, rejected from the strictly valid forms of thought while employed in reasoning. And our present sympathies lie with the ancients. We cannot in this place articulately set forth the grounds of our belief, and the processes by which we have arrived thereat, neither, perhaps, would it be right in us until farther study and maturer thought has certiorated our *belief* and made it *knowledge*.

One of the most important literary controversies of the age connects itself with the aforementioned system—viz., the discussion between Sir

William Hamilton and Professor Augustus De Morgan, regarding the prior publication of their respective systems, which are in some respects similar, although, in our opinion, the differentiating points exceed the agreeing ones, and that greatly to the disadvantage of the latter author. Indeed, while studying his "Formal Logic," the following passage of Brown's "Lectures" was forcibly recalled to our memory:—"If an Art of Reasoning is to be given us, it is surely to be an art which is to render the acquisition of knowledge more easy, not more difficult—an art which is to avail itself of the natural tendency of the mind to the discovery of truth, not to counteract this tendency, and to force the mind, if it be possible, to suspend the very process which was leading it to truth." (Lect. 49, p. 321.) We must confess that the above sentence precisely represented our thoughts on this subject, and, though admiring much many portions of the work—*e.g.*, Chapter II., "On Objects, Ideas, and Names;" Chapters IX. and X., "On Probability;" and Chapter XIII., "On Fallacies"—we apprehend that such *extensions* as those proposed by Professor De Morgan would be fatal to the possibility of studying Logic. The mnemonics of the system would occupy so much time in their acquisition, that there would be little left for the practical employment of so intricate an instrument. Of the controversy we may say that it has been conducted with very bad taste, and a greater development of bile than the topic warranted.*

The third Logic—J. S. Mill's (1843)—may fitlier be called "An Encyclopedia of philosophic tenets connected with, or resulting from, the Science of Logic." Its title is singularly indicative of its contents— viz., "A System of Logic, Ratiocinative and Deductive; being a Connected View of the Principles of Evidence and the Methods of Scientific Investigation."

"Logic comprises the science of reasoning as well as an art founded on that science." "The sole object of Logic is the guidance of one's own thoughts." "Logic is the judge and arbiter of all particular investigations." "Logic is the science of the operations of the understanding, which are subservient to the estimation [*i.e.*, judging of the value] of evidence." Reasoning is used in its most extensive signification—viz., the making of any kind of inference whatever in accordance with the laws of mind. Book I. treats of "Names and Propositions," including the *rationale* of Definition. Book II., "Of Reasoning." The proper subject of Logic is proof. Proof is that which makes opinions believable. Inference is capable from—1, The Conversion and Opposi-

* For farther information on this controversy the reader is referred to De Morgan's "Formal Logic," appendix i., and Hamilton's "Discussions," appendix ii., Logical (B).

tion of Propositions; 2, The Conjunctions of propositions in Syllogisms, *i. e.*, Demonstration; 3, Induction. This book contains an excellent exposition of "the nature and value of the Syllogism," and a discussion on the question of "Necessary Truths." Book III., "Of Induction." The chief teachings of this book we have abridged in the body of the present work.* Book IV., "Of the operations subsidiary to Induction." A most important topic ably treated; see especially the remarks on "Observation," "Abstraction," "A Philosophical Language." Book V., "On Fallacies;" most valuable. Book VI., "On the Logic of the Moral Science." This book treats of some of the results of Logic in its applications. It contains a very fair abstract of the Sociology of Auguste Comte. The speculations in this treatise are based on the associative theory of Hobbes, Hartley, Priestley, and the elder Mill, the theory of causation expounded by Hume and Dr. Thomas Brown, and on the fact that consciousness is to us the source of all philosophical truth. His doctrine of the Syllogism—viz., that Induction performs the inferring of Generals from Particulars, and that the Syllogism unfolds and develops this *register* of our inferences into the ground of new specializations—is equally deserving of notice; and although it has involved the author in a controversy regarding "necessary truths,"† we do not think that its importance is in any way lessened by the counter-notions which it disputes. Although we do not coincide, but are in fact diametrically opposed to this author on the Theory of Causation,‡ we can yet recommend the chapters which relate to this subject—viz., Book III., Chapters V., VI., X., XV., and XXI. —as full of clear, bold, and precise thinking. The whole work is characterized by strength, lucidity, terseness, and patient indefatigibility of thought. No man can read it without being vastly wiser and better.

The works of these three great speculators in logical science we specially commend to the earnest student; he will find therein intellectual *pabulum* of the most beneficial kind, which will serve for the well-uprearing of a race of strong-minded and accurate thinkers, whom few speculative difficulties need appal.

* Chapter VIII.

† For the grounds of this controversy, see Mill's "Logic," book ii., chap. v., and Whewell's "Philosophy of the Inductive Sciences," vol. i., as well as a small pamphlet "On Induction," by the same author.

‡ For an excellent abstract of the several theories of Causation, see Thomson's "Laws of Thought," p. 255.

SECTION II.

To mention the chief publications on logical science which have appeared within the last few years may be serviceable to the student, especially if accompanied by brief and reliable characterization—this is the object of the present section of this appendix.

Besides the works mentioned in connexion with, and as resulting from, the publication of Whately's "Logic," we may direct attention to the following works, viz. :—

B. H. Smart's "Outline of Sematology; or, an Essay towards establishing a new Theory of Grammar, Logic, and Rhetoric" (1831). Grammar includes nothing more than correct construction under the laws of concord and government; Logic provides that words in joining shall make sense, *i.e.*, express knowledge either real or supposed. "Inductive knowledge is the art or practice of gathering knowledge by the instrumentality of words;" "the process by which the knowledge so accumulated is spread again before the understanding, in words which, being joined together, make evident *sense*, that is to say, make one expression with one meaning, is called Deduction." If words *are* knowledge this theory is tenable; if, however, they are *not*, by what agency are we to know *the true* from *the false*? Many judicious and ingenious remarks are scattered through his little "Manual of Logic" (1849). Drobitsch's "Neue Durstellung der Logik" (1836) is worthy the attention of readers of German. Haughton's "*Prodromus*" merits a perusal. S. R. Bosquanet, in his "New System of Logic" (1839), publishes his discovery that Aristotle is a heathen, and that "the mind which has been trained and formed in the schools of Grecian wisdom *cannot* see the truths of Christianity." Hence the study of the Syllogism ought to be abolished. True's "Elements of Logic" (Boston, U.S., 1840) is a tolerable class-book. Tappan's "Logic" (New York, 1844) takes a higher place. This is really an admirable treatise. A student in the German school of thought, he has lucidly expounded the operations of the Reason—the relations between philosophy and the sciences and arts. The functions of the Reason are—Intuition, Abstraction, Generalization, Judgment, Invention, Mediate Perception, Induction, Memory, Recollection, Attention, Imagination, and Consciousness. To Thomson's "Outline of the Necessary Laws of Thought; a Treatise on Pure and Applied Logic" (1842), we have frequently referred. It is a work of singular breadth of view, clearness of thought, precision of style, and bears evidence of being the result of mature study and careful investigation. We can confidently recommend this treatise as a valuable addition to the philosophy of thought. It deserves and will repay study. J. F. Perrard's "Introduction à la Philosophie ou Nouvelle Logique Française" (1844); Duval Jouve's "Traité de la Logique (1844); B. S. Hilaire's "De la Logique d'Aristote" (1838), and the introduction and notes of his translation of Aristotle's "Organon" (1844); Javary's "De la Certitude" (1847); Tissot's "Logique de Kant" (1840); Kœnig's "La Science du Vrai" (1844), are all highly worthy of the attention of the French scholar. Kant's "Logic" has been translated into English by Richardson, and Aristotle's "Organon" by O. F. Owen (Bohn's Classical Library, 1853); the latter is very well rendered, and has a few admirable notes. Beck's "Psychologie und Logik" (1846) will repay and reward perusal. William Cairns, Professor of Logic, Belfast, published "Outlines of Lectures on Logic," for the use of his students. They exhibit a clear conception of the science, and an extensive acquaintance with the philosophy of the questions involved in it. His successor, Robert Blakey, in his "Essay towards an easy and useful System of Logic" (1846), has presented the public with many judicious observations regarding a few of the questions which arise in a logical course, but is very far from entertaining an adequate idea of the utility of the Science. Thomas Solly, Esq., has developed and applied the logical principles of Kant in combination with those of Aristotle. He has thus, like Sir William Hamilton, De Morgan, and William Thomson, been led to extend the boundaries of pure Logic. Logic is not an organon or instrument of science, but *the* truth-tester and the determinant of all the consequences contained in any one of the principles of science. We do not reason *in* syllogism, but *in accordance with* its laws. The Symbolism he employs as illustrative of conceptions and their intellectual limitations are clear and easily comprehended, although the Cambridge mathematics is rather too largely infused; his section on "The Modality of Syllogisms" is highly valuable and worthy of study. Boole's "Mathematical Analysis of Logic" is a work of considerable merit, although based upon the fallacy of supposing "Thought" a contained species under "Algebra," instead of regarding "Algebra" as one of the species of the genus "Thought." Hind's "Introduction to Logic" is an abridgment of Whately's work, adapted to the requirements of Oxford. The usual text-book in that University being Aldrich's "Artis Logicæ Rudimenta" * (an abridgement of a larger work, "Artis Logicæ Compendium," by the same author), a con-

---

* The best edition of this work is that edited by Mr. Mansel (1849), whose "Pro logomena Logica" deserves a high place in the catalogue of those *Logics* which have emanated from Oxford.

siderable degree of logical acuteness has been concentrated round that
work by the Rev. John Huyshe, in his "Treatise on Logic" (1840).
"The author's sole endeavour has been to render the study of the
science as easy as he could," and hence its real worth and utility is
greatly lessened by the emasculation of many of its most invigorating
elements. Moberly's "Lectures on Logic" (1848) is rather a superior
book. Upon the basis of Aldrich he makes many excellent remarks,
elucidative of the sense, or in extension of the principles of the "Rudimenta." Part V., we think, is the most valuable portion. Chrétien's
"Essay on Logical Method" (1848) is a laudable and meritorious
attempt to prove that Logic lies at the foundation of all scientific
investigation, and most imperatively operative in the human mind.
His general views of Logic itself, his manly opposition to the nominalistic school of logicians, his clear and exact powers of exposition, and
his extensive knowledge of logical topics, enhance the worth of the
work greatly. W. H. Karslake's "Aids to the Study of Logic" (1851)
is a work of considerable ability, and exhibits diligent study as well as a
mind highly capable of excelling in logical pursuits.* "Logic, designed
as an Introduction to the Study of Reasoning," by John Leechman,
A.M., has neither merit nor originality to recommend it. It is in great
part a clumsy version of Archbishop Whately's work, interspersed here
and there with a sentence borrowed from the writings of the Scottish
philosophy—Reid, Stewart, &c. Yet this is the popular text-book at
the University of Glasgow—the university of Hutcheson, Adam Smith,
Reid, Stewart, Jardine, Mylne—"*O tempora! O mores!*" Monro's
"Manual of Logic" is vastly superior to Leechman's work. It is
evidently the production of an acute mind; the style is plain, perspicuous, and concise, and is, as a whole, well calculated "to facilitate an
earlier and easier acquaintance with the science than is at present
attainable." We commend it willingly and conscientiously. G. W.
Gilbart's "Logic for the Million" will be found exceedingly useful to
the student of Logic who has attained an average acquaintance with
the methods and forms of thought which syllogistic exhibits, as a *praxis*
upon the accuracy of the rules thereby laid down for their guidance. It
is a collection of many of the best specimens of argumentative literature,
and not a little of our comic writing is herein shown to contain truths
whose influence *ought to be* more deeply beneficial than merely to excite
a laugh in an idle moment. During the years 1845-6 a series of
articles, entitled "The Science of Symbols; or, Reason, its Method,

---

* We have not had the second volume forwarded to us, and hence our remarks must
be understood to refer to the first only, viz., that " On Pure Analytical Logic."

Means, and Matter," from the pen of Dr. F. R. Lees, of Leeds, appeared in a little serial, called "The Truth-Seeker." These papers, despite of a certain quaintness and epigrammaticality of style, evince an admirable conception of a "Science of Reasoning," although we question the possibility of passing "from the more limited view of Logic" usually entertained, "to the whole field of human reasoning," without lessening the real formal value of a knowledge of Logic. There can be little doubt, however, that the classification adopted by this author would give, as its result, a considerable body of rules applicable both to discovery and formal thought, while it places in a clearer light than ever the important fact, that Logic, *i.e.*, the laws of formal thought, is capable of being usefully employed in all the possible processes of the mind. The following, with slight alterations in form, is a general view of the author's system. Reason has reference to three points, viz. :—

I. Sound Reasoning is reducible to a right METHOD—a certain form —the Syllogism.

False inferences are preventible by a knowledge of the laws which regulate this form.

II. True Reasoning must be certain of the distinctness and accuracy of its premisses. As the *matter* of the premiss is, so will that of the conclusion be.

Logic, therefore, practically connects itself with Language—the MEANS of all reasoning—the *signs* of thought.

III. True Reasoning requires real and sufficient *facts* for its foundation. These are gained by Induction and Experiment. These constitute the MATTER of thought.

Right Reasoning is consistent (and true?) predication.

The author differs from both Mill and Whewell regarding conception or ideation, and this will lead to various other differences. The distinct treatment of the three topics—Method, Means, and Matter—must be followed by beneficial results, and not the least of these will be the entire differentiation of formal and informal fallacies. The series has never been completed, but we believe that in the forthcoming edition of the works of Dr. Lees, this will be found one of the portions most worthy of being prized by his readers. We may here also refer to the article "Logic," in Chambers' "Information for the People," 1849, as deserving of high praise—concise, judicious, and, in great part, excellently abridged, from Mill's great work.

G. J. Holyoake's "Logic of Facts" contains several note-worthy observations on the province of Logic and the means of correct thought, although it savours too strongly of the "secular" principles, to the advocacy of which he is now devoting his life. We do not think it right, obtrusively, to urge peculiar opinions on such subjects in a work on a professedly scientific topic. Samuel Bailey's works, especially "The Theory of Reasoning," "Essays on the Pursuit of Truth and the Progress of Knowledge," and "Discourses on Various Subjects," VI., "On the General Principles of Physical Investigation," should command the careful perusal of every earnest student: he will find much that is instructive in them. We do not, of course, homologate his views, more especially on the value of the Aristotelic Syllogism, but we can nevertheless recommend the work honestly. We are so very catholic in our own tastes, that we can find good in almost any work, whether it accords with or contradicts our own opinions. *These* have been formed with some care, so doubtless have those of others; let us read and learn from all, whatever they are capable of yielding, nor be bound only to the intellectual acquaintanceship of those only whose "thoughts are like unto our own." That is the way to narrow and fetter the mind, not to expand and liberalize it.

Baynes' "Essay on the new Analytic of Logical Forms" (1850) is expositive of the logical theory of Sir William Hamilton. The notes are valuable. Mr. Baynes has also favoured the public with a most admirable translation of "The Port-Royal Logic," to which several important notes are affixed. Gray's "Exercises on Logic" form excellent topics for trying one's skill upon. J. J. Osborne's "Treatise on Logic" is a small tractate which will not be altogether without use to the reader. This is not the case, however, with Vale's "Logic in Miniature;" *that* is absolutely useless. Whately's "Easy Lessons on Reasoning" are more difficult than his large work. "A new Introduction to Logic," published by J. W. Parker, is a very excellent initiatory book.

Surely a subject, which has excited so much intellectual activity, cannot be the useless and valueless study which it has been the fashion to consider it. *Right thinking* is the source of *right acting;* both conjoined give to man the elements of happiness. Surely those who labour to increase the power of correct thought cannot be too numerous! Surely their labours ought not to be lightly esteemed! He is the true benefactor of his race who strives to purify the sources of thought and action, the co-efficients of individual happiness and national prosperity.

B.

NOTE A, INTRODUCTION, p. x.

The following rhymes may be regarded as conveying the *sense* of the schoolman's eulogium on Logic, viz.:—

> "Even as the golden Sun etherial fire out-flashes,
> When early Phoebus up heaven's archway dashes ;
> So Logic eminent among the arts appeareth ;
> Nay, it excels the Sun which at mid-day careereth !
> For it gives light alone when day's all colours blending,
> Not when pale Luna thro' the sky is wending.
> Ne'er does the light of Logic wane.   Its splendours
> By day and night alike to all it renders."

NOTE B, p. 14.

We adapt the following tabular scheme of Ideas from, 1°, a table subjoined to a "Translation from Leibnitz, of his tract entitled 'Reflections touching Knowledge, Truth, and Ideas,'" in T. S. Baynes' "Port-Royal Logic;" 2°, Dr. F. R. Lees' "Anatomy of Argument"—"Truth Seeker," vol. i., viz. :—

Ideas.

Ideas, *i.e.*, the elements of knowledge are

I. Clear, *i. e.* recognisable,
- i. Distinct, *i. e.*, sufficiently differentiated
  - (*a*) Inadequate, *i.e.*, incompletely analyzable.
  - (*b*) Adequate, *i. e.*, completely analyzable. } Perfect.
  - (*c*) Intuitive, *i. e.*, understood *per se*, but indefinable. } Perfect.
  - (*d*) Symbolical, *i.e.*, substitutive.
- ii. Confused, *i.e.*, not sufficiently differentiated.

II. Obscure, *i.e.*, irrecognisable.

NOTE C, p. 143.

The following is a table of conversion, viz.—

Conversion

Simple.			Accidental.			Contrapositional.		
E	to	E	A	to	I	O	to	I
I	to	I	E	to	O	A	to	E

NOTE D, p. 158.

"Four different criteria of Truth have been in different forms advocated by Logicians, viz.—

"1st Criterion.—*The principle of Contradiction.* 'The same attribute cannot be at the same time affirmed and denied of the same subject,' or 'the same subject cannot have two contradictory attributes,' or 'the attributes cannot be contradictory of the subject.' To illustrate this—at a particular time facts were observed as to the motions of the planets, which were inconsistent with the received theory, that these motions were circular. The theory was consequently modified, first by the introduction of epicycles, and finally by the substitution of the theory of elliptical revolutions, because otherwise the Astronomer must have affirmed of the planets a circular and a non-circular motion, or in other words, must have assigned to a subject, to which he had already given ' a circular motion,' a predicate contradictory of this.

"2nd Criterion.—*The principle of Identity*. Conceptions which agree can be united in thought, or affirmed of the same subject at the same time. This principle is the complement of the former.

"3rd Criterion.—*The principle of the middle being excluded* (*lex exclusi medii*). ' Either a given judgment must be true, or its contradictory; there is no middle course.' So that the proof of a judgment forces us to abandon its contradictory entirely, as would the disproof of it force upon us a full acceptance of the contradictory. This law, among other uses, applies to the dialectical contrivance known to Logicians as *reductio per impossibile*.

"4th Criterion.—*The principle of sufficient (or determinant) reason*. ' Whatever exists, or is true, must have a sufficient reason why the thing or proposition should be as it is and not otherwise.' From this law are deduced such applications as these— 1. Granting the reason, we must grant what follows from it. 2. If we reject the consequent, we must reject the reason. If we admit the consequent, we do not of necessity admit the reason."—*Thomson's* " *Laws of Thought*," p. 279—281.

Note E, p. 166.

The modes of true consequence are—

 1st. From the positing of the antecedent to the positing of the consequent.

 2nd. From the eviction of the consequent to the eviction of the antecedent.

The modes of false consequence are—

 1st. From the positing of the consequent to the positing of the antecedent.

 2nd. From the eviction of the antecedent to the eviction of the consequent.

SYNOPSIS OF THE PRINCIPLES OF PROOF.

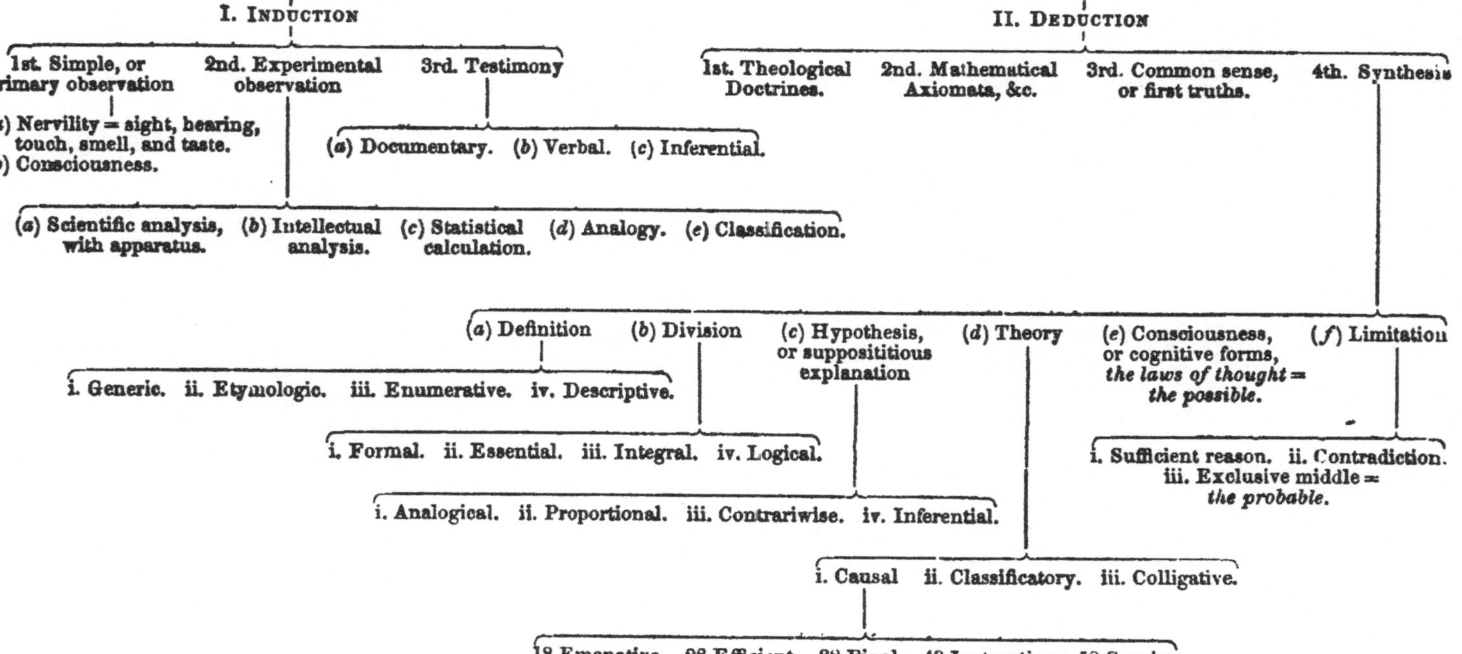

Made in the USA
Monee, IL
07 July 2026

56550025R00173